Endorsements

"David Barker has written a book in which he examines biblical accounts in light of current research theories. Many conventional scientists might be unsympathetic, but some of the questions he asks and the suggestions he proposes are thought-provoking and well worth pondering."
—Noel L. Owen, Emeritus Professor of Chemistry, PhD

"Interesting! Well documented. Thought Provoking."
—Bob Burton, JD

"Everything's well written. . . . I liked it all and it is very informative."
—John Richey, high school student

"I think it is important to show both sides of an 'argument.' He did a good job of showing, even with his strong beliefs, that believers have erred and do err."
—Douglas Horne, young adult

"It has made me realize that I need to be much more cautious about accepting contemporary thought. Specifically the points made regarding carbon dating, and uniformism have impacted me a lot. . . . I find his writing style easy to follow and understand."

—Tyler Knowlton, BS Engineering, RN

"Some of the ideas in this book were so amazing I had to share them with the family. . . . It is good enough to be published as a textbook. . . . I found that each chapter got more and more interesting as the book progressed. . . . There are so many great ideas that increased my understanding. This really is a needed book."

—Rebecca Birkin, JD

"This book has a lot of very interesting insights and he ties ideas together really well."

—Mark Jaster, former NASA engineer

"Almost thou persuadest me."

—W. Marvin Tuddenham, Chemist, PhD Fuel Technology

His writing represents decades of in-depth, profound research. In reality, it's . . . a veritable gold mine of information in its field! His focus is to provide rational explanations concerning wide differences between common scientific assumptions concerning earth's origins and age, as contrasted with explanations based on scriptural passages. His career experiences as a bank examiner have helped him spot numerous unsupportable assumptions, and weaknesses in logic and methodology, in presentations on both sides of the science vs. religion aisle. He repeatedly asks questions which cause one to ponder the validity of various interpretations and theories. The reader is led to look . . . [toward] identifying what actually is fact and what actually is correct and well-documented. . . . He has been willing to allow the questions he raises to speak for themselves rather than constantly insert his own opinions. The result is that he has written an understandable, faith-promoting book. It provides numerous evidences and bases for personal testimonies for many who wrestle with science vs. religion issues. His research is so deep, and the quotations he incorporates are so on-target and meaningful that this book will stand as a major bulwark in its field for years to come."

—Duane S. Crowther, author, editor, and publisher.

What do you do when you repeatedly read and hear your strongly held personal beliefs not only disputed but ridiculed and belittled? . . . David Barker . . . believes and accepts the scriptural accounts of creation. But everywhere he turns, he encounters those of the "scientific community" who discount his strongly held beliefs as mere nonsense. . . . Although not specifically schooled in science, he has . . . discovered numerous sources that demonstrate that much of the "scientific data" is itself based on assumptions, [and] estimates. . . . Through exhaustive research he has found facts and data that raise serious doubts about the supposed facts and data so many accept without question. . . . Undoubtedly, this work will be dismissed by "experts," but if judged in a court of law, it would have to be conceded that he has certainly "raised considerable doubt" about the validity of many scientific conclusions. Those who share his beliefs especially will find this work rewarding. It will help counter the continuing barrage of criticism of religious belief and testimony.

—Dale O Zabriskie, former President of the National Alliance of State Broadcasters Associations, and the

Utah Broadcasters Association, founder of Zabriskie &
Associates public relations firm.

"It's quite a gem—both, so well researched in breadth
and depth, and so well written that it carries the reader
along. I found myself wishing there was more to savor on
a particular subject, and yet champing at the bit to get on
to the next. . . . The tone and logical augmentation of the
entire book flows beautifully. . . . it isn't overbearing or
off-setting. . . . I laughed out loud several times at mild
jabs which pointed out unsupportable reliances. . . . The
author has been even-handed, thoughtful, and logically
honest. . . . This book is extremely well thought out,
researched, and crafted."

—Ken Barker, Ed.D.

SCIENCE

and

RELIGION

Reconciling the Conflicts

SCIENCE

and

RELIGION

DAVID M. BARKER

TATE PUBLISHING
AND ENTERPRISES, LLC

Published by Tate Publishing & Enterprises, LLC
127 E. Trade Center Terrace | Mustang, Oklahoma 73064 USA
1.888.361.9473 | www.tatepublishing.com

Tate Publishing is committed to excellence in the publishing industry. The company reflects the philosophy established by the founders, based on Psalm 68:11,
"The Lord gave the word and great was the company of those who published it."

Book design copyright © 2013 by Tate Publishing, LLC. All rights reserved.
Cover design by Jan Sunday Quilaquil
Interior design by Jomel Pepito

Library of Congress Control Number: 2013944330

Published in the United States of America

ISBN: 978-1-62510-379-6
1. Religion / General
2. Religion / Religion & Science
13.07.26

Acknowledgments

Occasionally, someone comes along, not only with the intellect and education to recognize shortcomings in popular theories but also with the fortitude to challenge them. Two such men were Hugh Nibley and Melvin Cook.

Nibley was a scholar extraordinaire with an amazing knowledge of languages, memory for details, and a voracious appetite for learning.[1] He graduated from UCLA and received a PhD from UC Berkeley as a University Fellow. It is said that he had a wealth of knowledge on almost any subject, and his knowledge continues to be shared through his extensive writings.

Cook received a PhD from Yale University in physical chemistry and was recognized as a man of genius. He wrote and published articles in scholarly and scientific journals and wrote several books. Cook's invention of slurry explosives, among other achievements, earned him worldwide acclaim. He was awarded

---

1. Knight. "Behind the Legend, There's a Man." *Deseret News.* Sept. 1, 1976.

the Nitro Nobel Gold Medal, and he received the American Chemical Society's prestigious E. V. Murphree Award in Industrial and Engineering Chemistry. Although some of Cook's theories were regarded as controversial by mainstream scientists, his logic, mastery of mathematics, command of chemistry, physics, and science in general set him apart as a scientist of distinction.

Much of the material presented in this book is based on or derived from the works of Hugh Nibley and Melvin Cook. I am deeply grateful to them for their research and scholarship. Many others have greatly stimulated my interest and added to my understanding. I give particular thanks to John P. Pratt and Larry Walker.

I also express appreciation to the staff of Tate Publishing for the excellent work and patience in bringing this book together—especially to Trinity Tate-Edgerton for her enthusiastic acceptance of the project. In addition, I give my thanks to those who have encouraged me and who have helped in preparing this book for publication: Darlene Barker, Alan Barker, Sam and Emily Barker, Paul and Ruth Barker, Rebecca Birkin, Bob Burton, Michael and Danielle Butterfield, Melissa Carmack, Evan and Emily Farrer, Clark Hodgkinson, Douglas Horne, Ralph Horne, Mike Hurlin, Pamela G. Jones, Yoshihiko Kikuchi, Tyler Knowlton, Noel L. Owen , David Read, Bonnie and Ken Rice, John Richey, W. Marvin Tuddenham, Eric Tuttle, Roy Vandermolen, and Miriam and Dale Zabriskie. I also express special thanks to Duane and Jean Crowther for sharing their talents as writers and editors. Most of all, I thank the Almighty for the occasional, but wondrous bursts of inspiration, the intense curiosity and the enthusiasm with which He has blessed me.

Contents

Preface

If... I seem to express myself dogmatically, it is only because I find it very boring to qualify every phrase with an "I think" or "to my mind". Everything I say is merely an opinion of my own. The reader can take it or leave it. If he has the patience to read what follows he will see that there is only one thing about which I am certain, and this is that there is very little about which one can be certain.

—W. Somerset Maugham,
The Summing Up (1938)

This book takes a step toward reconciling conflicts between science and religion. A vast amount of intriguing information is now available, and what is shared herein is merely a preview. I have a very high regard for, and an intense interest in science. What troubles me is when theory is presented as though it is precisely known fact—especially when it conflicts with my religious beliefs. In this book, I call upon the testimonies of numerous experts in their fields, many of which express ideas that are considered unorthodox and even radical by many of their colleagues. In my estimation, they are worthy of consideration, for they provide alternatives to more popular theories, and are much more harmonious with the scriptures.

The word "reconciling" in the subtitle of this book is used in the same manner as reconciling a bank statement. Those who have balanced a checkbook recognize that the goal is to identify the differences between their own records and those of the bank— usually, they are timing issues. A difference between the date a check was written and the date it was recorded by the bank is typically a result of such timing issues. The date a check clears the bank is rarely the same date it was written. Occasionally, errors are made. Is there anyone so meticulous as to have never made an arithmetic error? Once the differences are identified, and the numbers balanced, the reconcilement is complete. However, some discrepancies may still need to be resolved. When a mistake has been made, the resolution may be as simple as transferring funds between accounts. When timing issues are involved, sometimes all that is needed is to wait until a check clears.

In some dictionaries, the definition of "reconcile" includes the word "resolve." In this book, "reconcile" means to identify and understand the differences, but in many instances, more is needed before the issues can be fully resolved. No attempt is made herein to represent all the diverse ways believers seek to harmonize science and religion. Neither is there any presumption to present an official position of any church or denomination. What is intended is to share scientific evidence and theories that are in harmony with a literal reading of relevant scriptural accounts and to help readers be more able to distinguish between real facts and unproven theories.

In a sense, more questions are raised than answers given. Indeed, this book may be thought of as being more about what is not known than what is. More importantly, the questions raised are intended to be uplifting. They can be seen as complementing faith rather than detracting from it.

Much of this book is a collection of quotes. An avalanche of similar information is available as well as details of the research from which it is gleaned. I have attempted to include some of the most applicable portions of what has come to my attention. The information is from diverse sources; a number of which are not readily available to most readers. Many are from "peer-reviewed" journals. In some respects, peer-review is very positive—helping to ensure quality and accuracy. However, in other respects it is negative—serving as a strainer to filter out material unwanted in the main stream—particularly when the filtering excludes anything to do with God or the Bible. In fact, many peer-reviewed publications refuse to publish articles that mention ideas discussed in this book. Since a high percentage of collegiate science course papers are restricted to quotations from peer-reviewed sources,[2] even if the sole intent is to promote good scholarship, certain subjects are not addressed.

Not being under such constraints, I have gathered and shared what I consider valuable information from scientists and scholars from within the "mainstream," from "creationists" and "catastrophists." Although some of these sources are dismissed outright by various factions, I have found information from each of them that seems very relevant to reconciling the conflicts. I have chosen to include them even though I may disagree with some of what the particular authors have written. Furthermore, if we disregard all the writings of all the people with whom we have any sort of disagreement, who will we be able to quote?

Some of the references used herein are old but still seem pertinent, historically significant, and important in reconciling the conflicts. They have been used in good faith. A number of

---

2.   For example: http://web.utk.edu/~grissino/ltrs/lectures.htm. (Click on "Geography 432" in the 1st paragraph, then scroll down to the Final Term Paper requirements). (last accessed 9/17/12)

quotes are from literature some consider legend or myth. Some are from Bible-related books that are not part of the canonized scriptures of most religious groups. They have been considered sacred by some people and often add details, which—if true—add to the clarity of things described in the Bible.

The term "sic" is customarily used to signify spelling errors found in quotes. In this book, it is also used to call attention to words which appear to have been wrongly used.[3] The words in square brackets ([,]) within quotes are usually my additions. Less often, the original author or translator added the bracketed material, in which cases, that fact is stated at the end of the quotation.

---

3. "Sic may be inserted in brackets following a word misspelled or wrongly used in the original." *Chicago Manual of Style*, 15th Edition. 2003, p. 464.

Introduction

What seems to be proved may not be embraced; but what no one shows the ability to defend is quickly abandoned. Rational argument does not create belief, but it maintains a climate in which belief may flourish.

—Austin Farrer,
Light on C. S. Lewis

The wonders of nature are beautifully shown in science publications and documentaries. They provide spectacular views of all manner of interesting people, places, and things and include marvelous factual information. However, far too often, believers are startled when, in the midst of our enjoyment, comes a slap in the face in the form of information contradictory to our understanding of religious truths. The slap is usually portrayed in an attractive and convincing manner. It comes from well-respected scientists and scholars and includes exceptional photography and graphics. Unfortunately, such contradictory information, has contributed to the loss of faith in a startling number of people when a rational defense of faith has not been forthcoming.

In referring to theories that were so entrenched in the 1960s and 1970s, Hugh Nibley expressed his regret: "It is sad to think how many of those telling points that turned some of our best students away from the gospel have turned out to be dead wrong!"[4] To believers, it is truly sad when people lose faith; it is tragic when they do so because of a flawed theory.

The epigraph[5] at the top of the previous page is from a book about the role C. S. Lewis played in answering attacks on Christianity.[6] On a similar note, David Berlinski indicated that his book *The Devil's Delusion*

> is in some sense a defense of religious thought and sentiment.... A defense is needed because none has been forthcoming. The discussion has been ceded to men who regard religious belief with frivolous contempt. Their books have in recent years poured from every press, and although differing widely in their style, they are identical in their message: because scientific theories are true, religious beliefs must be false."[7]

Some say that resolving the conflicts between science and religion is not necessary for their salvation. Since they seem to have been blessed with unwavering faith, it is likely true for them. However, the personal salvation of others is certainly in peril.

Too often, both laymen and scientists assume that "scientific" means tested and proven so much so that processes given that label are beyond reproach. This is not always the case. A good

---

4.   Nibley. *Old Testament and Related Studies.* 1986, p. 57.

5.   Epigraph. "A motto or quotation, as at the beginning of a literary composition, setting forth a theme." *American Heritage Dictionary,* on CD. 1994.

6.   Farrer. "The Christian Apologist." In *Light on C. S. Lewis.* Jocelyn Gibb, ed. 1965, p. 26.

7.   Berlinski. *The Devil's Delusion.* 2009, pp. xiii–xiv.

example is the carbon-14 dating system. Although a valuable tool, it relies heavily on assumptions and, as will be discussed in the chapter titled Carbon Dating, it isn't nearly as reliable and accurate as most people suppose. Carbon-14 and other date-estimation techniques provide much of the material in conflict with religious teachings and especially with Bible chronology. Why? This and many other questions beg for answers—or at least logical alternatives to conflicting theories when definitive answers are not available. This book presents some promising possibilities for resolving such differences.

My position is: God is the greatest of all scientists, and what seems supernatural to mankind is natural to Him. Thus, I make no claim to be completely objective. Indeed, many will say I am biased by my religious beliefs. I do not dispute such a statement—but I have tried to present information accurately and fairly.

When conflicts appear between the wisdom of men and the revelations of God, it is man that is in error! It is either due to an inaccurate understanding of the revelations, of scientific truths, or of both. Truth is truth, and a main premise of this book is that truth in science is harmonious with truth in religion.

When truths are found in science (uncontaminated by false notions), there is no incompatibility with religious truths (also uncontaminated). The difficulty lies in finding the truths amidst the multitude of theories, suppositions, and misinterpretations. "After all," Nibley wrote, "how many wrong answers are there to a problem? As many as you want. But how many right ones? Very few."[8] In reality, there is only one way a particular event happened, and available descriptions are often vague, complicated, and confusing.

The more variables involved, the less likely it is for any particular theory to be completely accurate. Men propose theories, and one of those theories may be precisely correct. However, how an event

---

8.   Nibley. *Temple and Cosmos.* 1992, p. 504.

actually occurred is often not encompassed by the theory that is the most popular. J. Ward Moody wrote about what he called the Principle of Noncontradiction: "When two conclusions contradict each other, at least one conclusion, and possibly both, is wrong."[9]

Students in scientific fields, must learn certain theories in order to pass their exams—whether those theories are right or wrong. It would be well for them to heed the advice given to Dr. Henry Eyring by his father as he was leaving for college: "Learn everything you can, and whatever is true is a part of the gospel."[10]

Charles Hapgood and James Campbell[11] were privileged to confer with Albert Einstein. They reported: "After considerable discussion he [Einstein] added that it was not, however, necessary to take the present state of our knowledge very seriously. Future developments might show us how to reach a different conclusion from the evidence. Much of what we regard as knowledge today may someday be regarded as error."[12] Since Einstein's time, many answers have been found and new questions asked. The more we learn, the more we realize how little we know.

In a discussion about truth, it is important to consider the one who opposes truth. Of course, science does not recognize such a being as the devil, yet believers are aware that his role is part of the plan. He has great powers of deception and his aim is clear.

Within the religious community are those who express a belief that the Bible is literally true and unerring in every word. At the opposite end of the spectrum are atheists who completely

9. Moody. "Knowledge, Science, and the Universe." In *Physical Science Foundations*, 2nd Ed. 2006, p. 8.
10. Eyring. *Reflections of a Scientist.* 1983, p. 1.
11. Charles H. Hapgood completed his doctorate at Harvard. James H. Campbell was a chemist and electrical engineer. Hapgood. *Earth's Shifting Crust.* 1958, inside cover.
12. Hapgood. *Earth's Shifting Crust.* 1958, pp. 364–365.

disregard or even seek to discredit the Bible. Among believers, some take a figurative approach to the scriptures. Due to their belief in science, they attribute much of the Bible to allegory, myth, or fable. Of course, in the scriptures, there are parables meant to teach lessons. For instance, Matthew 13:18 begins with, "Hear ye therefore the parable of the sower." In such cases, it doesn't matter whether a specific event was being described. Since it was introduced as a parable, it is obviously the lesson of the story that is important. But is that the case for the rest of the scriptures?

For those who attribute scriptural descriptions that are contrary to their scientific beliefs to myth, questions perpetually arise. Was there a real prophet named Noah, and did a flood destroy "all in whose nostrils was the breath of life" other than those with him on the Ark (Genesis 7:21–23)? Was Jesus really born of a virgin named Mary? Was he really resurrected? Did his life and sacrifice really accomplish more than just setting a good example? Or are some or all of the scriptural descriptions just "faith promoting" fables? For those who attribute some to fable and some to truth, how do they determine which is which? It is especially perplexing to realize that most of the scriptures give no hint that they are anything but accounts of actual events. The problem seems to be that—for many people—they are "hard to believe."

How literally should the scriptures be viewed? In this book, I take a rather literal approach, supposing as Rodney Turner suggested: they generally "mean what they say and say what they mean"[13]—at least as far as they are accurately understood and translated correctly. Speaking of translation, a "most carefully thought-out definition is that of Willamowitz-Moellendorf: 'A

---

13. Turner (Personal communication).

translation is a statement in the translator's own words of what he thinks the author had in mind."[14]

Those of us who are literal believers in the truthfulness of the Bible need to take care against being overzealous in scriptural interpretation as many of the events are described only briefly and often in terms few modern people adequately understand. James E. Talmage cautioned: "We do not show reverence for the scriptures when we misapply them through faulty interpretation."[15]

14.   Nibley. *The Message of the Joseph Smith Papyri.* 1975, pp. 47–48.
15.   Kowallis. "Things of the Earth." In *Of Heaven and Earth.* 1998, p. 38.

Fact or Theory?

Facts, as usual, are very stubborn things—overruling all theory.

—Jules Verne,
Journey to the Center of the Earth

What Is Science?

The average individual's exposure to science seems a mix of news reports, documentaries, and a faint recollection of science classes from days gone by. It might also include remembering lab work, experiments, and something about testing hypotheses. Most people have a great admiration for science and scientists. Indeed, science is pictured as a high-tech, fact-filled realm beyond the reach of most intellects. In reality, it is comprised of a broad range of disciplines. They each make use of exceedingly high-precision technology, but some aspects of science are highly speculative and untestable.

Science may be thought of as the study of all things physical, or as John Pratt, PhD Astronomy, described it: "Science is the study of everything that can be observed, but true science makes no claim that it is the study of everything that exists."[16]

The root words of science—to know, to discern, to distinguish—imply knowledge of the truth. The beauty, usefulness, and sophistication are magnificent, and the inventiveness of scientists creates a mystique. William Broad and Nicholas Wade observed: "The conventional conception of science exerts a powerful fascination because it is based on a highly attractive set of ideals about how science should work. It can accurately be described as an ideology."[17]

Many restrict their definition of science to what they call "natural" phenomena, and seek explanations without any reference to God. Mainstream science seems to want it so, and some scientists have waged a war to restrict "science" from open consideration of God and his hand in nature. To believers, such an attitude is contrary to a sound approach to discovering truth.

Distinguishing Fact from Theory

The conflicts between science and religion are not a clash of facts with truths, but discrepancies between facts, inferences, theories, and misunderstandings. Scientists often use "hypothesis" to mean something such as an untested theory, and "theory" to mean a hypothesis "which has been verified to some degree." In this book, the common vernacular of the nonscientist is used, considering hypothesis and theory to be roughly synonymous. Indeed, the progression from "conjecture" to "hypothesis" to "theory" to "law" is very imprecise. It is intertwined with assumption, inference, surmise, and dependence on general acceptance. Although

---

16.   Pratt. "Has Satan Hijacked Science?" *MeridianMagazine.com*, 16 Nov 2005, p. 3.

17.   Broad and Wade. *Betrayers of the Truth*. 1982, p. 15.

theories are built using facts, it should be remembered that theories are heavily involved in organizing and trying to explain the facts.

John A. Widtsoe[18] stated: "The methods used by science to discover truth are legitimate." But he also cautioned:

> In this wholehearted acceptance of science, the Church makes, as must every sane thinker, two reservations:
>
> [1] The facts which are the building blocks of science must be honestly and accurately observed....
>
> [2] There must be a distinct segregation of facts and inferences in the utterances of scientific men. Readers of science should always keep this difference in mind. Even well-established inferences should not lose their inferential label.[19]

It is unfortunate that scientific presentations are frequently out of touch with Widtsoe's admonition. Scientists are typically bright intellectually, but descriptions of their findings are often poor in terms of distinguishing what is fact and what is inference. Making accurate distinctions is time-consuming and requires extra effort. When terms such as "estimated," "assumed," "surmised," "inferred," and "derived from" are frequently used, though they may be essential to clarity, those words tend to weaken the scientific argument. A scientist's intent in publishing often involves convincing others of the validity of his or her ideas, and such motives should be taken into account by readers. There is a significant element of salesmanship involved.

---

18. Widtsoe was a scientist, as well as a church leader from 1921 until his death in 1952.

19. Widtsoe. *Evidences and Reconciliations*. 1943, pp. 127–128.

Another barrier is that it is natural for people to simplify terms as they write. A "calculated estimate" is often written as "a calculation." "Derived from observations" might become "found," and so on. After all, a "calculation" sounds more convincing than "an estimate," and a "conclusion" sounds better than an "assumption." As you read or listen to scientific presentations, be alert to these expressions as well as others like "may be," "suggest," "appears to be," and "best explained by." There are often clues that can help in distinguishing between facts and theories, but don't expect to see them each time they are due. Also, be aware of other words that often imply more confidence than is deserved: words such as "determined" and "demonstrated."

Pratt put it this way: "It is extremely important to distinguish between facts and theories in science.... They are not always easy to differentiate, and even scientists forget to do it. And the people who write science textbooks nearly always forget to do it."[20] He also pointed out that in scientific usage, "the word 'fact' has several meanings, which can be very confusing.... It can mean either 'observation,' 'theory,' or 'truth.'"[21] Thus comes a startling message: if "fact" and "theory" are sometimes used as synonyms, how can anyone expect to adequately differentiate between them? Careful scientists don't confuse facts and inferences, and the point is this: too few are careful enough.

Those who wish to learn what part of a text is fact and what part is theory must usually do additional research such as checking the author's sources. Sometimes, it involves studying the origin and development of a scientific procedure. For example, in their work on geology, Judson and Kauffman published a discussion on time including a statement typical of many textbooks: "We now know that the Earth is about 4.6

---

20.   Pratt. "Fact or Theory?" (http://www.johnpratt.com/items/ astronomy/science.html. Last accessed 9/4/12). 1998, p. 1.
21.   Ibid., p. 4.

billion years old."[22] Such a statement implies that not only is there no doubt in the authors' minds that the earth is actually that old, but that it is in fact about that old. What evidence causes them to "know" it? How accurate is that figure? If true, what actually is 4.6 billion years old? Has the earth remained in its current state for that long? Or is the estimate of something else—such as the "age" of certain materials from which the earth was made? To understand the degree of truth behind their statement, one must study the geological date-estimation techniques and learn the theories and assumptions on which they are based, some of these are summarized in the chapter titled "Other Scientific Date Estimation Techniques."

It would be more accurate to say: "The Earth is estimated to be about 4.6 billion years old, based on the... dating system." The age of 4.6 billion is obviously not based on an actual record of observations over that span of years, but on calculations using facts, heavily reliant on theories, inferences, and assumptions.

A similar example emphasizes the point: Television programs often show archaeologists uncovering artifacts and stating their ages as though they were precisely measured. A site may be described in terms such as: "this settlement is ten thousand years old." On what basis are such age estimates made? How can people decide whether to take these statements literally? This problem is especially pertinent when it is remembered that Bible chronologies typically list Adam and Eve at about 4000 BC. If human settlements have really been around for 10,000 to millions of years, what does that imply about the Bible or at least chronologies derived from it?

The powerful role of assumption in science isn't adequately acknowledged. Pratt was keenly aware of the deficiency when he wrote: "All of science is based on various underlying assumptions. Often these are so deeply rooted that the scientists are unaware

---

22. Judson and Kauffman. *Physical Geology*, 8th ed. 1990, p. 3.

of just what they are. If they turn out to be wrong, then the entire edifice built upon them could fall."[23]

There is something about the human ego that causes people to personally cling to ideas and theories they've proposed, or beliefs they've espoused. "When scientific theories or religious opinions are repeated enough times people tend to accept them as facts."[24] When others criticize those thoughts, even if the criticism is appropriate, it takes effort on the part of the person whose ideas are being challenged to avoid becoming personally offended. David Suzuki stated: "Science is really in the business of disproving current models or changing them to conform to new information. In essence, we are constantly proving our latest ideas wrong."[25]

According to Phillip Johnson, it is essential to recognize our ignorance. Further, he indicated that showing something to be wrong "is not a defeat for science, but a liberation."[26]

Consensus Theory

Many theories have gained an almost consensus status in the scientific community. Popular acceptance can propel a theory to such a lofty realm that the line between fact and theory is further blurred. Pratt similarly expressed: "When a theory proves extremely successful in predicting observations, even scientists forget that they are supposed to be ready to discard the theory objectively and without regret when it fails. This is probably

23.   Pratt. "Strengths and Weaknesses of Science." *Meridian Magazine*. 28 Dec 2000, p. 7.
24.   W. Marvin Tuddenham, PhD Chemistry, (personal communication).
25.   Suzuki. In *If Ignorance is Bliss*. Lloyd and Mitchinson. 2008, p. 274.
26.   Johnson, P. *Darwin on Trial*. 1991, p. 154.

because they have come to believe their theory is actually 'true' rather than just a successful model."[27]

Theories which have achieved a consensus status may be thought of as lenses through which observations are viewed. If a lens is filtered to obscure certain things, then those who use that lens miss those details. Furthermore, when a theory is generally accepted, exerting the extra effort needed to distinguish the facts from the inferences is deemed unnecessary. "A 'law of nature' is one of those concepts that slips through your fingers the more you try to grasp it. The most that can be said about a physical law is that it is a hypothesis that has been confirmed by experiment so many times that it becomes universally accepted. There is nothing natural about it, however: it is a wholly human construct."[28] Consider Broad and Wade's analysis:

> When a hypothesis has been confirmed a sufficient number of times, it may take on the character of a law, such as the law of gravity.... Laws are valued principles in science because they predict and account for large bodies of facts. They describe important regularities in nature. But they don't necessarily explain the facts they describe. The law that chemicals combine with each other in fixed proportions doesn't explain why this is the case but simply states the regularity.[29]

Pratt made a profound observation:

> You cannot prove any theory to be true. You might think up a thousand totally different tests to try to disprove the theory, and it might pass every one. Does that mean

---

27. Pratt. "Strengths and Weaknesses of Science." *Meridian Magazine.* 28 Dec 2000, p. 6.

28. Editorial. "Breaking the Laws." *NewScientist.* April 29, 2006, p. 5.

29. Broad and Wade. *Betrayers of the Truth.* 1982, p. 16.

it is "true"? No, because the 1,001ˢᵗ test could prove it
false. While scientific theories are never supposed to be
considered to be absolute truth, some have passed so many
tests that they are called "laws." ... A scientific law is like
a theory that has been inducted into the "Science Hall of
Fame." But even then it might have to be modified.[30]

Relative to popular theories, it has been said, "A million
scientists can't be wrong." On the contrary, a million scientists
not only can be but are wrong at times about some ideas. Has
any mortal made it through life without being wrong on many
occasions? Has there ever been a scientist who postulated only
100 percent–correct theories?

Phillip Johnson noted a problem: namely, that scientists
recognize mistakes made by "their predecessors, but they find it
hard to believe that their colleagues could be making the same
mistakes today."[31] In 1954, Alfred North Whitehead wrote:

> Fifty-seven years ago... I was a young man in the University
> of Cambridge. I was taught science and mathematics
> by brilliant men and I did well in them; since the turn
> of the century I have lived to see every one of the basic
> assumptions of both set aside... and all this in one life-
> span, the most fundamental assumptions of supposedly
> exact sciences set aside. And yet, in the face of that, the
> discoverers of the new hypotheses in science are declaring,
> "*Now at last, we have certitude.*"[32]

Bernard G. Campbell of UCLA suggested: "We know that
we can never do more than present hypotheses on the basis of
the presently available evidence. As time-bound creatures, no

30.   Pratt. "Fact or Theory?" 1998, p. 2.
31.   Johnson, P. *Darwin on Trial.* 1991, p. 154.
32.   Nibley. *Temple and Cosmos.* 1992, p. 446.

ultimate truth about the origin and evolution of mankind can ever be known to us."[33]

> "If nothing else," Professor Pilbeam concludes his study, "perhaps the only thing that is certain is that the next decade will provide us many surprises." If that is certain, we should in all conscience postpone any further discussion or debate on such matters for at least another ten years. I could have saved myself a lot of trouble by simply ignoring the experts for thirty years.[34]

When a new theory is proposed (even if it better accommodates the facts), it is often met with resistance. There seems to be an inherent reluctance in human beings to accept change in thought. Someone once said that it takes one hundred years to displace an erroneous theory published in a textbook. The hundred years was likely an exaggeration, but the point should be taken seriously.

Rens van der Sluijs expressed: "Too often, standard textbooks and dictionaries do not offer a realistic picture of what is known about a given scientific subject. As they tend to suppress anomalous evidence, the illusion of solid proven fact is then allowed to lull the minds of the critical and the curious and slow down the progress of science."[35] Failure to disclose negative evidence is typically innocent. Writers and editors try to include only the most pertinent information and leave out that which would confuse the issue or require explanations perceived to be unnecessary.

---

33. Campbell. "Progress in Anthropology. In *Annual Review of Anthropology*" Vol. 1, 1972, p. 27.
34. Nibley. "Before Adam." http://maxwellinstitute.byu.edu/publications/transcripts/?id=73. 2011, (last accessed 9/4/12), p. 6.
35. Van der Sluijs. "The Unwavering Truth." *Chronology & Catastrophism (C&C) Workshop*. The Society for Interdisciplinary Studies (SIS), 2010:1, p. 40.

Evidence and Proof

Dr. Henry Eyring said, "For me, there has been no serious difficulty in reconciling the principles of true science with the principles of true religion."[36] However, many of us struggle with the inconsistencies. Eyring was a renowned scientist and, no doubt, had a better understanding of what parts in his realm of expertise had actually been tested sufficiently. He encouraged people to "believe everything scholars can strictly prove and suit yourself about the rest."[37]

What constitutes proof? Alasdair Beal wrote an article specifically criticizing individuals who he thought were misusing scientific evidence to try to prove their unorthodox points of view. However, his criticisms seem applicable more generally:

> In many areas of modern science, the interpretation of experimental data and the assessment of the validity of theories depends heavily on statistical analysis.... It certainly sounds convincing when someone claims that "the hypothesis... can be rejected at the 96.2% confidence interval" on the basis of a statistical reading of the experimental evidence. Yet it is surprising how often a careful, skeptical look at the information reveals that the Emperor's new statistical clothes are surprisingly threadbare. There is another... trap which sometimes catches even the most eminent scientists—it is the sin, often committed accidentally, with no ill intent, of trying to read more into experimental evidence than the quality of that evidence will support.[38]

---

36. Eyring. *The Faith of a Scientist.* 1967, p. 183.
37. Ibid., p. 183.
38. Beal. "Lies, Damned Lies and...." *C&C Workshop*, SIS, 1990:2, p. 20.

A pertinent statement about proof came from Peter Mere Latham:[39] "People in general have no notion of the sort and amount of evidence often needed to prove the simplest matter of fact."[40] In many realms of science, proof is not possible. Evidence can be found to support one scientific theory, while other evidence tends to refute it. Sometimes, the same evidence is used by one party to support a theory, while others use it to oppose the theory or at least support a different view. So with some exceptions, as in mathematics, proof is usually an individual perception rather than a scientific certainty.

Nibley observed: "When, indeed, is a thing proven? Only when an individual has accumulated in his own consciousness enough observations, impressions, reasonings and feelings to satisfy him personally that it is so. The same evidence which convinces one expert may leave another completely unsatisfied."[41] He also mentioned powerful examples: "The case of the radio can be taken as equally convincing evidence for or against miracles, depending on how one wants to take it."[42] And: "the Sophists said, 'Look, the stars are just moving up there; that proves there's no God.' Aristotle looked at the same stars moving and said, 'That proves there is a God. I don't need any more argument.'"[43]

Milton Friedman commented: "Factual evidence can never 'prove' a hypothesis; it can only fail to disprove it."[44] And, Berlinski added his view:

> By what standards might we determine that faith in science is reasonable, but that faith in God is not? It

39. Peter Mere Latham (1789–1875) was considered a great medical educator.
40. Bartlett. *Bartlett's Familiar Quotations*. 1980, p. 464.
41. Nibley. *Since Cumorah*. 1967, p. viii.
42. Nibley. *Old Testament and Related Studies*. 1986, p. 5.
43. Nibley. *Temple and Cosmos*. 1992, p. 512.
44. Bartlett. *Bartlett's Familiar Quotations*. 1980, p. 880.

SCIENCE AND RELIGION

may well be that "religious faith," as the philosopher Robert Todd Carroll has written, "is contrary to the sum of evidence," but if religious faith *is* found wanting, it is reasonable to ask for a restatement of the rules by which "the sum of evidence" is computed.... ... There are no such rules. The concept of sufficient evidence is infinitely elastic. It depends on context. Taste plays a role, and so does intuition, intellectual sensibility, a kind of feel for the shape of the subject... and much besides.... What a physicist counts as evidence is not what a mathematician generally accepts.[45]

Sir Isaac Newton, in addition to being a great scientist, was devoutly religious—although his religious beliefs were unconventional. "Dr. Ernest Jones commented: 'Most of Newton's biographers have suppressed the important fact that throughout his life theology was much more important to him than science.'" He took a literal approach to his religious beliefs, "which did not concur with the prevailing religious teachings of his time.... Newton thus becomes a highly unorthodox outcast of both camps: of the 'spiritual' and abstract." Further, he claimed: "'It is indeed, practically certain... that the true and ultimate cause of gravity is the action of the "spirit" of God.' Newton's own disciples would not tolerate his position; the very thing he took as proof of God, the force of attraction, they promptly converted into the opposite."[46]

Van der Sluijs wrote: "What causes otherwise intelligent thinkers to shut off their minds for alternatives that seem

---

45.   Berlinski. *The Devil's Delusion.* 2009, pp. 47–48.
46.   Nibley. *The Ancient State.* 1991, pp. 409–410.

genuinely possible, if not perfectly viable? A conspiracy? Ill will? Naivety? Or an intellectual blind spot?"[47]

Sometimes, things are rejected because their cause is not known. Nibley pointed out a curious case in point:

> All efforts by the geologists of Trinity College to discover water for a well on campus failed; a local dowser[48] was called in and succeeded immediately. "There is no doubt of the reality of the dowsing effect," wrote Trinity's J. J. Thompson, but the dowser could not be tolerated because no physical explanation had been found. "Although... the reality of dowsing" is conceded, "there is no agreement about its cause," and so the dons indignantly denounced the dowsing. We must necessarily view all things which we cannot explain "as unreal, as vain imaginings of the untrained human mind," which since "they could not be described scientifically... were in themselves contradictory and absurd."[49]

In a sense, dowsing is outside the realm of science. But if it works, it works, whether or not science can explain it.

Rejecting truth because neither "how" nor "why" are known goes back to ancient times. Hippocrates was known as the father of medicine.[50] According to Nibley, he debunked the thought "that garlic and onions have an effect on the human system, that the wearing of black has a depressing effect on people, that a religious state of mind can have an effect in fasting and healing." He rejected "all these 'superstitions' (though all are fully justified by centuries of testing) because he cannot explain in each case

47. Van der Sluijs. "An Aristotelian Hangover." *Chronology & Catastrophism Review.* The Society for Interdisciplinary Studies (SIS), 2009, p. 39.
48. Dowser: one who searches for water using a divining rod.
49. Nibley. *The Ancient State.* 1991, pp. 394–395.
50. Hippocrates (460?–377? BC) was regarded as the greatest physician of antiquity.

why it should be so." He insisted "that one should always use the scientific cure even when it does not work and avoid a traditional remedy even when it does."[51]

A famous Jewish scholar, Miamonides,[52] deplored "the prescribing of certain superstitious cures by the rabbis 'since though experience has shown that they work, reason cannot explain why.'"[53] In contrast, Nibley concluded: "Just because we can never prove that the matter of the brain produces thought is no reason for doubting that it does!"[54]

"Newton got the right answers, but scientists refused to accept his explanation, which embarrassed them: 'We cannot deny... that attraction belongs to matter just because we do not understand how it works.'"[55]

Religion Is Not Free of Error

It is obvious, now, that some things taught by religionists of the past are just plain wrong. And, of course, conflicting ideas demonstrate errors in the present. During Galileo's time, the religionists in power believed that the sun orbited around the Earth. Galileo wrote, "I cannot... express strongly enough my unbounded admiration for the greatness of mind of these men who conceived (the heliocentric system)[56] and held it to be true... in violent opposition to the evidence of their own senses."[57] He

51. Nibley. *The Ancient State*. 1991, pp. 395–396.
52. Moses ben-Maimon, called Maimonides 1135–1204 AD was a preeminent medieval Jewish philosopher.
53. Nibley. *The Ancient State*. 1991, p. 396.
54. Ibid., p. 415.
55. Ibid., p. 395.
56. Heliocentric: where sun is recognized to be at the center of the solar system and the planets orbit the sun.
57. Nibley. *Ancient State*. 1991, p. 446.

was forced to recant his belief that the Earth orbits the sun—no matter that he was right and the religionists were wrong.

Copernicus was fearful of sharing his conclusions on the subject of the revolutions of Earth and the solar system. His book on the subject wasn't published until he was on his deathbed. The preface states:

> As soon as some people learn that in this book... I ascribe certain motions to the Earth, they will cry out at once that I and my theory should be rejected. Accordingly... when I considered in my own mind how absurd... it must seem... that the Earth moves;... the novelty and apparent absurdity of my view nearly induced me to abandon entirely the work I had begun.... How did it occur to me to venture, contrary to the accepted view of mathematicians, and well-nigh contrary to common sense?[58]

Not only did Copernicus question his own theory, but one who "was an enemy of the Copernican hypothesis" expressed the prevailing view: "Don't theorize, he said, but open your eyes and observe without prejudice... and you cannot doubt that the Sun moves and that the Earth is at rest."[59] His argument was perfectly logical—after all, who has ever seen or felt the Earth spin on its axis?

Other questionable teachings crept into religious dogmas. Origen[60] declared:

> "The church rejects any involvement with a physical universe whatsoever.... According to an official... handbook, whoever says or believes that the physical heavens have any relationship whatever to God and the divine orders of Cherubim and Seraphim is anathema

---

58. Velikovsky. *Stargazers and Gravediggers*. 1984, p. 118.
59. Nibley. *The Ancient State*. 1991, p. 446.
60. Origen of Alexandria lived about 185–254 AD.

[accursed].... Whoever studies the Creation, the Chariot or asks what is above, below or beyond or what will be in the eternities, "it were better for him had he not come into the world!"[61]

Other religious precepts that turned out to be wrong were noted by Eyring. For instance:

> The Bible speaks of the four corners of the earth. In the time of Columbus, there were those who thought a flat earth was a religious necessity. When it turned out to be round, Christ's teachings were found to be just as consistent with the new view as the old.... When the smoke of battle cleared away and men looked at matters calmly, it became apparent that nothing essential had been lost. A lot of human philosophy disappeared, but it turned out to be unnecessary.[62]

Sir Isaac Newton's enlightened approach was described: "Newton, though firmly believing in God, could not accept the denatured and abstract religious teachings of his day, the result of centuries of eager accommodation by religionists to the prevailing science of their times.... Years of religious oppression and suppression have given all religion a bad name."[63]

An extreme example of a false religious belief was also mentioned by Nibley: "Some fathers of the church... declared that anything not specifically stated to have happened in the Bible could not possibly have happened anywhere."[64] Such a backdrop gives some understanding as to why Darwin and his associates recoiled so completely from religious teachings. Although many

---

61.   Nibley. *Enoch the Prophet.* 1986, note 215, p. 293.

62.   Eyring. *The Faith of a Scientist.* 1967, p. 63.

63.   Nibley. *The Ancient State.* 1991, p. 404.

64.   Nibley. *Old Testament and Related Studies.* 1986, p. 58.

of those teachings deserved to be rejected, it is as though the baby was thrown out with the bathwater.

Darwin's rise to popularity is amazing, even after the Inquisition and other oppressiveness of religionists. His publication of *The Origin of Species by Means of Natural Selection* was an immediate sensation: "The first day the publication went on the market, Oct. 1, 1859, the entire edition of 1500 was sold out. Thus it would seem that the book was received as a best seller."[65] After its publication "a controversy arose.... It was a struggle between the Christian theological conception of man and the conception held by science.... You were either for religion or you were for science." And, according to Huxley,[66] "the battle against the doctrine of inspiration... was the crucial engagement in the fight."[67]

Although religion is not free of error, it doesn't deserve the staggering blow given in the Presidential Address to the Utah Geological Society in 1957. Though it was delivered more than fifty years ago, similar sentiments are abundant today: "The most important responsibilities of the geologists involve... [freeing] people from the myths of Biblical creation. Many millions still live in mental bondage controlled by ignorant ranters who accept the Bible as the last word in science."[68] For those who believe in a literal approach to the Bible, *it is* the last word in some scientific matters. Such a belief is no more mental bondage than the dogmatically opposite approach taken by much of the modern scientific culture.

One day, all the grains of truth will be sorted out from the chaff of error. It is comforting to know that the current polarization of perspective is only temporary. Clues are available to help reconcile

---

65. Patten. *Biblical Flood and Ice Epoch.* 1966, p. 12.
66. Huxley, Thomas Henry (1825–1895), "British biologist, best known for his active support of Charles Darwin's theory of evolution." *Encarta Encyclopedia.* 2004.
67. Nibley. *The Ancient State.* 1991, p. 403.
68. Ibid.

the differences, but many of the conflicts will not be fully resolved until the Lord comes and reveals all things.

Science and Religion in Harmony

Individuals react to the conflicts in vastly differing ways. At the extremes are those who become hostile to either religion or science. Between those extremes many seek a comfortable mix with varying degrees of skepticism and belief. William D. Opperman suggested that seemingly incompatible ideas should sometimes be placed "on the shelf." Later, once more information is gathered, the ideas may be better understood and make perfect sense.[69]

A harmonious view was written in an ancient text known as the *Pistis Sophia*:[70] "Those who receive the mysteries of the gospel will also come to know the mysteries of the physical Cosmos."[71]

Mortality

Scientists are not in the business of trying to learn of immortality or spiritual matters. What can science reveal about the spirit? Eyring wrote: "Science has nothing to say one way or another about whether there is a spirit. This is simply to say that the evidence lies outside of our present scientific knowledge."[72] If a resurrected being allowed himself to be examined, would scientific equipment be able to detect anything about the composition of his body? Could his age be calculated? Could spiritual matter be detected by even the most advanced of modern technology?

---

69.   William D. Opperman is a scholar, historian, and a friend of mine, (personal communication).

70.   The *Pistis Sophia* is a "Gnostic text, possibly written as early as the 2nd Century." http://en.wikipedia.org/wiki/Pistis_Sophia.

71.   Nibley. *On the Timely and the Timeless*. 1978, p. 83.

72.   Eyring. *The Faith of a Scientist*. 1967, p. 66.

A curious tidbit relating to the Fall from a state of paradise came from an ancient manuscript titled "The Combat of Adam and Eve against Satan": "They [Adam and Eve] say 'Today our eyes having become terrestrial can no longer behold the things they once did.'"[73]

The temporal, or physical world is often thought of as the only world. In an article on *Science and Creationism*, Andrew Whipple described the naturalistic point of view that all reality is within the physical realm and that science is the real path to truth because he claimed, "there is no other reality beyond the physical." He went on to indicate that from a naturalistic perspective, any inclusion "of a deity or other supernatural activity… is firmly and logically denied."[74] "The trouble here," according to Nikolai Kozyrev, "is 'the deep discrepancy between the world of the exact sciences and the real world,' while all are taught to believe that the world of science is the real world and the only world."[75] If the scriptures are true, there is an entire realm beyond mortals' ability to explore.

A Puzzle

One of the immense challenges in science is determining which frameworks best accommodate the vast amounts of collected data. It can be compared to putting together a beautiful—but extremely challenging—jigsaw puzzle. One problem in the real-life puzzle is: only a relatively small number of the pieces are within reach, making it more difficult to discern how the available pieces should fit together—or how the overall picture should appear.

---

73.   Nibley. *On the Timely and the Timeless.* 1978, pp. 15–16.

74.   Whipple. "Science and Creationism." *Nature,* June 9, 1988, p. 492.

75.   Nibley. *The Ancient State.* 1991, p. 438.

So much scientific data has been accumulated that it is impossible for one person to learn it all in a lifetime. As Lynn E. Rose described it:

> "Science" is fragmented into disciplines, departments, and specialties in an arbitrary and artificial manner. Our "science" has fallen to these present depths under the sheer weight of its accumulated data and literature. Since no one of us can any longer hope to sift through all of the paper that has been accumulated, we face a choice: we can admit how little we know about nature as a whole—or we can restrict our areas of knowledgeability to fit our capacities, and thus continue to appear knowledgeable.[76]

The host of written, audio, and video resources, and almost unlimited and ever-expanding material on the Internet, is staggering.

Name-calling and Derisive Comments

To this day, the word "heretic" brings to mind horrible images. During the Dark Ages, religionists caused the death or imprisonment of many learned and wise men (beginning with the label "heretic"). In modern times, critics have also resorted to name-calling—especially when entrenched ideas are challenged. "Quack," "fruitcake," "nutcase," and other derogatory names are used. One, surprising to believers, is "creationist." Rather than simply referring to people who believe that God is the creator, within the scientific community it usually suggests naiveté and disqualifies one so labeled from being considered competent by mainstream science. Further, that all their work should be dismissed. To those of us who do believe that God created Earth

---

76. Rose. "Astronomy over Other Disciplines." *Kronos,* Vol. II, no. 4, 1977, p. 56.

and its inhabitants, the term need not be offensive (except for the negative baggage attached by critics). Although I don't believe every idea that each creationist has expressed, they ask questions and find plausible answers mainstream scientists are unwilling to entertain.

In 1963, Dr. Melvin A. Cook (who had been labeled a "creationist")[77] published an article in the alumnus magazine of the university where he was a professor of metallurgy. In it, he summarized some of his research into continental movement, scientific age estimations, and his opinion that Earth may be much younger than commonly believed. He wasn't able to provide full details in a three-page article—and his points were unconventional—but it seemed well-written and well-footnoted.[78] Subsequently, letters to the editor were exceptionally critical. One, signed by five scientists from the school's geology department, stated:

> The article is pseudo-science at its worst, scarcely worthy of serious scientific review... we must disclaim any connection with or sympathy for the fantastic conclusions of this article.... The geological arguments are so full of error as to be almost laughable. We hope that Dr. Cook will be able to elaborate in print on many of the side issues

---

77.   In 1954 Joseph Fielding Smith asked Dr. Cook to write an introduction to his anti-evolution book, *Man His Origin and Destiny*. Cook did, and almost overnight earned the title "creationist." As a result, many of his colleagues distanced themselves from him and refused to participate with him on other scientific ventures (personal communication). About his acceptance of the request from Smith, he wrote: "I complied, with a feeling of high honor but also with 'fear and trembling' fully realizing how my colleagues at the U and other academicians would take it." Cook. *The Autobiography of Melvin A. Cook*. Vol. 2. 1977, p. 31.

78.   Cook. "Continental Drift." *The Utah Alumnus*, Vol. 40, no. 1, Sept–Oct, 1963, pp. 10–12.

so that we get the documented facts and not just dogmatic conclusions. His revolutionary ideas on so many varied aspects of geology would be widely hailed if they could only be proved by field observation...

Let our alumni be assured that the members of the Department of Geology are engaged in careful study and are not wasting their time and taxpayers' money fighting the old battle of the age of the earth and universal catastrophes.... And we must naturally regard Dr. Cook's article as antithesis of sound scientific procedure.[79]

Were these geologists trying to brand Cook with a modern equivalent of "heretic"? Were they suggesting that he wasn't a bonafide scientist because he believed in catastrophes of biblical proportion and they didn't? Were they scorning him because he criticized generally accepted scientific dating techniques? Is any theory outside of the realm of "generally accepted" to be labeled "pseudoscience"? Were they serious when they wrote: "his revolutionary ideas... would be widely hailed if they could only be proved by field observation"? What would constitute proof to these men? Which of their theories have been proven? Could aspects of the same data set be used as both evidence for and against—as has happened many other times? If scientists simply reject unusual theories outright because they differ from those in vogue or because they are in harmony with the Bible, progress in reconciling the conflicts is stifled—for them.

It is ironic that a few years later, one of the geologists whose name appeared on that letter to the editor published a book with the following in its preface: "In writing and publishing this work I am risking more than time spent in writing it. In the first place I am mixing serious religion with serious science, something

---

79. Stokes et al. "... And Dissenting Voices." *The Utah Alumnus,* Vol. 40, no. 2. Dec./Jan. 1964, p. 4.

that will probably discredit me among my fellow scientists."[80] If mixing "serious religion with serious science" discredits competent scientists, something is wrong with the system!

Another letter to the editor, after calling Cook's article "pseudoscientific," added that it "would not be accepted by any reputable scientific journal."[81] It is noteworthy that Cook did publish many of the ideas summarized in the article in very reputable scientific journals.[82] One positive letter to the editor was printed in the *Utah Chronicle*:

> Dear Editor:
>
> Hurrah for Dr. Cook who has the scientific community up in arms!
>
> Methinks he may have something solid merely by virtue of the defensive hostile responses he has evoked.
>
> The status of the majority of traditionalists depends largely on their conformity and submission to "accepted" ways of looking at things.
>
> History reminds us that erroneous ideas evoke only mild concern in people secure in their understanding; but correct, though revolutionary, ideas usually cause anger, hostility and nervousness in the threatened, insecure, status quo.
>
> Thus the "dreamers" have moved true science onward while "scientists" of conformity are left behind, forgotten, in the debris of crumbled tradition.
>
> Time will verify ultimately, but for the meantime, Hurrah for Dr. Cook!
>
> —John Walden.[83]

---

80. Stokes. *The Creation Scriptures.* 1979, p. 9.
81. Kistler. "Dear editor." *The Utah Alumnus.* Vol. 40, no. 2, 1964, p. 4.
82. Although I don't know what the writer considered reputable, Cook's publications include over 200 articles in leading journals.
83. Walden. "Letters to Editor." The Daily Utah Chronicle. Feb. 3, 1964. In *Autobiography of Melvin A. Cook.* Vol. 2, 1977, p. 188.

47

The reasons scientists deride colleagues who express unorthodox views are complex. In part, it is due to their own fear of persecution—causing them to hold fast to the party-line and, for some, openly criticize those who don't. As he was retiring as president of the American Astronomical Society, Otto Struve said: "It is all too easy, step by step, to relinquish our freedom of scientific inquiry.... Fear of political persecution and of social ostracism is cropping up in unexpected places.... We should reaffirm our belief in the freedom of science."[84]

Another scientist who endured severe criticism was Dr. Immanuel Velikovsky. In an introduction to a book detailing many of the scorching attacks Velikovsky had suffered, Eric Larrabee observed: "Scholars and scientists must regularly remind themselves of how fragile their institutions of free and open discussion are unless unorthodoxy is tolerated, if not protected."[85]

Gordon A. Atwater was reportedly dismissed from both his position as curator of the planetarium and as chairman of the Astronomy Department of the American Museum of Natural History. This, he claimed, was due to his positive stance toward Velikovsky's book *Worlds in Collision*. Prior to his dismissal, he published an article in *This Week* and was preparing a planetarium show based on Velikovsky's theories. In his, article he said:

> You may have heard that Dr. Velikovsky's astronomy is rubbish, his geology nonsense and his history ridiculous. You will be hearing those things again and again.
>
> I do not intend to say that all Dr. Velikovsky's findings are correct—in fact, I disagree with many of them. But I do contend that, looking at it from an over-all point of view, the author has done a tremendous job, the effect of which is to link science and religion.[86]

---

84. Velikovsky. *Stargazers and Gravediggers*. 1984, p. 116.
85. Ibid., p. 14.
86. Ibid., pp. 114–115.

Perhaps the real controversy was the fact that influential scientists did not want science and religion linked in any way. The first edition of Velikovsky's *Worlds in Collision* came out in 1950. After succumbing to incredible pressure, George Brett, the president of Macmillan Publishing Company, informed Velikovsky of an awkward decision:

> In my thirty-three years in the publishing business... this situation is without precedent. I have to ask the author of a national best seller, number one on the best seller lists, to release us from our contract. Tremendous pressure is being exerted against our company by a group of scientists. We have secured for you an offer from another publisher... It has no textbook department and cannot be hurt...
> ... Seventy percent of... this company is in textbooks; it is the real backbone of our firm.... Professors in certain universities have refused to see our salesmen. We have received a series of letters declaring a boycott of all our textbooks.[87]

Angered over the scientists' boycott, George Sokolsky, a syndicated news columnist wrote a scathing description: "What the learned and liberal professors wanted really was the total suppression of a book which opposed their dogma. Scientists tend to become dogmatic like theologians, whom they denounce as dogmatic."[88] A journalist, Fulton Oursler, published an article with positive comments about Velikovsky's book in the *Reader's Digest*. For this, he was accosted by Dean B. McLaughlin, an astronomer at the University of Michigan:

> You had a part in advancing to the best-seller category a book that scientists confidently appraise as mere rubbish

87. Ibid., pp. 131–132.
88. Ibid., p. 145.

and the most flagrant intellectual fraud ever foisted upon the public...

We are aware which sections [of science] are certain, which are only probable, and which extremely uncertain...

... Please understand that I am speaking for a great number of experts collectively.... If this were merely a crackpot book about astronomy I would just laugh it off. But it is worse than that; worse than an attack on science; it is an attack on reason.... Many religious people are "falling for" this crazy "theory." I can appreciate their confusion about the modern world, with science and religion *apparently* in conflict. But what they do not see is this: if the Biblical miracles are explained as mere natural phenomena... then they are no longer miracles.[89]

Oursler responded:

This procedure horrifies me... Is not this book burning by intellectuals? And isn't that a matter of shame rather than pride?...

You go on to say that scientists admit the limitation of their knowledge but are aware of which sections are certain, which are only probable and which extremely uncertain. That, I take it, is a statement much more sweeping and infallible than you can possibly have intended...

... There is nothing in Velikovsky's theory that removes the miraculous intervention of God at just the right time, in full accord with the Biblical position.[90]

After learning the details of the letter, Velikovsky retorted: "The solution is apparently a permanent conflict between science and religion, with miracles or events that took place against

_____

89. Ibid., pp. 147–148.
90. Ibid., pp. 149–150.

natural laws assigned to the domain of religion, and natural phenomena to the domain of science."[91]

Not only were scientists up in arms over Velikovsky's book, but some religionists were also upset with him. They accused him "of being a rationalist—in explaining miracles as natural phenomena."[92] Indeed, what is a miracle? When the details are known and understood, it may not be the event itself that was miraculous but its timing. That a prophet knew just when to speak—and what to say—that may ultimately be the miracle.

Nibley observed that many consider anything described as "supernatural" to be unacceptable. That "our civilization today is... oriented" toward "solving problems without the aid of superhuman agency... No matter what one's field, whether science, scholarship, literature, or art, one must 'reject the supernatural' to be taken seriously."[93] What is the difference between "natural" and "supernatural?" The answer may be this: "natural" is applied to things and events which scientists think they understand, while "supernatural" is applied to events for which they do not yet have explanations.

Nibley also noted that relying too much on the word of people with prestige can have negative consequences: "Many eminent scientists, in fact, are today calling attention to the crippling effect of appeal to authority and position in science." Then he added some words from G. A. Kerkut who asserted that it is "a professional complacency that 'may in fact be the closing of our eyes to as yet undiscovered factors which remain undiscovered for many years if we believe that the answer has been already found.'"[94]

---

91.   Ibid., p. 148.
92.   Ibid., p. 280.
93.   Nibley. *The Ancient State.* 1991, p. 381.
94.   Nibley. *An Approach to the Book of Abraham.* 2009, pp. 43–44.

What happens when modern scientists actually take an objective look at unorthodox theories, particularly those that include God's influence? When they do, they often find that there is abundant factual data in support of such alternatives. But, if they pursue unorthodox positions, will they also be branded as heretics or pseudo-scientists? Although looking at field observations with a perspective different than the consensus view can be dangerous to scientists' careers, it could uncover a whole realm of understanding. What things previously undiscovered, or hidden by rigid blinders, could be learned by a more open perspective?

In the 2008 documentary *Expelled: No Intelligence Allowed*, it is alleged that freedom of speech in science is suffering. Although the star and narrator, Ben Stein, is a comedian, he has also been a speech writer for two presidents of the United States, a lawyer, and political commentator. The program contains some exceptionally pertinent and serious information. He interviewed several scientists who attribute their dismissal from scientific positions to their discussing Intelligent Design (the deliberate formation of life on Earth). The institutions from which they were removed have expressed differing viewpoints as to the reasons.

Stein interviewed Steve Fuller, Professor of Sociology at the University of Warwick, who said: "I'm actually a person of the left, and not even particularly religious. I think of myself as kind of a humanist. And I think it's sending a very bad message to religious people who are interested in science, that in some sense, in order to do science credibly they have to leave their religious beliefs at the door."[95] Dr. Gerald Schroeder observed: "There is academic freedom as long as you are on the correct side."[96]

Similar to the ideas expressed in Stein's DVD, Jeremy Dunning-Davies wrote:

95. "Expelled: No Intelligence Allowed." Premise Media Corp. DVD. 2008, 58:03.
96. Ibid., 1:25:53.

There can be little doubt in the minds of those who are involved in attempting to disseminate research results among the entire scientific community that major problems exist. It is well documented that adopting certain stances will result in an inability to publish in the majority of the so-called high impact academic journals...

People such as Wolfgang Kundt, Halton Arp and Tom van Flandern... each describes being ostracized by former so-called friends and colleagues after expressing views which did not accord with the commonly accepted view of things.... One is left with the question "What is Science supposed to be about?"[97]

The title of a book by G. Moran published in 1998 is alarming: *Silencing Scientists and Scholars in Other Fields*. In a brief description of the book, Jill Abery wrote: "Having experienced at first hand establishments' reaction to questioning of dogmas, Moran spent years examining... suppression in academia, science and the art world. This book reveals how far from ideals of truth and honesty is most research."[98]

According to Molly Farmer's report on a scholars conference May 9, 2009, David Collingridge, PhD, said:

God has been both passively and actively pushed out of the study of the natural world—and the shift happened despite the fact that some of the world's greatest scientists were also believers....... A few movements are responsible for rendering science "Godless and God-hostile." During the 18ᵗʰ century Enlightenment, writers such as Voltaire

97. Dunning-Davies. "Science in Turmoil—Are we Funding Fraud?" http://www.thunderbolts.info/thunderblogs/guest_jdd.htm (last accessed 9/4/12). p. 1

98. Abery. Review of *Silencing Scientists*, by G. Moran. *Chronology & Catastrophism (C&C) Review*. The Society for Interdisciplinary Studies (SIS) 2001:1, p. 50.

"downplayed references to God" when they rewrote the treaties of past scientists and made them available to the masses.

Consequently, many people aren't aware of the way these scientists coupled scientific beliefs with spiritual.... One evidence of the movement is the way it turns "freedom of religion into freedom *from* religion."

Collingridge said that when he was a student at two different liberal-arts colleges, he was surprised at how all points of view were accepted so long as they weren't religious in nature.[99] (emphasis added)

Fraud—In Science?

In 1610 Galileo saw four of the moons of Jupiter through his telescope. Those of us who have similarly "discovered" the awesome sight can imagine his excitement. However, "astronomers and philosophers declared that these moons were a fraud" and refused to look.[100] It is now clear that Galileo was right, and they were wrong.

Unfortunately, as in any profession, there are unscrupulous people who are willing to falsify data for power, prestige, and/or gain. Some attorneys are notorious for leading questions, and twisting words in order to try to get people to say things they don't intend to say. Or at least, focus on favorable details in order to better their clients' position. Indeed, an attorney hired to defend someone who has committed an illegal act is expected to try to find ways to shed a positive light on a negative set of facts. As advocates, they are expected to try to get a guilty party "off the

99.   Farmer. "Science Should Include God." *Deseret News.* May 14, 2009.
100. Velikovsky. *Stargazers and Gravediggers.* 1984, p. 104.

hook" or at least a minimal punishment.[101] In science, some are similarly prone to trying to justify negative evidence. Some even twist evidence to support their positions.

In their book *Betrayers of the Truth*, William Broad and Nicholas Wade documented cases of fraud among scientists and analyzed reasons for that abhorrent behavior:

> The term "scientific fraud" is often assumed to mean the wholesale invention of data. But this is almost certainly the rarest kind of fabrication. Those who falsify scientific data probably start and succeed with the much lesser crime of improving upon existing results. Minor and seemingly trivial instances of data manipulation—such as making results appear just a little crisper or more definitive than they really are, or selecting just the "best" data for publication and ignoring those that don't fit the case—are probably far from unusual.[102]

In their preface they described:

> This is a book about how science really works. It is an attempt to understand better a system of knowledge that is regarded in Western societies as the ultimate arbiter of truth. We have written it in the belief that the real nature

---

101. Years ago, I was called to jury duty in the trial of a mass-murderer. Even though the defendant confessed to the crimes and led police officers to the places where he had buried the bodies, his attorney spent almost four weeks in court trying to show reasons he shouldn't be held responsible for his crimes. In my opinion, the only significant argument to try to justify his actions was that the defendant was addicted to pornography. For this, the jury was supposed to be lenient? I was shocked that such time and effort was taken to show so little. After the trial, I spoke with the judge, asking him why. He said that the defense attorney was just doing her job—it was expected of her.

102. Broad and Wade. *Betrayers of the Truth*. 1982, p. 20.

of science is widely misunderstood by both scientists and the public.

According to the conventional wisdom, science is a strictly logical process, objectivity is the essence of the scientist's attitude to his work, and scientific claims are rigorously checked by peer scrutiny and the replication of experiments. From this self-verifying system, error of all sorts is speedily and inexorably cast out.

We began to doubt this view in the course of reporting some of the recent cases in which scientists had been discovered publishing results that were fictitious... How could a researcher, committed to discovering the truth, betray the central principle of his profession by publishing false data? ...

... Logic, replication, peer review, objectivity—all had been successfully defied by the scientific forgers, often for extended periods of time.... ... Cases of fraud provide telling evidence not just about how well the checking systems of science work in practice, but also about the fundamental nature of science... about the relation of fact to theory, about the motives and attitudes of scientists.[103]

They added some revealing details about the reality of careers in science and the pressures scientists are subjected to:

Our conclusion, in brief, is that science bears little resemblance to its conventional portrait.... In the acquisition of new knowledge, scientists are not guided by logic and objectivity alone, but also by such nonrational factors as rhetoric, propaganda, and personal prejudice. Scientists do not depend solely on rational thought, and have no monopoly on it.... ... Scientists are not different from other people. In donning the white coat at the laboratory door, they do not step aside from the passions, ambitions, and failings that animate those in other walks

---

103. Ibid., pp. 7–8.

of life. Modern science is a career. Its stepping-stones are published articles in the scientific literature.[104]

The pressure to publish is a very real challenge for scientists. A friend of mine who was an engineer at NASA indicated that the "publish or perish mentality" creates an atmosphere causing scientists to avoid spending time or interest in looking "into things that may discredit or weaken their work."[105]

A specific instance of fraud in science was reported by Abery:

> A fossil first heralded in the *National Geographic,* Nov. 99, as a missing link between dinosaurs and birds, has been revealed as a fake with the tail of one fossil specimen from the famous Chinese deposits having been glued to the body of another... An investigation by the *Geographic* revealed "a tale of misguided secrecy and misplaced confidence, of rampant egos clashing, self-aggrandizement, wishful thinking, naïve assumptions, human error, stubbornness, manipulation, backbiting, lying, corruption and, most of all, abysmal communication."[106]

She also noted that "a Japanese archaeologist admitted planting stone artifacts at 2 palaeolithic sites, casting Japanese archaeological history into doubt, including the site where 500,000 yr old post holes were supposed to mark the world's oldest building."[107]

More recently, Michael Shermer discussed David Goodstein's book *On Fact and Fraud.* He described some perceptions about science as "myth" in real life:

---

104. Ibid., pp. 8–9, 19.
105. Mark Jaster, (personal communication, Oct. 27, 2010).
106. Abery. "Fakes." *C&C Review.* SIS, 2001:1, p. 38.
107. Abery. "Japanese Fraud." *C&C Review.* SIS, 2001:2, p. 46.

"A scientist should never be motivated to do science for personal gain, advancement or other rewards.". . . "Scientists must never believe dogmatically in an idea or use rhetorical exaggeration in promoting it." "Scientists should never permit their judgments to be affected by authority."[108]

It is unfortunate that these "myths about science" don't reflect the reality more often.

Some scientists become very defensive when any aspect of science is criticized. They are offended even if the criticism is not directed toward their specialty. Those who do point out weaknesses in some of the popular theories and procedures are often branded with another label: "anti-science." Contrary to that view, because someone criticizes a specific concept or procedure in science doesn't necessarily mean he is "anti-science"—only that there seems to be a problem with that particular aspect of science.

Conclusion

There is no intent in this book to reject either science or religion or to be hostile to the truths found in either; indeed, they are two of my intense interests. Much of science is incredibly accurate. Technology has reached astounding levels of precision and sophistication. If not, how could it be used to do such incredible feats—as sending satellites into orbit and permitting almost instantaneous communication all over the world? Much of modern science involves theories trying to explain physical things. Some preach that "science is not atheistic—it is non-theistic." Either way, it generally tries to explain things without recognizing God's hand. Why must it be so? Who made such an exclusive definition? And why should it be upheld?

108.   Shermer. "When Scientists Sin." *Scientific American.* July 2010, p. 34.

It is my desire: (1) to help people by giving them some keys by which they can be better able to distinguish the truths in science from the unproven theories—particularly those that are in direct conflict with my religious beliefs, (2) to help people be more aware of the inability of science to adequately test some of the very popular theories, and (3) to help them realize that no matter how persuasively a theory is presented, it must not be taken as disproof of truths found in religion.

Reid E. Bankhead wrote:

> There is danger in confusing facts and theories. Let it not be held, however, that theories are in themselves objectionable. They play an important part in human progress. They are man's best inferential explanations of existing facts. The history of theories is largely the history of the world of thought. They have been steppingstones to the discovery of truth. Only when theories have been held aloft as unchanging facts or guides to life, have they become dangerous in the search for truth.[109]

---

109. Bankhead. Fall of Adam. (undated), p. 12.

Why the Conflicts?

The necessity of reconciling the constantly accumulating facts... with a basic error has produced a multiplicity of theories which are, in fact, a veritable cloud castle of conjectures, without substance.

—Charles Hapgood (1958)

Prominent Conflicts

The conflicts between science and religion arise, not between real facts and truths, but scientific fact and religious error, faulty scientific theory and religious truth, or misunderstandings in one or both realms. Many of the conflicts are due to assumption differences. Two examples are: (1) assuming uniform processes in Earth's history for events that were catastrophic and (2) different perceptions as to whether God plays a role in human affairs. These differences result in frequent and substantial inconsistencies.

Numerous descriptions found in the scriptures are either ignored, discounted, or ridiculed by a large number of scientists. The list below is by no means complete, but it does include descriptions from the Bible that are in conflict with popular scientific theories:

1. Creation
2. the Fall of Adam
3. Noah's Flood
4. lifespans of the ancients
5. Exodus miracles[110]
6. Joshua's long day
7. Bible chronology

The scientific method is regarded as the foundation of science, and it is a good and appropriate approach. A simplified version is this: (1) observe and record data, (2) propose hypotheses to explain what was observed, (3) test the hypotheses, and (4) use the hypotheses to predict future outcomes. When used well, these steps are performed in as scrupulous and objective a manner as is possible. But unfortunately, it seems beyond human ability to be completely objective in anything.

In actual practice, the testing of hypotheses and the replication of experiments often fall short of the ideal. Why? One problem was described by Broad and Wade:

> The short answer is that replications are not significant and therefore are rarely performed. The reasons for this at first surprising situation are rooted in the reward system of science. The prizes go for originality; being second wins nothing.... There is no credit to be won in replicating and

---

110. For an interesting view of the Exodus miracles, see Velikovsky. *Worlds in Collision*. 1950.

validating someone else's experiment except in unusual circumstances."[111]

In some realms of science, testing is a necessity—for practical application. However, their point is valid, especially in other disciplines that are particularly dependent on theories which cannot be tested. Cosmology (the study of the universe, its origin and structure) is one in particular. Cosmologists can propose grand theories, record observations, collect enough data to fill warehouses and make wondrous calculations, but how can the origin of the universe be known?

A news article in 2009 reported a revealing comment by physicist Ron Hellings: "In the last 20 years, we have learned so much about the universe that we are now mystified and profoundly confused.... This is no time for anyone to criticize anyone else's beliefs based on what cosmologists know."[112] Astrophysicist Martin Lopez-Corredoira commented: "We might wonder whether cosmology... is a science like other branches of physics or just a dominant ideology."[113]

A pertinent observation about the testability of theories in other disciplines was shared by Nibley:

> Meteorology... is quite as "scientific" as geology and far more so than archaeology—it actually makes more use of scientific instruments, computers, and higher mathematics.... Yet we laugh at the weatherman every other day; we are not overawed by his impressive paraphernalia, because we can check up on him any time

---

111. Broad and Wade. *Betrayers of the Truth.* 1982, pp. 76–77.
112. Shill. "New Look at Prophet's Cosmos." *Deseret News.* Aug. 27, 2009.
113. Thornhill. "Astronomy has little to celebrate in 2009." *C&C Workshop.* SIS, 2009:1, p. 27.

we feel like it: he makes his learned pronouncements—
and then it rains or it doesn't rain.[114]

He continued by emphasizing the inability to test theory
in archaeology:

> No scientific conclusion is to be trusted without testing—
> to the extent to which exact sciences are exact they are
> also experimental sciences; it is in the laboratory that the
> oracle must be consulted. But the archaeologist is denied
> access to the oracle. For him there is no neat and definitive
> demonstration; he is doomed to plod along, everlastingly
> protesting and fumbling through a laborious, often
> rancorous running debate that never ends.[115]

Astrophysics is another field that, although dealing with
complicated math and physics, is highly dependent on theory.
Astronomers Victor Clube and Bill Napier[116] wrote: "In
astrophysics, where experiment is not usually possible, there is a
danger of uncontrolled theoretical speculation untested against
predictions."[117]

Frank Wolfs, professor of physics at the University of Rochester,
went so far as to state: "Theories which cannot be tested, because,
for instance, they have no observable ramifications... do not
qualify as scientific theories."[118] And John Baumgardner wrote:
"It is fairly obvious that if a hypothesis cannot be tested, it should

114. Nibley. *Old Testament and Related Studies*. 1986, p. 21.
115. Ibid., 21–22.
116. Victor Clube is an astrophysicist and professional astronomer.
     Bill Napier is also a professional astronomer and holds a PhD in
     philosophy.
117. Clube and Napier. *Cosmic Serpent*. 1982, p. 68.
118. Wolfs. 1996. http://teacher.pas.rochester.edu/phy_labs/AppendixE/
     AppendixE.html.

more properly be called a conjecture or speculation, in which case the scientific method can say little about it."[119]

After an exploded star became visible from Earth in 1987 (called Supernova 1987A), all manner of scientific data was collected. That data could be interpreted in a number of different ways. A prominent astronomer, Stan Woosley, is reported to have said, "It's what you might call organized scientific chaos. When it's all over, we'll have a better idea of what causes a supernova, but the one rule now is that you shouldn't trust the theoreticians. Expect the unexpected."[120]

Paul Sukys asserted that:

> The process of scientific research is not quite as cut and dry as it is made to appear in most introductory science courses. On the contrary, the scientific process is fuelled by creativity, and without that creativity there would be little value to scientific research. However, creativity must be balanced by the day-to-day activity of the scientific establishment, the function of which is to clarify, confirm, and complement.[121]

In Suky's article, he discussed Thomas Kuhn's book, *The Structure of Scientific Revolutions*, and concluded: "Kuhn's work represents the idea that scientists are just as prone to subjective influences as other professionals."[122]

---

119. Baumgardner. "Exploring the Scientific Method." *Acts & Facts*. March 2008, p. 4.
120. Lemonick. "Supernova!" *Time*, March 23, 1987, p. 67.
121. Sukys. "Velikovskian Catastrophism." *C&C Review*. SIS, 2009, p. 18.
122. Ibid., p. 26.

Uniformity vs. Catastrophe

"Uniformity" is typically described in textbooks as "the present is the key to the past." It is a major component of many of the conflicts between science and religion. If it is used to mean that the present provides clues to the past, no problem. However, the meaning has been predominantly interpreted more narrowly—almost to the point of assuming that past processes were *only* slow and steady, while ignoring important catastrophes, and particularly—to the exclusion of those mentioned in the Bible.

More detailed definitions of uniformity often include the expression "natural causes." This too need not be troubling to those who believe that God is the master of nature. However, when the belief in "natural causes" becomes a rationale for ignoring things beyond mankind's understanding, conflicts loom heavy. Nibley commented:

> We have all grown up in a world nurtured on the comfortable Victorian doctrine of uniformitarianism, the idea that what happens in this world is all just more of the same:... the same forces that are at work on the earth today were at work in the same manner, with the same intensity and the same effects at all times past and will go on operating inexorably and irresistibly in just the same way forever hereafter. There is no real cause for alarm in a world where everything is under control beneath the watchful eye of science.[123]

Uniformity is mentioned in nearly all geology and geography textbooks as a foundational assumption on which modern geology is built. In Tom L. McKnight's *Physical Geography*, he stated: "Fundamental to any logical understanding of topographic

---

123. Nibley. *Temple and Cosmos.* 1992, p. 451.

development is acceptance of the doctrine of *uniformitarianism*."[124] Isn't he suggesting that anyone who doesn't accept the assumption of uniformity is not logical and cannot understand Earth's topography? And isn't that dangerously presumptuous? It is true that during long periods of Earth's history, physical processes (like the laying down of sediments) have been slow and reasonably steady. However, evidence is mounting in support of the idea that sudden and catastrophic events have caused substantial changes in Earth's features.

Mortals face a major obstacle in their search for the truth of the past: the inability to go back in time and see how things really happened. Professor Rodney Turner commented: "How can we determine the exact nature of this planet in its primordial state when we cannot replicate that state? The answer provided by uniformitarianism is that we must assume that nature's law-controlled processes are essentially constant and unchanging— the unknown past can be extrapolated from the known present."[125] As more and more catastrophes have been recognized and understood, it has become clear that the slow, steady, "normal" processes" cannot be relied upon as the sole means of interpreting the past.

It is now commonly believed that a large asteroid or meteor slammed into the earth at Chicxulub, off the coast of the Yucatan Peninsula. It is thought to have caused more worldwide extinctions (including the dinosaurs) in a few weeks than many thousands of years of "normal" processes.

Volcanoes are another example of important catastrophic events. Mt. Pinatubo, in the Philippines, erupted violently in 1991. More geological changes in its vicinity took place in a few weeks than did in hundreds of years by means of all other natural

---

124. McKnight. *Physical Geography*, 3rd ed., 1990, p. 366.
125. Turner. *This Eternal Earth.* 2000, p. 28.

processes. Evidence suggests a large area in what is now called Yellowstone National Park was once a "super-volcano."[126]

> Ask a geologist, "What is Yellowstone National Park?" and you are likely to get the answer, "Yellowstone is a gigantic collapsed volcano." That is the new story now popular at the visitor center at the national park. The size and scale of the collapsed volcano are so huge that they prevented the earlier generation of geologists from properly appreciating the ancient explosions which formed Yellowstone's landscape. Aided by satellite photos and detailed geologic maps, a new generation of geologists has recently outlined an elliptical depression which is now interpreted as a caldera, the collapsed crater structure formed after an extremely explosive volcanic eruption. That colossal structure is 75 by 45 kilometers (47 by 28 miles), comprises one-third of the area of the national park.[127]

Additionally, the site of Lake Toba in Indonesia is believed to have been another super-volcano. Its eruption apparently blanketed the earth with clouds of sulfuric acid, causing mass extinctions.[128]

After an interview with Albert Einstein, Hapgood and Campbell reported that he did not support uniformity: "The gradualistic notions common in geology were, in his opinion, merely a habit of mind, and were not necessarily justified by the empirical data."[129]

---

126. Savino and Jones. *Supervolcano: Could Yellowstone be Next?* 2007.

127. Austin. "The Declining Power of Post-Flood Volcanoes." *Impact*, Aug. 1998, p. i.

128. Savino and Jones. *Supervolcano.* 2007, pp. 11–12.

129. Hapgood. *Earth's Shifting Crust.* 1958, p. 364.

The Origin of Uniformity

Donald Patten, M.A. Geography, described: "Even as uniformitarianism has been an integral part of humanism for the last 150 years, so catastrophism has been an integral part of the Judeo-Christian heritage for the past 4,000 years. Biblical events bearing upon the Flood, the fire and brimstone days of the prophets... have all been of primary import to Judaism and Christianity."[130] Although "natural catastrophes" are now being recognized, many scientists are still reluctant to publicly mention any that might be thought of as vindicating biblical descriptions.

It is helpful to understand the roots of uniformity and how it became the dominant rule in so many aspects of science. It seems to have been contrived as an alternative to catastrophes; particularly those mentioned in the scriptures. Patten expressed his view:

> Anti-spiritual humanists, like Voltaire or Kant, usually applauded anything which tended to discredit the Genesis record of catastrophes. Thus the doctrine of uniformitarianism was born and nurtured.... Evolution and uniformitarianism practically require agnosticism, and they made atheism increasingly respectable.... The viewpoints of the early catastrophists became outmoded and were gradually discarded, and then they were all but forgotten. Thus our century has received an almost pure heritage of uniformitarianism.[131]

Why was there such a radical shift from the catastrophist viewpoint? Prior to the time of Lyell, Hutton, and Darwin, clues found in the Bible dominated scientific thinking in the Western

---

130. Patten. *Biblical Flood and Ice Epoch.* 1966, p. 8.
131. Ibid., p. 2.

world. Lemon and others attribute the sweeping acceptance of uniformity to the "persuasive teachings of Charles Lyell."[132]

The shift may be compared to the cutting of a cord holding a pendulum that had been tied at one extreme position, namely, that of religionists' dominance. Once free to swing, the pendulum moved to the other extreme, where it became tied to the scientific uniformitarian position, and where it remained for more than a century. David Salkeld described the shift in a rather negative manner:

> Lyell's theory triumphed over a common-sense approach to the geological evidence and this victory of theory over common-sense was perhaps his most pernicious legacy, because we find it appearing throughout scientific disciplines today...
>
> Another of Lyell's legacies is the "million years syndrome": the way in which, where other people had talked of thousands of years, he spoke of millions—just like that! He didn't bother to say how he got to millions; he just added three noughts.[133]

Lyell verbalized thoughts which had been suppressed by powerful religionists. Mounting evidence was suggesting that many religious dogmas—inferred from Bible teachings—were false. For centuries, people had been persecuted, tortured, or even put to death for teaching things that contradicted the prevailing beliefs. Finally, people were able to express dissenting views without fear of such dire consequences. It is not suggested herein

---

132. Lemon. *Principles of Stratigraphy*, 1990, p. 30. Charles Lyell (14 November 1797 – 22 February 1875) "was a British lawyer the foremost geologist of his day. He is best known as the author of *Principles of Geology*, which popularized... uniformitarianism." http://en.wikipedia.org/wiki/Charles_Lyell.
133. Salkeld. "Genesis and the Origin of Species." *C&C Review.* SIS, 2002:1, p. 10.

that what Lyell and other dissenters taught was correct, but that freedom to teach and believe as one desires is fundamental to religious thought.

Even in the recent era which includes an intensely anti-religion version of science, the swing was not to such an extreme position. Although many fine scientists have been labeled as quacks, and some have lost their positions, they have not been forced to recant their beliefs under threat of imprisonment, torture, or death. Nevertheless, there still remains a dominant uniformitarian theme, which most scientists are hesitant to challenge.

What if catastrophes in the past have done more to sculpt Earth's crust in short bursts of time than all the slow processes combined? Without having the actual documentary history of the earth, we are left to speculate and assume whatever we wish based on what limited knowledge we can gather.

The real "laws of nature" may be unchanging, but there are plenty of natural processes that are not well understood, and scientists' perceptions of them are definitely changing. There is no doubt that the rates of many physical processes vary over time and that natural laws such as gravity may be overcome (temporarily) by one means or another.

A passage in the New Testament seems to refer to uniformity— and not in a positive light:

> Knowing this first, that there shall come in the last days scoffers, walking after their own lusts,
>
> And saying, Where is the promise of his coming? for *since the fathers fell asleep, all things continue as they were from the beginning of the creation.*
>
> For this they willingly are ignorant of, that by the word of God the heavens were of old, and the earth standing out of the water and in the water. (2 Peter 3:3–5) (emphasis added)

This passage was described as a reference to uniformity by Reid E. Bankhead. He was only one of many who have considered this to be so. In Elmer G. Homrighausen's commentary on these verses, he stated: "Have all things continued as they were? Has history gone on as usual? A great many things have taken place which do not conform to the iron-clad law of uniformity."[134]

> "One of the most exciting results of the radio-carbon dating," writes Piggott, "... has been to emphasize how rapidly and severely the environment was modified." Extreme and rapid changes... have long been anathema to science. "Darwin's secret, learned from Lyell," according to H. F. Osborn, was (in Lyell's own words) that "all theories are rejecting that which involves the assumption of sudden and violent catastrophies." In a world of nuclear explosions this seems downright funny, but it "was a perfect expression," as Egon Friedell has written, "of the English temperament and comfortable middle-class view of the world that refused to believe in sudden and violent metamorphoses, world uprising, and world calamities."[135]

Uniformity need not be so contradictory to the scriptures—if a less rigid approach is taken. Trevor Palmer commented:

> Setting aside the rhetoric, the geology debate in Britain in the 1830s was between two scientific models: one catastrophist and directionalist (the face of the Earth changing significantly with time) and the other gradualist and essentially steady-state (the Earth remaining much the same, with minor fluctuations). In 1831, the first Director of the Geological Survey, Henry de la Beche, wrote, "The difference in the two theories is in reality not very great;

---

134. Homrighausen. "The Second Epistle of Peter." In, *The Interpreter's Bible.* Vol. 12, 1957, p. 198.

135. Nibley. *Old Testament and Related Studies.* 1986, pp. 28–29.

the question being merely one of intensity of forces, so that probably, by uniting the two, we should approximate nearer the truth. . . ."

When addressing the Geological Society in 1869, Huxley stated: "To my mind there appears to be no sort of theoretical antagonism between Catastrophism and Uniformitarianism; on the contrary, it is very conceivable that catastrophes may be part and parcel of uniformity."[136]

Unfortunately, the concept of a mix of uniformity and catastrophism was overwhelmed by the strictly uniformitarian view.

A humorous treatment of the rigid uniformitarian view came from Mark Twain. Although the shortening of the Mississippi River he referred to was the result of engineering projects eliminating many of the bends in the river, it is a thought-provoking spoof:

> The Mississippi between Cairo and New Orleans was twelve hundred and fifteen miles long one hundred and seventy-six years ago... Its length is only nine hundred and seventy-three miles at present.
>
> Now, if I wanted to be one of those ponderous scientific people, and "let on" to prove what had occurred in the remote past by what had occurred in a given time in the recent past... what an opportunity is here! Geology never had such a chance, nor such exact data to argue from!... In the space of one hundred and seventy-six years the Lower Mississippi has shortened itself two hundred and forty-two miles. That is an average of a trifle over one mile and a third per year. Therefore, any calm person, who is not blind or idiotic, can see that in the Old Oolitic Silurian Period, just a million years ago next November, the Lower Mississippi

---

136. Palmer. "Uniformitarianism, Catastrophism and Evolution." *C&C Review*. SIS, 1996:1, pp. 7, 13.

River was upwards of one million three hundred thousand miles long, and stuck out over the Gulf of Mexico like a fishing-rod. And by the same token any person can see that seven hundred and forty-two years from now the lower Mississippi will be only a mile and three-quarters long.… There is something fascinating about science. One gets such wholesale returns of conjecture out of such a trifling investment of fact.[137]

Catastrophes

Some have suggested that the thought of catastrophes happening in the past conjures up fear that they might also happen in the future. Clube and Napier emphasized the point:

> If then, in part, it is the thought of catastrophism that disturbs, we feel bound to remind the reader that the real, objective world is not in the end a matter of taste; it works only one way and no amount of wishful thinking can alter the reality. The aim of the scientific analyst, be he astronomer, geologist, archaeologist, historian or whatever, is simply to sift the evidence and search for that reality.… The catastrophists' views were popular in the early part of the nineteenth century… The uniformitarian view gradually prevailed so that by the middle of the nineteenth century catastrophism was dead in scientific circles. Of course the advent of Darwinism was apparently the final blow.[138]

The rigid view of uniformity, although tenaciously held to by many scientists, seems to be steadily losing ground. Even back in 1975, Nibley noted the change in trend:

137. Twain, Mark. *Life on the Mississippi*. 1874, p. 156. http://www.online-literature.com/twain/life_mississippi/ (last accessed 9/4/12).
138. Clube and Napier. *Cosmic Serpent*. 1982, pp. 13, 94.

Nigel Calder, who works for the British Broadcasting Corporation, goes all around the world getting up television programs of very high caliber. Thus, while surveying recent astronomical developments, he consulted with major astronomers in every part of the world and so built up the programs... The *Violent Universe, Restless Earth,* and *Supernature*—that is not the way I heard it when I went to school.

In my day, everything was pretty well under control. At best we had a tolerant scientific smile for anything suggesting catastrophism or any dramatic or spectacular event in history or in nature... things classed in the lunatic fringe.[139]

Contrary to the doctrine of uniformitarianism, numerous verses of scripture seem to refer to sudden catastrophes. Below is a partial list with brief excerpts. If any of their descriptions are reasonably accurate accounts of what actually happened, they have profound scientific implications. Such events would have greatly altered the "normal" rates and manners in which certain "natural processes" sculpted the landscape.

- "And the waters prevailed... and all the high hills, that were under the whole heaven, were covered" (Gen 7:19).
- "So the sun stood still in the midst of heaven, and hasted not to go down about a whole day" (Joshua 10:13).
- "The mountains melted" (Judges 5:5).
- "And he brought the shadow ten degrees backward by which it had gone down in the [sun] dial of Ahaz" (2 Kings 20:11).
- "Which shaketh the earth out of her place, and the pillars thereof tremble. Which commandeth the sun, and it riseth not; and sealeth up the stars" (Job 9:6–7).

---

139. Nibley. *Temple and Cosmos.* 1992, pp. 1–2.

In addition to being described in the scriptures, catastrophes are also mentioned in other ancient sources. Nibley commented that some scientists are now taking them seriously: "An unfailing aspect of apocalyptic[140] literature in general and the Enoch writings in particular is the reverberation through their pages of vast upheavals in the natural world. This aspect of apocalyptic has begun to be taken seriously only within very recent years, and it is the scientists rather than the theologians who are impressed by the ancient records."[141]

Scientific Evidence of Catastrophes

According to John Lewis, "The end of the Cretaceous was marked by the second-largest mass extinction of all time. Over 90 percent of the species then living on Earth vanished abruptly and nearly simultaneously. The final fall of the dinosaurs at this time was only a tiny part of the extinction story."[142]

For at least a century, scientists rejected any possibility of extra-terrestrial impacts having had any significant effect on the Earth since the time of its formation.

> In 1981 a team of physicists and geologists headed by Luis Alvarez of Berkeley discovered that a thin, global sediment layer... contained the unmistakable signature of an asteroid or comet impact. A number of metals, such as iridium, that are very rare in Earth's crust but common in meteorites, were found to be dramatically enriched in that layer. Further, ... the layer, which is dominantly composed of a very fine-grained clay, was found to contain tiny particles of minerals that had experienced extremely high shock pressures. The layer also contains a large amount of soot, and in some locations a generous admixture of tiny glassy

---

140. Apocalyptic: prophetic visions of eminent destruction.
141. Nibley. *Enoch the Prophet.* 1986, pp. 193–194.
142. Lewis. *Rain of Iron and Ice.* 1996, p. 102.

beads called microtektites. The layer is at least a millimeter thick over the entire planet… but is considerably thicker at some locations in the Americas. In Haiti it is found in association with, and painted on top of, a rubble layer tens of meters thick. Recently the "smoking gun" has been found: a huge… crater over two hundred kilometers in diameter, buried under more recent sediments on the north shore of Mexico's Yucatan Peninsula.[143]

Since Luis Alvarez's theory became so well accepted, things have changed. It is as though a dam broke—behind which was a lake of evidence. Paul Weissman[144] noted:

> Prior to the Alvarez paper, scientists who invoked singular, catastrophic events were described… as plucking answers out of thin air, or simply as crackpots. But suddenly it became a bit more respectable to speculate whether improbable events had figured in the history of the Earth or other bodies in the solar system. And once it was acceptable to look at problems this way, pieces of evidence began to fall into place.[145]

David Keys's[146] interest in catastrophes was sparked at a lecture by the tree-ring expert Michael Baillie who suggested that a major cold spell hit the earth in about 536 AD based on extremely narrow tree rings believed to have formed at that time. It resulted in his 1999 book called *Catastrophe*. Keys found evidence from all over the world that for about two years the sun was dimmed, plagues spread, civilizations fell, and starvation was

---

143. Ibid., pp. 5-6.
144. Paul Weissman: a Planetary scientist at the Jet Propulsion Lab.
145. Weissman. "Cosmic Catastrophes." *Sky & Telescope.* January, 1990, p. 46.
146. David Keys is an archaeology correspondent for a London daily paper.

rampant. He quoted the *Nihon Shoki*, an early chronicle of Japan: "Food is the basis of the empire. Yellow gold and ten thousand strings of cash cannot cure hunger. What avails a thousand boxes of pearls to him who is starving of cold?"[147] In about 535–536 AD, a Syrian bishop, John of Ephesus, reported:

> There was a sign from the sun, the like of which had never been seen or reported before. The sun became dark and its darkness lasted for 18 months. Each day it shone for about four hours, and still this light was only a feeble shadow. Everyone declared that the sun would never recover its full light again.... It wasn't just the sun's light that appeared to be reduced. Its heat seemed weakened as well. Unseasonable frosts disrupted agriculture. "We have had a spring without mildness and a summer without heat," wrote Cassiodorus. "The months which should have been maturing the crops have been chilled by north winds. Rain is denied and the reaper fears new frosts."[148]

Keys learned of evidence from ice-core analysis pointing toward a volcanic source of the catastrophe. His research suggested that the culprit may have been a volcano "in the Sunda Straits area (between Sumatra and Java), where Krakatoa is located."[149]

Dallas Abbott, of Columbia University, also noted the 536 AD disaster. As reported by Ker Than:

> Historical records tell us that from the beginning of March 536 AD, a fog of dust blanketed the atmosphere for 18 months. During this time, "the sun gave no more light than the moon", global temperatures plummeted and crops failed.... The cause has long been unknown,

---

147. Keys. "Catastrophe." 1999, p. 172.
148. Ibid., pp. 239, 282.
149. Ibid., p. 253.

but theories have included a vast volcanic eruption or an impact from space.

Now Abbott and her team have found the first direct evidence that multiple impacts caused the haze. They found tiny balls of condensed rock vapour or "spherules" in debris inside Greenland ice cores dating back to early 536 AD. Though the spherules' chemistry suggests they did not belong to an impactor, they do point to terrestrial debris ejected into the atmosphere by an impact event, Abbott says. "This is the first concrete geological evidence for an impact at 536 AD."[150]

A more recent example of a multi-year cold spell was just after the eruption of Mount Tambora in Indonesia on April 10, 1815. That eruption has been described as "the world's worst volcano disaster in recorded history."[151] It did not cause as much devastation, or have after-effects as long-lasting as the 536 AD disaster, however 1816 became known in New England as "the year without a summer." Snow fell in June and ice formed on ponds and lakes, and severe crop failures ensued.[152]

---

150. Than. "Comet Smashes Triggered Ancient Famine." *NewScientist.* January 7, 2009. http://www.newscientist.com/article/mg20126882. 900-comet-smashes-triggered-ancient-famine.html?full =tru&print=true (last accessed 9/4/12).

151. Fleury. "The Year without a Summer 1816." http://www.suite101.com/ content/the-year-without-a-summer-1816-a54675 (last accessed 9/4/12). May 21, 2008, p. 1.

152. Foster, Lee. "1816 – The Year Without Summer." http://www.erh. noaa.gov/car/Newsletter/htm_format_articles/climate_corner/ yearwithoutsummer_lf.htm. (last accessed 2/4/13).

Conclusion

The assumption of uniformity has had an extremely strong hold on mainstream science for more than a century. Until recently, that grip has been tight enough to exclude most catastrophic events—and all things biblical. Although progress has been made, there are still barriers to overcome.

3

Carbon Dating: How Old is it Really?

Radiocarbon dating is not employed to test theories, but to support them... radiocarbon always gives a scattered set of dates.

The theorists then pick the ones they believe to be correct.

—Charles Ginenthal (1997)

Many of the most obvious conflicts between science and religion involve timing issues—the dating of events in Earth's history. Bible chronologies typically list Adam and Eve at about 4000 BC. In contrast, science textbooks can hardly be found that do not refer to human or "prehuman" remains ten thousand to millions of years old. Why the discrepancy?[153]

---

153. The information in this chapter is based primarily on the writings of Dr. Melvin A. Cook, and his sources. This is a simplified version intended to be understandable to non-scientists. For more details, see his publications listed in the bibliography.

A Valuable Tool, but with Limitations

Since the 1950s, the carbon-14 system has achieved a particularly high prominence. Thomas Higham described it:

> Radiocarbon dating has been one of the most significant discoveries in 20th century science. Renfrew (1973) called it "the radiocarbon revolution" in describing its impact upon the human sciences. Oakley (1979) suggested its development meant an almost complete re-writing of the evolution and cultural emergence of the human species. Desmond Clark (1979) wrote that were it not for radiocarbon dating, *"we would still be foundering in a sea of imprecisions sometime bred of inspired guesswork but more often of imaginative speculation"*…
>
> According to one of the scientists who nominated Libby as a candidate for this honour [the Nobel Prize in Chemistry]; *"Seldom has a single discovery in chemistry had such an impact on the thinking of so many fields of human endeavor. Seldom has a single discovery generated such wide public interest."*[154]

Theoretically, carbon dating can be used to estimate the ages of once-living samples as old as 40,000 years although some earlier claims were as high as 100,000 years.[155] Due to the minute amounts of carbon-14 in any specimen, it is difficult to distinguish "the radioactive emanations from background radiation."[156] After seven half-lives, less than 1% of the C14 remains undecayed.[157]

---

154. Higham. "Radiocarbon Web-info." http://www.c14dating.com/int. html (last accessed 9/4/12), p. 1.
155. Baillie. *Tree-Ring Dating and Archaeology.* 1982, p. 223.
156. Hedges and Gowlett. "Radiocarbon Dating by AMS." *Scientific American,* Jan. 1986, p. 100.
157 Pipkin. *Geology and the Environment.* 1994, p. 36.

(Note: for simplicity, in this book carbon-14 is usually written "C14," however, when variants such as "C^{14}," "14C" or "C-14" appear within a quote, they are shown as they were published.)

Contrary to popular perception, carbon dating is not a precise answer-all to chronology questions. This fact is openly recognized by scientists involved in the field. For instance, T. C. Aitchison and E. M. Scott wrote: "It has long been acknowledged, though not always fully acted upon, that radiocarbon dating measurements are not definitive, i.e. they do not produce precise age estimates."[158]

Failing to acknowledge this lack of precision, a Nova program that aired in 2009 showed a paleontologist who had found a skeleton of an extinct animal deep in a cave. The narrator indicated that they have samples dated "because they want to know exactly how old the skeleton is."[159] Sorry—but scientific dating methods are tools for estimating ages—not determining them exactly.

At the Proceedings of the Twelfth Nobel Symposium on carbon dating, an important detail about how carbon-14 dates are actually used was shared:

> A famous American colleague, Professor Brew, briefly summarized a common attitude among archaeologists.... "If a C14 date supports our theories, we put it in the main text. If it does not entirely contradict them, we put it in a foot-note. And if it is completely 'out of date,' we just drop it."
>
> Few archaeologists who have concerned themselves with absolute chronology are innocent of having sometimes applied this method."[160]

---

158. Aitchison and Scott. "A Review of Calibrating." In *Applications of Tree-Ring Studies*. 1987, p. 188. Both T. C. Aithchison and E. M. Scott are PhDs.

159. Nova: *Bone Diggers*. Air Date June 19, 2007.

160. Säve-Söderbergh and Olsson. "C14 Dating and Egyptian Chronology." In *Proceedings of 12th Nobel Symposium*. 1970, p. 35.

Although the symposium was held in 1970, the point is still relevant. It would seem that practices should have improved as technology advanced—but more recent accounts suggest that the accuracy of the results hasn't changed much. For example: "Nobody cites the many hundreds of C14 dates... from Thera. According to C14, Thera erupted c. 1660 BC... a date which is more than 110 years too early for even conventional historians. C14 dates are still only cited when they agree with your chronology!"[161]

How Carbon Dating Works

Carbon-14 is radioactive—therefore, it decays over time. It can be used as a dating tool because creatures and plants accumulate it during their lifetimes and cease doing so when they die. The system is conceptually very simple. If four essential facts are known, an age can be calculated with precision. They are (1) the C14 concentration in a specimen at its time of death, (2) the decay rate of C14, (3) the current C14 concentration in the specimen being "dated," and (4) if anything else has affected the specimen's C14 content. Note: only third of those four necessary facts can be measured; the other three must be estimated.

Radioactive decay causes once-living specimens to lose half of their C14 atoms in about each 5,730-year half-life. Thus, if its level today is half of its estimated original content, it is said to be 5,730 years old. If its current level is only one quarter of the original, 11,460 years, and so on. See figure 3.1.

---

161. Notes and Queries. "Tutankhamun radiocarbon dates." *C&C Review.* SIS, 1996:1, p. 34.

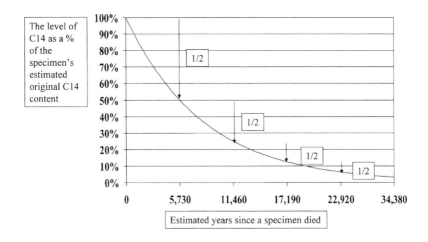

Figure 3.1. Radioactive decay of C14. The curved line represents the declining amount of C14 atoms over time due to radioactive decay. During each half-life (~5,730 years), about half of the remaining C14 atoms in a specimen are expected to decay.

Essential Fact #1: The Original Content

Since scientists aren't able to take sophisticated equipment back in time to actually measure the C14 concentration when a plant or animal died, it is necessary to estimate. It was natural for Willard Libby, the inventor of the method, to assume *uniformity* in this estimation.[162] No doubt, he had been taught it from his youth, and he reasoned that living things in the past must have had the same C14 levels as seen in living things in modern times. Therefore, he used modern C14 levels to approximate the ancient.[163] This is graphically represented in figure 3.2.

---

162. Libby. "Accuracy of Radiocarbon Dates." *Science*, Vol. 140, no. 3564, April 19, 1963, p. 278.

163. Otlet. "Impact of Atmospheric Carbon-14." In *Radiocarbon after Four Decades.* 1992, p. 529.

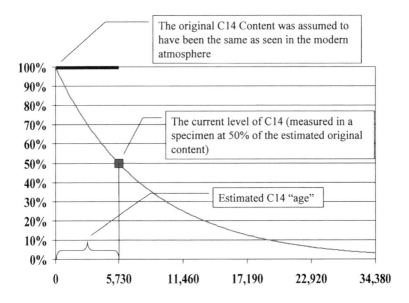

Figure 3.2. The curved line represents the loss of C14 over time due to radioactive decay. The bold line at the 100% level represents the generally accepted assumption that for thousands of years the original content has been at roughly the same level as what is observed in the atmosphere in modern times. The small box on the decay curve represents the current level of a particular once-living specimen, in this instance measured at 50 percent of its assumed original content. The technique suggests that the specimen died about 5,730 years ago (one half-life).

Testing has not verified Libby's assumption of uniformity. Indeed, experiments have led to a startling conclusion: that C14 levels in the past were lower than they are now. If the experimental data was correctly collected and interpreted, Libby's assumption in estimating the original content is wrong.[164] That assumption error causes C14 dates to appear "older" than the actual ages of

164. See Cook. *Scientific Prehistory*. 1993, pp. 10–22.

the specimens dated. (See the "Assumption Error" section later in this chapter for more details.)

Essential Fact #2: The Decay rate of C14

The decay rate of C14 is estimated by comparing measurements taken in the recent past with C14's current radioactivity levels. Early estimates of C14's half-life ranged from 1,000 to 25,000 years.[165] The 5,730-year half-life was selected as the standard at the Fifth Radiocarbon Dating Conference at Cambridge University, July 1962. Immediately prior to that time, some labs had been using 5,568 years, which introduced undesirable discrepancies in age estimates.[166] More recently, 5,715 years was published for C14's decay rate.[167]

Beal noted a frailty in estimating the half-life: "It is worth remembering that the half-life of C14 used in the calculations (5,730 years or thereabouts) has been calculated from measurements taken over only a few decades. It is also worth remembering that in a sample from 3000 BC the C14 content is now only diminishing at a rate of 0.0066% per year,… it would take only slight contamination to affect the result."[168]

Although there is still some uncertainty regarding the precise decay rate of C14, perhaps a more important question is whether the decay rate is consistent over time. Experiments have been performed to try to determine if radioactive decay rates can be affected when the materials involved are subjected to unusual conditions. As early as 1954, Kalervo Rankama reported: "the decay constant may be slightly altered by putting the nuclide in

---

165. Arnold. "Early Years with Libby at Chicago." In *Radiocarbon after Four Decades.* 1992, p. 3.

166. Libby. "Accuracy of Radiocarbon Dates." *Science*, April 19, 1963, p. 278.

167. *CRC Handbook of Chemistry and Physics*, 72nd ed. 1991, p. 11.29.

168. Beal. "A Bit Creaky?" *C&C Review.* SIS, 1991, p. 40.

a different chemical combination or physical state."[169] A more recent report suggests:

> The constancy of rate of radioactive decay in all physical and chemical conditions is the mainstay of radiometric dating. However, "changes in radioactive decay constant depending on the physical and chemical environment of the nuclide have been known for 40 years." In particular a researcher... found that with a mixture of titanium and radioactive tritium "its radioactivity declined sharply" as it was heated from 115 to 160 degrees C. As the discovery was not of direct relevance to the research involved it was not published until 1994, when it appeared to have relevance to the problem of "cold fusion."[170]

That test involved other radioactive elements, but it showed that radioactive decay rates can be altered, thus creating more uncertainty regarding the second of the facts essential to precise C14 dates. Other things affecting decay rates were mentioned by G. Brent Dalrymple, including electric fields, pressure, and chemical combination.[171]

Radioactive decay is described as "spontaneous." In other words, "not due to any known cause."[172] What if a cause is identified some day? Some scientists already favor the idea that sub-atomic particles such as neutrinos may affect radioactive decay. Frederic Jeuneman expressed this thought in 1972. He suggested that a supernova—one that is believed to have exploded about 11,000 years ago and only 1,500 light years away—could have thrown dating measurements into a "cocked hat!" "Being so close, the...

169. Rankama. *Isotope Geology.* 1954, p. 63.
170. Monitor. "Radioactivity declines with temperature." *C&C Workshop.* SIS, 1994:2, p. 30.
171. Dalrymple. *The Age of the Earth.* 1991, p. 89.
172. Curie. *Radioactive Substances.* Reprint edition 1971, p. 6.

neutrino flux of the superexplosion must have had the peculiar characteristic of resetting all our atomic clocks."[173]

Fifteen years later, scientists observed Supernova 1987-A. It was the first exploded star close enough to Earth and large enough for detailed analysis—made possible by the emplacement of modern neutrino-detection equipment. Roland Pease reported that it was the only supernova that could be seen well since 1604.[174] Although it was outside our galaxy, estimated to be 160,000 light-years away, "a 100-fold spike in the neutrino counting rate, a peak never seen before or after"[175] was discovered by detectors both in the Japanese Alps and in a salt mine under the shore of Lake Erie. Thus, neutrinos and other subatomic particles from nearby supernovas may have had an important effect on radioactive decay.

Another unknown is whether there are any processes, yet undiscovered, which might affect radioactive decay rates. The decay rate may not be certain or everlastingly set; however, it appears to be consistent enough to be useful in the formula for C14 date estimates during historical times.

Essential Fact #3: Measuring Current Levels

Measuring the current levels of C14 in a specimen is—by far— the most precisely determined of the four essential facts. With the

---

173. Jueneman. "Will the Real Monster Please Stand Up." *Industrial Research*, Sept., 1972, p. 15.

174. Pease. "Supernova Brightens the Horizon." *Nature*, April 15, 1993, p. 585.

175. Morrison, "Wonders: On Neutrino Astronomy." *Scientific American*, Nov. 1995, p. 108.

advent of AMS technology,[176] scientists can determine the current composition of a sample with an impressive level of precision. However, "AMS tends to be significantly more expensive than decay counting,"[177] and the less-precise technique is often employed.

Essential Fact #4: Has Anything Else Affected the Specimen's C14 Content?

This component of the formula is the most difficult to estimate due to numerous variables and unknowns. Contamination of some samples has been identified, leading scientists to take extra precautions in order to protect specimens. Testing the accuracy of this required fact is limited and subject to a vast array of possible assumptions. (More details are provided in Appendix 1.)

Where Does Carbon-14 Come From?

Carbon-14 is rare,[178] and it forms when nitrogen-14 (N14) reacts with free neutrons.[179] Neutrons are "freed" from their nuclear bonds

---

176. AMS: Accelerator Mass Spectrometry. A highly sophisticated scientific technique designed to measure different elements, and even to distinguish their rare isotopes. Of particular interest is its ability to identify quantities of the rare C14 relative to the abundant C12, and do so using smaller amounts of sample material.

177. Rafter Radiocarbon Laboratory GNS Science. http://www.gns.cri.nz/Home/Services/Laboratories-Facilities/Rafter-Radiocarbon-Laboratory/Measuring-Radiocarbon/Accelerator-Mass-Spectrometry (last accessed 9/4/12).

178. There are several isotopes of carbon, with C12 being the most abundant (98.90%), C13 next at (1.10%), *CRC Handbook of Chemistry and Physics*, 72nd ed. 1991, p. 11.29. Radioactive C14 is less than 0.0000000001% of total carbon on the earth, Higham. "Radiocarbon Web-info." *http://www.c14dating.com/int.html*, (last accessed 9/14/12), p. 1.

179. Nitrogen-14 is the most abundant element in earth's atmosphere, about 78 percent by volume. *CRC Handbook of Chemistry and Physics*, 72nd ed. 1991, p. 4.19.

in chain reactions when cosmic rays collide with atoms in Earth's atmosphere.[180] C14 has the same chemical properties as C12 and C13 (stable isotopes of carbon),[181] and any of the carbon isotopes can react with oxygen to form carbon dioxide, which enters plants "as a result of photosynthesis and by absorption through the roots."[182] Plants are eaten by animals, and living things on Earth become ever-so-slightly radioactive due to ingesting things containing C14. When something dies, it no longer assimilates C14, at least not by the means described above. If an artifact is preserved from physical decay and leaching of chemicals, radioactivity may be the sole means whereby it gradually loses its C14.

---

180. Cosmic rays are high-energy nuclear particles which continuously bombard the earth from all directions. *CRC Handbook of Chemistry and Physics.* 1991, p. 11.133. Cosmic rays travel at nearly the speed of light. These collisions cause cascades of secondary nuclear particles, some of which are free neutrons. *McGraw-Hill Concise Encyclopedia of Science.* 1997, pp. 501, 1289–1290.

181. Hedges and Gowlett. "Radiocarbon Dating by AMS." *Scientific American,* Jan. 1986, p. 100.

182. Faure. *Principles of Isotope Geology.* 1977, p. 307.

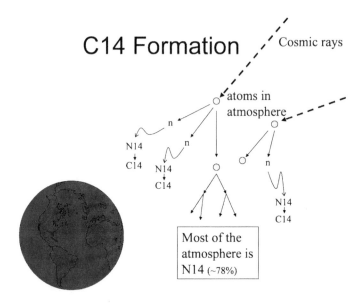

Figure 3.3. Carbon-14 formation. Cosmic rays continually bombard the earth. When they strike atoms in the atmosphere, chain reactions occur, some of which result in free neutrons (n) that readily react with nitrogen-14 to form C14.

Assumption Error

Libby assumed that C14 levels must have remained constant during at least the last 20,000 to 30,000 years.[183] Therefore, "a steady-state condition should have been established, in which the rate of formation of carbon-14 would be equal to the rate at which it disappears to reform nitrogen-14."[184]

To test the assumption, the rate that C14 forms in Earth's atmosphere was estimated (based on measurements from various locations around the globe). This was compared with C14's decay

---

183. Libby. *Radiocarbon Dating*, 2nd Ed. 1955, pp. 8–9.

184. Libby. "Radiocarbon Dating." *Science*, March 3, 1961, p. 622.

rate. The testing indicated that C14 is forming faster than it is decaying. A simple analogy may be helpful: Suppose water is steadily dripping into a large tub. As long as water drips in faster than it escapes, the water-level increases. If it reaches a point where the rate water is dripping in is matched by the rate it escapes, it is in a steady-state or equilibrium. Similarly, for C14 to be in a state of equilibrium, its formation rate would need to be matched by its decay rate.

Initial estimates indicated the formation rate was "about 10 percent" higher than the decay rate. This difference was attributed to "experimental errors."[185] Other measurements were made, and a startling conclusion was reached. In 1963, R. E. Lingenfelter (one of Libby's collaborators) wrote: "There is strong indication, despite the large errors, that the present natural production rate exceeds the natural decay rate by as much as 25%."[186] Here is a perplexing question: If this was true in 1963, what logical deduction can be made about the distant past? Isn't it that C14 has likely been building for some time, and thus, past levels were lower than current?

It seems an odd twist of logic to ignore the strong experimental evidence, and instead assume that C14 levels have been constant for many thousands, if not millions of years. Are there any compelling reasons to continue to assume what appears to be erroneous? There is one that is very persuasive: if C14 has been building for thousands of years, the assumption of uniformity in the atmosphere is wrong, and the current concentration of C14 is not an acceptable estimate for the past levels. What a horrible thought for staunch uniformitarianists! Could this be the main reason most scientists ignore the evidence for non-equilibrium?

---

185. Ibid.
186. Lingenfelter. "Production of Carbon 14 by Cosmic-Ray Neutrons." *Reviews of Geophysics*. 1963, p. 51.

Perhaps it is—but the most common cause is likely ignorance of these details.

Another compelling reason seems to be that the C14 dating system has already been adjusted (calibrated) to fit better with tree-ring dating—which has been used to adjust conventional chronology. Changing it would upset the apple cart—that is, it would again cause the C14 dates to be out of sync with the claimed "historical dates."

If C14 levels have, in fact, been building for say at least the past four thousand years, the original C14 content in an ancient specimen would have been significantly less than current levels. Therefore, failure to recognize buildup causes specimens to appear older than they actually are, and it introduces a significant error into the first of the four components of the calculation formula. Would it be better not to buck the system and continue using an established—but invalid assumption? No. It appears that a revamping of the radiocarbon dating technique is needed.

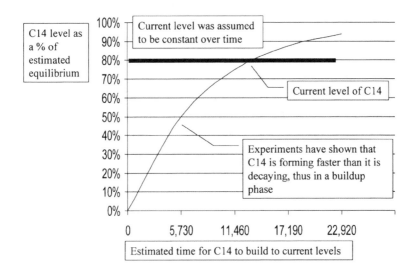

Figure 3.4. A buildup curve contrasted with the assumed constant level. The curved line going up from 0 percent

represents a rough estimate of the C14 levels in the atmosphere over the past 12,000 years or so. It is based on the 30,000 years Libby suggested was needed for C14 to build to a level close to equilibrium. The bold horizontal line represents the popular assumption that levels have remained constant over at least the past 12,000 years and are expected to remain the same in the future. Since current levels are about 80 percent of the equilibrium as calculated from the difference between the formation and decay rates, the line is drawn at 80 percent rather than the 100 percent of equilibrium used in figure 3.2.

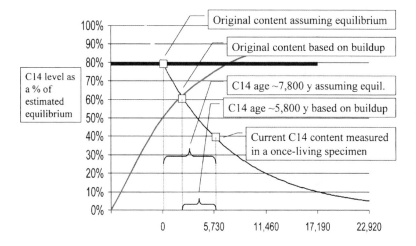

Figure 3.5. A carbon-14 "date" based on buildup versus the commonly assumed uniformity. The bold horizontal line represents the common assumption that C14 levels remain constant in the atmosphere (at about 80 percent of estimated equilibrium). The downward curve represents the decay of C14 over time. The curved line going up from 0 percent represents a rough estimate of the buildup of C14. If it is actually building as depicted, a specimen that died about 3,700 years ago would be "dated" by

conventional means 5,730 years—more than 2000 years too old—simply because of an assumption error.[187]

Since the C14 levels appear to be increasing, how does one correctly estimate the original content of a specimen? Using the difference between the formation rate and the decay rate, a buildup curve may be derived—as Cook has done.[188] Simplified versions of his graphs are presented in figures 3.4 and 3.5.

If the buildup curve as shown is reasonably accurate, the original C14 content of the specimen would have been only about 60 percent of equilibrium rather than the assumed 80 percent. Thus the older the artifact, the less C14 it originally contained at its time of death, and the greater the error of those C14 "ages" which fail to take this into consideration. Cook wrote: "I raised an issue [non-equilibrium] in 1955 that to this day has not been successfully rebutted."[189]

"Known" Historical Dates

From the beginning of the C14 system, discrepancies were found between its dates and the supposed "known dates" from historical and archaeological sources. The "historical dates" were often "older" than the ages obtained from C14. In 1965, Libby wrote:

> At the present time, radiocarbon dates seem to be accurate within one or two centuries back to about 3500 years ago and possibly to 4000, but beyond that there appears to be a discrepancy between the Egyptian historical and radiocarbon dates which increases to some 500 years or

---

187. See Cook. *Scientific Prehistory.* 1993, p. 11. This is a simplified version of Cook's Figure 2-1.
188. Cook. *Scientific Prehistory.* 1993, p. 11.
189. Cook. *The Autobiography of Melvin A. Cook.* Vol. 2. 1977, p. 72.

more…. It may be, of course, that this is historical error rather than error in the radiocarbon dating method."[190]

Since then, evidence has been amassed showing that many of the "known historical dates" were wrong by a significant margin. Serious studies by chronologists have led to major revisions of the Egyptian dating (see the chapter titled "History or Myth" for some specifics). In the mean time, scientists had adjusted the C14 system to fit erroneous Egyptian dates.

It is ironic that since C14 dating was "corrected" (calibrated) to fit the older dates, it is now out of sync with the corrected historical dates. Paul Damon et al. wrote: "The key date for fixing the time the Egyptian Middle Kingdom and the periods preceding it is the seventh year of the reign of Pharaoh Sesostris III of the Twelfth Dynasty. This date is fixed by a heliacal rising[191] of the star Sirius."[192] Although Damon referred to it as a "fixed" date, a number of contrary estimates for the age of this event have been claimed. I have collected thirty-two different dates from published sources attributed to the beginning of Sesostris III's reign. They range from 1300 to 2099 BC. Nineteen of them were radiocarbon dates that range from 1300 to 1895 BC. This so-called fixed date is by no means certain.

Calibration from Tree-ring Dates

As carbon dating gained acceptance it was believed necessary to calibrate the results of the technique to agree with tree-

190. Libby. "Natural Radiocarbon and Tritium." In *Radiocarbon and Dating.* 1965, p. 749.
191. Heliacal: of or near the sun; the apparent rising, or setting, of a star or planet just after conjunction with the sun. *Webster's College Dictionary*, 4th ed. 2005.
192. Damon et al. "Fluctuation of Atmospheric C14." In *Radiocarbon and Dating.* June 7–11, 1965, p. 417.

ring dates.[193] Pearson, Pilcher, and Bailey. suggested more than one calibration was needed.[194] However, calibration has led to dates substantially older than those from uncalibrated C14 date estimates.

R. M. Porter criticized an introductory statement made at the Seventeenth International C14 Conference by H. Bruins indicating his "confidence in ^{14}C's ability to solve all problems overlooks the fact that ^{14}C dates have to be corrected by dendrochronology [tree-ring dating]."[195] Bernard Newgrosh was also critical of the C14 calibrations when he wrote: the "adoption of calibrated radiocarbon dates has led to artificially stretched chronologies and non-existent 'dark ages.'"[196] Porter noted:

> By 1977 calibration had arrived. Callaway and Weinstein…. admitted that they had to reject almost all of the previously published Ai dates as "deviant". For some of these they had sent fresh test pieces—from the same specimens—for a retest at Texas and also at Pennsylvania. Both laboratories gave results which again roughly agreed with conventional dates. These results, however, incorporated radiocarbon calibration. If one looks at the "raw" radiocarbon results, before calibration, there is effectively a 600 year difference between the later and earlier results on the very same specimens![197]

---

193. Becker. "History of Radiocarbon Calibration." In *Radiocarbon after Four Decades.* 1992, pp. 34–48.

194. Pearson, Pilcher, and Baillie. "High-Precision 14C Measurement." *Radiocarbon,* Vol. 25, 1983, p. 184.

195. Porter. "Recent Developments in Archaeology." *C&C Review.* SIS, 2002:1, p. 14.

196. Newgrosh. "Calibrated Radiocarbon.'" *C&C Review.* SIS, 1991, p. 37.

197. Porter. "Ai, Jericho and 'Deviant' C14 Dates." *C&C Review.* SIS, 1992, p. 26.

Circulation Lag in the Oceans

In the early days of carbon dating, it was assumed that various segments of the biosphere would contain roughly equal levels of C14. Libby noted that one predicted difference was that "sea shells should differ and be richer in C-14 than organic matter in general; yet we find... that this is not so."[198] Goodfriend and Hood noted: "Shell organic carbon is largely derived from plant material but apparently also contains carbon derived from... bicarbonate. This makes it subject to a small age anomaly (estimated at up to ca 150 years) due to incorporation of carbon ultimately derived from limestone."[199]

Libby estimated that it would take about one thousand years for C14 to mix with and spread throughout the oceans after forming in the atmosphere.[200] More recently, Shackleton et al. presented actual lag time data for surface water in the eastern Pacific Ocean indicating it "has an 'age' of ~580 yr whereas deep water has an 'age' of ~2,100 yr."[201] In addition, "errors in radiocarbon age may be as much as 3000 years for shell samples from rivers."[202]

Certain other watery environments can cause the carbon levels of some samples to contain diluted amounts of C14, depending on the nature of the source of the water.[203] A specific instance

---

198. Libby. "Natural Radiocarbon and Tritium." In *Radiocarbon and Dating*. 1965, p. 747.

199. Goodfriend and Hood. "Carbon Isotope Analysis." *Radiocarbon*, Vol. 25, No 3, 1983, p. 827.

200. Libby. "Radiocarbon Dating." *Science*, March 3, 1961, p. 622.

201. Shackleton et al. "Radiocarbon Age of Deep Water." *Nature*, Oct. 20, 1988, p. 709.

202. Keith and Anderson. "Radiocarbon: Fictitious Results." *Science*, Vol. 141, no. 3581, 1963, p. 636.

203. Hedges. "Sample Treatment in 14C Dating." In *Radiocarbon after Four Decades*. 1992, p. 173.

was mentioned by Libby: "It has recently been shown that a New England lake whose bed was entirely ancient limestone and which was fed mainly by water leached through ancient limestone... whose radiocarbon content was only 77 ± 2 per cent of the value for the carbon in modern wood."[204] Thus something living in that lake would have a C14 content only about 77 percent of expected, and an uncorrected radiocarbon "age" of about 2,200 years.

Charcoal and Bones

Charcoal and bones are favorites among archaeologists as carbon dating candidates. Although bones are often dated, the accuracy of their age estimates is in question. J. Van der Merwe reported: "Charcoal which is buried in the ground is subject to contamination by rootlets, carbonates, and humic acid."[205] Jesse Lasken also noted difficulties:

> "The same standard techniques are too frequently used in ignorance to combine the results of determinations of dissimilar events or materials (e.g. heartwood charcoal and animal bone). Such combinations give an unjustified air of precision to a date, and they disguise real uncertainty.". . .
> ... Since the wood could have come from the inner rings of an old tree,[206] its radiocarbon age could vary by centuries from the time of the historical event with which it is associated.[207]

R. E. Taylor indicated:

---

204. Libby. *Radiocarbon Dating*, 2nd Ed. 1955, p. 11.
205. Van der Merwe. *Carbon-14 Dating of Iron*. 1969, p. 66.
206. The inner rings are the oldest while the outer rings are the most recently grown.
207. Lasken. "Misusing Radiocarbon." *C&C Review*. SIS, 1992, pp. 17–18.

Discussions concerning the reliability of ^{14}C-based age determinations on bone have occurred throughout all four decades of radiocarbon research... Despite the amount of attention given... a tradition of skepticism concerning the general reliability of bone ^{14}C values remains.... From the point of view of the archaeologist or paleoanthropologist, this is an unfortunate situation, since bone material is present in many sites where other organics are not.... ... Carbon-containing inorganic materials... are transported into the bone matrix from the groundwater and soil environment by chemical exchange.[208]

In other words, since bones can absorb minerals containing carbon through soil and groundwater, their C14 content can be altered—causing "dates" to appear younger, or older, than the actual age of the bone. Can other materials be similarly affected by chemical exchange?

Inconsistencies with Other Methods

Although most of the geologic dating procedures are used to estimate ages believed to be much older than the C14 dating, one that is claimed to overlap is the uranium-thorium (U-Th) method. Unfortunately, the results have not been consistent. For things that lived more than nine thousand years ago, according to Bard et al., "the ^{14}C ages are systematically younger than the U-Th ages, with a maximum difference of ~3,500 yr at ~20,000 yr BP." They then suggested that the uranium-thorium technique can be used to calibrate carbon dating beyond the realm of tree-ring calibrations.[209] Here is another example where a different dating

---

208. Taylor. "Radiocarbon Dating of Bone." In *Radiocarbon after Four Decades.* 1992, pp. 375, 377.

209. Bard et al. "Calibration of the [14]C Timescale." *Nature.* May 31, 1990, p. 405.

method produced older dates than C14, and it was assumed that the C14 method was less accurate.

Bard et al. also noted that various techniques produce different "dates" for the same samples. Large discrepancies have been found between Carbon-14 and potassium(K)-argon(Ar) "ages" as well as between C14 and thermoluminescence.[210] What causes people to suppose that less-testable methods such as U-Th, and K-Ar, are more accurate than the C14? Could it be a preference for "older" dates? What historical dates can be used to check their validity? There are none. Wouldn't it be more logical to first fix the C14 system for known problems and then use it to calibrate the other overlapping methods?

Misleading Terminology

Two terms frequently used in describing scientific age estimations are misleading, namely "absolute date" and the "±" (plus or minus) symbol. "Absolute date" gives the impression—at least to non-scientists—that the age listed is certain or assured to be correct. However, in common usage, it simply means the age estimate is expressed in years. The following definition is fairly typical in science texts: "We can consider geologic time from two points of view: as relative or as absolute. Relative time—that is, whether one event in Earth history came before or after another event disregards years.... On the other hand, if we can determine [estimate] how many years before the present an event took place—whether it was 10,000 years or 60 million years—we deal in absolute time."[211]

The definition of "absolute time" found in the *Dictionary of Scientific and Technical Terms* states: "Geologic time measured

210. Ibid., p. 408.
211. Judson & Kauffman. *Physical Geology*, 8th ed. 1990, p. 3.

in years, as determined by radioactive decay of elements."[212] The words "absolute," "measured," and "determined" imply much more confidence than the dating processes deserve. The definition would be more accurate if the terms were replaced by some that depict the uncertainty. In her introductory remarks to *Nuclear Methods of Dating*, Etienne Roth expressed more clearly that "absolute" referred to "an estimate... expressed in years." She also noted that "the term is questionable because of the uncertainties which still affect established time scales."[213]

When the plus or minus symbol (±) is used to portray the margin of error in C14 dates, it is particularly misleading. For example, a C14 age expressed as "3,000 ± 100 years" leads readers to believe that the age is assured to be accurate within 100 years of 3,000; that the thing being dated almost certainly died some time between 2,900 and 3,100 years ago. What it really represents is the laboratory's estimate of the accuracy of their measurement of current levels of C14 in the specimen. Thus, the margin of error is based on only one of the four essential facts for accurate date calculations—and the most precise one at that. Aitchison and Scott described an additional concern:

> Every radiocarbon age has an associated error term of which a major component is the counting error of the radioactive measurement process.... The quoted error terms are estimated in different ways by different laboratories...
> ... Analysis of the results from twenty laboratories throughout the world suggest that commonly quoted counting errors should be approximately doubled and that several of the laboratories which participated in the study

---

212. Absolute time. *McGraw-Hill Dictionary of Scientific and Technical Terms.* 1974.

213. Roth. "Dating Using Radioactive Phenomena." In *Nuclear Methods of Dating.* 1989, p. 4.

were systematically biased with respect to others and to the overall trend by an amount up to several hundred years.[214]

Although only taking into account a small portion of the many uncertainties, scientists are at least recognizing that the stated precisions (±) are not to be relied on.[215] Pearson, Pilcher, and Baillie noted: "The error associated with the ^{14}C date, ie, the precision quoted... should include all inaccuracies, the error in the calibration, the choice of sample material and knowledge of the growth period."[216] Although they only listed three out of the large number of factors which can contribute to inaccuracy, they were at least on the right track.

Scientists presumably do not use this terminology to deliberately mislead readers, nevertheless laymen and scientists who haven't studied the details can, in fact, be misled. I remember being intimidated by such terms in my early chronology studies, particularly when a date I was working on was outside the claimed precision range of a corresponding carbon date or an "absolute date" contrary to my findings—not so now.

Conclusion

Of the four facts essential to precise carbon dating: The first (the original C14 content) is based on an assumption—one that is contradicted by experimental evidence. The second (the C14 decay rate) appears to be accurate enough to support the system during historical times. The third (the current content) is by far the most sure of the four (when AMS is used). And the fourth (other factors that may have affected the process) presents serious

214. Aitchison and Scott. "A Review of Calibrating." In *Applications of Tree-Ring*. 1987, pp. 188–189.
215. Beal. "A Bit Creaky?" *C&C Review*. SIS, 1991, p. 40.
216. Pearson, Pilcher, and Baillie. "High-Precision 14C Measurement." *Radiocarbon*, 1983, p. 184.

problems. Newgrosh expressed his concern: "Radiocarbon dating is based on assumptions which are now known not to hold true. If we were going to re-invent the method, knowing what we do about those assumptions, there is a real possibility that the method would now be deemed inadmissible."[217]

Despite its weaknesses, radiocarbon is a valuable tool for estimating dates of once living things—as long as people realize that it produces only estimates, not precisely accurate dates. Although the errors increase with the actual age of the specimen, dates of things that died after about 2000 BC are usually close enough to be useful. Earlier dates appear to be grossly inaccurate and should be "put on the shelf." Until more facts are built into the estimation formula and the known problems are corrected, the inaccuracies will persist. The C14 dating technique would be much better if many of the so-called corrections made in the past, which were based on faulty information, were abandoned. Then revisions could be made to account for non-equilibrium and other known effects. Dates prior to about 4000 BC (the time usually attributed to Adam) should be considered spurious (to those of us who believe that the Fall of Adam introduced profound physical changes into the world).

Those who have read and understood this book thus far should be able to see inconsistencies in the following quote:

> We know very little about the earliest inhabitants of the Nile Valley because no human remains have been found from that period. We do know that the area was first inhabited around 500,000 B.C. by settlers who had as their only tool the hand ax. This marked the beginning of the Paleolithic, or Stone Age, Period. By modern standards change was slow. When we think of the changes in our civilization in the last hundred years, it is almost

---

217. Newgrosh. "Scientific Dating Methods." *Journal of the Ancient Chronology Forum*, Vol. 2, 1988, p. 67.

inconceivable that in the first 450,000 years of Egyptian civilization the only improvement was a better hand ax![218]

I do not wish to demean the author of the preceding quote because much of the information in his book is excellent, but he has obviously been indoctrinated by the assumptions popular in dating. Two of his statements deserve criticism:

1. "We know that the area was first inhabited around 500,000 B.C." How is this known? This statement cannot be based on carbon dates since realistic estimates only claim theoretical ages up to about 40,000 years. On what then was it based? Particularly, what assumptions? Wouldn't it have been more accurate to say something like: "The... [naming the estimation method used] suggests that the area was first inhabited around 500,000 B.C."? Yes, it would! Was he concerned that such wording, though more accurate, would inspire a lack confidence among his readers?
2. "It is almost inconceivable that in the first 450,000 years of Egyptian civilization the only improvement was a better hand ax!" Almost inconceivable indeed! On what basis was this almost inconceivable idea conceived?

Even after realizing that the C14 dating technique has been calibrated by tree-ring dating and by conventional Egyptian chronology (indirectly), some fail to recognize the significance. For example, Paul Standring reported an odd position held by Baillie: "I believe the revisionists [of Egyptian chronology] are wrong because calibrated radiocarbon dates broadly support the conventional Egyptian chronology. For the revisionists to be correct, calibration and dendrochronology would have to be

218. Brier. Ancient Egyptian Magic. 1981, p. 14.

wrong and that is not possible [sic] given the degree of tree-ring replication."[219] If one method has been adjusted to fit the other because the other was thought to be more accurate, then when they agree, it is merely a tautology.[220] (See the next chapter for issues regarding tree-ring dating.)

Another question has been raised: had Libby—earlier in his studies—openly acknowledged that the formation rate of C14 was significantly higher than its decay rate as experiments have shown, what would have been the ramifications? Had he done so, his system would have directly challenged the fundamental assumption of uniformity. Would it then have been the means of his receiving a Nobel Prize, which it was, or might he have been ostracized and labeled a pseudo-scientist like many others who challenged popular thinking?

Once the deficiencies in C14 dating are recognized, the conflicts between radiocarbon dates and those from the scriptures are reconcilable. However, a resolution of the problem is a challenge for scientists who ask out-of-the-ordinary questions and dare to pursue the answers.

---

219. Standring. "Pot Pourri." *C&C Review*. SIS, 2001:2, p. 50.
220. Tautology: a needless repetition of an idea. Often, the restated version is intended to sound like it establishes the validity of the first, or visa versa.

Other Scientific Age Estimation Techniques

When the experts went about dating the recently discovered Dead Sea Scrolls, the specialists in each field... all came up with different answers, sometimes many centuries apart.

—Hugh Nibley (1964)

Scientists use many techniques to estimate ages. Several are briefly discussed in this chapter along with indications as to their strengths and weaknesses. They include tree-ring dating, helium dating, crustal rebound, ice core, waterfall recession, and radiometric dating of rocks. Since they provide much of the information in conflict with Bible chronology, it is helpful to understand some of the basics.

Willard Libby wrote about some of the conflicts between various scientific dating techniques:

109

In both archeology and geology it has been held that several sequences of radiocarbon dates do not allow enough time for specific series of events... In geology, some... criticisms of the radiocarbon dates are based upon inferences concerning the behavior of a presently nonexistent ice sheet. There is no way of proving or disproving assumptions concerning the speed of advance or retreat of the ice.... Similarly in archeology, opinions concerning time... are based largely upon assumptions concerning the rate of change in cultural processes.[221]

Thus Libby's radiocarbon system was challenged by what he recognized as techniques based on inferences and assumptions.

Tree-Ring Dating (Dendrochronology)

Tree-ring dating seems to be a straightforward means of age estimation. For years, we've been taught that trees grow "annual rings." Although trees in tropical regions generally do not produce growth rings,[222] in other parts of the world, they typically do. These can be counted to estimate ages.

A crucial question is: do all tree-rings correspond to annual growth periods? The answer is no. Ring growth is not directly tied to annual cycles. It is affected by temperature, water availability, insect infestation, competition from nearby plants, light intensity, and other factors.[223] N. T. Mirov indicated that "The term 'annual ring' is not accurate; it originated in the northern countries where the periods of summer growth and winter rest are well defined, but... formation of rings does not always coincide with the calendar year." Furthermore, he found that "in semi-

---

221. Libby. *Radiocarbon Dating*, 2nd Ed. 1955, p. 148.
222. Speer. *Fundamentals of Tree-ring Research*. 2010, p. 253.
223. Ababneh. "Growth Patterns of Bristlecone Pine." PhD Diss. University of Arizona, 2006, p. 11.

arid parts of the world, such as the southwestern United States, where precipitation during the growing season is in the form of occasional violent cloudbursts, several rings may be formed in pines during one year."[224]

Growth in one tree may be different than trees nearby, and even in different parts of the same tree. Some rings are labeled "false rings," "frost rings," "locally absent," or "missing rings." Or less often: "partial," "multiple," "intra-annual," or "sub-annual" rings.

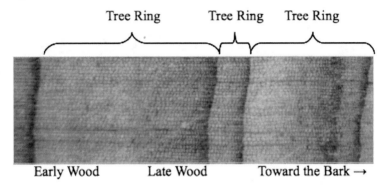

Figure 4.1. A microscopic image (~2mm) of a cross-section of a fairly typical tree-ring growth pattern. Wood sample provided by Gordon Thomas, photo by the author.

Using a microscope, clues are found. Figure 4.1, shows a very small section of three distinct growth rings. Note: a tree-ring consists of thin-walled cells (lighter in color, called "earlywood"), and thicker-walled cells (darker colored called "latewood"). But according to a textbook on tree-ring research by James H. Speer (2010): "A tree may produce micro rings that are only two cells wide, with one cell of earlywood and one cell of latewood."[225]

---

224. Mirov. *The Genus Pinus.* 1967, pp. 354, 413.

225. Speer. *Fundamentals of Tree-ring Research.* 2010, p. 47.

Some rings are barely distinct, even under high magnification. Figure 4.2 shows a microscopic image of a wood cross-section (believed to be of a bristlecone pine) with some exceptionally narrow rings.

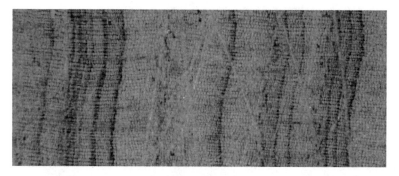

Figure 4.2. A micro-photo showing ~2mm of a cross-section with some indistinct, and very narrow rings only a few cells wide. Which represent annual growth periods, and which do not? Photo by the author.

Tree-ring dating techniques may be divided into three main categories: (1) tree-stump or cross-section ring-counts, (2) living-tree age estimates, and (3) cross-dating (a method used to try to identify matching ring patterns in two or more wood samples). Although there is little conflict between Bible chronology and tree-stump ring-counting, some age estimates of living trees and cross-dating provide more contradictory results.

Tree-Stump or Cross-Section Ring-Counts

If it is known when a tree ceased growing and a cross-section is intact, the ring-count is used to estimate how long the tree lived. Some fantastic claims of Giant Sequoia ring counts appear to be spurious. Nathan Stephenson of the US Geological Survey wrote: "Early claims of up to 11,000 rings counted on stump tops cannot be taken seriously."[226]

The tree slabs with the highest actual ring counts appear to be:

Giant sequoia CBR26[227]	3,290
Fitzroya[228]	3,622
Bristlecone pine WPN-114 called "Prometheus"	4,862

All the cross-section ring counts seem to be well within the range of Bible chronology except for one. It is the bristlecone pine WPN-114 known as Prometheus. It is commonly cited as having lived about five thousand years. Prometheus was cut down in 1964 and is said to have been the oldest living thing on Earth at that time. A count made by the Laboratory of Tree-Ring Research at the University of Arizona yielded 4,862 rings.[229] This count did not include the oldest rings—at the heart of the tree—since they had weathered away. If that tree grew one, and only one, ring in each of 4,862-plus years, and if the Flood really occurred in about 2344 BC as listed in many Bible chronologies, then it was at least 554 years old when the Flood took place.[230]

If Noah's Flood was as widespread and devastating as the scriptures suggest, could a tree have survived it? That is a possibility, especially a resilient tree like the bristlecone. Bristlecones grow in high, arid, mountainous regions of the western US, just below the

---

226. Stephenson. "Estimated Ages of Giant Sequoias." *Madrono*, Vol. 47, no. 1, 2000, p. 65.
227. Ibid., p. 64.
228. Speer. *Fundamentals of Tree-ring Research*. 2010, p. 275.
229. Cohen. *A Garden of Bristlecones*. 1998, p, 64.
230. 1,964 + 2,344 = 4,308. 4,862 − 4,308 = 554 years.

timberline. Their growing season is short, and "Bristlecone, [is] loaded with pitch and tight-grown."[231] Rather than Prometheus having survived the Flood, to those who take the Flood account literally, another explanation seems more likely. As mentioned earlier, Mirov noted that due to peculiar conditions in the southwestern region of the United States—where bristlecone pines grow—more than one ring may be formed in a year.

---

231. Hall. "Staying Alive." *San Francisco Chronicle*, 23 Aug. 1998. http://www.sfgate.com/default/article/Staying-Alive-High-in-California-s-White-2995266.php, (last accessed 9/4/12)

Figure 4.3. Partially-living Bristlecone Pines. The first photo is a Rocky Mountain Bristlecone showing strip bark growth.[232] The second is of a bristlecone one in Cedar Breaks National Monument, Utah.[233]

Ancient bristlecones are famous for their unusual strip bark growth patterns. Parts of the trees are dead and relatively small

---

232. Photo courtesy of the U.S. Forest Service: http://www.fs.fed.us/rm/ highelevationwhitepines/About/photo-tour/strip-bark.htm. (last accessed 9/4/12).
233. Photo courtesy of the National park Service: http://www.nps.gov/ cebr/images/20070823131458.jpg. (Photo by Paula Hamilton) (last accessed 9/7/12).

strips of bark and portions of branches reveal their living sections. The trees shown in figure 4.3 are examples.

Warm temperature is often thought of as the main factor initiating ring growth. However, in her PhD dissertation dealing with the Prometheus tree, Teresa Halupnik, after comparing the ring widths of Prometheus with climatic records, noted: "the ring widths were wider during the cooler period, and narrower during the warmer period." She concluded "water stress during the warm period and abundant water availability during the cool period were the likely causes of the variable ring widths."[234] Might it also have been the cause of some sub-annual rings?

Experiments were performed by Walter E. Lammerts on bristlecone seedlings he had planted. He found that withholding water from a select group of them in his greenhouse for a period of three weeks in August caused that group to form an extra ring.[235] Thus—if Prometheus reacted similarly—water stress would have been the means of it growing at least some sub-annual rings.

Of particular interest is that the bristlecones with the largest numbers of rings generally grow in rocky areas where the soil is poor and moisture is scarce during some parts of the summer. Ronald M. Lanner observed that Prometheus "grew in a relatively moist region but was located on a ridge of permeable rocky material that held very little water."[236]

"One season's growth increment may be composed of two or more flushes of growth, each of which may strongly resemble an annual ring" according to C. W. Ferguson. However, he went on to state that "such multiple growth rings are extremely rare in bristlecone

234. Halupnik. "Analysis of Tracheid Length Vs Age in Prometheus." PhD Dissertation UTA, 2008, pp. 5, 3.
235. Lammerts. "Are Bristle-cone Trees Really so Old?" *Creation Research Quarterly* 20(2). 1983, p. 108.
236. Lanner. *The Bristlecone Book.* 2007, p. 92.

pine."[237] This seems an odd conclusion since he also mentioned "in some instances, 5 percent or more of the annual rings may be missing along a given radius" in bristlecones.[238] Were there really that many years in which no annual ring grew in the tree, or did sub-annual rings grow in some parts of trees but not in others?

Waldo S. Glock et al. documented numerous instances of multiple rings having grown in various species within specific years. Some of the rings were incomplete (only extending part way around the center). The examples they cited were from areas subject to stress from large fluctuations in water availability but in a warmer region than the habitat of the bristlecones. They wrote about the controversy over whether or not rings are strictly annual, discussing how either position "is an assumption unless supported by adequate evidence."[239] Describing the gist of each position: one may assume that growth always (1) "begins in the spring and goes to completion" or that it "can slow down and cease completely within a single season... [and] can begin anew." (2) Annual rings are either always signaled "by a sharply defined outer surface" or sometimes not. (3) The "growth factors present... in the spring can also be present later during the general growing season," or they cannot. (4) Either all of the rings that formed more frequently than annually "are diffuse, never sharp" or there are exceptions. (5) "The maximum number of sharply bounded growth layers in a tree [either] reveals the true number of years involved," or it doesn't. If it doesn't, the ring count "exaggerates" the "true number of years involved."[240]

---

237. Ferguson. "A 7104-Year Chronology for Bristlecone." *Tree-Ring Bulletin.* Vol. 29, no 3–4, 1969, p. 6.
238. Ibid., p. 7.
239. Glock, Studhalter, and Agerter. "Multiplicity of Growth Layers." *Smithsonian Miscellaneous Collections,* Vol. 140, no. 1. June 17, 1960, p. 123.
240. Ibid., pp. 123–124.

Figure 4.4. The Prometheus stump. The heart of the tree is missing but appears to have been to the right of the remaining stump. Photo by James R Bouldin.[241]

Figure 4.5. The Prometheus slab at the Ely Convention Center (photo inverted).[242] It is about 82" × 12" × 3". The left end includes some bark, and the heart of the tree

241. Courtesy of J. R. Bouldin and http://en.wikipedia.org/wiki/File:Prometheus_tree1.jpg.
242. Photo courtesy of Meg Rhoades, White Pine County Tourism and Recreation Board.

(where the oldest rings grew) was apparently near the top right of this slab.[243]

I had the privilege of going to Great Basin National Park in April 2011 to take some microphotos of the Prometheus slab at the visitor's center there. See Figures 4.6, 4.7, and 4.8.[244]

Figure 4.6. The Prometheus slab at the Great Basin National Park (GBNP) Visitor's Center. It is about 54" long and 3" thick. Photo by Darlene Barker.

243. Cohen. *A Garden of Bristlecones*. 1998, p, 64.
244. More of the photos can be seen at www.davidmckaybarker.com.

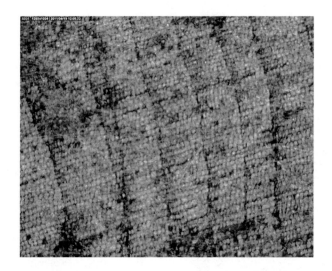

Figure 4.7. Image of a ~2mm section of the Prometheus slab at GBNP showing an unusual ring wedging out and back in. (second from the left). Photo by the author.

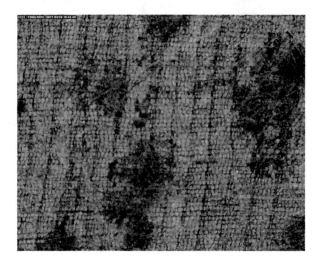

Figure 4.8. Image of a ~2mm section of the Prometheus slab at GBNP showing unusually narrow rings. Which were annual, and which were not? Photo by the author.

From examining the Prometheus slab and taking numerous micro-photos, I learned that discerning which of its rings were annual and which were not is difficult if not impossible. None of the "rings" on the GBNP slab make a complete circuit around a center—either due to strip bark growth, or portions of the tree having weathered away. Donald Currey described that in Prometheus, "die-back had left 92 percent of the circumference devoid of bark."[245]

At least one tree may have survived the Flood. However, to those who accept a literal reading of the biblical account, it seems more likely that the contradicting ring counts don't accurately represent the actual age of the particular tree(s) in question. If Prometheus grew a sub-annual ring an average of once every eight years, the difference between the common dating of that tree and typical Bible chronologies is resolved.

Estimating the Ages of Living Trees

More frequent conflicts appear when comparing age estimates of living trees with Bible chronology. In order to avoid causing serious damage to aged living trees, bore holes are made, and pencil-sized core samples are extracted. The rings are counted and then used along with data on the size and shape of the tree to estimate its age.

The age of a tree called Methuselah was listed as 4,789 years in 1957 (thus, it was supposed to have been a seedling about 2832 BC). It was claimed that this was verified by cross-dating.[246] Later, Tom Harlan dated the tree's innermost ring at 2800 BC.[247]

---

245. Cohen. *A Garden of Bristlecones*. 1998, p. 64.
246. Bailey. "Pinus Longaeva." http://www.conifers.org/pi/Pinus_longaeva.php (last accessed 9/4/12).
247. Lanner. *The Bristlecone Book*. 2007, p. 87. Tom Harlan is a Research Technical at the Laboratory of Tree-Ring Research at the University of Arizona.

Figure 4.9. Photos of the tree called General Sherman, a giant sequoia believed to be the largest tree in the world (by

volume). At its base, it measures 102.6 feet in circumference.[248] The first photo (showing a man leaning against the trunk) was taken in 1909.[249] The second photo was taken in 2009 from a more distant vantage point.[250]

Age estimates for the tree called "General Sherman" range from about 2,000 to 6,000 years. Although the 6,000-year estimate seems contradictory to the dating of the Flood, it is not accurate according to Nathan Stephenson who studied the techniques used to estimate that age. The more reliable estimation method yielded the 2,150 years.[251]

If trees were perfectly symmetrical, age estimates would be less cumbersome and more accurate. Since they are not, trying to discern the age of ancient living trees is somewhat speculative.

Other extraordinary claims have been made for the ages of living trees. For instance, scientists in Sweden say they've found "the world's oldest known living tree."

> Its root system has been growing for 9,550 years.... The spruce's stems or trunks have a lifespan of around 600 years, "but as soon as a stem dies, a new one emerges from the same root stock."[252]

---

248. http://en.wikipedia.org/wiki/General_Sherman_(tree).
249. Photo courtesy of USGS http://libraryphoto.cr.usgs. gov/cgi-bin/search.cgi?search_mode=noPunct&free_ form=general+sherman&free_form=&free_form=&free_form (last accessed 9/4/12).
250. Photo of "General Sherman." Courtesy of Famartin at http:// en.wikipedia.org/wiki/File:General_Sherman_Tree_wide.jpg (last accessed 9/4/12).
251. Stephenson. "Estimated Ages of Giant Sequoias." *Madrono*, Vol. 47, no. 1, 2000, p. 61.
252. Owen. "Oldest Living Tree Found in Sweden." *National Geographic News*, April 14, 2008, p. 1. http://news.nationalgeographic.com/ news/2008/04/080414-oldest-tree.html, (last accessed 9/4/12).

If the root stock is really as resilient as suggested, perhaps it truly is one of the few survivors of the Flood. However, the age was not estimated from ring-counts, but by radiocarbon dating.[253] Those familiar with the information in the preceding chapter can recognize that such an estimate is far from certain.

The apparent conflict between living tree age estimates and Bible chronology may thus be due to (1) errors in estimates, (2) the tree having survived the Flood, (3) multiple rings grown in some years, or (4) confusion in Bible chronology. The most likely explanation of the differences seems to be errors in the estimations.

Cross-Dating

When wood samples from trees with overlapping lifespans are found, if portions of their ring patterns are distinct enough to be recognizable matches, longer ages can be derived. Although it sounds quite simple, those who have compared the rings of wood samples have learned that cross-dating is no easy task.

Many trees are particularly difficult to cross-date. Some ring patterns are so uniform as to make cross-dating infeasible. Other trees have patterns that seem to match in parts but not in others. In Figure 4.10, different segments of the same slab of wood are shown. Some sections are easily recognizable matches while others are not.

M. A. Stokes and T. L. Smiley described: "One complication which sometimes arises in the process of cross-dating is the absence of an annual ring at the location in the tree where the sample was taken."[254] Was their assumption of absent annual rings correct, or, as seems more likely, did an extra ring form in a particular year in at least a part of a tree?

---

253. Ibid.
254. Stokes and Smiley. *An Introduction to Tree-Ring Dating.* 1968, p. 13.

Figure 4.10. Photos of the same slab of wood. Near the left end of the top two images are three narrow rings

(marked by arrows) separated by wider rings. These are the same rings seen in different parts of the slab. Some of the patterns farther away from the center do not have the appearance of a match. Wood slab provided by Gordon Thomas, photos by David Barker.

The Belfast "long chronology" claims to span over 7,000 years by cross-dating one thousand different timbers.[255] Other tree-ring schools claim counts as high as 8,200 years, and "the known occurrence of samples 9,000 years old (dated by radiocarbon only) lends hope that in time an absolute chronology may be available covering at least 10,000 years."[256] These claims do appear to be in conflict with Bible chronology. Note that the term "absolute chronology" is used in the same manner as "absolute date" to signify that the estimates are in years, and it should not be interpreted to mean absolutely certain.

Alasdair Beal noted some of the difficulties encountered in cross dating:

> No one tree records the whole of history, so a master chronology must be built up by linking pieces of wood from different trees in sequence and then matching samples to be dated against this; this is not easy and it is made harder by the fact that although the growth of the various individual trees responds to a common climatic signal, there are considerable local variations... It is part science, part art.[257]

255. Baillie and Pilcher. "Belfast 'Long Chronology.'" In *Applications of Tree-ring Studies*. 1987, p. 203.

256. Baillie. *Tree-Ring Dating and Archaeology*. 1982, p. 37.

257. Beal. "A Bit Creaky?" *C&C Review*. SIS, 1991, p. 39.

Figure 4.11. "A rare signature pattern in samples from Trinity College, Dublin... The arrowed ring is the year AD 1580."[258]

Beal also noted inconsistencies in the ring patterns shown in Baillie's photo (Figure 4.11):

At first sight it looks very impressive.... However, look again with a little care: the rings on the left hand timber above the arrowed ring do not appear to match those on

---

258. Baillie. *Tree-Ring Dating and Archaeology.* 1982, frontispiece. Used with permission.

the centre timber at all and the same is true of the rings below the bottom 'signature' ring. On the right hand timber, the rings above the arrowed ring don't look much like those on the central timber either. In this instance, the historical context of the samples appears to have been carefully checked and the match is probably genuine, but had this not been done who would have been able to say? If only tree-ring evidence had been available, an element of doubt would have been in order.

The Belfast team rightly took great care cross checking the modern end of their chronology against historical and archaeological evidence—after all, if this went adrift the whole chronology would be useless. However, for earlier periods this is not possible and there are only the tree rings to go by... It is a daunting task, faced with a vast collection of oaks recovered unstratified from bogs. Understandably, the researchers resorted to radiocarbon dating to give approximate dates to help them make progress... but in the process the independence of their dates from radiocarbon dates must have been compromised. The fact that they also used other tree-ring chronologies (English, German and Californian) to help as the work proceeded means that the chance of a truly independent check of the validity of their chronologies has also been lost.

There is no doubt that a great deal of work has gone into the Belfast bog oak chronology and it may well be absolutely, precisely, correct but the above considerations suggest that a bit of caution is in order; it may not be the last word on the matter.[259]

Jesse Lasken pointed out that some of the data used to support the Irish and German oak cross-dates "actually contradicts them":

---

259. Beal. "A Bit Creaky?" *C&C Review.* SIS, 1991, pp. 39–40.

This, in combination with other factors... suggests the need for an independent re-examination of the European oak dendrochronologies.

Several studies... that were used to bridge the Irish chronology at c. 940 BC, have suggested that English and Irish oaks exhibit multiple (false) matches on a relatively frequent basis...

The theoretical basis for matching trees as far apart as Northern Ireland and Germany, particularly given the differences in the two climates and other factors, is non-existent.[260]

Due to the difficulties in matching ring patterns, dendrochronologists have devised methods to convert ring widths to mathematical indexes. Baillie described one process:

> Visual comparison of ring width plots involves superimposing the two patterns under study and shifting their relative positions until such a time as significant agreement is obtained between them. In practice the observer looks at significant features in one pattern and attempts to duplicate them in the second.... However, visual matching is subjective and the ability of a trained observer to find sufficient similarities, in two long ring patterns, to establish a cross-correlation, is not a measurable quantity.[261]

Statistical Analysis

In regards to the statistical methods, dendrochronologists use in cross-dating wood samples, Lasken made an astounding observation:

---

260. Lasken. "Should the European Oak be Re-examined?" *C&C Review.* SIS, 1991, p. 30.
261. Baillie. "A Recently Developed Irish Tree-ring Chronology." *Tree-ring Bulletin,* 1973, p. 20.

Theoretically, a random distribution is 50%....

It was reported that for a 4700 year period the south German and Irish oak chronologies yield an agreement of 54%...

Thus, it is by no means certain that 54% is a truly significant result.... ... The authors [Pilcher et al.] acknowledge, and they admit, it is not "a rigorous statistical test."[262]

With computer programs designed specifically for tree-ring cross-dating, now available, claims of high precision have been made. Some dendrochronologists are convinced that statistical analysis provides proof positive—especially when computerized. My experience with computers has taught me that once programmed correctly, computers can "crunch the numbers" accurately and almost instantly—even complex mathematical formulas and vast amounts of data that would take days to calculate by hand. However, the programs don't remove the need for data input, assumptions, and reasoning built into their models. Nor do they eliminate the necessity to interpret the results obtained.

A tree ring expert, Dr. Henri Grissino-Mayer, describing one of the popular programs in use, indicated that it is "powerful in its diagnostics and functions, but its operation and the interpretation of its output remain complex." He also mentioned "the program should not be used as a substitute for visual crossdating on the wood sample. The ultimate decision concerning whether or not a tree-ring series is dated must lie with the dendrochronologist based on both graphical and statistical techniques."[263] Still, the confidence dendrochronologists have in the results are astonishing. He indicated that they use "correlation and autoregressive modeling

---

262. Lasken. "Should the European Oak be Re-examined?" *C&C Review.* SIS, 1991, p. 31.

263. Grissino-Mayer. "Evaluating Crossdating Accuracy." *Tree-Ring Research.* Vol. 57(2), 2001, pp. 205–206.

techniques to ensure a sequence is dated to 99.99% accuracy."[264] Could this claim be overly optimistic? According to Edward R. Cook and Neil Pederson, within the statistical modeling used for cross-dating:

> significant uncertainty exists due to our incomplete... understanding of radial growth.... This biological uncertainty cascades into the realm of statistical uncertainty in ways that are difficult to quantify.... Therefore great care must be taken to apply the many well-developed and tested statistical methods of dendrochronology in ways that reduce the probability of making false inferences. This is especially true in the case of.... uncertainty that arises from the way in which trees as complex organisms can have properties expressed in their ring widths that are impossible to predict.[265]

Thus, the programs depend on subjective input have built-in assumptions, modeling, variable choices, and rest on the foundation of statistical probability theory. They rely on measurements and data derived from observations of relative ring-width sizes and the surmises derived there from. An independent audit of the long chronologies and the statistical techniques used in their formation, seems needed.

Skeleton Plot

One cross-dating method is intended to focus on unusually narrow ring patterns. It is known as the skeleton plot. Stokes and Smiley discussed the way it works and then acknowledged a critical weakness:

264. Henri D. Grissino-Mayer (personal communication).
265. Cook and Pederson. "Uncertainty and Statistics in Dendrochronology." In *Dendroclimatology*. 2011, p. 77.

> In skeleton plotting the narrow rings are the ones primarily
> being compared… The decision of narrowness is based on
> the comparison of each ring with its immediate neighbors.
> The narrower the ring, the longer the line is drawn. The
> narrowest rings are arbitrarily represented with a line 2 cm
> in height…
>
> … Since these lines are not measured, these averages,
> like the individual plots, are a matter of judgment…
>
> … Unfortunately, the actual practice is mastered by
> trial-and-error experience and cannot be adequately
> described.[266]

If a process is not precise enough to be adequately described,
or sufficiently measurable, how can it be relied upon with
confidence? They also acknowledge that even after this process of
reducing the data to paper,

> while several of the patterns match, there are many
> individual rings which do not match from plot-to-plot.
> *This variation is typical.* It is logical to ask how many such
> unmatched rings can be accepted in what we call matched
> plots. Our answer would have to be that, *when most of the
> rings match*, the fit is considered correct. While this may
> sound like a very unscientific answer, the experienced
> dendrochronologists using these methods are able to
> duplicate each other.[267] (emphasis added)

The fact that experienced tree ring experts can duplicate each
other does not necessarily mean both are right.

Another world-renowned dendrochronologist, M. G. L.
Baillie, acknowledged an important weakness of tree-ring
dating: "It is very easy to make the results… seem excessively

---

266. Stokes and Smiley. *An Introduction to Tree-Ring Dating.* 1968, pp. 47,
     49.
267. Ibid., p. 50.

tidy. This is usually the result of attempting to present the results in too logical a fashion. The fact of the matter is that dendrochronological research is not all that logical in itself, it is only logical with hindsight... Here the 'art' of dendrochronology becomes apparent."[268]

James Speer also mentioned the skeleton plot method, and the "master chronology" derived by comparing a number of wood samples. "For a ring to be represented on the master chronology it has to appear on 50% of the plots, and the length of the lines are averaged together (usually only counting the trees that represent that ring)."[269]

Speer also noted: "Dendrochronologists use the principle of uniformitarianism when we reconstruct past climate.... For this reconstruction to be possible, dendrochronologists have to assume that the processes affecting tree's response to these environmental factors have not changed.... This is a common assumption made in the natural sciences, but it has some drawbacks of which the researcher should be aware."[270]

Beal concluded his article critiquing tree ring dating techniques with: "There is a great tendency amongst historians of all persuasions to treat tree-ring dates or radiocarbon dates as gospel when they suit but to reject them out of hand when they don't. This is not helped by the tendency of the scientists who do the measurements to claim far more certainty than is reasonable for their findings."[271]

The scholarly research—including mainstream dendrochronologists—shows that there is a significant amount of subjectivity and uncertainty associated with tree-ring cross-dating. Therefore, the fantastic claims of the contradictory long counts do not appear to constitute a viable challenge to Bible chronology.

---

268. Baillie. *Tree-Ring Dating and Archaeology*. 1982, p. 23.
269. Speer. *Fundamentals of Tree-ring Research*. 2010, p. 14.
270. Ibid., pp. 10–11.
271. Beal. "A Bit Creaky?" *C&C Review*. SIS, 1991, p. 42.

Helium Dating and the Age of the Atmosphere[272]

Helium was once used to try to estimate the age of rocks in a manner similar to radioactive methods. Although helium is not radioactive, it is radiogenic (produced by the radioactive decay of heavier elements). Cook noted: "It was discovered that not only was helium removed as the rock underwent erosion but helium leakage from the igneous rock was also taking place... [and] even such hard, non-porous minerals as magnetite lose a considerable portion... It is now generally realized therefore that the helium method cannot be relied upon to give a true measure of the age of rocks."[273]

Although not effective for dating rocks, Cook noted that helium is useful in estimating the age of the atmosphere—at least calculating minimum and maximum ages.[274] Helium is continuously being released from rocks into the atmosphere. Based on the rate it is escaping from Earth's crust, the atmosphere should be highly concentrated in helium—that is, if processes have been roughly uniform for millions of years, as is commonly supposed.[275] Nevertheless, the current concentration of helium in the atmosphere is only about .0005 percent.[276]

For many years, it was assumed that the reason the helium concentration is still low was due to atoms escaping from Earth's atmosphere into space as quickly as they were entering.

---

272. This section represents a simplified version of Dr. Melvin A. Cook's findings on the subject. For a more detailed and technical treatment, see his books *Scientific Prehistory*, 1993; *Prehistory and Earth Models*, 1966; and "Where is the Earth's Radiogenic Helium?" *Nature*, no. 4552, Jan. 26, 1957, p. 213.

273. Cook. *Scientific Prehistory*. 1993, p. 278.

274. Ibid., pp. 41–42.

275. Cook. "Where is the Earth's Radiogenic Helium?" *Nature*, no. 4552, Jan. 26, 1957, p. 213.

276. *CRC Handbook of Chemistry and Physics*, 72nd ed. 1991, p. 14.11.

A term was coined for the outermost region of the atmosphere, namely the "exosphere," suggesting that was where the lighter elements exited Earth's realm. Although it was once believed to be the "region of escape,"[277] high-altitude studies have shown that hydrogen and helium "do not concentrate significantly in the upper atmosphere as has previously been supposed."[278] Therefore, it does not appear to be a place where a significant amount of helium exits Earth's domain as had been supposed. Although the name exosphere is still used, it should no longer be used to imply that particles such as helium are escaping into space.

Using helium, Cook calculated variations for the maximum age of the atmosphere. In estimating helium's original concentration in the atmosphere, the least possible amount would have been zero, while the logical maximum would be near current levels. Since helium is being produced by radioactive decay of other elements and released into the atmosphere—with no significant escape there from—it is in a buildup phase. The production rate has been estimated by measuring amounts exuded from rocks. Using that rate, depending on which assumptions are made for the original concentration, the calculations of how long it has taken to build to its current level, range between 12,000 and 350,000 years.

A calculation was made by M. Garfield Cook. He indicated that "helium is estimated to be entering the atmosphere [from rock] at a rate of about 100,000 tons per year. The total helium content of the atmosphere is about 3.5 billion tons."[279] Therefore, if there was no helium in the atmosphere when it was formed, and there is no significant escape into outer space, it would only take

---

277. Exosphere. *McGraw-Hill Dictionary of Scientific and Technical Terms.* 1974.

278. See Cook. "Where is the Earth's Radiogenic Helium?" *Nature.* Jan. 26, 1957, p. 213, and *Prehistory and Earth Models,* 1966, pp. 41–42.

279. Cook, M. G. *Science and Modern Revelation.* 1981, p. 197.

about 35,000 years to build to its current level (3,500,000,000 ÷ 100,000 = 35,000). If the primordial atmosphere did contain some helium, which seems likely, and since there are other sources of helium, the age of the atmosphere is apparently less.

Of what relevance is this? To those who believe that the earth and its atmosphere have remained in their present configuration for millions of years, even the upper limit of 350,000 years is a major contradiction. The more likely estimate of 35,000 is so contrary to popular assumptions that it is also generally ignored. For those who adhere to the belief that each day of Creation was only twenty-four hours long, even the lower limit of 12,000 years is a bit problematical. However, to those who will entertain the suggestion that each "day" of Creation was at least one thousand years, the lower calculation is on target.

Six "days" of Creation	at least	6,000 years
Adam to Jesus	about	4,000 years
Jesus to present	about	2,000 years
Estimated total	at least	12,000 years

These rough estimates do not take into account the physical composition of the atmosphere during the days of Creation, nor the "seventh day." Nevertheless, the helium method is a scientific time estimate worthy of note.

Age Estimations by the Rebound of Earth's Crust

The weight of the huge ice sheets that once covered Earth's polar regions created depressions in the crust beneath them. Much less ice is there now and, surprisingly, the crust is still rebounding. The depression and rebounding of the crust is called isostasy. Bernard Pipkin described it:

> The Ice Age continental glaciers and ice caps, with thicknesses of two miles or more, were so massive that the crust beneath them was depressed.... Uplift of the crust

due to unweighting is caused by isostatic rebound, the slow transfer by flowage of mantle rock to accommodate uplift of the crust.... Above the modern shorelines of the Gulf of Bothnia in Finland and Sweden are raised beaches that show a maximum uplift of 275 meters (900 ft).... The rise is so rapid in some places in Scandinavia that docks used by ships are literally rising out of the sea. Uplift in Oslo Fjord, Norway, is about 6 millimeters (0.25 in) per year.... Similar uplifting is recorded along the northern shores of Hudson Bay.[280]

This rebound effect has been measured at various other locations as well, and correlated with palynology (the study of microorganisms), and varved-clay studies.[281] Based on those correlations, scientists have estimated the duration of the isostatic rebound in Norway to be about 10,000 years. In other areas in Europe and North America, using C14 dates, ages were estimated between 10,000 and 12,000 years.[282] Although these estimates do not synchronize well with Bible chronologies, they seem to be relatively minor timing conflicts which will be rectified as more knowledge is gained.

Another example of dating by isostatic rebound is the former Lake Bonneville (of which the Great Salt Lake is a small remnant). Max Crittenden of the US Geological Survey noted:

Lake Bonneville... [which] occupied some 50,000 km² in western Utah, is an almost ideal natural experiment in the loading and unloading of the earth. Its clearly defined shorelines reveal both the magnitude and the distribution of the now-vanished load.... The fact that the shorelines

---

280. Pipkin. *Geology and the Environment*. 1994, p. 318.
281. Varve: thin layers of sediments, often thought to be annual layers.
282. Peteet. "Contributions of ¹⁴C Dating." In *Radiocarbon after Four Decades*. 1992, pp. 458–459.

of Lake Bonneville are bowed upward in the center of the
lake basin was recognized by Gilbert in 1890 and correctly
ascribed to isostatic adjustment in response to removal of
the load......... The once-level shorelines have undergone
a broad domical [dome shaped] uplift of about 210 feet
(64 m) in the center.... The observed 64-m uplift of the
Bonneville shoreline indicates that T_r [the time the lake
drained] cannot be greater than about 4000 years and may
be slightly less.[283]

This date estimate is harmonious with Bible chronologies.

Ice-Core Dating

Another dating technique uses ice cores from holes bored deep
into ice caps. When layers are detectable, they are counted to
estimate ages. Scientists measure chemical compositions at various
depths and try to learn clues about past climate conditions. John
E. Dayton described the process:

Dust, volcanic ash, rare gases, sulphuric acid, nitric acid, lead
from petrol and radioactive materials settle... at the Poles
in the form of dirty snowflakes.... Because of the polar
climate this snow does not all melt away and is covered
by next year's dirty snow. Over time the snow layers are
compressed and become polar ice......... The yearly layers
of compressed snow can then be counted and each layer
analysed for its tell tale dust, atomic fallout, sulphur, and
oxygen 16 and 18 ratios, rather like tree rings. The results
are dramatic. Events of known dates such as nuclear tests
and, for our purpose, volcanic eruptions can be clearly
seen.... Volcanic events produce both dust and droplets
of sulphuric acid which act as snow nuclei. This secondary

283. Crittenden. "Effective Isostatic Loading of Lake Bonneville." *Journal
of Geophysical Research,* Oct. 1, 1963, pp. 5517, 5520, 5526.

aerosol creates bands of acid in the ice, and those from Krakatau (1883) and Agung (1963) are notably sharp.... It must be pointed out that only very large volcanic eruptions where the dust reaches the stratosphere would show up in the cores from both poles.... More recently we have Mount St. Helens and El Chichon. The explosion of Tambora in 1814.... All these eruptions are clearly visible in the ice cores and in the tree rings of the following year.[284]

Lynn E. Rose noted some difficulties in ice core dating:

It must be emphasized from the outset that when geologists approach ice cores they are already "convinced" that the past nine or ten millennia have been routinely peaceful and that the last major geological event in Earth's history was the termination of the Wisconsin Ice Age roughly ten millennia ago.... Many of the problems involved in the study of ice cores are analogous to the problems that arise in the use of other techniques that attempt to count—whether directly or by calculation— some sort of annual variation that seems to extend back many thousands of years.... ... Some years are "double", for example, and it is not always easy to discriminate these double years from two single years. Other years may not be recognizable at all.... I'm not suggesting that these procedures necessarily were wrong, or that interpolation and extrapolation are *always* to be avoided. I am simply stressing the fact that much of what is presented in the literature is calculation, interpolation, extrapolation, curve smoothing, flow modeling and the like. It is not all hard observational fact.[285]

---

284. Dayton. "Ice Cores and Chronology." *C&C Review*. SIS, 1995, pp. 17–18.

285. Rose. "The Greenland Ice Cores." *Kronos*, Vol. XII, no. 1, 1987, pp. 56, 58, 61.

Beal published an article titled "How Old Is Greenland's Ice Cap?" In it, he pointed out weaknesses in some of the ice-core claims: "deep boreholes now being drilled to a depth of 3000 metres through the Greenland ice cap should yield samples of 'the oldest ice in the world', with an estimated age of 300,000 years. If this is true, it means that the ice cap survived all the climatic upheavals of the ice age and before."[286]

David Slade wrote about how ice cores are used to estimate dates and some of the challenges in doing so:

> The snowfall in the Polar regions (averaging 20 cm per annum) of successive years becomes compacted under its own weight. The upper stratifications are easy to distinguish but as the layers become thinner at depth, these are more difficult to identify... until the layers are too thin to distinguish.... ... It has also been found that precipitation nuclei such as particles, dust and various chemicals are recorded but attempts to correlate dust and acid traces with known dates of volcanic eruptions have had mixed success.
>
> It would be useful to be able to use such markers as historic milestones to underpin the History of Mankind. Because of the fragmentary nature of the archaeological record throughout the inhabited regions of the world, the evidence is often ambiguous and easily mis-read, leading to confusing chronologies worsened by the changing sequences of calendars devised by man.[287]

Donald Patten proposed a theory that a huge quantity of ice was dumped suddenly on the earth from a close encounter with

---

286. Beal. "How Old Is Greenland's Ice Cap?" *C&C Workshop.* SIS, 1992:1, p. 10.
287. Slade. "The Dust-up over Ice-cores." *C&C Workshop.* SIS, 1994:2, p. 6.

a comet.[288] If Patten's theory is reasonably close to reality, ice core dates based on the assumption of uniform deposition rates are invalid for periods prior to that event.

Comets are believed to contain a great deal of ice. A recent news report described how NASA's Deep Impact spacecraft encountered minute quantities of ice as it passed within 435 miles of a comet. It appeared to have been hit nine times by tiny icy particles.[289]

From Beal's review of details from the Greenland Icecore Project results, he concluded:

> It seems that out of the whole 250,000 year ice core, at least 235,000-237,000 years (94-95% of the total) were not determined by counting rings. According to the *New Scientist* report,
> "The rest of the core has been dated by calculations based on ice flow models describing the stretching and thinning of the annual layers as they move downward through the ice sheet, as well as knowledge of how rainfall decreases with cold climate and increases in warm periods."[290]

After reading the information above as well as similar reports, the conclusion seems appropriate that the ages claimed in ice-core drilling are securely established only during the recent past. The assumptions on which the deeper ice cores rely undermine any serious threat they may otherwise pose to Bible chronology.

---

288. Patten. *Biblical Flood and Ice Epoch.* 1966.

289. Chang. "NASA craft braved comet ice storm." Associated Press. *Deseret News.* Nov. 19, 2010.

290. Beal. "The Great 250,000 Year Ice Core." *C&C Workshop.* SIS, 1993:2, p. 7.

Receding Waterfalls

The receding of the Niagara River gorge makes a unique means for estimating the time of the "ice age." The Niagara is a short but powerful river, running from Lake Erie into Lake Ontario—a distance of only thirty-six miles.[291] The land over which it flows is a crystalline structure underlain by limestone. As the water cascades over the falls, the turbulence erodes the softer limestone underneath the upper strata, which ultimately collapses and falls into the gorge below.

Charles Lyell, in his geological "time scale" dated the Ice Age at about one million BC. To test his theory:

> Lyell measured the lineal distance of the Falls from its original location. He interviewed the inhabitants of the area regarding the rate of erosion. They affirmed that the rate of erosion was about 3 feet per year, on the average. This rate did not check with Lyell's time scale... of 1,000,000. Therefore, Lyell impulsively concluded that the inhabitants must have been exaggerating, and he set the rate of erosion at 1 foot per year, not 3. After further calculations, Lyell announced that the Ice Epoch had ended at 35,000 B.C., and not his previous estimate of 1,000,000 B.C.[292]

Other estimates of the recession of Niagara gorge run from about 5,000[293] to 18,000 years,[294] with about 12,000 years seeming to be the most popular. Although the higher estimates conflict with Bible chronology, the 5,000-year estimate of Delair is quite

291. http://www.niagaraparks.com/media/geology-facts-figures.html, (last accessed 9/4/12).

292. Patten. *Biblical Flood and Ice Epoch.* 1966, p. 11.

293. Delair. "Planet in Crisis." *C&C Review.* SIS, 1997:2, p. 7.

294. http://www.niagaraparks.com/media/geology-facts-figures.html, (last accessed 9/4/12).

close. Furthermore, who is to say whether physical conditions remained constant and that the falls receded at the same rate during periods prior to detailed historical records? Certainly before strata completely solidify they are much more vulnerable to rapid erosion.

Geological Dating

Bernard Poty described a difficulty with popular techniques used to date rocks: "A chronometer does not usually give the formation age of a mineral or a rock, but the date after which a particular clock began to count time with efficiency, i.e. when it is not continuously or episodically reset."[295] When geological dates are derived, it isn't certain what event the estimate represents.[296]

Scientists use long-lived radioactive isotopes to estimate the age of rock. The rate of decay of a radioactive nuclide such as uranium 238 into its daughter products is used in a manner similar to the relatively short-term C14 dating—only the decay sequences are more complicated. The fact that their half-lives involve vastly longer time periods also means a greater potential for small discrepancies in the estimates to create large errors in age calculations. Their accuracy, like in C14 dating, is dependent on knowledge of four essential facts:

1. The original concentrations of the radioactive *parent and daughter* nuclides.[297]
2. The radioactive decay rates of the isotopes involved.
3. The current concentrations of the *parent and daughter* nuclides in the mineral.

---

295. Poty. "Geological Dating Methods." In *Nuclear Methods of Dating.* 1989, p. 39.

296. Hamilton and Farquhar. *Radiometric Dating for Geologists.* 1968, p. 5.

297. Poty. "Geological Dating Methods." In *Nuclear Methods of Dating.* 1989, p. 35.

4. Whether any processes other than radioactivity have altered the composition of any of the rocks, or elements involved.

Essential Fact No. 1: Original Composition

Scientists have devised methods to estimate the initial concentration of the radioactive parent and radiogenic daughter nuclides. They have considered such questions as the following: can it be determined how and when the radioactive "clock" was last set, and was it before, after, or during a solidification process? They've tried (1) assuming a beginning composition based on what is seen in cosmic rays, (2) assuming that it was the same as what is now seen in meteorites, and (3) using model ages believed to be correct from other estimation techniques and extrapolating back to a compatible original content. Who can say which technique produces the most accurate results?

Essential Fact No. 2: The Decay Rates of the Isotopes Involved

As with C14, it is not certain whether other processes have altered the "spontaneous" decay rates of the radioactive materials used in the technique. Thus, possible changes in the decay rate are generally ignored.

Systems of dating by radioactive decay require assumptions. According to Salkeld, "all radioactive-dating methods depend upon constancy and as there is no reliable alternative means of testing constancy, all radio ages for rocks should be viewed with some reserve."[298]

Essential Fact No. 3: The Current Measurement

Again, as with C14, the third of the essential "facts" is the most precise (when AMS is used). However, the complexity of rocks and minerals causes additional challenges. Sometimes different

---

298. Salkeld. "Shamir." *C&C Review.* SIS, 1997:1, p. 21.

minerals within the same rock sample display conflicting "ages." Bernard Poty pointed out an example of the problem in the attempt to date rock: "If these minerals may be easily separated two distinct ages will be calculated. If they cannot be separated an intermediate age will be obtained and this age will have no geological meaning."[299] This invokes a question: how does one interpret dates when individual minerals within a rock produce differing results?

Essential Fact No. 4:
Have Other Factors Affected the Radioactive Elements Involved?

The fourth of the essentials is difficult to estimate. If a particular rock shows signs of deformation, changes have obviously taken place. If a rock specimen is taken from an apparently undisturbed strata, it is assumed to have been in a "closed system" (free of changes which might have affected the relative abundances of the elements involved). Nevertheless, this does not rule out other possible changes. It is prudent to recognize that current knowledge is insufficient to determine with assurance all the possible variables that may have affected the radioactive and radiogenic elements within.

Commonly Used Radioactive Decay Series

Popular methods make use of several radioactive decay series. Some are shown below.

Radioactive Nuclide	Daughter Product	Half-Life (billion years)
uranium-238 →	lead-206	4.5
uranium-235 →	lead-207	.71
thorium-232 →	lead-208	15

---

299. Poty, "Geological Dating Methods." In *Nuclear Methods of Dating.* 1989, p. 38.

| rubidium-87 | → | strontium-87 | 48.8 |
| potassium-40 | → | argon-40 | 1.28 |

Many geochronologists claim that "independent time clocks" substantiate one another. However, contradictory results are often acknowledged. Henry Faul reported: "In the instances where it has been possible to date a rock by more than one method, serious discrepancies between the various results are observed in some cases. For instance, the lead : thorium ages are usually different from the lead : uranium and lead: lead ages of the same rock."[300]

Potassium-Argon Dating

Potassium (K) argon (Ar) dating has perhaps the best means available for estimating the beginning composition. Since argon is a gas, when rock is in a molten state, it easily escapes. Therefore, even though some argon may be locked into place within crystals, it is thought that no significant amount of it would have been present at the time a rock solidified. After solidification, argon is produced by the decay of radioactive potassium within the rock.

A complicating factor is that potassium-40 (K40) also decays into calcium-40 (Ca40). "In 1290 m.y.... half of the atoms of ^{40}K in existence today will have decayed to either ^{40}Ca or ^{40}Ar."[301] Scientists have not been able to independently determine what proportion of K40 decays to Ca40 and what to Ar40. J. Laurence Kulp wrote:

> The branching ratio posed, and is still posing, the largest problem. In addition to this matter of the physical constants, there is also the difficulty of releasing all of the argon from a mineral at the time of fusion and the possible leakage of argon from the lattice during the lifetime of

---

300. Faul, *Nuclear Geology.* 1954, p. 257.
301. Hamilton and Farquhar. *Radiometric Dating for Geologists.* 1968, p. 3.

the mineral.... During the past decade the branching ratio Ar^{40}/Ca^{40} has been estimated all the way from .05 to 1.9 by various investigators. Because this quantity must be known with precision for any absolute age determination, this is a very immediate problem.[302]

According to Joan Engels, "The K-Ar dating of more than one mineral from a single rock sample has often revealed widely discordant ages.... It is not uncommon to find situations where purity levels of 95% or more do not suffice to give geologically meaningful ages."[303]

Raymond Montigny reported:

A rock can be subjected to a polythermal history [heating more than once]. In that case... [if] the last thermal event was of moderate intensity and caused a partial argon loss.... the calculated age has no geological meaning.

In summing up, the ability of the potassium-argon clock to yield meaningful ages is essentially governed by two factors, the thermal history of the investigated samples and the variable retentiveness of minerals towards argon.[304]

Although he only mentioned two of the factors governing meaningful age estimations, the points are valid and need to be addressed.

John Morris and Steven Austin described astonishing results from samples "dated" from Mount St. Helens:

302. Kulp. "Geological Chronometry." In *Advances in Geophysics.* 1955, p. 207.
303. Engels. "Discordant Ages Found in K-Ar Dating." *Journal of Geology,* Vol. 79, 1971, p. 609.
304. Montigny. "The Potassium-Argon Method." In *Nuclear Methods of Dating.* 1989, pp. 305–306.

Samples gathered have now been dated using the potassium-argon method. According to radioisotope dating, certain minerals in the lava dome are up to 2.4 million years old. All of the minerals combined yield the date of 350,000 years by the potassium-argon technique. However, we know that these minerals and the rocks that contain them cooled within lava between the years 1980 and 1986.[305]

If this report is accurate, the K-Ar method is grossly unreliable for such rocks.

Perhaps a better use of argon is to estimate the age of the atmosphere—in a manner similar to the helium-dating method. Since argon is a gas, it exudes from rocks as it is formed by potassium decay. Based on measurements and estimates of the rate argon is escaping from minerals on Earth, if the atmosphere was as old as scientists usually suggest, argon would now be its most abundant component. People wouldn't be able to get enough oxygen by breathing unprocessed air. Cook estimated that it would take only about 100,000 years for argon to get to such a stifling concentration.[306]

---

305. Morris and Austin. *Footprints in the Ash.* 2003, p. 67.
306. Cook. (Personal communication, May 6, 1994.)

Uranium/Lead Dating

Another of the commonly used techniques makes use of uranium-238 (U238), which, in a fourteen-step sequence, ultimately decays to lead-206 (Pb206). It is believed to span more than 4.5 billion years. Is there any room for error?

Element	Half-life
Uranium-238	4.5 billion years
Thorium-234	24.1 days
Paladium-234	1.14 minutes
Uranium-234	25,200 years
Thorium-230	80,000 years
Radium-226	1,622 years
Radon-222	3.825 days
Polonium-218	3.05 minutes
Lead-214	26.8 minutes
Bismuth-214	19.7 minutes
Polonium-214	.0000137 seconds
Lead-210	25 years
Bismuth-210	5.02 days
Polonium-210	4.23 minutes
Lead-206	Stable

Figure 4.12 The radioactive decay series from uranium-238 to lead-206 (simplified).

A scientist who challenged the U238/Pb206 method was Earl R. Milton, professor of physics at Lethbridge University. He wrote:

> For the uranium-238 radiometric dates to be valid some 30 'ifs' must be true.... To begin with, *we do not know the initial chemistry*—this puts 15 of the 'ifs' into doubt. Here

assumption, disguised as a "logical deduction", is invoked to make the unknown appear to be known.[307]

Another problem with the reliability of systems involving lead is that of lead loss. J. Laurence Kulp and Walter R. Eckelmann, speaking of a detailed study of certain ores, wrote: "the lead removal was most probably due to temperature rises at certain periods during the history of the mineral." They also spoke of another complicating factor: "the present isotopic composition in any sample, therefore, is dependent on the pressure, temperature and chemical environment to which a particular mineral lattice has been subjected at different periods in its history as well as the initial crystal structure."[308]

Early attempts to use the technique assumed minerals started with no original radiogenic lead. Faul reported that they "found that the premises on which the method rests are not valid for most uranium minerals … and it is now known that most radioactive minerals contained some lead when they were formed."[309] The initial amount of lead in the minerals is a matter of speculation, and whatever amount is supposed greatly affects the age estimates.

Neutron Promoted Transformations

Recall that the C14 dating technique is made possible by reactions of free neutrons with nitrogen-14 to form C14. The neutron reaction with N14 is the most common since nitrogen is the most abundant element in the atmosphere and readily reacts with free neutrons. Cook found that many less-abundant isotopes also react with free neutrons. Some of those reactions affect the results

---

307. Milton. "Physics, Astronomy and Chronology." *C&C Review*. SIS, 1987, p. 27.

308. Kulp and Eckelmann. "Discordant U-Pb Ages." *American Mineralogist*, 42, 1957, pp. 154, 156.

309. Faul. *Nuclear Geology*. 1954, p. 282.

of other radioactive-decay series. For instance, he indicated that neutron reactions are adding to thorium "probably as fast as it is decaying—upsetting the time clocks."[310] Rankama reported that "the uranium isotope ^{235}U is fissionable by neutrons of almost any energy."[311] Without accounting for the neutron reactions and their effect on other isotopes, such systems appear to be invalid—even if all other components of the calculation formula were accurately determinable.

Rubidium Strontium Dating

Another popular method of estimating the ages of certain rocks is the rubidium (Rb) strontium (Sr) time clock. Beal pointed out a very important weakness:

> ^{87}Rb decays to ^{87}Sr with a half-life of 48,800 million years. The problem with the method is that most rocks contain not only ^{87}Sr formed by radioactive decay of ^{87}Rb but also ^{87}Sr present as an isotope of the initial strontium.
>
> ... Scientists have devised a technique known as the "isochron method" which "completely eliminates the problem" and is "elegantly self-checking".... The reasoning goes that when rocks are first formed, they will all have the same ratio of $^{87}Sr/^{86}Sr$, no matter what their ratio of rubidium to strontium....... However, a closer examination reveals that all is not quite what it seems.... The idea that this can be described as "elegantly self-checking" and that it fixes the age of the rock with a precision of +/- 1.5% takes a bit of swallowing.
>
> ... Who is to say that the ratio $^{87}Sr/^{86}Sr$ is constant to this degree of accuracy in natural rocks?... Of course it is possible that the tiny variations in strontium isotopic ratios analysed by Dalrymple are, as he claims, significant and caused solely by radioactive decay over time, making

---

310. Cook. (Personal communication July 30, 1998.)
311. Rankama. *Isotope Geology*. 1954, p. 103.

them an accurate measure of rock age.... However... great ingenuity... [has] been applied to extract useful meaning from problematic data; but ultimately the data are just too weak to support the confident conclusions. Far from being an "elegantly self-checking" reliable technique, the isochron method is a brave and limited attempt to rescue an otherwise useless dating method from oblivion.[312]

Conclusion

In spite of the large number of dating techniques used in science today, many are so heavily reliant on assumptions as to render them spurious in spite of the confident manner in which they are cited. Results of testing suggest that many of the assumptions are invalid. They are certainly not the "self-checking time clocks" they are commonly purported to be. Considering the reliance on inference and estimation, it is astounding that so often estimated dates and ages are spoken of as though they are precisely-known facts.

In 1965, G. W. Wetherill of the Institute of Geophysics and Planetary Physics at UCLA summarized the weak status of geological dating at that time. In spite of significant improvements in technology, a most important problem remains:

> The result of... increased understanding has not been the fulfillment of some geologists' dreams, wherein specimens collected in the course of mapping would be sent into a laboratory from whence would soon issue answers to his major geochronological questions....... All these methods have in common the assumption that at some time in the past... the amount of this radiogenic daughter isotope in the sample can be calculated... and that since that time the quantity of the parent and daughter isotope has not

---

312. Beal. "Lies, Damned Lies and. . . ." *C&C Workshop.* SIS, 1990:2, pp. 21–22.

changed for any reason other than radioactive decay.... There is no a priori reason[313] why this assumption should be valid for any rock or mineral.[314]

If Adam really fell from a paradisiacal state at about 4000 BC, any estimations of dates prior to that time are simply guesswork based on untestable assumptions.

This chapter concludes with a remark by Earl R. Milton:

> The whole façade of radiometric chronometry is based upon being able to claim an initial chemistry for the Universe.... We cannot know any of these chemistries so how can we date the Universe, the Earth, or the time when its rocks formed? If we cannot assume that all of the uranium minerals have the same composition at time "zero" we have no way to get a date from the present state of the minerals.[315]

---

313. A priori. A self evident deduction based on logic.

314. Wetherill. "Present Status of Methods." In *Geochronology of North America*. 1965, pp. 1–3.

315. Milton. "Physics, Astronomy and Chronology." *C&C Review*. SIS, 1987, p. 28.

5

Comets, Asteroids, and Meteorites

Cosmic catastrophism has hardly been out of the news recently: since Comet Shoemaker Levy 9's collision with Jupiter... [it] is now firmly on the scientific agenda.

—Alasdair Beal (1997)

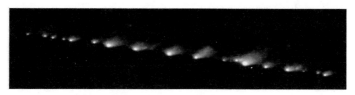

Figure 5.1. Photo of Comet Shoemaker-Levy 9 taken after it broke apart but before its fragments collided with Jupiter.[316]

---

316. This photo was taken by the Hubble Space Telescope, courtesy of NASA, ESA, H. Weaver and E. Smith (STSci). http://hubblesite.org/gallery/album/solar_system/pr1994026c. (last accessed 9/4/12)

Since one of the primary conflicts between science and the scriptures is differing accounts of how quickly physical processes have taken place, it is important to be aware of things that can alter normal speeds. Comets, asteroids, and meteorites have played a significant role, and likely will do so in the future. Until relatively recently, modern science has generally been reluctant to give them serious consideration. And when recognized, such events have usually been attributed to ages long past.

Rens Van der Sluijs summed up the effect an extraordinary comet has had on scientific thought: "When comet Shoemaker-Levy 9 visibly impacted on Jupiter in 1994, any illusions that impacts only recurred millions of years in the past were firmly dispelled."[317]

In July 1992, the comet broke into pieces as it passed close to the giant planet. "The gravitational (tidal) attraction of Jupiter at the surface of Shoemaker-Levy 9 must have been significantly larger than its own surface gravity. In effect, it was pulled apart by Jupiter's powerful gravity."[318] Twenty-one major fragments circled, and then slammed into the giant planet causing huge explosions and making distinct marks visible through telescopes on Earth.

Beal observed: "The spots which can now be seen on Jupiter's surface have jogged some memories: Thomas Hockey of Northern Iowa University noted that several spots were reported from 1690 to 1872 by observers including William Herschel and Giovanni Cassini." He continued: "Brian Marsden of the Harvard-Smithsonian Center found notes

---

317. Van der Sluijs. "An Aristotelian Hangover." *C&C Review*. SIS, 2009, p. 39.
318. Lewis. *Rain of Iron and Ice*. 1996, p. 7.

about a row of five dots" on Jupiter's surface on July 28, and ten on August 2, 1927.[319]

Not only did Comet Shoemaker-Levy 9 demonstrate that impacts happen within the solar system in modern times, but that they occasionally come in clusters. Studies of craters on Venus also concluded that "there is a clear tendency for large craters to form pairs and clusters."[320] Further, H. J. Melosh and P. Schenk reported that during January 1979 as the Voyager 1 spacecraft flew near Jupiter, it took photos of "several prominent chains of impact craters on the surface of the moon Callisto."[321] Clusters of impacts on Earth have also been suggested. According to Richard Grieve the evidence is formidable for the large (124-mile diameter) impact crater at Chicxulub (just off the Yucatan Peninsula). However, he also mentioned other craters (Manson, Kara, Kamensk, and Gusev). Recognizing them has led some to believe that the K/T event[322] "was, in fact, a series of impact events produced by a number of comets, perhaps due to the break-up of a large comet as was observed recently."[323]

Tiny meteorites penetrate Earth's atmosphere many thousands of times each day, usually with no disruptive consequences.[324] On many nights each year, one may gaze into the heavens and see at

319. Monitor. "Death of a Comet." *C&C Workshop.* SIS, 1994:2, p. 19.
320. Lewis. *Rain of Iron and Ice.* 1996, p. 6.
321. Melosh and Schenk. "Split Comets and Crater Chains." *Nature.* Oct. 21, 1993, p. 731.
322. KT event: Acronym for the impact that is commonly believed to have caused the dinosaur extinction. It is named for the boundary between the Cretaceous and Tertiary geologic strata. The "K" in K/T is from the alternate spelling of Cretaceous and the T stands for Tertiary.
323. Grieve. "When Will Enough Be Enough?" *Nature.* June 24, 1993, p. 671.
324. Pendleton and Cruikshank. "Life from the Stars?" *Sky & Telescope,* March 1994, p. 36.

least one bright meteor streaking across the sky. Most are very small and burn up in the atmosphere, but occasionally, an object is large enough to make it through and collide with Earth. James Trefil wrote about impacts:

> Only in recent years have astronomers realized how often Earth is still being hit, and how certain is the probability that it will be hit again.
>
> We have known for a long time that our planet is constantly being pelted with small particles, mostly the size of grains of sand and pebbles. We know that sometimes the projectiles are larger—the size of golf balls, bread boxes, even office desks. Twenty tons a day come filtering down through the atmosphere, the detritus [rock fragments] of interplanetary space.[325]

Van der Sluijs noted: "Comet impacts remained taboo until [1980 when] Alvarez & Alvarez identified iridium[326] in the extinction layer of the Dinosaurs."[327] And, Michael L. McKinney and Robert L. Tolliver, observed: "During the 1980s this idea [the Alvarez hypothesis] caught the attention of the general public in a way that few scientific theories ever do.... The impact hypothesis has renewed 'catastrophism' as an important element in the evolution of the Earth. Not all major changes in Earth history are due to slow processes."[328]

It is obvious now that direct hits of large objects such as comets, meteorites, or asteroids do happen occasionally, and when large enough, they are devastating to life on Earth. In 1992, a *Newsweek*

---

325. Trefil. "Stop to Consider the Stones that Fall." *Smithsonian*. Sept. 1989, p. 82.
326. Iridium: a metal that is very rare in Earth's crust but common in meteorites.
327. Van der Sluijs. "An Aristotelian Hangover." *C&C Review*. SIS, 2009, p. 39.
328. McKinney and Tolliver, editors. *Current Issues in Geology*, 1994, p. 65.

article reported that "geologists have discovered 139 craters left by comets and asteroids. Some were big enough to have killed much of life then on the planet."[329] An eminent astrophysicist, Ernst J. Opik, suggested that some have hit with such force that they "could penetrate the continental crust." He also proposed that they may have triggered huge lava flows "flood basalts such as those in the Deccan Traps in India and the Columbia River basin in the American northwest."[330] John Lewis suggested that "massive volcanism might make more sense as a consequence of, not an alternative to, impact."[331]

Figure 5.2. A car seat and muffler hit by the Benld meteorite in 1938, with the meteorite shown in the inset.[332]

Why were such ideas considered to be scientific heresy for so long? Why should scientists have had such difficulty recognizing

329.   Begley. "The Science of Doom." *Newsweek*, Nov. 23, 1992, p. 59.
330.   Lewis. *Rain of Iron and Ice.* 1996, p. 107.
331.   Ibid.
332.   Photo   courtesy   of   Wikipedia.   http://en.wikipedia.org/wiki/
       File:Benldmeteorite.jpg, (last accessed 9/4/12).

influences from beyond the earth? It is true that catastrophic impacts were a threat to the theory of uniformity, but don't comets follow "laws of nature"?

Even though impacts have now been firmly established in science, the lingering tendency to attribute them to ages far distant is noteworthy: "This intellectual preference is never explicitly stated" says Van der Sluijs. "It rather acts on the unconscious mindsets of theoreticians...when evidence for cratering on the planets is immediately, without a second thought, relegated to the eventful 'early days' of the solar system."[333]

Victor Clube and Bill Napier wrote a book seeking to "bring together hitherto unconnected strands in astronomy, biology and geology, and in the early history and mythology of man."[334] In it, they gave a historical perspective:

> The belief that... comets might sometimes crash on to the Earth took root in the minds of scientific people almost 300 years ago. Thomas Wright wrote around 1755: "That comets are capable of destroying such worlds as may chance to fall in their way is... not at all to be doubted." Fifty years later Laplace thought that "The seas would abandon their ancient positions, ... a great portion of the human race and the animals would be drowned in the universal deluge, or destroyed by the violent shock imparted to the terrestrial globe; entire species would be annihilated."
>
> ... These ideas... were soon lost, submerged by the bold concepts of uniformity and evolution. But the great explosion of astronomical and other knowledge of the past few years has enabled us to put such early speculations on a scientific footing.[335]

---

333. Van der Sluijs. "An Aristotelian Hangover." *C&C Review*. SIS, 2009, p. 39.
334. Clube and Napier. *Cosmic Serpent*. 1982, p. 11.
335. Ibid., pp. 11–12.

Meteor Crater

Figure 5.3. Meteor Crater, Arizona: approximately one mile across and 750 feet deep. It was caused by the Canyon Diablo meteorite estimated to have weighed 300,000 tons and been 135 feet in diameter.[336]

For many years, scientists refused to consider the possibility that comets, meteors, and asteroids played an important role in Earth's history. John Lewis,[337] noted:

> One reason for the reticence of the educated to accept impact cratering on Earth is that the debate... was

---

336. Weaver. "Meteorites: Invaders from Space." *National Geographic.* Sept., 1986, pp. 392–394. Photo by David J. Roddy, USGS, Branch of Astrogeology. http://libraryphoto.cr.usgs.gov/cgi-bin/show_picture. cgi?ID=ID.%20Project%20Apollo%20%281960-1973%29%20001, (lat accessed 9/4/12).
337. John Lewis: Codirector of the NASA/University of Arizona Space Engineering Research Center and Commissioner of the Arizona State Space Agency. Lewis. *Rain of Iron and Ice.* 1996, inside cover.

written in the shadow of the greatest conflict in the history of geology, the uniformitarian-catastrophist debate.... Unanimity had finally been achieved in the nineteenth-century geology community that the uniformitarian principle was valid: catastrophes were not only unimportant factors in geological change, they were nonexistent. In the context of such an attitude, Meteor Crater was a serious embarrassment, a mile-wide hole in their most fundamental theory.[338]

A mineral dealer, Dr. A. E. Foote, examined Meteor Crater and surrounding area in 1891 and found no trace of volcanic activity. He did find evidence of impact—recovering 137 iron meteorites in the vicinity of the rim. In his written report, he stated his position that it was not due to volcanic activity but didn't mention his belief that the crater was due to impact. Was this because he was reluctant to buck the scientific thinking in his day? He did express to a friend that he believed the crater was a consequence of impact.[339]

For some reason, scientists found it less troubling to think the crater was formed in a catastrophic volcanic eruption than in catastrophic impact. They were so reluctant that they coined a new term "cryptovolcanic," meaning volcanic in origin—but with supporting evidence hidden, or cryptic.[340]

Meteor Crater turned out to be "the first documented impact crater on Earth. Its authentication opened the door to hundreds of others."[341] According to Clube and Napier, "geological studies, which included the discovery of about 30 tons of meteoric iron in the vicinity, have settled the matter."[342] If there was any

338. Lewis. *Rain of Iron and Ice.* 1996, p. 34.
339. Ibid., p. 31.
340. Ibid., p. 33.
341. Ibid., p. 71.
342. Clube and Napier. *Cosmic Serpent.* 1982, p. 83.

lingering doubt, it seems to have been resolved by what Nancy Hendrickson described:

> In 1957, geology student Eugene Shoemaker began investigating the crater.... He found shock-melted glass embedded with meteoritic bits. His work convinced geologists that a huge impact shattered and fused the rocks. By studying Meteor Crater, Shoemaker essentially founded the science of impact geology. His work prompted scientists to reinterpret the surface of the moon. Previously they thought that the craters on the moon were remnants of old volcanoes. But Shoemaker's work showed that impacts caused the craters.[343]

Coesite is a mineral named after the chemist Loring Coes. He identified it as a product of "extreme conditions... it is found in nature only where silica-rich rocks have experienced the extremely violent compression of a meteorite impact."[344] Since then, the meteoritic origins of craters all over the earth have been recognized, and using satellite imagery, scientists have identified gigantic impact sites.

One reason for scientists' reluctance to recognize impacts has been the inability to observe them as they happened. Even when impacts have occurred in modern times, most often, no one saw them. "The natural tendency of meteorites [is] to fall randomly to Earth (and hence to sink without a trace into the oceans 72 percent of the time)." And, "those that fell on land more than a few centuries ago were most likely to fall in uninhabited areas."[345]

---

343. Hendrickson. "Arizona's Meteor Crater." *Astronomy.* Nov. 1998, p. 96. An intriguing account of Shoemaker's involvement may be seen in the National Geographic Society's DVD "Asteroids: Deadly Impact."
344. Lewis. *Rain of Iron and Ice.* 1996, p. 71.
345. Ibid., p. 16.

Clube and Napier wrote: "One can open almost any text book on palaeontology or geology to find the evolution of the Earth discussed as if the planet existed in isolation.... On the contrary, far from being negligible, collisions are a major determinant of Earth history."[346] Lewis also commented: "Fortuitously, a number of exciting but seemingly unrelated twentieth-century discoveries in many different fields of science have converged into a single vast drama.... Our understanding of astronomy, geology, and biology is illuminated by this new insight: we see Earth's surface... subject like other bodies to rare, cataclysmic change."[347]

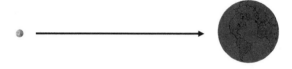

Figure 5.4. A depiction of the path of a direct impact.

Figure 5.5. A Depiction of one of innumerable possibilities for paths of close encounters.

Which is more probable, a direct impact or a close encounter? Although Earth seems very large to its inhabitants, it is less than

346. Clube and Napier. *Cosmic Serpent.* 1982, p. 92.
347. Lewis. *Rain of Iron and Ice.* 1996, p. 2.

tiny compared to the solar system. Thus, by a gigantic margin, more interplanetary objects miss Earth than collide with it, just as most comets are seen to fly into and out of the inner regions of the solar system without collision.

In 1989, Trefil noted that not only do huge objects "strike Earth with catastrophic effect," but "a few months ago, one barely missed us."[348] It is startling to realize that astronomers haven't known much about a large number of objects within the solar system until recently. Since Eugene Shoemaker and David Levy discovered their famous comet, thousands of other objects have been identified whose orbits cross that of the earth.[349] Comet Hale-Bopp, the most spectacular comet I have seen, wasn't even discovered until July 1995—just one year before it so majestically appeared in the sky.[350] It "could be seen without optical aid for 15 months—from July 1996 to October 1997—a record for any comet"[351] and its orbital period is now estimated to be 2,533 years.[352]

There are practically unlimited variations of the sizes and trajectories of the possible objects that might pass close to the earth. Relatively small objects have come close enough to skim Earth's atmosphere. This was the case with the fireball of 1972 shown in figure 5.6.

---

348. Trefil. "Stop to consider the stones that fall from the sky." *Smithsonian.* 1989, p. 81.

349. *National Geographic* DVD. "Asteroids: Deadly Impact." 2003.

350. Gibbs. "Great Expectations." *Scientific American*, Dec. 1995, p. 18.

351. Talcott. "Great Comets." *Astronomy.* May 2004, p. 41.

352. http://en.wikipedia.org/wiki/Comet_Hale-Bopp, p. 4, (last accessed 9/4/12).

Figure 5.6. The Great Daylight Fireball.[353] This photo
was taken August 10, 1972. It shows a streaking object
(marked by the oval), visible in daylight, near Jackson
Lake, Wyoming. It was reportedly sighted from Utah to
Alberta, Canada,[354] and estimated to weigh about one
thousand tons.

Another close encounter occurred in 2002 when an asteroid
came within 288,000 miles of the earth. It wasn't observed until
four days later.[355] In 2011 two small asteroids, one called MD
2011, and the other 2011 CQ1, came within 7,500 and 3,400

---

353. Photo copyright: James M. Baker of Lillian Alabama, used with
     permission.
354. Nemiroff and Bonnell. http://apod.nasa.gov/apod/ap090302.html,
     (last accessed 9/4/12).
355. Associated Press. "Asteroid zips by unseen." *Deseret News*. Salt Lake
     City, March 21/22, 2002.

miles of Earth,[356] and the orbit of MD 2011 was altered by Earth's gravity.[357]

It is helpful to realize that the earth is traveling at about sixty-five thousand miles per hour in its orbit around the sun.[358] Comet Hale-Bopp was estimated to be traveling at 33,800 miles per hour as it hurtled past the Earth toward the Sun.[359] Comets travel anywhere from slowly (at the outer edge of their elliptical orbits) to exceedingly fast as they whip past the sun. Comet Shoemaker-Levy 9's speed as it slammed into Jupiter was estimated to be close to 135,000 miles per hour.[360]

Traveling on a highway, one can't help but observe cars passing one another. When two vehicles are traveling at the same speed, say 65 mph, in the opposite direction, their relative speed is 130 mph. If they are traveling in the same direction and one is moving at 65 and the other at 67 miles per hour, their relative speed is only 2 mph. Similarly, two objects approaching one another in space could have relative speeds anywhere from very slow to extremely fast, depending on their velocities and directions.

Roche's Limit

Roche's Limit[361] is a method for estimating how close two massive objects can be without one being broken apart by

356. http://news.nationalgeographic.com/news/2011/06/110627-asteroid-earth-close-pass-weiss-moon-space-science/.
357. http://www.huffingtonpost.com/2011/06/27/asteroid-today-2011_n_885052.html (last accessed 9/4/12).
358. Wiley. "Phenomena: This Time the Comet Alarm was False." *Smithsonian.* March, 1993, p. 21.
359. Gibbs. "Great Expectations." *Scientific American*, Dec. 1995, p. 18.
360. Wiley. "Phenomena: Comet Shoemaker-Levy 9." *Smithsonian*, Jan., 1995, p. 14.
361. Roche limit: "named after the French mathematician Édouard Roche (1820–1883) who described the theory behind it." From: http://www.daviddarling.info/encyclopedia/R/Rochelimit.html (last accessed 9/4/12).

the gravitational forces of the other. Its formula is complex, considering mass, density, and rigidity of the objects. A simplified version is this: if two massive bodies of similar composition come within about 3 radii of the larger, the smaller will likely break apart. A demonstration of the reality of Roche's Limit was seen in the breakup of Comet Shoemaker-Levy 9 mentioned at the beginning of this chapter.

Joshua's Long Day

The Bible story of what became known as Joshua's long day has been hard to comprehend even for literal believers of the scriptures. However, until some simple questions can be answered, it is wise to refrain from attributing the story to fable. Did the sun really "stand still" as described in Joshua 10:12, or did the description express the way the events appeared to men on the earth? After all, every day in modern society someone mentions a "sunrise" or "sunset" even though it is not the sun's movement being observed.

Some have used faulty logic to try to debunk the description of the sun appearing to stand still. They argued that the consequences of a stoppage of the earth's rotation would reap total destruction. Velikovsky encountered such logic:

> Exact science requires exact figures. If the earth stopped rotating suddenly or in a very small fraction of a second, unattached objects would move away at a velocity of 900 miles an hour at the latitude of Egypt since that is the linear velocity of terrestrial rotation at that latitude. But if... the earth decelerated within the space of six hours.... a man weighing 160 pounds would experience a forward push equal to 5 ounces. Of course he would not fly off into space, for his weight is much greater than the push. Nonetheless, atmosphere and oceans would be set in motion.... ... An airplane that is stopped suddenly on

hitting a rocky mountain disintegrates, but one that is
slowed down in the course of twenty minutes does not.[362]

Although the gradual stoppage of the rotation of the earth
makes more sense than an abrupt one, no mechanism for such a
stoppage (and re-starting) comes to mind. Velikovsky proposed
an alternative which has the ring of possibility: "If rotation
persisted undisturbed, the terrestrial axis may have tilted in the
presence of a strong magnetic field, so that the sun appeared to
lose for hours its diurnal movement."[363]

A number of scientists now hold to the theory that Earth's
poles have shifted, tilted, or flipped. Of course, they usually
attribute such events to slow processes, millions of years ago, but
maybe ancient texts can provide some clues. An early Egyptian
text, Papyrus Salt 825, contains messages with peculiar scientific
implications: "O make lamentation…. The earth is desolate, the
Sun does not come forth, the moon is reversed in her course;
Nun [the watery firmament] trembles, the earth is overturned, all
mortals shall weep and morn."[364] (brackets by Nibley)

Suppose Earth's axis tilted so the North Pole pointed toward
the sun. What would conditions be like? In the northern
hemisphere the sun would not set. It would appear in the sky at
about the relative position where the North Star is now seen. The
southern Hemisphere would be dark. What might this have to
do with Joshua's long day? Maybe a lot. Consider the following:

> And he [Joshua] said…Sun, stand thou still upon Gibeon;
> and thou, moon, in the valley of Ajalon.
> And the sun stood still, and the moon stayed. (Joshua
> 10:12–13)

---

362. Velikovsky. *Stargazers and Gravediggers.* 1984, pp. 92–93.
363. Ibid., p. 93.
364. Nibley. *Enoch the Prophet,* 1986, pp. 193–194.

Not only have scientists ignored Joshua's description but so have most believers. Indeed, it is extremely peculiar. But, if it is a representation of a real event, it has significant scientific implications and deserves to be studied. Charles Totten published a small book on the subject in 1877. In his introductory remarks, he addressed the lack of attention paid to Joshua's long day:

> Most commentators regard the matter as a mere quotation from a poetical book called Jasher,[365] and without exception, so far as the author knows or can find out, the Theological library of to-day contains no volume in which the absolute integrity of the account is candidly admitted and fairly argued.
>
> The result is that this battle ... has fallen entirely out of serious thought, and now-a-days serves merely as a text wherewith to point the shaft of ridicule and doubt.[366]

The book of Jasher includes an intriguing detail, absent from the Bible's account of Joshua's long day: "*The day was declining toward evening*, and Joshua said in the sight of all the people, Sun stand thou still" (emphasis added) (Jasher 88:63). Take note of

---

365. Whether the 1887 edition of the book of Jasher available today (*The Book of Jasher*. Salt Lake City: J. H. Parry & Company, 1887, Photo Lithographic Reprint 1973) is an accurate rendering of the book referred to in Joshua 10:13 is uncertain. On the Title Page, it is claimed that it is a translation from the "Orginal Hebrew" The full text may be found at: (http://www.sacred-texts.com/chr/apo/jasher/index.htm.) A number of things suggest that it is authentic. John Pratt compared many specific details in Jasher which are not in the Bible but are mentioned in ancient texts which have come to light in modern times (Pratt. "How Did the Book of Jasher Know?" *Meridian Magazine*, 2002. http://www.johnpratt.com/items/docs/lds/meridian/2002/jasher.html, last accessed 9/4/12). His work lends credence to the authenticity of that book.

366. Totten. *Joshua's Long Day*. 1968, p. 4.

the phrase "the day was declining toward evening" because if true, it is important to what follows.

Suppose a body such as a large comet or asteroid with a magnetic field passed close to the earth; close enough, and large enough, to cause Earth's axis of rotation to temporarily tilt from pointing toward the North Star to pointing toward the sun. If the encounter was beyond Roche's Limit—neither body would have broken apart. Later, as the object moved away from Earth and the influence of its magnetic field diminished, Earth's axis shifted back to its current orientation.

Not long ago, such a hypothesis would have been immediately dismissed as nonsense. In fact, it was. When Velikovsky proposed it, he was denounced, ridiculed, and scorned.[367] But with more and more astounding discoveries regarding objects within the solar system, it now seems worthy of serious scientific scrutiny.

Consider a simple experiment: a straight bar magnet is placed into a small bowl. Together, they are placed into a larger bowl of water—so they float. If the magnet is not already oriented with the Earth's magnetic field, it slowly moves into alignment. When another magnet is slowly moved past the bowl of water, if near enough and strong enough, it temporarily changes the orientation of the floating magnet. Several passes at different speeds and distances reveal interesting results. When the small magnet passes very close to the bowl, its field temporarily overrides the effect of the Earth's.

Let the magnet in the small bowl represent the earth, and the magnet passing by, a comet or other massive object with a strong magnetic field. Of course, the likelihood of the astronomical version of the demonstration above is extremely remote. But if it happened, it happened—no matter how unlikely. G. Brent

---

367. See Velikovsky. *Worlds in Collision.* 1977, p. 60. Also *Stargazers and Gravediggers.* 1984.

Dalrymple made an impressive statement concerning the slight probability of unlikely events:

> Calculating the odds of an event, especially after it has happened, can be misleading. As an illustrative experiment, deal yourself a "hand" of 52 cards from a shuffled deck and lay them out on a table in the order dealt. The odds of dealing that particular sequence of cards is... 1.2 x 10^{-68}. From this exceedingly small probability you might conclude that the hand you just dealt was impossible, yet there it is before you.[368]

This probability is staggeringly remote: one chance in 52 x 51 x 50... x 1, a product with 68 digits.[369] Bennison Gray posed a question worth consideration: "Who is to say when one kind of gross improbability in the very distant past outweighs another?"[370] Who indeed?

Isaiah suggests an abnormal physical event that seems relevant to the long day of Joshua:

> Behold, the Lord maketh the earth empty, and maketh it waste, and turneth it upside down, and scattereth abroad the inhabitants thereof....
>
> The earth is utterly broken down, the earth is clean dissolved, the earth is moved exceedingly...
>
> The earth shall reel to and fro like a drunkard, and shall be removed. (Isaiah 24:1, 19, 20)

Now, more questions to ponder:

---

368. Dalrymple, *The Age of the Earth*, 1991, p. 197.

369. Hamburg. *Statistical Analysis for Decision Making*. 1970, p. 52. Multiplying the numbers yields: One chance in 80,658,175,170,943 ,900,000,000,000,000,000,000,000,000,000,000,000,000,000,000, 000.

370. Gray. "Alternatives in Science." *Kronos*, Vol. VII, no. 4, 1982, p. 20.

1. Why are nearly all planets of the solar system in the same orbital plane?
2. What causes gravity?
3. Why does the earth rotate on its axis?
4. Is the earth's spin-rate constant, or does it change over time?
5. Why does the earth's axis point toward the North Star?
6. Why is the axis of rotation of other planets oriented differently than Earth's?
7. What causes the earth's magnetic field?
8. Why isn't Earth's magnetic north pole the same as the rotational North Pole?

If the answers to these questions were better understood, answers to other questions might be within reach.

Now, back to Joshua's long day. Compare figure 5.7 with the description in Joshua.

> And the Lord discomfited them before Israel, and slew them with a great slaughter at Gibeon, and chased them along the way that goeth up to Beth-horon, and smote them to Azekah, and unto Makkedah.
>
> And it came to pass, as they fled from before Israel, and were in the going down to Beth-horon, that the Lord cast down great stones from heaven upon them unto Azekah, and they died: they were more which died with hailstones than they whom the children of Israel slew with the sword.
>
> Then spake Joshua to the Lord in the day when the Lord delivered up the Amorites before the children of Israel, and he said in the sight of Israel, Sun, stand thou still upon Gibeon; and thou, moon, in the valley of Ajalon....
> ... So the sun stood still in the midst of heaven, and hasted not to go down about a whole day. (Joshua 10:10–12)

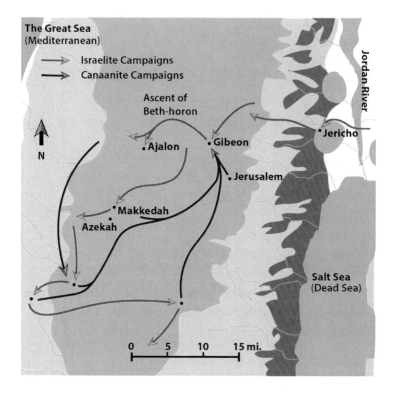

Figure 5.7. Sites mentioned in Joshua 10:10–12.[371]

It appears that at the time Joshua spoke the words "Sun, stand thou still upon Gibeon; and thou moon, in the valley of Ajalon" he was in the vicinity of Makkedah and Azekah (lower left in figure 5.7). If so, the sun and moon would have been roughly north and northeast of his location. Since neither the sun nor the moon are normally seen in those positions at the latitude of Israel, it is singular that his description mentions those directions. This orientation—the sun observed in the northeast—would be

---

371. This map is based on similar maps published by Hammond, Incorporated, and titled "Israel's Entry into Canaan."

particularly strange, if, as recorded in Jasher 88:63, "the day was declining toward evening."

To illustrate how a temporary polar tilt could cause physical phenomena matching the description of Joshua's long day, a small-scale demonstration may be useful:

1. An Earth globe is positioned so its North Pole points toward the North Star (simulated by a spot on the ceiling about 23 degrees from vertical above the globe). As the globe is slowly rotated on its axis from west to east, a flashlight is positioned at the farthest corner of the room pointed at the world globe (simulating the sun shining on the earth).

2. As the world globe continues to rotate on its axis, an object (representing a comet) is moved from the corner of the room opposite the "sun" and toward it. Have the object pass close to the earth globe when the "sun" is "declining toward evening" in the Middle East. As the object passes, tilt the globe so its North Pole points toward the "comet" in its path toward the "sun."

3. While the globe's North Pole is pointing toward the "sun," continue the earth globe's rotation "about a whole day." Then, as the "comet" moves farther away, and its "magnetic influence" on the earth globe diminishes, slowly tilt the globe back to its original position with the North Pole pointing toward the "North Star."

The "hailstones" that caused so much destruction to the enemies of Israel are another clue that should not be ignored. Normal hailstones don't destroy large armies, but debris from cometary interaction certainly could. When things are seen as they actually happened, it will be intriguing to learn how close this theory is to reality.

If the future is also a key to the past, Isaiah's prophecy may provide important clues: "The earth shall reel to and fro like a

drunkard, and shall be removed like a cottage" (Isaiah 24:20).
If the earth is going to "reel to and fro" in the future, might
not something similar have happened in the past? Could the
"reeling" be a description of a polar tilt and reorientation? If so,
this idea may have merit. If Joshua's long day actually happened as
described in the scriptures, surely there would have been people
in other parts of the world who observed the extremely unusual
phenomena. One description that may fit was recounted at a
meeting of the Society for Interdisciplinary Studies in June 1996:

> Margaret Grant said there is a Greek legend about two
> twins quarrelling over who was going to be king of Thebes
> and one said "if the sun goes backwards, will you agree that
> I should be king?" His twin said "of course, what nonsense"
> whereupon the sun went so far back that it actually set
> before it rose again. Where was that particular Thebes?
> Was it the same event as Joshua's Long Day?[372]

Robert H. Chappell Jr. discussed some other accounts that
seem to refer to Joshua's long day from different vantage points.[373]
Laplace[374] discussed and described what he envisioned the
effects would be if a large comet passed close to Earth: "He said
that for his own generation the chances of such an encounter
must be very small, but 'the small probability... must accumulate

372. SIS Study Group. *C&C Review.* SIS, 1997:1, p. 54.
373. Chappell. "The Day the Sun Stood Still." *Catastrophism and Ancient History,* Vol. 13, July 1991, pp. 102–112.
374. "Pierre-Simon, marquis de Laplace (23 March 1749–5 March 1827)... was a French mathematician and astronomer whose work was pivotal to the development of mathematical astronomy and statistics." http://en.wikipedia.org/wiki/Pierre-Simon_Laplace. (last accessed 9/4/12).

during many centuries and will become very great.... The axis and the movement of rotation would be changed."[375]

The theory of polar shift, if considered at all, is commonly attributed to ages millions of years ago. In 1958, Charles Hapgood described:

> The occurrence of this kind of polar shift has seldom been supposed, for the reason that no force capable of shifting the axis has ever been imagined, other than, possibly, a major interplanetary collision......... The principal obstacle to a shift of the earth on its axis lies in the existence of the earth's equatorial bulge, which acts like the stabilizing rim of a gyroscope. The early writers on this question, such as Maxwell and George H. Darwin, all recognized that a shifting of the planet on its axis to any great extent would require a force sufficient to overcome the stabilizing effect of the bulge. But they were unable to see what could give rise to such a force, and dismissed the idea.[376]

Hapgood noted that the dismissal of the idea "left the evidence unaccounted for," and he continued:

> Fortified by their very strong conviction that a shift of the planet on its axis was impossible, astronomers and geologists insisted that all this evidence, such as fossil corals from the Arctic Ocean, coal beds and fossil water lilies from Spitzbergen, and many other evidences of warm climates in the vicinity of both poles, simply must be interpreted in accordance with the assumption that the poles had never changed their positions.... This placed quite a strain upon generations of geologists, but their imaginations were usually equal to the task. They were fertile in inventing theories to account for warm climates

375. Velikovsky. *Stargazers and Gravediggers.* 1984, pp. 106–107.
376. Hapgood. *Earth's Shifting Crust.* 1958, pp. 24–25.

in the polar zones at the required times, but these theories were never based on substantial evidence.[377]

Later in his book, Hapgood pointed out the weak position of assuming that the poles were permanently fixed in their orientation:

The sum total of the contradictions in this theory, and in the various theories advanced to explain ice ages, mountain formation, the history of continents and ocean basins, or evolutionary theory, will appear as we proceed, to be essentially the result of the *impasse* between the evidence and the doctrine of the fixity of the poles. The necessity of reconciling the constantly accumulating facts in a number of fields with a basic error has produced a multiplicity of theories which are, in fact, a veritable cloud castle of conjectures, without substance.[378]

Gordon Williams wrote of a late-1600s reference to polar shift made by Thomas Burnet:

Before the geological timetable was established to suit the Uniformitarian School, [Burnet] found the following "observation or doctrine among the Ancients":
"They say, The Poles of the World did once change their situation, and were first in another posture from what they are now, till that inclination happen'd; this the ancient Philosophers often make mention of... and the stars, they say, at first were carried about the Earth in a more uniform manner."[379]

---

377. Ibid., p. 25.
378. Ibid., p. 31.
379. Williams. "Our Tilted Earth." *C&C Workshop.* SIS, 1994:1, p. 9.

Conclusion

In recent years, science has taken an about-face from ignoring the possibility of close encounters and impacts to one of enthusiastic acceptance. Although this has caused a swing from the uniformitarian way of thinking in some circles, uniformity is still clung to tenaciously in others.

It is interesting to note how the time estimates over the years have jumped from thousands to millions of years and how that leap has influenced modern thinking. David Salkeld noticed the predisposition as it came out in a TV interview:

> The Palomar 200 inch telescope, used to reach out into the farthest ends of space, was focused for the very first time on.... the asteroid belt [where] it found something that had never and could never have been seen before. Two blobs of material had hit and fused together.... A few weeks later Patrick Moore (now Sir) and a chap from JPL [Jet Propulsion Lab] were discussing this on TV. "These two things must have collided a million or more years ago," said Moore. Now the only logical thing one could say was that they must have collided more than three months earlier but nobody corrected them. "A million or more years ago" has locked into people's minds.[380]

---

380. Salkeld. "Genesis and the Origin of Species." *C&C Review.* SIS, 2002:1, p. 10.

6

Continental Drift or Shift?

The "Moho" line... shows evidence of viscosity which, under extreme stress, could permit or assist the crust, either wholly or as large blocks, to slide considerable distances.

—J. B. Delair (1997)

It is well attested that the continents have moved from their earlier positions. J. Tuzo Wilson reported: "Between 1910 and 1912, Frederick B. Taylor, H. D. Baker, and Alfred L. Wegener all advanced views about continental drift quite similar to those that are widely held today."[381] Although there is apparently no dispute between science and the scriptures regarding continental movement, the inferences regarding when it happened and how long it took do not seem to be in harmony.

---

381. Wilson, J. Tuzo. "Mobility in the Earth." In *Continents Adrift.* 1970, p. 1.

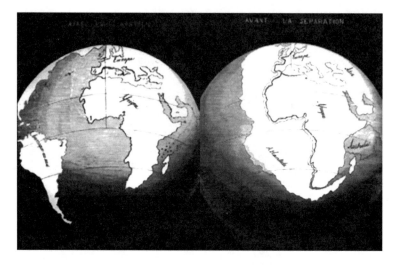

Figure 6.1. "In 1858, geographer Antonio Snider-Pellegrini made these two maps showing his version of how the American and African continents may once have fit together."[382]

Slow Drift or Sudden Shift?

Scientists were at first reluctant to recognize continental movement partially due to the lack of a plausible cause. Its popularity skyrocketed once the theory of mantle convection currents as the driving force captured the imagination. It has become one of those almost universally accepted theories. Continental drift is taught in schools from elementary to collegiate levels as though the narrated audio-visual library going back millions of years was available and had been studied thoroughly.

Claims that America and Europe have been drifting apart at a rate of a few centimeters per year have been made for decades.

---

382. Kious and Tilling. *This Dynamic Earth*. U. S. Geological Survey. http://pubs.usgs.gov/gip/dynamic/historical.html (last accessed 9/4/12). Reproductions of the original maps courtesy of University of California, Berkely.

While in junior high school (in the early 60s), I asked how such small movements could be measured across the ocean. Nobody had a good answer. Surely an extra-long tape measure would expand, contract, sink, or be distorted by water movement and temperature changes, thus preventing precise measurements of such vast distances. A Nova program seems to have provided the answer: "In 1995, the first truly world-wide navigation system was realized. GPS, the Global Positioning System, now provides navigators their latitude and longitude within a few feet anywhere on Earth."[383] If it wasn't until 1995 that measurements on a global scale could be made to within a few feet, on what basis was it confidently taught that the continents were moving less than an inch each year prior to then?

In 1997 Larson et al. made what appears to be another overly optimistic claim:

> We have analyzed 204 days of Global Positioning System (GPS) data... spanning January 1991 through March 1996. On the basis of these GPS coordinate solutions, we have estimated velocities for 38 sites.... The GPS velocities agree with absolute plate model predictions within 95% confidence. For most of the sites in North America, Antarctica, and Eurasia, the agreement is better than 2 mm/yr.[384]

What factors were used to calculate their statistical confidence level? How were the estimates made? Was this just another speculation couched in sophisticated terminology as though it was sure and accurate? Based on a report in 2010, that seems to be

383. Nova. "Lost at Sea—The search for Longitude," airdate 10/6/98. http://www.pbs.org/wgbh/nova/transcripts/2511longitude.html (last accessed 9/4/12).

384. Larson et al. "Plate Velocities from GPS." *Journal of Geophysical Research*, May 10, 1997, p. 9961.

the case. In describing an upgrade to the GPS system (which cost about 8 billion dollars): "The new system is designed to pinpoint a location within an arm's length, compared with a margin of error of 20 feet or more today."[385]

Other high-tech methods of estimating the relative positions of the continents include very long baseline interferometry (VLBI) and satellite laser ranging (SLR). Certain measurements from these techniques are claimed to be within a few millimeters. The methods are very promising, but as Collilieux et al. reported, they are susceptible to "modeling errors," "systematic errors," "range biases," and estimations.[386] Thus, it appears these claims are also overly optimistic. More research is needed.

Furthermore, if the small movements claimed to be ongoing are real, it could be a result of the crust readjusting after calamitous and sudden shifting. Or as Phillip Clapham put it: "If Europe is moving away from North America, this may have involved episodes of enhanced or rapid spread, in contrast to the uniformitarian idea of continuous slow drift."[387]

An example of sudden shifting, although relatively small, was described as a result of the 2011 earthquake off the coast of Japan. Numerous news sources reported that the island of Honshu shifted eight feet to the east.

The evidence firmly establishing continental movement comes from diverse sources. However, the theory that mantle convection currents was its cause does not have the same degree of factual support. Such currents no doubt exist, but a number of scientists cast doubt on whether they create a sufficient force to accomplish the movement of the continents. They also suggest

385. Hennigan. "Capabilities: GPS Upgrade Aims for Accuracy." In *Deseret News,* May 30, 2010.

386. Collilieux et al. "Satellite Laser Ranging." *Journal of Geophysical Research,* Vol. 114. 2009, pp. 14–15.

387. Clapham. "Sea Level Changes." *C&C Review.* SIS, 1997:2, p. 12.

that the currents fail to account for other geological phenomena, particularly overthrusting.[388] Further, if mantle convection currents exist in sufficient strength to cause ongoing continental movement, what would cause them to remain at fixed positions relative to the crust?

The Ninety East Ridge is the long slender north/south, underwater ridge along the eastern part of the Indian Ocean floor (see figure 6.2.) Its cause is uncertain, however, scientists believe it provides clues to the path of India as it moved from the southern hemisphere to the northern. Other features on the Indian Ocean floor appear to be remnants which had broken off and been left behind as India moved.

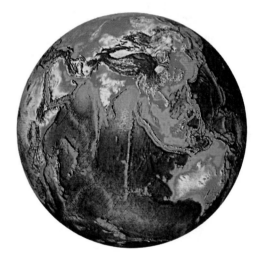

Figure 6.2. An illustration of Earth and the ocean floor from a perspective above the Indian Ocean. Scars along the ocean floor seem to provide clues as to the path taken by India as it moved.[389]

---

388. See Orowan. "The Origin of the Oceanic Ridges." *Scientific American.* Nov. 1969, pp. 103–119.
389. Image courtesy of NOAA. http://www.ngdc.noaa.gov/mgg/image/ relief_slides2.html (last accessed 9/4/12).

Does reason dictate that a peculiar, localized mantle convection current behaved like an extremely slow conveyor belt—causing India to gradually move through the Indian Ocean thousands of miles over millions of years? Has it slowly crumpled the crust of Asia? Or is it more reasonable that a sudden sliding ended in a collision of stupendous proportions?

Hapgood was one who challenged the popular slow-motion view of continental movement. He noted: "Gutenberg has shown that the various forces that Wegener depended upon to move the continents are either nonexistent or insufficient, while another geophysicist, Lambert, has stated that they amount to only one millionth of what would be required."[390]

Others have been advocates for sudden continental movement. "A large body approaching Earth could cause currents in the Earth so large that they would affect Earth's crust in such a catastrophic way that the geological record would later be interpreted as having taken millions of years to produce."[391] McKinney and Tolliver indicated: "A recent report has suggested that impacts may have caused not only the mass extinction at the end of the Permian,[392] but the breakup of Gondwana[393] as well."[394]

Perhaps tilting of the poles similar to that described in the preceding chapter was the main force causing continental movement. If a change in polar orientation happened relatively suddenly, huge segments of the crust could not have resisted movement.

390. Hapgood. *Earth's Shifting Crust.* 1958, p. 30.
391. Monitor. "Conductive and Energetic Earth." *C&C Workshop.* SIS, 2009:1, p. 22.
392. Permian: one of the many geologic "periods" or stata.
393. Gondwanaland: a name given to the southern part of an ancient continent before it broke apart. It is believed to have existed before the present continents came to be.
394. McKinney and Tolliver, editors. *Current Issues in Geology,* 1994, p. 65.

J. Ward Moody, although not addressing the possibility of sudden shift, made a relevant point in his discussion of Archimedes's Principle of Buoyancy: "An object immersed in a fluid experiences an upward buoyant force caused by contact interactions with the surrounding fluid. The strength of this force equals the weight of the displaced fluid." He added: "An interesting example of buoyancy occurs between Earth's crust and mantle. The outer layer of the mantle is hot enough to have some characteristics of a fluid. The continents and ocean basins actually float in the upper mantle in much the same way that ships or icebergs float in water."[395] If flotation is a reality on a continental scale as Moody indicated, the amount of force necessary to cause huge land masses to shift is much less than most people would suppose.

Plate Tectonics

The term "plate tectonics" is used for the predominant theory of crustal deformations around the earth. But since it is so generally associated with the theory of slow and steady mantle convection currents over millions of years, it should be accepted only with reservation. Paul Lowman of the Goddard Space Flight Center wrote:

> Plate-tectonic theory is an enormously powerful and helpful conceptual framework for teaching geology, whatever else may be said about it. First, it is fundamentally simple and easy to understand, even by students in the lower primary grades. An indirect benefit of this simplicity is that the theory is easy for teachers to assimilate, an important factor because many grade and high school earth science teachers have no background in geology, being pressed

---

395. Moody. "Forces in Fluids." In *Physical Science Foundations*, 2nd Ed. 2006, pp. 70, 74.

into service for lack of anyone else. A second pedagogical [educational] strength of plate tectonics is that the concept is easily visualized.... The very strength of plate-tectonic theory... is also a major weakness. The plate maps and attendant explanations found in all modern texts are over-simplified, in that they concentrate on features that actually may be well-explained by the theory.... But they omit, because plate tectonics does not explain them, many major crustal features and characteristics...

The most serious charge against plate tectonics as an educational device is also the simplest: the theory may be wrong. This suggestion would be dismissed by most western geologists, students, and recent graduates. But ruling theories have been overthrown before.[396]

Dan McKenzie expressed a growing concern: in spite of the general acceptance of plate tectonics, "it has been clear since the earliest days of the theory that it provides a poor description of continental deformation."[397] Jill Abery reported that "S. Keshov of Bombay's Indian Institute of Technology asserts that it is 'a myth that has paralysed our thinking.'"[398]

A study by K. M. Storetvedt of the Institute of Solid Earth Physics cast another doubt when he mentioned "the inadequacies of the current model to explain predominant structural features of our globe, the undue complexity of geophysical processes in the wake of the model, and despite two decades of ocean drilling, an adequate verification of the theory appears more remote than ever." He continued that these factors: "raise the question

396. Lowman. "Plate tectonics in geologic education." In *New Concepts in Global Tectonics,* 1992, pp. 3–6.
397. McKenzie. "Spinning Continents." *Nature,* March 8, 1990, p. 109.
398. Abery. "Tottering Tectonics." *C&C Review.* SIS, 2001:1, p. 40.

of whether orthodox plate tectonics represents a realistic approach.... [Or,] is it just another fallible theory?"[399]

How the original continent broke apart is another speculative topic. Could impacts have cracked the continental crust? According to Verne R. Oberbeck:

> Impact... may also provide clues to the cause of continental breakup. Supposed glacial deposits often occur in the same places as massive flood basalt deposits and along ancient continental breakup boundaries. Many scientists now believe that continental breakup is associated with mantle plumes emanating from the boundary between Earth's core and mantle, and that mantle plumes cause the flood basalt eruptions and continental breakup. For the past 20 years, however, some geologists have advocated that impacting asteroids and comets produced craters that released overburden pressure on magma chambers and caused melting of mantle material and flood basalt eruptions.[400]

Hapgood, at one time, suggested that pressure from ice caps caused the continent to crack and the segments to slide, but experiments have shown that ice caps would not have created sufficient driving force to move the continents.[401] Einstein expressed his view that the pressure of the ice wasn't enough to cause Earth's crust to shift. Hapgood listened, and modified his theory accordingly.[402] Indeed, after revision, Albert Einstein

399. Storetvedt. "Rotating plates." In *New Concepts in Global Tectonics*, 1992, p. 204.
400. Oberbeck. "Impacts and Global Change." *Geotimes*, Sept. 1993, p. 17.
401. Hubbert and Rubey. "Role of Fluid Pressure in Overthrust Faulting." *Bulletin of the Geological Society of America*, Vol. 70, Feb. 1959, pp. 115–166.
402. SIS Study Group. *C&C Review*. SIS, 1997:1, p. 54.

wrote the Foreword to Hapgood's book titled *Earth's Shifting Crust*. He began:

> I frequently receive communications from people who wish to consult me concerning their unpublished ideas. It goes without saying that these ideas are very seldom possessed of scientific validity. The very first communication, however, that I received from Mr. Hapgood electrified me. His idea is original, of great simplicity, and—if it continues to prove itself—of great importance to everything that is related to the history of the earth's surface.
>
> A great many empirical data indicate that at each point on the earth's surface that has been carefully studied, many climatic changes have taken place, apparently quite suddenly. This, according to Hapgood, is explicable [explainable] if the virtually rigid outer crust of the earth undergoes, from time to time, extensive displacement over the viscous, plastic, possibly fluid inner layers. Such displacements may take place as the consequence of comparatively slight forces exerted on the crust, derived from the earth's momentum of rotation, which in turn will tend to alter the axis of rotation of the earth's crust.[403]

Sea-Floor Spreading and Subduction Zones

Fundamental to the popular plate tectonics theory is the concept of gradual sea-floor spreading in the Atlantic basin, and subduction of plates in other locations, such as the west coast of the Americas. One typical sketch is shown in figure 6.3.

---

403. Hapgood. *Earth's Shifting Crust*. 1958, p. 1.

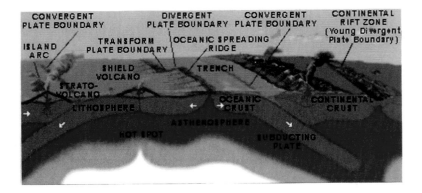

Figure 6.3. A portrayal of the theorized seafloor spreading and subduction zones.[404]

Storetvedt discounted sea-floor spreading "as an important mechanism of oceanic crustal evolution."[405] As with so many popular theories, they are—of necessity—based on assumptions. Meyerhoff et al. questioned a number of the assumptions on which plate tectonic theory is built.[406] A. C. Grant of the Geological Survey of Canada concluded a report on his study of sea-floor spreading with:

> Nares Strait is a unique place to test the validity of the plate-tectonic theory, and on geological grounds the theory fails the test. Geological and geophysical data in Labrador Sea and Baffin Bay do not support a plate-tectonic interpretation there, and highlight weaknesses in the... theory.

404. Courtesy of http://science.nasa.gov/science-news/science-at-nasa/2000/ast06oct_1/ (last accessed 9/4/12).
405. Storetvedt. "Rotating Plates." In *New Concepts in Global Tectonics*, 1992, p. 203.
406. Meyerhoff. "Origin of Midocean Ridges." In *New Concepts in Global Tectonics*, 1992, p. 167.

... An enormous edifice of interpretations has grown around the assumptions of the plate-tectonic theory; it would be unfortunate if its shadow obscures the exciting implications of these new observations.[407]

In a similar study of the crust beneath the northwestern Pacific Ocean, Choi et al. cast doubt on one of the so-called subduction zones: "Finally, this study focuses on the validity of the assumed subduction and accretion of Pacific plates. The observations... across the Wadachi-Benioff zone, and the crustal structure across the Japan Trench, indicate that neither accretion nor subduction of the Pacific plates has taken place along the present Japan Trench."[408]

Ice Buildup

It is a fact that huge quantities of ice now exist in the polar regions of the earth. In the past, there was even more. The evidence for this conclusion has led to the popular theories about "ice ages." Important questions are: How much of the ice was a result of a normal slow and steady buildup processes? How much of it was from other sources? How, when, and why did the vastly larger ice sheets appear and disappear? What has caused the global cooling, and then warming since the "ice ages"?

According to Derek Allan, permafrost deposits in the Arctic regions appear to have been "laid down as the result of a single event of enormous size and power, not as a series of separate lahar [layered] incidents." He added:

407. Grant. "Intracratonic Tectonism." In *New Concepts in Global Tectonics,* 1992, p. 72.

408. Choi. "Paleoland, Crustal Structure." In *New Concepts in Global Tectonics,* 1992, p. 188.

The extraordinary depths to which these deposits have been penetrated so far show that the event responsible for the deposition of the permafrost as a whole must have been frighteningly large: e.g. when drilling for oil through the Alaskan "muck" on one occasion, part of a frozen (not fossilized) tree came up in a core from the amazing depth of 308 m. In a second instance, goldminers drilling through permafrost in northern Siberia stopped at 1231 m below the surface when they failed to reach bedrock. Such thick deposits surpass any elsewhere known.... Some other agency must have been responsible for their deposition.[409]

In whichever way the ice caps formed, their weight undoubtedly stressed the super-continent, making it susceptible to cracking.

Shock Waves

Experiments have shown that when two or more waves collide, an intensified wave occurs at their interface. In an article titled "Rogue Waves," Bruce Stutz described some of the research done regarding these unusual wave patterns. He indicated that scientists in Europe gathered everything they could find on the subject. They concluded: "rogue waves not only exist but are also more common than previously thought. They can be described with nonlinear physics and reproduced in a wave tank."[410] Although the rogue waves referenced in that article were in water, shock waves similarly travel through Earth's crust. Consider the damage done in a few moments by the shock wave from slippage of a major fault and how much greater the shockwaves would be if continents shifted suddenly!

---

409.   Allan. "An Unexplained Arctic Catastrophe." *C&C Review*. SIS, 2001:2, p. 5.
410.   Stutz. "Rogue Waves." *Discover.* July 2004, p. 55.

Rock Mechanics

Dr. Melvin A. Cook was an expert in rock mechanics, brittle fracture, and metallurgy. He observed fractures and, with explosives, caused them in hard rock. His practical application of scientific knowledge suited him particularly well for understanding the mechanics of the breakup of the original continent. Cook's research demonstrated that it is not long periods of time under low stress that causes rocks to deform, but the key factors are high temperature and/or pressure. Soil can "creep" when it is subjected to mild to moderate pressure, but hard rock, like the granite layer in the lower portion of the earth's crust, does not. It becomes pliable only when it is exposed to high pressure and/or heat. For instance, at some point beneath Earth's surface, the weight of many layers of rock and dirt provides sufficient pressure to cause what is called "plastic failure" of solids. The estimated depth for such failure varies depending on the nature of the rock and the weight of the overburden. Cook suggested that the level of the failure of the crust at the time of continental shift approximately coincided with what is now the Atlantic sea floor (beneath the sediments that have since accumulated).[411]

Numerous renditions have been proposed as to how the original continent may have appeared before continental breakup and movement. One is shown in Figure 6.1. A precisely accurate preshift map is not currently within reach due to massive distortions as a result of the stresses associated with the movement of the continents. However, viewing various versions does provide intriguing possibilities.

---

411. Cook. (Personal communication).

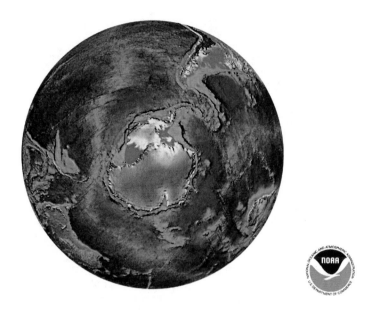

Figure 6.4. An image of Earth from above Antarctica. Also shown are Australia and New Zealand and the southern parts of South America and Africa.[412]

In S. Warren Carey's work revising Wegener's continental drift model, he proposed that India had underthrust the Tibet region. See Figures 6.5 for a recent map. The incredible height and ruggedness of the Himalayan mountains, particularly the 29,000 ft. Mount Everest, and its neighbors, suggests forces were at work other than slow and gradual. In order to underthrust, crumple and raise to such astounding heights such a sizeable segment of land, the forces involved had to have been extreme.

---

412. Courtesy of NOAA. http://www.ngdc.noaa.gov/mgg/image/relief_slides2.html (last accessed 9/4/12).

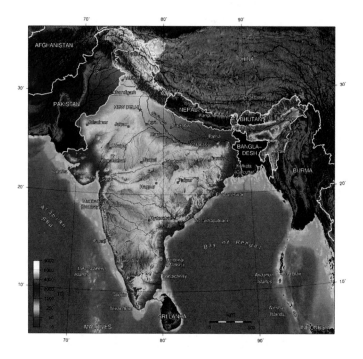

Figure 6.5. A topographical map portraying the crumpling
effect in the regions north and east of India.[413]

A physical property of solids known as spallation or scabbing
may have important implications regarding some crustal features
at the edges of Asia.[414] John Rinehard, a research physicist and
John Pearson, a research engineer, published photos showing the
effect shockwaves had on steel plates. The shock from a small
explosive charge on one side of the plates caused portions on the
opposite sides to spall or literally be blown away. Depending on

---

413. Courtesy of http://en.wikipedia.org/wiki/File:India_topo_big.jpg
      (last accessed 9/4/12).

414. Nemes and Eftis. "Impact and Post-Spall Behavior." In *Shock-Wave
      and High-Strain-Rate Phenomena in Materials*. 1992, p. 723.

the intensity of the charge, materials used, and their condition, the degree of spallation varied. See Figure 6.6.[415]

Figure 6.6. Photo of cross-sections of two steel plates (approximately three inches in diameter and two-inches thick) spalled by shockwaves from explosive charges. Top left: showing the spall (the bulged portion on the top of the plate in this photo). The explosion sent a shockwave through, and partially spalled, the opposite side of the plate. Top right: another plate cross-section showing where a spalled portion had been. Bottom: fragmented material which was spalled off a plate.[416]

Maps which show the topography of the ocean floors and continental shelves reveal features having the appearance of spalls at or near the edges of some continents. Examples can be seen

---

415. Rinehart and Pearson. *Behavior of Metals under Impulsive Loads.* 1954, pp. 154, 189. Reprinted with permission of ASM International. All rights reserved. www.asminternational.org.
416. Ibid., p. 154.

in figure 6.7. Note the shape of some of the islands and portions of the continental shelf east and southeast of Asia. If they really are spalls, what explosive force could have caused them? Cook proposed they were spalls—caused by the shockwaves created when India and Asia collided. If true, that constitutes strong evidence in support of the proposal that the collision was sudden rather than slow and steady. Elias, Rios, and Romero's work on spalls suggest that "materials submitted to high strain rates behave very differently from materials deformed slowly."[417] Thus it seems Cook's theory has possibilities worth considering.

Figure 6.7. Eastern Asia/Australia showing possible spall effects of the shockwaves caused when India slammed into Asia.[418]

---

417. Elias, Rios, and Romero. "Spall of Differently Treated Steel." In *Shock-Wave and High-Strain-Rate Phenomena.* 1992, p. 733.
418. Image courtesy of NOAA. http://www.ngdc.noaa.gov/mgg/image/ etopo1_large.jpg (last accessed 9/4/12).

Erosion

David J. Des Marais of NASA's Ames Research Center and his colleagues noted some details about the collision of India and Asia and the erosion that followed:

> Geological upheaval can have such a dramatic effect because, whether rifting or crashing, continents generate vast amounts of sediments that pour into the oceans. As an example, Des Marais points to India which is currently ramming [sic] into Asia and raising the Himalaya mountain range. As it grows, the range continually sheds its outer skin, turning the rivers of India turbid with sediment. The collision creates so much erosion that the Ganges River carries four times more sediment than the Amazon, even though the South American river is three times the size of the one in India.[419]

Although Des Marais supposed the slow, ongoing ramming of India into Asia, the fact that the sedimentation of the Ganges River remains high can also be used in support of a sudden collision in relatively recent times.

Christopher Newhall published an article describing rapid erosion "as a result of the explosive eruption of Mount St. Helens in 1980... runoff and erosion increased sharply, and annual sediment yields were among the highest ever observed. Today, the river draining the debris... of Mount St. Helens still carries one to two orders of magnitude [10 to 100 times] more suspended sediment than before the eruption."[420]

---

419. Monastersky. "Oxygen Upheaval." *Science News*, Dec. 12, 1992, p. 342.
420. Newhall. "Mount St. Helens, Master Teacher." *Science*, May 19, 2000, p. 1181.

Conclusion

Sudden shifting of continents seems revolutionary due to the nearly overwhelming acceptance of the theory supposing slow and steady processes. One of the challenges facing proponents of sudden shifting is understanding how such large land masses could slide. A force much greater than convection currents seems needed in order to move objects as huge as continents. Perhaps the process is better explained by catastrophic close encounters. Gravitational and/or magnetic interaction between two massive bodies passing close enough, would be tremendous. Under certain circumstances, sudden movement of huge land masses would not only be possible but inevitable.

David L. Clark, PhD, although not teaching this unorthodox approach to continental movement, nevertheless made some points that are relevant:

Earth's continental areas have histories that include different kinds of events than those of the major modern ocean basins, and together the story of the origin of each of Earth's oceanic and continental features comprise the history.... Some parts... are better understood than are other parts, and Earth scientists are constantly reminded of the place of humility in their studies because they realize that today's dogma may become tomorrow's discarded theory.[421]

Hapgood noted:

The Wegener theory involved the corollary that, as the continents had drifted very slowly across the smooth ocean floors, these floors had accumulated sediment to great thicknesses. It was thought that this sediment should provide an unbroken record for the whole period

---

421. Clark. *Of Heaven and Earth.* 1998, p. 131.

of geological time since the formation of the oceans. The greatest surprise of recent oceanographic exploration, however, has been the discovery that this supposed layer of sediment is nonexistent. The layer of sediment on the ocean bottom is uneven, in some places only a few feet or a few inches thick, and is rarely of great thickness.[422]

Sudden shifting not only has scientific backing, but depending on which timing is assumed, it may be in harmony with Bible chronology.

---

422. Hapgood. *Earth's Shifting Crust.* 1958, p. 29.

7

The Flood: A Radical New Theory, Age-Old History, or Myth?

> The grand fact of an universal deluge... is proved on grounds so decisive and incontrovertible, that had we never heard of such an event from Scripture or any other authority, Geology of itself must have called in the assistance of some such catastrophe.
>
> —William Buckland (1819)

The story of Noah's Flood is one of the most obvious conflicts between popular scientific theory and the scriptures. Few scientists openly consider the biblical account of the Flood. Rodney Turner expressed his opinion: "While most geologists reject Moses' account of a global deluge outright, there are others who simply edit it down to a regional affair. However, Moses' account, combined with other inspired testimony, simply do not allow for such."[423]

Vast amounts of evidence can be used in support of a global flood, but much of that same evidence is also used to support theories that exclude the Flood. The epigraph on the previous page is one example of scientists in the nineteenth century who still regarded the Flood as an integral part of their studies. Patten wrote about such Bible-based science:

> When people began finding fossils in every province of Europe... and at virtually every elevation, the literature of Genesis was recalled. Marine fossils were found high in the Swiss Alps.... This they attributed to the Flood. Terrestrial fossils, often of extinct forms, were found in widely separated locations, and again, this pointed to the Flood.... Many, such as Cuvier, felt that some sort of gigantic, watery cataclysm... had indeed engulfed the past. This possibility immediately suggested the Biblical Flood. Yet others cast about for an alternative explanation. Modern humanists, increasingly anti-Genesis in outlook, were growing in numbers and in positions of importance, especially in academic circles. To Voltaire, for instance, any mention of the Flood was offensive.[424]

Because few scientists during the past century have felt comfortable expressing any views positive toward biblical events, relatively little scientific attention has been paid to the Flood. Modern geology seems to deliberately exclude theories contemplating the Flood.

Years ago, I asked an acquaintance who was completing his PhD in geology if he had seen any geological evidence for Noah's Flood. He answered that he had not. And added that geologists

423. Turner. *This Eternal Earth.* 2000, p. 166.
424. Patten. *Biblical Flood and Ice Epoch.* 1966, pp. 33, 2.

don't see a "flood layer" like they do the iridium layer all over the world.[425] Since then, after much study and reflection, I have come to the conclusion that if the descriptions of the Flood in the scriptures and related sources are reasonably accurate, geologists have been ignoring what is right before their eyes. No surface feature on Earth would have escaped significant alteration, and in many places, the changes would have been extreme! There would be no "flood layer," but there would be many diverse strata and features providing clues. If the Flood occurred in conjunction with sudden continental shifting, the changes in the crust would have been even more pronounced. "Then I shall bring down the flood onto the earth, and the earth itself will be overwhelmed by a great quantity of mud" (2 Enoch 34:3).[426]

A Flood Hypothesis

Here is a hypothesis to consider:

1. The Flood really did happen as described in the scriptures and other ancient sources.
2. It was much, much more than just a local or regional event.
3. The forty days of rain were only a small part of the catastrophe.
4. Every part of Earth's surface and many subterranean features were drastically altered.

---

425. The layer of iridium-containing sediment is believed to be from impact(s) marking the extinction of the dinosaurs.
426. In *The Old Testament Pseudepigrapha*, Vol. 1. 1983, p. 159. Although the book of Enoch is not part of the modern editions of the Bible, it appears to have been highly esteemed by the people of the scrolls based on the number of fragments found in the Dead Sea Scrolls. The New World Encyclopedia gives a list of books ranked according to number of manuscripts found: Psalms, 39; Deuteronomy, 33; 1 Enoch, 25; Genesis, 24; Isaiah, 22; etc. http://www.newworldencyclopedia.org/entry/Dead_Sea_scrolls.

5. No one survived except those with Noah on the ark, some aquatic life, and possibly some plants and seeds.
6. Before the Flood, there was one main landmass. It cracked into pieces and shifted—substantially contributing to the catastrophic effects of the Flood.
7. Continental breakup was primed by stresses on the crust from ice buildup on the northern and southern regions of the original continent, and fracturing was initiated by comet and/or asteroid impacts.
8. Most of the continental movement and mountain-formation took place during and in the aftermath of the Flood/continental-shift event.
9. The mechanism of the catastrophe involved a temporary tilting of Earth's axis.
10. Shockwaves bounding and rebounding dwarfed even the most powerful earthquakes known in modern times.
11. Unprecedented volcanism took place during the Flood/continental shift event.
12. Much, if not most, of the erosion and sedimentation seen on and near Earth's surface took place in a relatively short time—during and after the Flood.
13. Most of the details attributed to "ice ages" can be explained by the effects of the Flood, and its related catastrophes.

Flood Stories from All over the World

Stories similar to the biblical account of Noah's Flood are found in nearly all parts of the world. From Philo of Alexandria,[427] came this account:

> The vast ocean being raised to an height which it had never before attained, rushed with a sudden inroad upon

---

427. Philo (20 BCE–50 CE) was a Jewish philosopher born in Alexandria. http://en.wikipedia.org/wiki/Philo, (last accessed 9/4/12).

islands and continents. The springs, rivers and cataracts, confusedly mingling their streams, contributed to elevate the waters... For every part of the earth sunk beneath the water and the entire system of the world became... mutilated and deformed.[428]

Nibley described an account from an earlier period: "The 178th chapter of the Book of the Dead contains a flood story text that the ancient scribes profess themselves at a loss to explain, lost as it is in the mists of the remote past."[429] He also noted:

A certain great lady... came to the Nile Valley immediately after the Flood and established herself and her son as rulers in the land. Since this is the same story that is told in the Book of Abraham 1:21-27, it is fortunate that the Egyptian sources are both abundant and specific. It was Hermann Junker who first called attention to them in 1911; in short order the eminent Egyptologists Sethe and Spiegelberg joind in the hunt, and by 1917 the most important sources had been brought together and published.... ... The Egyptian story of earthly dominion begins with the Flood. And there can be little doubt that it was the Flood...

As the curtain rises we see all nature in upheaval as the skies darken and the waters descend... violent atmospheric disturbances and world disorder... attests the reality of those early catastrophes.[430]

"Herodotus recounts an ancient tradition that all Upper Egypt was a marsh until the reign of the first king of the first dynasty, whom he called Menes."[431]

---

428. Patten. *Biblical Flood and Ice Epoch.* 1966, p. 9.
429. Nibley. *Enoch the Prophet.* 1986, p. 45.
430. Nibley. *Abraham in Egypt.* 1981, pp. 149, 151.
431. Johnson, Paul. *Civilization of Ancient Egypt.* 1978, p. 26.

An interesting twist on the Flood story came when the Babylonian version was unearthed. Nibley expressed his view:

> Secular scholars... have been quick to take any resemblance between heathen traditions and the Bible as absolute proof that the scriptures are simply ordinary stuff. The classic example of this was the Babylonian flood story, discovered by Layard in the mid-nineteenth century. It resembled the biblical account closely enough to show without doubt that they were connected, but before any search for the source of either version was undertaken, it was joyfully announced that the biblical account was derived from the Babylonian and was, therefore, a fraud. The experts were wrong on both points—the Assurbanipal version is really a late redaction [edition], and the duplication of the flood story, instead of weakening it, actually confirms it.[432]

Dorothy Vitaliano, apparently a subscriber to the conventional geological view, nevertheless recognized that flood stories abound. She noted traditions from almost every part of the world: "These are the traditions of a great flood which destroyed either all mankind, or at least a substantial number of the earth's inhabitants."[433] Rather than using those traditions to support the authenticity of the biblical account, she concluded by saying: "All in all, then, from the purely geologic point of view we should *expect* independent flood traditions to have arisen almost anywhere in the world at almost any time, engendered by flood catastrophes stemming from perfectly natural causes."[434] The mechanisms of the Flood suggested herein easily fit the definition of "natural"— though far from ordinary.

---

432. Nibley. *Old Testament and Related Studies*. 1986, pp. 39–40.
433. Vitaliano. *Legends of the Earth*. 1973, p. 142.
434. Ibid., p. 150.

Mechanisms for the Flood

What possible mechanisms could account for such an extraordinary event as a worldwide flood? It should be remembered that about 70 percent of the earth's crust is now covered by oceans and another 3 percent by ice. Nevertheless, a huge amount of water would have been necessary to cover the remaining 27 percent. Many different mechanisms have been proposed. Several have merit, though it seems, none of them alone could account for all the water needed for a complete inundation. It is likely that many sources contributed. In addition to the "40-days of rain," several seem particularly impressive:

1. subterranean chambers releasing huge quantities of water
2. water directly from comets
3. water blasted high into the atmosphere from oceanic impacts of comets, meteors, and/or asteroids
4. a collapsing vapor canopy
5. water from the original ocean overwhelming portions of the continents as they slid and opened up the Atlantic basin

Forty Days of Rain

Those who have read the Bible have encountered the description: "And the rain was upon the earth forty days and forty nights" (Genesis 7:12). Even if that was all that happened, it would have caused significant topographical changes on parts of Earth's surface. People who haven't seen flooding, tsunamis, or the destruction caused in torrential rainstorms or when a dam or a levee fails may not be aware of the incredibly destructive power water can have. For them, an image may come to mind of a calm lake developing around a peaceful ark. Water gradually rising and gently floating the ark, then slowly decreasing until it serenely rested on Mt. Ararat. This is not the picture portrayed by the ancient accounts. There would have been raging torrents, perhaps all over the earth, particularly as floodwaters came, and again during the lengthy period as they subsided.

The Fountains of the Great Deep

What did Moses envision when he recorded, "the same day were all the fountains of the great deep broken up"? (Genesis 7:11). Whatever they were, they must have played an important role in the Flood—much more than a few artesian wells spouting up. A picture painted by Dr. Walt Brown has some intriguing possibilities. In his Hydroplate theory, he postulated that a huge amount of water had been trapped under the crust of the earth during its formation. At the time of the Flood, the cracking of the crust allowed the highly pressurized water to shoot high into the stratosphere.[435]

The wording of Enoch's dream in Martinez's *Dead Sea Scrolls* translation may shed some light: "And behold, the reservoirs in the interior of the earth opened and they began [to spout and lift up the water over it.] I continued to watch until the earth was covered by the water [and by darkness and mists(?) which] hung over it"[436] (brackets by the translator).

It is interesting to compare these ideas with some of the data gathered by the Cassini spacecraft in 2005. "Enceladus is a tiny, frozen moon of Saturn, supposedly too cold and small to be geologically active in any way, but near its south pole it shoots up geysers of vapor and ice-particles from deep fractures. The composition of the material is surprisingly similar to that of a comet and scientists are all agog."[437] Dan Vergano also reported that Enceladus was "caught

435. Brown, W. *In the Beginning*, 7th ed, 2001, pp. 87–120.
436. The Books of Enoch. In Martinez, *Dead Sea Scrolls Translated*, 2nd ed. 1994, p. 257.
437. Monitor. "Enceladus—Mystery Moon." *C&C Workshop*. SIS, 2009:1, p. 21.

in the act of spewing a watery geyser.... [It] was blasting 270 miles into space, actually hitting the orbiting spacecraft."[438] Robert Alder described some research by planetary scientists and concluded: "A global ocean almost certainly lurks beneath the surface of Europa, Jupiter's fourth-largest moon."[439]

Wording in the book of Enoch provides some other intriguing details with scientific implications:

> After he showed me the angels of punishment who are prepared to come and release all the powers of the waters which are underground to become judgment and destruction unto all who live and dwell upon the earth.... Those waters shall become in those days a poisonous drug of the body and a punishment.... the temperatures of those fountains of water will be altered (and become hot), but... those waters of the fountains shall be transformed and become cold.
>
> 1 Enoch 66:1, 67:8-11 [440]

Vapor Canopy

Something about the atmosphere was apparently very different before the Flood. According to Rodney Turner:

> God not only confirmed the reality of the Flood, he also confirmed Moses' testimony that the rainbow originated "in the days of Noah." We assume that the presence of water vapor and sunlight always has the potential to create a rainbow.... Had the rainbow been a common phenomenon [before the Flood], it would not have been employed as a unique sign.[441]

---

438. Vergano. "Saturn Holds a Tiny New Secret." *USA Today.* July 23, 2007.

439. Alder. "Under the Ice." *NewScientist.* May 6, 2000.

440. In *Old Testament Pseudepigrapha*, Vol. 1. 1983, pp. 45–46.

441. Turner. *This Eternal Earth*, 2000, p. 176.

Genesis 2:6 may give an important clue as to what the atmosphere was like prior to the Flood: "There went up a mist from the earth, and watered the whole face of the ground." Patten proposed that the earth—prior to the flood—was watered in a different manner than today. He suggested a "dew regime."[442] Such a theory fits with the hypothesized vapor-canopy, and together, they may help explain why the rainbow was significant after the Flood, but apparently not before:

> And I will establish my covenant with you; neither shall all flesh be cut off any more by the waters of a flood; neither shall there any more be a flood to destroy the earth.
> And God said... :
> I do set my bow in the cloud and it shall be for a token of a covenant between me and the earth.
> And it shall come to pass, when I bring a cloud over the earth, that the bow shall be seen in the cloud.
>
> Genesis 9:11-14

Other modern theories suggest that Earth was once enveloped in clouds, and at some point, the canopy collapsed. This intriguing concept has promise, particularly since gaseous cloud canopies surround other planets such as Venus and Jupiter. Cook calculated that Earth's atmosphere could not hold sufficient water vapor to be the sole cause of a worldwide flood,[443] but he did not rule out the possibility that it could have been a significant contributor.

Professor of Geology, John J. Renton, taught about a vapor-canopy in his 2006 DVD lecture series for The Teaching Company. In his study outline, *The Nature of Earth: An Introduction to Geology*, he wrote:

> As the crust continued to form, the surface of Earth was highly volcanic.

---

442. Patten. *Biblical Flood and Ice Epoch*. 1966, p. 197.
443. Cook. (Personal communication.)

1. The volcanic activity released enormous volumes of gas into the atmosphere consisting primarily of water vapor, which condensed to form a thick cloud cover that enclosed Earth in much the same fashion that clouds now enclose Venus.

2. Within 3½ to 4 billion years, Earth's crust solidified and cooled to the point that the water vapor could condense and fall as rain.[444]

Of course Renton's time estimate, based on common geological assumptions, is vastly different than that suggested by Bible chronology, but his concept fits.

Windows of Heaven

What is meant in Genesis 7:11 by: "the windows of heaven were opened"? Perhaps it was something more than just a long-lasting torrential rainstorm. Again, Enoch may have provided some clues: "[I was] watching and behold, seven streams pouring out [abundant water over the earth]"[445] (brackets by translator). "They shall open all the storerooms of water in the heavens above, in addition to the fountains of water which are on earth. And all the waters shall be united with (all) other waters" (1 Enoch 54:7).[446]

If the flood hypothesis proposed herein is a reasonably close depiction of the actual events, no one would have been able to see the details based solely on physical observations. During much of the flood-year, conditions would have prevented a clear view of the events taking place. Furthermore, how could the survivors have known the extent of the Flood? The prophecy of Enoch and

---

444. Renton. *The Nature of Earth*. 2006, p. 15.

445. The Books of Enoch. In Martinez. *Dead Sea Scrolls Translated*, 2nd ed. 1994, pp. 256–257.

446. In *The Old Testament Pseudepigrapha*, Vol. 1. 1983, p. 38.

the testimonies of those who saw it in vision, may be the only accurate sources for much of what took place.

Another book, Jubilees, although not in the modern canon, ranked sixth in the number of copies found among the Dead Sea Scrolls—only behind Psalms, Deuteronomy, 1 Enoch, Genesis, and Isaiah.[447] Thus, it appears to have been highly revered among the people of the scrolls. Jubilees also includes a variation of the account of the Flood:

> And the Lord opened the seven floodgates of heaven, and the mouths of the springs of the great deep were seven mouths in number;
> And these floodgates sent down water from heaven forty days and forty nights, and the springs of the deep sent up water until the whole world was full of water.…
> And in the fourth month the springs of the great deep were closed and the floodgates of heaven were held shut.
>
> Jubilees 5:24, 25, 29[448]

Possible Contributions of Asteroids, Meteors, and Comets

Remember Patten's theory that Earth had interacted with a large comet which literally dumped vast quantities of water and ice on the globe.[449] Late in his life, after reading the Book of Enoch, Cook modified his theory of continental breakup to include at least seven impacts. His conclusions were based not only on clues from Enoch but also from fracture patterns and rock mechanics. They seem worthy of further study.[450]

---

447. http://www.newworldencyclopedia.org/entry/Dead_Sea_scrolls (last accessed 9/4/12).

448. In *Old Testament Pseudepigrapha*, Vol. 2. 1985, pp. 65–66.

449. Patten, *Biblical Flood and the Ice Epoch*. 1966.

450. Cook. *Noah's Flood, Earth Divided*. 1995, pp. 13–25.

Research by Bruce Masse was discussed in a 2007 article titled "Did a Comet Cause the Great Flood?" He noted that only about 185 craters had been identified on Earth and that since the oceans cover about 70 percent of the surface, a large majority of impacts would have been left unnoticed. He believes he has found evidence indicating a comet that impacted in the Indian Ocean near the coast of Madagascar was devastating to life on Earth. It sent

> 600-foot-high tsunamis crashing against the world's coastlines and injected plumes of superheated water vapor and aerosol particulates into the atmosphere. Within hours, the infusion of heat and moisture blasted its way into jet streams and spawned super-hurricanes that pummeled the other side of the planet.[451]

As Masse pointed out, a substantial majority of the impacts would have taken place in the ocean. A portion of the remainder would have occurred in polar regions, thus affecting ice caps. In those regions, they would have caused instantaneous vaporization of huge quantities of ice, and would have sent shockwaves throughout the icecaps—undoubtedly causing massive ice surges. Jill Abery described some of the work of geologists Alexander and Edith Tollmann. They wrote of "Lyellism[452] as an obsolete

---

451. Carney. "Did a Comet Cause the Great Flood?" *Discover Magazine*, Nov. 2007, p. 66.

452. "Charles Lyell, in his 1830 book *Principles of Geology*, further developed the uniformitarian view with such success that the opposing school of catastrophism ceased to have influence in mainstream geology.... Transformed from empirical evidence to dogma by succeeding generations of geologists, uniformitarian thought degenerated into yet another –ism. The latest crop of Guardians of Truth and Traditional Wisdom had found a new line to defend, and they dug in deep enough to hold their position for [nearly] two centuries." Lewis. *Rain of Iron and Ice*. 1996, p. 23.

thought pattern. In the light of the recent discoveries of cataclysmic asteroid and comet impacts they are advocating a return to Cuvier's catastrophism. They suggest that the most recent catastrophe has been the Universal Deluge around 7552 BC [sic], caused by oceanic impacts by fragments of a great comet."[453] Later, Abery added:

> A detailed article gives their geological evidence for a recent large impact which gave rise to the catastrophic phenomena depicted in flood mythology the world over. They suggest that myths indicate the impactor was a comet which broke into seven fiery pieces. Caustic blood-coloured rainfall would have been fallout of impact-generated nitric acid. All the major fragments appear to have landed in oceans, with minor pieces on land.[454]

One early reference to scientific theories about the Flood was from Newton's successor at Trinity College in Cambridge, William Whiston. He "advanced a theory of a comet's colliding with the earth. According to him, the collision brought about the Noachian deluge."[455]

Perplexing Questions

Even believers of the story of the Flood wonder how Noah and his family were able to accomplish their daunting tasks. It is encouraging to realize that some of the answers just might be within reach. Here are some possibilities: How could they build such a huge ship? Or as some skeptics put it: the technology to build that large of a ship out of wood wasn't available until the late 1800s. Anyone who has spent much time on a farm or ranch,

---

453. Abery. "Return to Catastrophism." C&C Workshop. SIS, 1993:2, p. 29.
454. Abery. "The Flood did happen." C&C Review. SIS, 1996:1, p. 43.
455. Velikovsky. Stargazers and Gravediggers. 1984, p. 42.

has learned about wilderness survival, or engineering, has had a glimpse of people's ingenuity. Couple that creativity with Divine help, and Noah would have had all the technology needed. The scriptures indicate that Noah was given particulars by revelation (Gen. 6:14-16), and no doubt he had more help than just from his wife, three sons, and their wives.

So Many Creatures

Just to gather all of the creatures seems an insurmountable task. "And of every living thing of all flesh, two of every sort shalt thou bring into the ark, to keep them alive with thee; they shall be male and female" (Gen. 6:19). "Of every clean beast thou shalt take to thee by sevens, the male and his female" (Gen. 7:2). A passage from the Book of Jasher adds some detail:

> I will gather to thee all the animals of the earth, the beasts of the field and the fowls of the air, and they shall all come and surround the ark.
> And thou shalt go and seat thyself by the doors of the ark, and all the beasts, the animals, and the fowls, shall assemble and place themselves before thee. (Jasher 6:1-2)

Even if the question of the gathering of the creatures is solved, it seems that no matter how large a ship was built, it could not have held at least two of all the species living on the earth today. What did God mean by "two of every sort"? Could the King James translators have used "species" in that passage? What is a species? Carl Zimmer commented on how surprising it is to realize that there are many different concepts as to what a species really is. He suggested that three things may have "misled the public into thinking the rules are simple." One is using Latin, "that gives species names the whiff of absolute certainty." Another "is the 1.8 million species that scientists have named." And a third "is laws like the Endangered Species Act, which take for granted that we know what species are." In addition, that trying to standardize the definition of "species" has been the subject of debate for many years. Further, he quotes biologist Jonathan Marshall: "There is no general agreement among biologists on what species are," and suggested that there are "at least 26 published concepts in circulation."[456]

As recently as 1999, the National Academy of Sciences (NAS) listed Darwin's study of "13 species of finches" on the Galapagos Islands as "evidence supporting biological evolution."[457] Aren't all thirteen of those "species" still finches? And aren't finches still birds? The NAS booklet also mentions "more than a thousand species of snails and other land mollusks... found only in Hawaii."[458] Aren't different varieties of snails still snails? Could it be that there were just two snails on the ark, and from them came all the varieties?

Jay Gould remarked about the species controversy within the scientific community:

> If all life is interconnected as a genealogical continuum, then what reality can species have? Are they not just arbitrary divisions of evolving lineages?... In fact, the two greatest evolutionists of the nineteenth century, Lamarck and Darwin, both questioned the reality of species on the basis of their evolutionary convictions. Lamarck wrote, "In vain do naturalists consume their time in describing new species"; while Darwin lamented: "we shall have to treat species as... merely artificial combinations made for convenience."[459]

---

456. Zimmer. "What Is a Species?" *Scientific American*. June 2008, p. 74.
457. National Academy of Sciences. *Science and Creationism*, 2nd Edition. 1999, p. 10.
458. Ibid., p. 17.
459. Gould. "What Is a Species?" *Discover Magazine*, Dec. 1992.

Did Noah take with him every breed of dog—Chihuahuas, German Shepherds, St. Bernards, Great Danes, etc.? Certainly not! Many dogs have been bred in recent times. It seems reasonable that Noah took a minimum number of dogs, cats, cows, horses, etc. This is where one aspect of evolution—diversification— seems to fit well with the biblical picture. After the Flood, as the population of living things increased and dispersed over the earth, not only environmental factors but inbreeding would have played an important role in diversification.

Luis Ginzberg collected and published legends of the Jews. From them came some details worth considering: "No less than thirty-two species of birds and three hundred and sixty-five of reptiles he had to take along with him.... Then Noah led the two cubs into the ark. The wild beasts, and the cattle, and the birds which were not accepted remained standing about the ark all of seven days."[460] If Ginzburg's account represents the truth, it provides some impressive answers. It suggests that all the varieties of birds now on the earth sprang from about "thirty-two species," and all of the reptiles came from 365 on the ark.

Recall another clue from Ginzberg's quote above: "Then Noah led the two cubs into the ark." Jasher 6:5 indicates that "a lioness came, with her two whelps, male and female... and she went away." The beasts entering the ark are often portrayed as fully grown, but the accounts in Jasher and Ginzberg suggest the more likely version, namely, that very young creatures would have been taken.

---

460.   Ginzberg, *Legends of the Jews*, Vol. 1, 1909, p. 157. A similar account is mentioned in Jasher 6, with an interesting twist: "The sons of men approached in order to break into the ark, to come in on account of the rain, for they could not bear the rain upon them. And the Lord sent all the beasts and animals that stood round the ark. And the beasts overpowered them and drove them from that place" (Jasher 6:24–25).

And every beast after his kind, and all the cattle after their kind, and every creeping thing that creepeth upon the earth after his kind, and every fowl after his kind, and every bird of every sort.

And they went in unto Noah into the ark, two and two of all flesh, wherein is the breath of life. (Genesis 7:14–15)

How Did They Feed the Creatures?

"And take thou unto thee of all food that is eaten, and thou shalt gather it to thee; and it shall be for food for thee, and for them" (Gen. 6:21). How was Noah able to gather, store, and distribute the vast quantities of food needed to keep the creatures alive for a year on the ark? And how did they dispose of the huge amounts of waste that surely accumulated? These are questions that remain unresolved. However, one clue may have come from apocryphal sources that indicate it was very cold on the Ark. Is it reasonable that many of the animals hibernated during much of the time on board? From Nibley:

> If we fancy Noah riding the sunny seas high, dry and snug in the ark, we have not read the record.... The family [was] absolutely terrified, weeping and praying "because they were at the gates of death," as the ark was thrown about with the greatest violence by terrible winds and titanic seas. Albright's suggestions that the Flood story goes back to "the tremendous floods which must have accompanied successive retreats of the glaciers" is supported by the tradition that the family suffered terribly because of the cold, and that Noah on the waters "coughed blood on account of the cold."[461]

---

461. Nibley. "A New Look." *Improvement Era.* October, 1969, p. 89.

The description in Jasher also speaks of great peril. "And great anxiety seized all the living creatures that were in the ark, and the ark was like to be broken" (Jasher 6:29).

Myth or Reality?

Many people relegate the account of the Flood in Genesis to myth or allegory. However, in context, the scriptures give no hint that it was anything less than a catastrophe of wondrous proportions. Christians may turn to the New Testament for additional testimony of the reality of the Flood.[462]

Ancient Greek accounts also refer to the Flood. The figure "Deukalion" has similarities to, and is often associated with Noah. He seems to represent the Greek rendition of Noah. In *Hamlet's Mill*, Giorgio De Santillana described a part of a Greek tale that may provide insight: "Zeus… in tilting the 'table' caused the Flood of Deukalion, the 'table,' of course, being the earth-plane through the ecliptic."[463] Salkeld commented on de Santillana's description of the event: "If earth's equatorial-plane tilted fairly rapidly (i.e. in a matter of days rather than millennia), then a catastrophic flooding would certainly occur. Whether the Flood of Deukalion event was separate from the Flood of Ogyges, or the two stories represent the same event as remembered by two different races or tribes, is an open question."[464]

Could the Mountains Have Been Covered?

And the waters prevailed exceedingly upon the earth; and all the high hills, that were under the whole heaven, were covered.

---

462. See Matthew 24:37–39, Hebrew 11:7, 2 Peter 2:5, and 2 Peter 3:5–6.
463. de Santillana and von Dechend. *Hamlet's Mill.* 1977, p. 279. The ecliptic is the plane of earth's orbit around the sun.
464. Salkeld. "Mythological/Historical Evidence for Earth Tilting?" *C&C Review.* SIS, 1996:2, p. 15.

Fifteen cubits upward did the waters prevail; and the
mountains were covered. (Genesis 7:19–20)

Many have claimed that not only is a global flood unsupportable,
but one covering the tops of tall mountains such as Mt. Everest,
impossible. It is truly an intellectual challenge to suppose that
the huge mountains might have been covered with liquid water.
Could frozen water (snow and ice) have been considered part
of the covering? Perhaps. However, it is also possible that the
high mountains had not yet been formed, as suggested in the
flood hypothesis earlier in this chapter. Evidence is abundant
in support of the premise that the great mountain ranges were
formed as a result of buckling and fracturing as the continents
shifted and collided.

According to ancient writings, catastrophic changes were
taking place on the earth even before the Flood began. One of
Ginzberg's "legends," may be pertinent to the Flood hypothesis:
"During this time [the week before the Flood]... the laws of
nature were suspended, the sun rose in the west and set in the
east."[465] Nibley noted the same tradition from the ancient Jewish
Zohar: "But the Lord altered the order of creation, making the
sun rise in the west and set in the east, so that all their plans came
to naught."[466] If these are descriptions of real events, there was a
catastrophic encounter of apparently extraterrestrial proportions.
A shifting of Earth's axis similar to the events associated with
Joshua's long day comes to mind (see the chapter titled "Comets,
Asteroids, and Meteors"). Could such an event have caused the
sun to appear to rise in the west and set in the east? If this event
involved a relatively sudden tilting of Earth's axis, it may well
have been what set the continents in motion.

465. Ginzberg, *The Legends of the Jews*, Vol. 1, 1909, p. 154.
466. Nibley. *Enoch the Prophet*. 1986, p. 184.

Another detail, relevant if true, about the beginning of the Flood, is provided in Jasher 6:11: "And on that day, the Lord caused the whole earth to shake, and the sun darkened, and the foundations of the world raged, and the whole earth was moved violently."

The book of Enoch provides another peculiar description. Its wording in E. Isaac's 1983 translation is: "In those days, Noah saw the earth, that she had become deformed, and that her destruction was at hand" (1 Enoch 65:1).[467] A hundred years earlier, Richard Laurence[468] translated it: "In those days Noah saw that the earth became inclined, and that destruction approached."[469] If either translation represents an accurate account, whether the earth became "deformed," "inclined," or both, the event would have had major scientific implications.

Nibley was familiar with these texts and was likely referring to them when he wrote: "The terrors of the book of Enoch reach their culmination when the upheavals of nature extend to the entire cosmos. Many apocalyptic accounts of the disturbed heavens suggest to some scientists today an actual shifting of the earth on its axis."[470]

Van der Sluijs mentioned: "the likes of William Whiston and Sir Edmund Halley felt no compunction to entertain the thought of comets precipitating the global flood of Noah or tilting of the rotational axis."[471] If such an event actually set the continents in motion, once started, inertia would have tended to keep them moving. A great deal of resistance would have been needed to stop them. That would have come in the form of obstacles

---

467. In *Old Testament Pseudepigrapha*, Vol. 1, 1983, p. 45.
468. Laurence was a professor of Hebrew at Oxford. Laurence. *The Book of Enoch*, 1883, inside cover.
469. Laurence, trans. *The Book of Enoch*. 1883, p. 78.
470. Nibley. *Enoch the Prophet*. 1986, p. 203.
471. Van der Sluijs. "An Aristotelian Hangover." *C&C Review*. SIS, 2009, p. 39.

encountered as portions of the original continent slid out over the ocean floor, and some slammed into other land masses. For instance: India colliding with Asia forming the Himalayas and crumpling the crust in that part of the world.

And All Flesh Died

And, behold, I, even I, do bring a flood of waters upon the earth, to destroy all flesh, wherein is the breath of life, from under heaven; and every thing that is in the earth shall die.

And all flesh died that moved upon the earth, both of fowl, and of cattle, and of beast, and of every creeping thing that creepeth upon the earth, and every man:

All in whose nostrils was the breath of life, of all that was in the dry land, died.

And every living substance was destroyed which was upon the face of the ground, both man, and cattle, and the creeping things, and the fowl of the heaven; and they were destroyed from the earth: and Noah only remained alive, and they that were with him in the ark. (Genesis 6:17, 7:21–23)

Did the fish die in the Flood? John Pratt seems to have identified the answer:

The account clearly states, "And all flesh died that moved upon the earth... All in whose nostrils was the breath of life, of all that was in the dry land, died... "

Fish use gills instead of breathing with nostrils, and fish are not listed among the dead after the Deluge.[472]

Although the Bible doesn't mention fish perishing in the Flood, there is no doubt that huge numbers of them did die.

---

472. Pratt, "Did the Fish Die in the Flood?" *Meridian Magazine.* 26 Mar 1999, pp. 1–2.

This conclusion is based on the devastation done by tsunamis, relatively minor flooding, fossils, and the vast coal and oil deposits from once-living things. Of course, mainstream geological theory presents a different picture.

The End of the Flood

And the waters prevailed upon the earth an hundred and fifty days.

And God remembered Noah, and every living thing, and all the cattle that was with him in the ark: and God made a wind to pass over the earth, and the waters asswaged.

The fountains also of the deep and the windows of heaven were stopped, and the rain from heaven was restrained;

And the waters returned from off the earth continually: and after the end of the hundred and fifty days the waters were abated.

And the ark rested in the seventh month, on the seventeenth day of the month, upon the mountains of Ararat.

And the waters decreased continually until the tenth month: in the tenth month, on the first day of the month, were the tops of the mountains seen.... And in the second month [of the 601st year of Noah's life], on the seven and twentieth day of the month, was the earth dried. (Genesis 7:24, 8:1–5, 14)

Where did all the water go? According to 1 Enoch 89:7–8, much of it sank into the depths of the earth: "The fountains of the earth were normalized, and other pits were opened. Then the water began to descend into them until the ground became visible."[473] Ancient myths refer to gigantic whirlpools—large enough to swallow

473. In *The Old Testament Pseudepigrapha*, Vol. 1. 1983, p. 64.

sailing vessels. Although there are conflicting opinions as to their reality, some were likely actual places where water drained into great subterranean caverns left in the aftermath of continental shifting. In 2002, Motohiko Murakami et al. published an article saying that even now "earth's lower mantle may store about five times more H_2O than the oceans."[474]

A small-scale modern example of a powerful whirlpool happened when Lake Peigneur in Louisiana suddenly drained on November 20, 1980. A drilling rig trying to find oil beneath the lake accidentally penetrated into a salt mine. The borehole was quickly enlarged by rushing water, so much so that barges on the lake were literally sucked down into the hole. Amazing video clips of the event may be seen on the Internet.[475] Although that example was short-lived, and the result of human engineering mistakes, it shows that powerful whirlpools and the rapid draining of vast quantities of water are possible.

The story of Noah's sending forth the raven and the dove has interesting implications. After releasing the raven, which did not return to the ark,

> He sent forth a dove from him, to see if the waters were abated from off the face of the ground.... And the dove came in to him in the evening; and, lo, in her mouth was an olive leaf pluckt off: so Noah knew that the waters were abated. (Genesis 8:6, 11)

Thus, it seems that even before the ark landed, an olive leaf had sprouted. Had an olive tree survived the Flood, or was the leaf from a new seedling? It is noteworthy that the dove with the olive branch is a symbol of peace to this day.

---

474. Murakami et al. "Water in Earth's Lower Mantle." *Science*, 2002, p. 1885.
475. Search on Lake Peigneur whirlpool video.

After the Flood

It appears that Noah and those with him were on the ark for one year and seventeen days. Five months was spent floating on the water and seven after landing on Ararat. This is based on:

- Noah entered the ark seven days before the Flood began (Genesis 7:1–10)
- On the 17th day of the 2nd month of Noah's 600th year the Flood began (Genesis 7:11)
- On the 17th day of the 7th month of Noah's 600th year the ark rested on Ararat (Genesis 8:4)
- On the 27th day of the 2nd month of Noah's 601st year they went forth from the ark (Genesis 8:14, 18)

Why did they remain in the ark for seven months after it "rested… upon the mountains of Ararat"? Winter may have been approaching as the ark landed, and in whatever season, at first landing, the only area they could have settled would have been higher on the mountain. It stands to reason that they would have needed to stay within the shelter of the ark. As the floodwaters subsided, the habitable land would have been muddy and unstable.

Furthermore, according to 1 Enoch 89:8, "that boat settled upon the earth, the darkness vanished, and it became light."[476] It suggests that Earth was enveloped in darkness during at least a portion of the Flood year. If true, the cold would indeed have been a major consideration, and seven months may have been a necessity. In addition, earthquakes, tsunamis, and volcanic activity were probably still frequently occurring as the crust settled into its new position.

During the subsequent years, the floodwaters decreased, and as the population increased, life began to spread abroad. Water

---

476. In *Old Testament Pseudepigrapha*, Vol. 1. 1983, p. 64.

was found in abundance. Dale F. Murphie described: "Of the pre-dynastic Nile, 'geological studies by Arkell, and others, of the high benches bordering the river show that it was then a moving lake like the Amazon, filling the valley.' It is interesting to note that the first eye-witness accounts of the Hathor migration... depict the Nile Valley as brim full of water."[477] A related description is found in the Book of Abraham (1:23–24):

> The land of Egypt being first discovered by a woman, who was the daughter of Ham, and the daughter of Egyptus...
> When this woman discovered the land it was under water, who afterward settled her sons in it.

Receding Floodwaters

Huge ancient lakes are well-attested in many parts of the world. Several are known to have been in the now arid western United States. Could they have been due to water from the Flood which was trapped for a time in valleys? Consider T. William Field's description of Lake Bonneville: "At its highest level... [it] had an area of 19,000 square miles compared to the 1,500 square mile area of Great Salt Lake today. Also, the ancient Bonneville shoreline indicates that the lake once had a depth of 1,000 ft." This he compared to the present level of the Great Salt Lake which is shallow—only about 45 ft. at its deepest.

> The catastrophe that occurred... was a sudden breaching of the Bonneville shoreline at Red Rock canyon, at the northeast end of the lake. During this event a 330 ft deep canyon was incised, which has a width up to 1.8 miles. The water pouring through the breach spilled out on the Snake River Plain, and savagely attacked the deep lava formations that form that plain. The erosional effect on

---

477. Murphie. "Critique of David Rohl's *A Test of Time*." *C&C Review*. SIS, 1997:1, p. 32.

the lava was incredible, with new spillways and channels 1,000 ft. wide and 330 ft. deep having been cut into the surface for up to 18 miles.... It is estimated that in a 6 week period the depth of Lake Bonneville was reduced by over 350 ft.... Mankind would be amazed if an event such as this were to occur today. It would be as if one of the Great Lakes suddenly drained.[478]

Vitaliano mentioned a prevailing theory:

There was a time not too long ago (geologically speaking) when the world's climate was generally wetter than now. When glaciers covered northern North America and Eurasia, precipitation was heavier in the areas outside as well as within the regions of snowfall; rivers were larger, and many huge lakes existed beyond the ice front. Great Salt Lake in Utah is the remnant of Lake Bonneville, an ancient body of fresh water which once filled part of the Great Basin; several lakes in the Nevada desert, including Pyramid Lake and Walker Lake and recently dried-up Winnemucca Lake, are remnants of ancient Lake Lahontan.[479]

What caused the wetter conditions? The Flood is certainly a prime candidate for those who will seriously consider it.

In the 1920s, another great lake became a source of controversy. Geologist J. Harlen Bretz stirred up a heated debate. He presented a paper on the Channeled Scablands at a meeting of the Geological Society of America in which:

He took special care not to call upon cataclysmic origins.... He did note, however, that the indicated channel erosion

---

478. Field. "Evidence of an Inversion Event?" *Aeon*, Vol. II, no. 1, 1989, pp. 18–19.

479. Vitaliano. *Legends of the Earth.* 1973, p. 145.

required prodigious quantities of water.... The idea of a
truly catastrophic flood appeared in Bretz's second scabland paper.[480]

In the words of Michael Parfit, the conflict that ensued "was
an argument that represented both the best and the worst of
the way science works, and it helped to change the discipline
of geology."[481] Bretz described distinct landscape patterns in the
Pacific Northwest. Features that were a result of rushing water—
gigantic versions of those caused by rivers. Parfit described Bretz's
story and the reactions of other geologists:

> It's ironic that the very qualities that turned Bretz away
> from his strict religious background helped him kick
> some pins out from under the geological theory that had
> undermined the biblical view of creation. This theory of
> Earth's development was Uniformitarianism.... [it] had
> discredited the theory known as Catastrophism, which
> explained Earth's shape through a series of upheavals far
> more violent than any seen today—events like Noah's
> flood.... ... He was invited to present his theory to a group
> of geologists in Washington D.C., and was clobbered by
> objections.[482]

Bretz continued to be discredited until 1940. At a meeting
of the American Association for the Advancement of Science
devoted to geology of the region "many papers were presented...
which strongly supported a non-catastrophic origin.... Finally,

---

480. Baker. "Pardee and the Spokane Flood Controversy." *GSA Today*, V. 5, no. 9, Sept. 1995, p. 2. http://gsahist.org/gsat2/pardee.htm, (last accessed 9/4/12)

481. Parfit. "The Floods That Carved the West." *Smithsonian*. April 1995, p. 50.

482. Ibid., pp. 51–52.

[Thomas] Pardee, the eighth speaker of the session... "[483] caused a sensation:

> [He] had written a paper describing a large lake that the evidence suggested had filled several valleys in western Montana during the Ice Age. It was called Glacial Lake Missoula.... Pardee estimated that the lake had been about the volume of Lake Erie and Lake Ontario combined.... Lake Missoula began a few miles east—just upstream—of the channeled scablands.
>
> ...The ripple marks Pardee had seen and described were up to 50 feet high and had a wavelength of between 200 and 500 feet. They were enormous. The marks could have been made only by a vast pouring of waters over the slope.... Here was the source of Bretz's flood.
>
> "When he [Pardee] stopped speaking," wrote scientist Howard Meyerhoff, "there were several moments of silence as the significance of his observations sank in...."
>
> So Uniformitarianism had been challenged by, of all things, a flood.[484]

Also speaking of the draining of Lake Missoula, Field mentioned some details of the fantastic proportions involved:

> Suddenly, the ice dam at Sandpoint ruptured releasing a flood estimated at 388 million cubic feet per second, which is roughly 65 times the flow of the Amazon, or about 10 times the volume of all the rivers in the world.
>
> The head of water at the ice breach was about 1950 ft. high, and water depth is estimated to have still exceeded 800 ft. at the Idaho-Washington state line.... The water poured across the loess plateau of southeastern Washington

483. Pitman. "The Great Scabland Debate." http://www.detectingdesign. com/harlenbretz.html (last accessed 9/4/12), pp. 9–10.

484. Parfit. "The Floods That Carved the West." *Smithsonian.* April 1995, pp. 54–55.

devastating about 15,000 square miles, forming an amazing network of channeled scabland. Many short-lived falls and cascades were formed, one cascade being 9 miles in width.[485]

Numerous other places in the world, now arid, once had abundant water. David Collingridge wrote about the region of modern southwestern Iraq: "Although a desert region today, in postdiluvian[486] times it had an abundance of wetlands and fertile soil capable of producing vast amounts of grain. These ideal conditions played a major role in this region becoming the location for one of the earliest high civilizations."[487]

How did the enormous amounts of water necessary to fill huge lakes and areas that are now vast deserts get there—especially those high in the mountains? Was it by slow, steady climate change, or an abrupt catastrophe like the Flood?

Did Men Really Live Longer Before the Flood?

According to the Bible, men lived substantially longer before the Flood—some having lived over 900 years.[488] After the Flood, lifespans abruptly dropped to 400, then 200, then typically less than 100 years.[489] Why? One likely reason was suggested by Cook: namely that radioactive carbon-14 was less concentrated in the biosphere prior to the Flood. Since radioactive emanations can damage living cells, and since C14 levels still appear

485. Field. "Evidence of an Inversion Event?" *Aeon*, Vol. II, no. 1, 1989, p. 19.
486. Postdiluvian: After the Flood.
487. Collingridge. *Truth and Science.* 2008, p. 12.
488. Adam lived 930 y (Gen. 5:5), Seth 912 y (Gen 5:8), and Mahalaleel 895 y (Gen. 5:17).
489. Arphaxad 438 y (Gen. 11:12–13), Eber 464 y (Jsr 30:15), Peleg 239 y (Jsr 10:1–2), Abraham 175 y (Jsr 26:29), Jacob 147 y (Gen. 47:28), Joseph 110 y (Gen 50:22), and so on.

to be increasing, C14 may have been a significant factor in decreased longevity.

In studying chronology, I found a strange account saying the pre-flood Sumerian kings reigned for fantastic periods, with the longest reign listed as "43,000 years."[490] Not understanding, I set it aside awaiting more information. Years later, it was provided by Hildegard Wienke-Lotz who recognized what seems to be the solution to the mystery:

> Sumarian kings… ruled efficiently for 36,000 years—at least, that is what the historian Berossus had to report of Sumerian kings who lived before the flood…. The main reason for the confusion, or misunderstanding lies with the interpretation of the word mu…. The key to the numerical system of the Sumerians is the word for 1 = 60. Sixty is their most perfect number, the base of their number system. Values less than sixty are expressed as fractions, thus 1/60, 3/60 etc just as numbers less than one are currently expressed as fractions. The number 60 plays a key role in the Sumerian system: in Sumerian ten was expressed as 1/6; twenty was written as 1/3; and thirty as 1/2, and so forth. Sixty was expressed by the cuneiform sign <…. The goal of this paper is to describe the length of reigns of the Sumarian kings in our language and terms. It is not reasonable to translate *mu* as "year" and generate a statement from the King List claiming that King Alulimak reigned for 28,800 years.[491]

She divided 28,800 mu by 60 to get 480 years. That reign-length (480 years) is within reason for preflood patriarchs who,

---

490. Woolley. *The Sumerians*. 1965, p. 21.

491. Wiencke-Lotz. "Length of Reigns of Sumerian Kings." *C&C Review*. SIS, 1992, pp. 20–21.

according to Genesis 5:25-26, lived as long as 969 years.[492] An Internet search brought up articles substantiating her assertion that the Sumerians' number system used a base of 60. One by Michael Lombardi titled, "Why is a minute divided into 60 seconds?" attributes the use of 60 in our time-measuring system to the Sumerians and Babylonians.[493]

In C. Leonard Woolley's book, *The Sumerians*, he showed a king-list with a section titled "The Kings before the Flood."[494] His first three are listed below along with a column added for conversions from the Sumerians' base 60:

Sumarian King's Name	Reign-Lengths according to Woolley's List	Reign-Lengths Converted from a Base of 60
A-lu-lim	"8 sars = 28,000 years"	÷ 60 = 480 years
A-la(l)-ga	"10 sars = 36,000 years"	÷ 60 = 600 years
En-me-en-lu-an-na	"12 sars = 43,200 years"	÷ 60 = 720 years

Woolley also listed "Kings after the Flood":

Ga-ur	"1,200 years"	÷ 60 = 20 years
Gul-la-Nidaba-an-na	"960 years"	÷ 60 = 16 years

---

492. Wiencke-Lotz went one step further and divided the result by thirty supposing that there was not significant difference in longevity before and after the Flood.

493. Lombardi. "Why Is a Minute Divided into 60 Seconds?" *Scientific American.* March 5, 2007. http://www.scientificamerican.com/article.cfm?id=experts-time-division-days-hours-minutes. (last accessed 9/4/12)

494. Woolley. *The Sumerians.* 1965, p. 21.

Thus, it appears that the mystery of the fantastic reign-lengths listed for the Sumerian Kings before the Flood was solved by the realization that the Sumerians used a number system with a base of 60.

The book of Jubilees may shed some light on the subject of the decrease in longevity after the Flood (note: a "jubilee" in this context was forty-nine years):

> And after the Flood they began to be less than nineteen jubilees and to grow old quickly and to shorten the days of their lives due to much suffering and through the evil of their ways...
>
> And all of the generations which will arise henceforth and until the day of the great judgment will grow old quickly before they complete two jubilees, and their knowledge will forsake them because of their old age. And all their knowledge will be removed. And in those days if a man will live a jubilee and a half, they will say about him, "He prolonged his life."[495]

Cook commented that another factor in the decrease in longevity after the Flood was likely due to viruses and bacteria. He noted that for many centuries before Louis Pasteur developed the pasteurization process, the average lifespan was significantly less than it is now.[496]

Drought after the Flood?

The post-flood period included some very difficult times. Here are a few curious references:

---

495. In *Old Testament Pseudepigrapha*, Vol. 2. 1985, p. 100.
496. Cook. (Personal communication.)

- "Many ancient sources recall that after the waters of the Flood had subsided there came a great 'Windflood' which converted large areas of the world to sandy deserts."[497]
- In every case, the land is turned into a desert.[498]
- A huge area of Nebraska is covered by a thick deposit of sand, formed like giant ripples. It is usually explained by wind deposits laid down during the late Pleistocene. One or two ... however, think they were laid down by a wall of water sweeping in from the north after the impact of an asteroid. Similar giant ripples are visible in a river valley in the Altai mountains of southern Siberia and these appear to have been formed... when a late ice age ice dam broke, causing catastrophic flooding down-stream.[499]

The Division in the Days of Peleg

Many have wondered if Genesis 10:25 refers to continental movement: "And to Eber were born two sons: the name of one was Peleg; for in his days was the earth divided." According to Bible chronology using the KJV, Peleg (a 3rd great grandson of Noah) was born 100 years after the Flood and lived 239 years. Although the scriptures are unclear as to what is meant by this "division," the eighth chapter of Jubilees suggests that the division was not referring to continental movement. It is described as a division of the land among the people as they multiplied after the Flood: "And he called him Peleg because in the days when he was born the sons of Noah began dividing up the earth... in an evil (manner) among themselves."[500] However, Jasher adds a phrase: "for in his days the sons of men were divided, and in the latter

---

497. Nibley. *The Ancient State.* 1991, pp. 33–34.

498. Ibid., note 2, p. 70.

499. Monitor. "Wind or Water and Impact?" *C&C Workshop.* SIS, 1994:2, p. 28.

500. Jubilees. In *Old Testament Pseudepigrapha*, Vol. 2. 1985, p. 71.

days [of his life?], the earth was divided" (Jasher 7:19). Did the phrase "the earth was divided" simply reiterate what was already said, or did it mean something different?

Ice Age

The ice age history of North America, according to Professor Reginald Daly of Harvard, "'holds ten major mysteries for every one that has already been solved' and that 'the very cause of excessive ice-making on the lands remains a baffling mystery.'"[501] Although Daly's words were published in 1934, many such unresolved mysteries are still troublesome to popular theory and may find resolution in the flood model.

If the Flood really covered the earth and made most of it uninhabitable for more than a year, it stands to reason that floodwaters in polar-regions would have frozen. There would have been severe global cooling, caused by massive amounts of debris thrown into the atmosphere by volcanic activity and impacts blocking the sunlight. Did the events associated with the Flood cause what is commonly called "the ice age"? Likely they did.

Perhaps some of the evidence for multiple "ice ages" would be more accurately described as ice surges. Modern examples of ice surges have been seen although on a much smaller scale. A news article in 1994 reported that the Bering Glacier in Alaska had surged, and during one period had moved at the rate of 300 feet in a day. Another one had moved at least six miles in a nine-month period, after having retreated during the previous twenty-five years.[502]

Another report came from William Hoesch:

---

501. Velikovsky, Immanuel. *Stargazers and Gravediggers*, 1984, p. 167.
502. Associated Press. "Huge Alaska Glacier Halts Seaward Surge." *Deseret News.* Dec. 7, 1994.

A curious thing happens from time to time in glacier-filled valleys around the world. A minority of glaciers that usually flow at rates measured in centimeters per day are sometimes known to surge... The significance to geology is that the erosion done in a single, day-long gallop may be far more extensive than what the normal rate of erosion can accomplish in a year.

Glacial misbehavior like this is sometimes hazardous to normal human activities. For example, when central Asia's largest valley glacier (the Fechenko Glacier) recently surged, the inhabitants of several villages watched helplessly as the ice mass plowed over their homes.[503]

In a paper describing a major advance of another glacier in Alaska, Robert Sharp mentioned that "in its latest advance Malaspina Glacier overrode a mature spruce forest... In this forest trees as much as 5 feet in diameter and about 250 years old must have been growing."[504]

The huge ice caps that existed before the continental breakup would likely have experienced similar surges, but vastly larger than those of the glaciers mentioned above. Thus, ice surges may better explain many of the geological features usually attributed to multiple ice ages. Note: most of the Northern ice cap now floats on the Arctic Ocean. Therefore, since continental movement much of the land mass on which Arctic ice once accumulated is gone. See figure 7.1.

503. Hoesch. "Galloping Glaciers." *Acts & Facts*. December, 2007, p. 14.
504. Sharp. "Latest Advance of Malaspina Glacier." *The Geographical Review*. Vol. XLVIII, no. 1, 1958, p. 26.

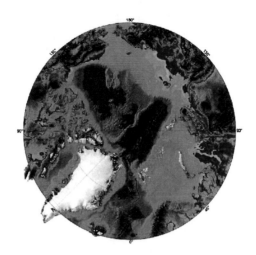

Figure 7.1. An image of Earth from above the North Pole (not showing the floating ice cap). It shows the submerged Arctic Basin which appears to be where Greenland and parts of northern Canada were located before continental movement.[505]

Conclusion

Does it make sense to disregard the many depictions of the Flood from ancient sources and instead invent a picture based on interpretations drawn from theories specifically designed to exclude the Flood? If the descriptions of the Flood in the scriptures and related sources are reasonable approximations of what actually happened, popular geological theory is in need of a major overhaul. Of course mainstream geologists reject such a suggestion. However, it seems likely that at least some, and perhaps all of the mechanisms described in this chapter contributed to

---

505. Image courtesy of NOAA. Image of the IBCAO v.2 grid of the Arctic. Amante, C. and B. W. Eakins, ETOP01 1 Arc-Minute Global Relief Model: Procedures, Data Sources and Analysis. NOAA Technical Memorandum NESDIS NGDC-24, March 2009. p, 11.

the deluge, and that it did happen. If true, any earth-scientist who fails to recognize the Flood/continental-shift event, is missing extremely important clues—and overlooking the single greatest geological event since Creation.

When the Flood is seriously considered, views of the topography of the earth take on a new perspective. Places like the Scablands of the Pacific Northwest, the Badlands of South Dakota, and Bryce Canyon in Utah seem consistent with areas having once been covered by water which suddenly drained.

Geology: Rock-Solid, or Theory?

One of the challenges in reading Earth's history, as it is recorded in the rocks, is that the record is incomplete. It's a little like trying to make sense of a novel after someone has ripped out every third page, or even occasionally large sections.

—Bart J. Kowallis (2006)

How solid is modern geology? Certain aspects of geology are amazingly precise and technologically advanced. They typically involve sophisticated equipment and current measurements. Other parts are heavily reliant on theory. They are assumed from current observations. Many of Earth's features do appear to have been formed slowly and steadily, but not all. Nibley wrote:

> If we could check up on the geologist... when he tells us with perfect confidence what has happened... in the

remotest ages, what would the result be? Actually, in the one field in which the wisdom of geology can be controlled, the finding of oil, it is calculated that the experts are proven right only about 10 percent of the time. Now if a man is wrong 90 percent of the time when he is glorying in the complete mastery of his specialty, how far should we trust the same man when he takes to pontificating on the mysteries?[506]

Referring to the preceding quote, a geologist recently observed: "This example is great—it illustrates that finding oil is difficult and has a big element of art."[507] I was expecting him to be critical of the quote. After all, it dates back to 1958, and surely the process of finding oil has improved since then. Apparently it has improved. In August of 2011, a petroleum geologist told me the odds of finding oil at a scientifically predicted site have now improved to about 50 percent.

What Lies Deep Below Earth's Surface?

The colorful pictorial representations of the earth down to its center may be seen in any number of science programs. They seem so clear and convincing, but what is really known of the bowels of the earth? When layers are not exposed at the surface, the picture is inferred. Estimates of the depth of the crust range from ten to twenty-five miles. The deepest boreholes have only been to about eight miles, and the center of the earth is almost four thousand miles beneath the surface.

When an earthquake or an explosion occurs, not only can surface shockwaves be measured at numerous sites, but echoes or reflections off boundaries between dissimilar layers beneath

506. Nibley. *Old Testament and Related Studies.* 1986, p. 21.
507. Personal communication from a retired geologist who did not want to be named in this book.

the ground are also recorded. When a shockwave encounters an abrupt change in composition (for example, at the interface of a solid and a liquid), it rebounds. A simple demonstration can be seen when an object is dropped into a calm pool: a wave moves radially, and when it encounters the bank of the pool it is reflected. Also, if a shockwave is initiated in the ground, it can reflect off of the bank of the pool. Seismologists try to interpret shockwave behavior in solids to estimate conditions deep below the surface.

Some of the representations of the inner core of the earth suggest it is liquid; others—solid. If gravity is truly a function of mass (which it seems to be), wouldn't a weightless condition exist at the center of the globe? That idea was presented in *The Planet Earth* by World Book Inc.: "Gravity beneath the Earth's surface... decreases steadily to zero at the center of the core, where the gravitational force is equal in all directions."[508] Therefore, if gravity is zero at the center of the earth, which seems the logical conclusion, doesn't that also mean zero pressure from the overburden? Interestingly, in the same book (p. 48), a drawing depicts a cross-section of the earth to its core suggesting that the pressure and density increase with depth. At Earth's center, it shows the pressure to be 3.750 million times that of the atmosphere at the surface. What is it really like?

Another example indicating the limited knowledge of Earth's inner regions came from McKnight's section in his geography text titled *The Unknown Interior*: "Our knowledge of the interior of the Earth is scanty and is based entirely on indirect evidence. No human activity has explored more than a minute fraction of the vastness beneath the surface. No person has penetrated as

---

508. *The Planet Earth*. 1984, p. 21.

much as one-thousandth of the radial distance from the surface to the center of the Earth."[509]

Deep drilling projects have revealed some unexpected details. A. C. Grant wrote about the deepest: "On the continents, results from deep drilling are astonishing; the 12 km hole drilled on the Kola Peninsula failed to detect the Conrad Discontinuity,[510] encountered much higher temperatures than expected, and found circulating fluids and gasses—including hydrocarbons, throughout."[511]

Nearly as deep, the KTB deep borehole in Germany revealed some more surprising results. Richard A. Kerr described its goal—of gaining "access to a region of the Earth's crust whose nature has so far only been guessed at." He added:

Geologists had previously inferred a picture of the crust under the drill site by... making electrical and seismic measurements that probe deep beneath the surface. Since drilling began in September 1987, however, they have had to redraw large parts of that picture. The subsurface faults and folds look quite different than predicted.... ... The expectation of moderate temperatures in the deep rock... would have allowed drilling to a depth of 12 kilometers before heat overwhelmed the drilling equipment. But the first surprise from KTB—temperatures far higher than predicted—forced a retrenching to a target depth of 10 kilometers. The other attraction seemed to be an opportunity to drill through the buried boundary between

---

509. McKnight. *Physical Geography.* 1990, p. 355. Since then, two deep boreholes have extracted material from about two one-thousandths of Earth's radius.

510. The Conrad Discontinuity is some sort of region about seven to twelve kilometers beneath earth's surface. It is a nonuniform region which reflects seismic waves.

511. Grant. "Intracratonic Tectonism." In *New Concepts in Global Tectonics,* 1992, p. 72.

two tectonic plates... But the suture, first predicted to slant under the KTB site at a depth of about 3 kilometers on the basis of surface geology, failed to show up at 3 kilometers, or at 5 kilometers as later hoped. And at 7.5 kilometers, researchers still "haven't seen any sign of a dramatic change" which would mark the boundary between the two plates.[512]

Kerr noted other unexpected findings associated with the borehole:

Other predicted boundaries in the rock have proven equally elusive. One object of the hole was to provide a kind of ground truth for seismic reflection profiling, the radar-like technique that creates images of subsurface structures from the manmade seismic waves that they reflect. "You see all kinds of reflectors around the world," says KTB operations leader Peter Kehrer, "but we don't know what they are." Distinguishing among faults, changes in rock type, fluid-filled cracks, or other possibilities has been largely guesswork—and the KTB hole suggests an extra measure of caution. Seismic profiles predicted the position of some—but not all of the structures encountered so far, and even those that showed up where expected were often different from what researchers had assumed they were.[513]

The discovery of large quantities of fluids deep underground was a big surprise to most scientists:

At 4 kilometers... more than half a million liters of gas-rich, calcium-sodium-chloride brine twice as concentrated as seawater poured into the well. Abundant fluids gushed

512. Kerr. "Looking Deeply into Earth's Crust." *Science,* July 16, 1993, p. 295.
513. Ibid., p. 21.

from depths as great as 6 kilometers... ... "There are large amounts of highly saline brine in the crust that migrate, carrying metals around and depositing them as minerals."

A minority of geophysicists, including Lawrence Cathles of Cornell University, had suspected that at least some permeability would remain at great depths, enough to allow fluids to circulate. But the large volumes flowing into the KTB hole are welcome confirmation. "It's beginning to look like the lower parts of the crust can be fairly permeable," Cathles says.[514]

How are Mountains Formed?

New mountains are not seen suddenly coming into existence today, with few exceptions—like when a mountain quickly rises, due to volcanic activity. Therefore, "geologists assume that the formation of mountains... must have occurred so slowly that observers in ancient times would have been unaware that they were watching new mountains... develop."[515]

The idea of a mountain slowly pushing up seems contrary to the nature of solids. Similarly, slow continental drift, powered by mantle convection currents, seems to be woefully inadequate to explain things like overthrusting and mountain-building. If two long railroad trains collide—one moving at a rate of one inch per day and the other stationary—how much damage will be done? If the moving train is going 70 mph, buckling and crumpling would be seen, perhaps involving all of the cars of both trains.

A continental movement theory more consistent with rock mechanics involves mountain formation as a result of sudden continental shifting. The terrific buckling and crashing that would have happened if rapidly sliding continents collided could

---

514. Ibid., p. 21.
515. Rose. "Astronomy over Other Disciplines." *Kronos,* Vol. II, no. 4, 1977, p. 61.

explain many of the questions unanswered by the more popular theories. "Campbell is responsible for the elaboration of a theory of mountain building based on the premise that the original active factor in the process is crust displacement."[516] Patten and Windsor wrote:

> Astronomers, geographers, geologists and others search for theory that addresses the causation of mountains. Mountain ranges, mountain systems, mountain cycles, volcanoes, and basaltic outflows all cast shadows over a culture unable to explain their existence.... Most of the ideas suggested for crustal deformation over the last 150 years offer explanation for only one type of deformation. They cannot address the variety on our planet."[517]

Mel Acheson mentioned an unusual perspective regarding mountain building:

> Geologists say mountains were formed gradually over millions of years. Native peoples say their ancestors saw mountains form in their lifetimes. It's a choice between speculation and hearsay.
> The uniformist/gradualist revolution erased the concept of suddenness from the geological vocabulary. Because a person tends not to see what he doesn't have a concept for, geologists for two centuries couldn't see evidence for suddenness as suddenness.

516. Hapgood. *Earth's Shifting Crust.* 1958, p. 90.
517. Patten and Windsor. "Catastrophic Theory of Mountain Uplifts." *Catastrophism and Ancient History.* Vol. XIII, Jan. 1991, p. 17.

Immanuel Velikovsky's books, *Worlds in Collision* and
Earth in Upheaval, hit geologists like a 2x4 between the
eyes of a somnolent mule. Velikovsky got kicked into
the mud of crackpotism for it, but the hit got geologists'
attention. After the mule had settled down, the concept
of suddenness reappeared: Alvarez's asteroid, Clube and
Napier's comet... mass extinctions, lava floods, ... [and]
climate disruptions.[518]

Stratification

One of the principles commonly used by geologists in trying to
understand various features on Earth was described by Kowallis
as the Principle of Original Horizontality. "Sedimentary rocks
form on Earth's surface, and they often hold clues—pieces of
stone, bones, and other evidence that help us understand past
events. We can use time symmetry to observe how and where
sedimentary rocks are forming today and apply this knowledge
to our study of sedimentary rocks that formed in the past."[519]
(Note: his use of "time symmetry" is another way of saying
"uniformity.") Many levels of Earth's strata are horizontal, but
some formations are tilted, some are vertical (see Figure 8.1), and
some have folded. How can layers have gotten to such distorted
positions without catastrophic forces?

---

518. Acheson. "Suddenly." *C&C Workshop.* SIS, 2010:1, p. 33.
519. Kowallis. "Geologic Time." In *Physical Science Foundations,* 2nd Ed.
2006, p. 316.

Figure 8.1 Devil's Slide in Weber Canyon near Morgan, Utah, showing nearly vertical strata. Photo by Darlene Barker.

Although the same rates at which geological processes are happening now have been operative much of the time in the past, it is now clear that they were not the prevailing processes all throughout Earth's history. Abery reported: "Lake sediments are often used as evidence for past events on the assumption that they have remained undisturbed but every spring in Lake Michigan millions of tons of silt are stirred up by winds and currents and carried along the shore for several weeks."[520]

_____

520. Abery. "Factors to Take into Account." *C&C Review.* SIS, 2001:2, p. 46.

Erosion

Popular assumptions about erosion need scrutiny. How did nearly vertical erosion occur at places like the Grand Canyon and Zion National Park? As recently as November of 2010, the recorded message played during the shuttle ride through Zion Canyon in southwestern Utah described how the stream had carved the canyon over millions of years as the land thrust upward. If land thrusts upward, doesn't the stream change direction and follow the course of least resistance? No mention was made that the description was theory, but it was stated as though fact. How does a small stream cut vertically through thousands of feet of rock? How did layer upon layer of limestone, sandstone, and shale form—many of them hundreds of feet thick—separated by abrupt and distinct changes? What caused the sudden stop of one sediment, then restart with a different composition? These realities seem contrary to the uniformitarian point of view.

A small-scale example of unusual erosion was described in an article by Michael Lamb and Mark Fonstad. They mentioned the common view that deep canyons are typically believed to have formed over vast periods of time and then described a small canyon that was carved rapidly by a Texas flood in 2002. They indicated that sophisticated measurements before and after the event showed that about seven meters of limestone had been eroded in only three days.[521]

What if many of the deep canyons were formed during events involving receding floodwaters—while at least some of the layers were saturated or before they had fully solidified? Much of it could have happened very quickly. Bennison Gray mentioned a related issue:

---

521. Lamb and Fonstad. "Rapid Formation of a Canyon." *Nature Geoscience* 3, 2010, p. 477.

GEOLOGY: ROCK-SOLID, OR THEORY?

Some big jobs can be accomplished little-by-little over long periods of time, but many cannot. Erosion (by water, wind, or ice) is an excellent negative explanation: everything can be worn away given enough time. But it is of little positive value. Geologists cannot convincingly explain with little-by-little how a huge rock formation is lifted in a single piece from its place of origin and left resting much higher on top of newer strata.[522]

According to Donald U. Wise, "geologists have long recognized many deposits that represent rapid burial by pulsating events which may last a few minutes to a few years. These rapid events are followed by thousands of years in which there is little or no deposition."[523]

Although the description of Principle of Original Horizontality deals specifically with layers of sediments, there are examples of other layers forming prior to, or in the process of, solidifying. One example, according to Francis Birch, is: "In the process of crystallization, the radioactive elements were segregated toward the top of the mantle."[524]

Another geologic assumption, the doctrine of superposition, supposes that the reason small life-forms are found in lower layers, is evolution. There are other explanations. No doubt each of the following processes played a role in the layering of parts of Earth's strata:

1. Roche's limit
2. layered solidification (based on chemical properties and melting temperatures)

522. Gray. "Alternatives in Science." *Kronos*, Vol. VII, no. 4, 1982, p. 13.
523. Wise. "Creationism's Geologic Time Scale?" *American Scientist*, Vol. 86, March–April 1998. p. 170.
524. Birch. "Heat from Radioactivity." In *Nuclear Geology*. Ed. Henry Faul. 1954, p. 168.

3. liquefaction (an effect of shock waves causing soil to temporarily behave like a liquid)
4. elutriation (the tendency of small particles in solution to be removed, leaving the heavier ones behind)
5. levitation (raising of particles in a froth to the surface, separating selected minerals)[525]
6. acoustic fluidization[526]

Creation Scientists John Morris and Steven Austin have discovered some stunning details by studying the 1980 explosion of Mount St. Helens. They learned from very precise data and measurements that substantial layers were formed extremely rapidly.

> Thin stratification (technically called lamination) was thought to form very slowly, as sediment was delivered by rather sluggish agents.... At Mount St. Helens, we saw a living laboratory for the rapid formation of strata. An abundance of coarse and fine particles was produced by the explosive eruptions. Pyroclastic flows, mudflows, and river floods distributed the particles widely and accumulated strata [rapidly]...We learned that the flow process creates a sweeping action as particles roll or bounce along at Earth's surface, quickly separating the particles by size, shape and density and forming even micro-thin laminae. Particles with similar size, shape, or density are deposited together at a specific horizon within the bed.... Some thicker layers of coarser sediment appear to possess internally a rather homogeneous texture. With closer study, however, these beds display a progressive particle size variation upward

525. Levitation. *McGraw-Hill Dictionary of Scientific and Technical Terms.* 1974.
526. Melosh. "Acoustic Fluidization?" *American Scientist*, March–April, 1983, pp. 158–161.

within the bed, with larger particles on the bottom grading
into finer particles above...
Moving fluids tend to sort their sediment load out into
layers. Particles which are denser and rounder settle out
first, with lighter ones settling only as the velocity of the
fluid decreases.[527]

The Book of Enoch contains some incredible descriptions of
events associated with Noah's Flood. Nibley quoted from it: "The
order of the entire earth will change, and every fruit and plant
will change its season, awaiting the time of destruction... the
earth itself will be shaken and lose all solidity."[528] It is interesting
to compare the phenomenon of liquefaction occurring during
strong earthquakes with this passage. And, if sudden continental
shifting actually took place at the time of the Flood, much of
the erosion would have been almost instantaneous due to the
explosive effect of crashing continents and shockwaves associated
with massive crustal movement. In Anthony Larson's view:

> Some early scientists, like Cuvier, Agassiz, Sedgwick,
> and Murchison, reasoned that such layering could have
> happened much more quickly, in cataclysmic inundations—
> like that of the Deluge. But other scientists would have
> none of that. Such thought, they reasoned, smacked of
> the stifling and stultifying dogmas of religion, which they
> abhorred. Hence, the theories of uniformitarian scientists
> such as Lyell, Hutton, and Darwin prevailed in a scientific
> community seeking to divorce itself completely from any
> religious ideas.[529]

---

527. Morris and Austin. *Footprints in the Ash.* 2003, pp. 50–51, 61.
528. Nibley. *Enoch the Prophet.* 1986, p. 72.
529. Larson. *And the Earth Shall Reel To and Fro.* 1983, p. 62.

Is there a way for scientists to determine which strata were formed in the typical slow, steady processes seen most days and which were laid down suddenly and catastrophically? When scientists ask bold questions, they often find bold answers. One clue to determining suddenness was described by Abery:

> The Green River formation in Wyoming shows more than a million varves (thin layers) of shale, each supposedly indicating one year's lake sediments. However, fossil catfish are found over a large area in excellent state of preservation, which indicates rapid burial as dead fish normally decay rapidly on a muddy lake bottom.... It is also hard to imagine any lake surviving over a million years, through ice ages and climate changes, yet never varying its rate of sedimentation, nor even becoming eventually silted up.
>
> ... A Mexican geologist pointed to a thick bed of sediment and suggested it might have been laid down during a single tidal wave. With the increasing numbers of examples like these how is it possible for geologists to maintain that the depth of any layer is indicative of even decades of slow deposition, let alone the millions they usually attribute to them? Bernard Newgrosh raises again the question of how it can be glibly assumed that the very thick layers necessary to cover a large dinosaur bone can have taken thousands of years to be deposited.... All thick layers of sedimentary rock should really be viewed as possible indicators of rapid and catastrophic deposition.[530]

Other indications of suddenness come from what are called polystrate fossils. See Figure 8.2 for an example of a tree which was buried rapidly.

---

530. Abery. "Suspicious Sedimentation." *C&C Review*. SIS, 1997:2, p. 44.

Figure 8.2. An example of a fossilized tree obviously buried by rapid deposition of material.[531]

David Salkeld also mentioned the problem:

> If anyone admits that the Cretaceous ended with a catastrophic event, why aren't all the other sudden cut-offs in the fossil record due to sudden events? It is difficult to say this one took a week but all the others took 250,000 years. That is what worries paleontologists, particularly having written their names on to a minimum of 250,000 years between one layer and the next.[532]

Brian Thomas presented logic worthy of consideration:

---

531. "Specimen is from the ... Cumberland Basin, Nova Scotia." Photo courtesy of Michael C. Rygel via Wikimedia Commons. http://en.wikipedia.org/wiki/Polystrate_fossil, (last accessed 9/4/12).

532. Salkeld. "Genesis and the Origin of Species." *C&C Review.* SIS, 2002:1, p. 11.

Do the rocks and fossils testify to millions of years, so that the thousands-of-years history of the Bible must be rejected?

The answer is no, and here is why. First, each sedimentary rock layer containing fossils had to have formed rapidly because that's the only way the fossils would have been preserved. Second, upper layers formed soon after the lower ones were deposited, since there is no sign of erosion in the razor-sharp contacts between them. Therefore, whole sections of the rock column were deposited in rapid succession.[533]

Could this be true? If so, couldn't some of it be a result of Roche's limit-type events and/or the Flood?

Geological Periods

For many years, geology students have memorized the names of the geological "periods," "eras," and "epochs." The names given them seem to have cast an aura of credibility around the assumptions and surmises used to derive the ages associated with them. Monastersky pointed to one of the weaknesses: "When it comes to reconstructing prehistory in the Cambrian, the problem is that scientists see the effect, but they have many causes to choose from—and not a lot of clues about the correct choice to make. 'You are looking at a unique event,' Raff says, 'so you don't have the ability to replicate it.'"[534]

The Geological Column or Geologic Time Scale was introduced as a reference standard for the various geological strata, and their so-called ages. Once radiometric dating gained acceptance, the ages were modified to accommodate the new

---

533. Thomas. "The Stones Cry Out." *Acts & Facts.* Jan. 2011, p. 17.
534. Monastersky. "Mysteries of the Orient." *Discover Magazine,* April 1993.

techniques, and the assumptions underlying the new techniques were adjusted to fit the theory. Although the Geological Column is not without variations, it has become the dominant framework on which geological data is organized.

Strickling observed: "The Standard Geological Column... presents a very precise picture of the geological record and events recorded in the earth's crust. And I hasten to add that *precise* does *not* imply *accurate*. It is a highly subjective representation, constructed piece-meal under uniformitarian assumptions."[535]

Geological Dating

As mentioned earlier, several geological age estimation techniques claim dates millions or billions of years in the past—assuming that "all things continue as they were from the beginning." Since so little is known about the creation process, how can one determine whether such dates are in conflict with the scriptures, or how things really happened? To literal Bible believers, any method trying to determine a date prior to the Fall is highly speculative at best, and contrary to revealed Scripture at worst.

Prior to radioactive dating techniques, geological ages were estimated by measuring the rates matter was carried by rivers and deposited in lake and ocean bottoms. Etienne Roth described:

> Observation of sedimentation rates and rates of erosion together with assessments of the amount of salt brought down by rivers to the oceans led to the age of the Earth being increased by anything from several centuries to millions of years. This method may have been inspired by a reading of Herodotus (≈ 400 B.C.), who by comparing the volumes of alluvial deposits accumulating at the annual sedimentation, estimated that it would have taken 20,000

535. Strickling. "The Signature of Catastrophe." *Aeon*, Vol. 1, no. 2, Feb. 1988, p. 54.

years for the Nile to form its delta. Naturalistic observations of this sort still form the basis of the methods used to establish geological ages, i.e. the succession of events that has led to the present-day formations. Such ages can only be relative, however: even experiments limited to historical times are enough to show that the rates at which geological processes have taken place cannot be taken as constant.[536]

If it did take about twenty thousand years for the Nile Delta to form, what does that say about millions of years of uniformity? What changed twenty thousand years ago? Who can say whether the materials being eroded and deposited have been in the same physical condition during the whole process? Certainly some material started out in a liquid state or a saturated condition prior to solidification. In those cases, they would have been much more susceptible to rapid erosion.

Extinctions

Estimates of fossilized remains of once-living things suggest that life forms today constitute less than one-tenth of the many varieties that once lived on, or have been incorporated into, Earth's strata. However, some creatures and plants thought to have been extinct for millions of years have been found alive and well. McKinney and Tolliver reported:

> Graptolites... are especially useful in biostratigraphy (correlating rocks) because they often occur in deep water shales where other fossils are rare. As floating organisms, they often sank into poorly oxygenated sediments where few other organisms could live. Graptolites were thought to have died 300 million years ago, but a recent sample of the seafloor off New Caledonia revealed that they are

---

536. Roth. "Dating Using Radioactive Phenomena." In *Nuclear Methods of Dating.* 1989, p. 2.

apparently still alive. This find is similar to that of the coelacanth fish in 1938, which was known only from fossils over 100 million years old. And like that find, it provides a rare opportunity to study soft tissues of creatures heretofore known only by the incomplete remains of the fossil record.[537]

"'Living Fossil' Tree Found in Australia." is the headline of a news article December 16, 2000. It mentions another example of living things thought to have been extinct for millions of years.[538] Does the fact that scientists occasionally find life-forms believed to have been extinct have any implications as to the validity of the million-year bias?

Petrified Wood and Fossils

A popular assumption was shown to be invalid. A number of researchers found that "petrified wood" (really wood components replaced by minerals) can be produced rapidly.[539] At least one firm has contemplated producing it as a building material.[540]

Multi-layered petrified forests are another phenomenon commonly interpreted in support of long periods for Earth processes. A striking example is that of Specimen Ridge in Yellowstone National Park. In 1960 Erling Dorf, described the area:

> In many respects these fossil forests are the most remarkable of their kind known in the world.... They

---

537. McKinney and Tolliver, editors. *Current Issues in Geology,* 1994, p. 190.

538. Associated Press. "'Living Fossil' Tree Found in Australia." *Deseret News.* Dec. 16, 2000.

539. Associated Press. "Lab Makes Petrified Wood in Days." *USA Today,* Jan. 1, 2005.

540. www.dinosaurc14ages.com/hughpet.htm. (last accessed 9/10/12)

consist of hundreds of petrified trees of which the great majority are still standing upright...

They include, in one locality, a vertical succession of up to 27 separate petrified forests, one upon the other, in a total sequence of about 1,700 feet of volcanic tuffs and breccias.[541]

The so-called 27 separate petrified forests were estimated to have taken about twenty thousand years to form,[542] and Dorf's description has been the dominant view since that time. See Figure 8.3.

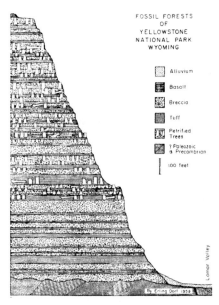

Figure 8.3. The once-popular depiction of Specimen Ridge showing the supposed multiple forests. From Erling Dorf, 1959.[543]

541. Dorf. "Fossil Forests of Yellowstone." *Billings Geological Society.* Sept. 7–10, 1960, p. 253.

542. Ibid., p. 254.

543. Ibid., p. 256. Used with permission of the Montana Geological Society.

An alternate view has been proposed by Morris and Austin. In their study of Mount St. Helens, and particularly nearby Spirit Lake, they noted that soon after the 1980 eruption, a floating log mat was found obscuring the lake. It was estimated to be comprised of over a million logs. From careful study, including underwater exploration, they learned that many of the logs had sunk but were standing upright on the bottom of the lake. The logs were deposited at various depths due to their sinking at different times as the debris from the volcanic cataclysm accumulated. They noted that many of the trees had been uprooted by the volcanic blast and still had a root ball which tended to weigh down one end and deposit them in the vertical position. They commented that "the natural system through which water is drawn into the tree is through the roots, and thus the trees tended to waterlog root end first."[544] (See Figures 8.4-8.6)

Figure 8.4. "Spirit Lake from the crater of Mount St. Helens. Nearly half of the surface of the lake is covered

544. Morris and Austin. *Footprints in the Ash*. 2003, pp. 83, 96–97.

with logs and debris. Note the vegetation stripped from all hills extending 18 miles northeastward."[545]

Figure 8.5. Huge logs floating in nearly vertical positions (mostly submerged) in Spirit Lake. Photo by John Morris.[546]

Morris and Austin reported that once officials at Yellowstone became aware of the data observed at Mount St. Helens, a sign at Specimen Ridge describing multiple fossil forests (based on Dorf's theory) was removed. At the location of another upright petrified tree stump, a sign was placed which was more consistent with the newly found data, "to indicate that the trunk had

545. Courtesy of the USGS. http://libraryphoto.cr.usgs.gov/cgi-bin/show_picture.cgi?ID=ID.%20CVO-A.%20%2066ct, (last accessed 9/4/12.

546. Morris and Austin. *Footprints in the Ash.* 2003, p. 96. Used with permission from the publisher Master Books.

been relocated by moving muds similar to those at Mount St. Helens."[547] This is to the credit of the Yellowstone officials.

Coal Formation

Any scientific approach seriously considering scriptural descriptions of the Flood will benefit from details about the process of coal and oil formation.[548] Popular theories assume long time-frames for accumulation of vegetation, partial decay, then slow burial as the carbon-containing material sinks and compresses.[549] Removal of water, by means of compression and heat, changes vegital matter to various grades of coal, from lignite (brown coal), to bituminous (medium grade), to anthracite (high-grade coal), graphite, and ultimately to diamond. Diamond is the product of extreme compression—sufficient to remove everything but carbon.

If it can be demonstrated that coal could have formed suddenly, although not "proof," it would certainly constitute evidence lending credence to the possibility that much of it formed in conjunction with the Flood. Cook proposed that most of the earth's coal deposits were formed by sudden burial of vegetal matter due to ice-cap surges, mountain building, overthrusting, continental shifting, and the Flood.[550]

Experiments have confirmed that coal can be formed in a short time using clay as a catalyst—even at temperatures commonly found in nature.[551] In one series of experiments, "the scientists heated lignin in the presence of the clays, for periods ranging

---

547. ibid. pp. 96–97, 103.
548. This section is based on Cook's research on coal formation—simplified and updated. See Cook. *Scientific Prehistory*. 1993, pp. 185–197.
549. Francis. *Coal*. 1954, p. 145.
550. Cook. *Scientific Prehistory*. 1993, pp. 185–197.
551. Hayatsu et al. "Artificial Coalification Study." *Organic Geochemistry*, Vol. 6, 1984, pp. 463–464.

from two weeks to a year. Longer heating times produced a higher grade coal.... They also found that lower grade natural coals could be converted to a higher grade by heating them with the clays at 300° F. Clays appear to catalytise the conversion of lignin to coal."[552] Clays, or shales (clay compressed into rock), are commonly found at or near coal seams.

Compression, as an important factor in coal formation from wood, was strikingly illustrated by a discovery more than a century ago:

> Petzoldt (1882) describes very remarkable observations which he made during the construction of a railway bridge... near Freiburg [Germany]. The wooden piles which had been rammed into the ground were compressed by overriding rocks. An examination of these compressed piles showed that in the center... [it] was a black, coal-like substance. In continuous succession from center to surface was blackened, dark-brown, light-brown, and finally yellow-colored wood. The coal-like substance corresponded, in its chemical composition, to anthracite, and the blackened wood resembled brown-coal."[553]

Referring to this observation, Cook commented: "In cylindrical compression the highest pressure is generated [at the center] with progressively lower pressures radially outward. This observation thus demonstrates temperature and pressure, not long time, are the essential factors in coal formation."[554] More evidence of his assertion is found where coal comes into contact with volcanic lava or molten igneous rock. Profound changes in the grade of coal are caused when it is exposed to high temperatures.[555] Another example of coal produced relatively quickly:

---

552. Monitor. "Lignin + Clay = Coal." *New Scientist.* Sept. 1, 1983, p. 623.
553. Stutzer and Noe. *Geology of Coal.* 1940, pp. 105–106.
554. Cook. *Scientific Prehistory.* 1993, p. 188.
555. Stutzer and Noe. *Geology of Coal.* 1940, p. 299.

In the vicinity of Scranton, Pennsylvania.... A mine prop left standing and surrounded by mine refuse was subjected for about 30 years to high pressure from the roof and for a time to high temperature from a mine fire, although the fire did not actually reach the prop. Different parts of the prop suffered varying degrees of alteration. The lower portion was well-preserved wood; about half-way up it was a little charred externally, and above this it was turned into friable, soft charcoal. The upper part and especially the cap wedge, which had suffered from great compression and had been crushed down, was greatly altered and had a conchoidal fracture like anthracite, a jet-black color, [and] a bright glossy luster.... It would appear that although heat aided this change the pressure was necessary to produce the coaly character, as distinguished from charcoal.[556]

Consistent with these findings, depth of burial had been found to be a significant determinant of the grade of coal formed. "Carl Hilt in 1873 observed that a coal seam increases in rank with increasing depth in a coalfield. This phenomenon, known as Hilt's Law, is related to the increase in both pressure and temperature."[557]

Not only does depth of burial affect the grade of coal, it also alters other sediments. Where bituminous (medium-grade coal) is found, the surrounding materials, subject to the same conditions, yielded various grades of rock rather than the unconsolidated matter from which those rocks form.[558]

Since geologists typically assume that the ages of formations also increase with depth, they generally suppose that coals with higher grade are older than those with lower. Although this has the appearance of sound reasoning, the evidence shows that the

---

556. Moore. *Coal.* 1940, p. 176.

557. Ross and Ross. *Geology of Coal.* 1984, p. 187.

558. Stutzer and Noe. *Geology of Coal.* 1940, p. 214.

assumptions are often inappropriate. A spectacular example is "the gradual increase in grade… in the Pittsburgh coal seam from Ohio to Pittsburgh. In this sequence… the strata dip down 20 to 40 feet per mile, the coal on the east side being several thousand feet deeper than on the west and considerably higher in rank. This involves a single general deposition of coal and thus shows clearly the predicted influence of depth of burial (pressure) on grade."[559]

One highly questionable use of assumption in trying to understand coalification was mentioned by Wilfrid Francis: "Bergius, assuming that the 'coal-forming reaction' took place at an average temperature $10°C$ above atmospheric, calculated that the time required to produce bituminous coal would be about 8 million years."[560] Bergius could have estimated the time in weeks or months if he'd chosen temperatures and pressures associated with catastrophic processes and recognized that clay acts as a catalyst for coal formation.

By now, some statements should be easily recognizable as erroneous, such as "a series of many hundreds of coal beds can be explained *only* on the assumption that the coal basins at the time of their formation were regions of subsidence. The organic and inorganic deposits were sinking, during and after their deposition, *slowly* but *steadily* into the depths"[561] (emphasis added). What caused the supposed sinking? What caused Stutzer and Noe to assume it was slow and steady? Why were they presumptuous enough to suppose that those assumptions provide the *only* explanation? Why isn't the supposed prolific plant growth—followed by subsidence in vast forest moors—evident today to any significant degree?

559. Cook. *Scientific Prehistory*. 1993, p. 188.
560. Francis. *Coal*. 1954, p. 448.
561. Stutzer and Noe. *Geology of Coal*. 1940, pp. 164–165.

Contrary to their assertion, other explanations of course have been postulated, and do seem more consistent with the facts.

Amount of Raw Material Needed to Form Coal

Estimates of the amount of peat needed to produce a coal seam one-foot thick range from three to twenty feet.[562] Using the low-end three-to-one estimate of Ashley,[563] it would take sixty feet of peat to produce a coal deposit twenty feet thick. Where did the raw materials come from to produce very thick coal-beds such as a brown-coal bed in the Fortuna strip-mine? It had a thickness of sixty-five meters (about 213 feet).[564] "At Morwell, Victoria, Australia, there are three seams of brown coal which are 266, 227 and 166 feet, respectively, in thickness. They are the thickest so far known in the world."[565]

Large volumes "of peat and associated sediments [form] in equatorial ever-wet climates."[566] "[The] largest tropical peatlands found on Earth [are] in the lowlands of Indonesia and Malaysia."[567] Yet, these deposits are less than 15 meters (~50 feet) deep.[568] These are some of the most promising of all modern peat deposits in terms of their potential for forming commercially

---

562. Moore *Coal.* 1940, p. 159. Cook estimated about sixteen feet—based on comparison of average densities. Cook. *Scientific Prehistory.* 1993, p. 192.

563. Stutzer and Noe. *Geology of Coal.* 1940, p. 177.

564. Ibid., pp. 198, 200.

565. Moore. *Coal.* 1940, p. 228.

566. Cobb and Cecil. *Coal-Forming Environments.* 1993, p. 1.

567. Neuzil et al. "Inorganic Geochemistry in Indonesia Coal." In *Coal-Forming Environments.* 1993, p. 23.

568. Supardi et al. "Peat Resources, Indonesia." In *Coal-Forming Environments.* 1993, pp. 50, 54.

workable coal beds,[569] and they are only a fraction of the thickness required to form coal beds as vast as those mentioned above. If the average of the estimates of raw materials needed is accurate, a peat deposit 1,660 feet thick would have been required to form the 166 foot thick coal bed.

Also noteworthy is the absence of any evidence of coal or even lignite deposits in the strata below modern peat beds. If neither the theorized subsidence nor the gradual coalification is seen in the most promising parts of the world now, why are they assumed to have been in the past? That seems a breach in etiquette for geology's doctrine of uniformity.

According to James Cobb and Blain Cecil: "Although some attempts have been made to model coal formation on the basis of modern peat deposits, most of these deposits have not had the thickness, lateral extent, or purity necessary to produce a coal bed of commercial interest."[570] Another recognition of the inadequacies of the popular theories came from Cecil et al.: "Although the origin of coal has been studied and debated for over a century, models that can be used to predict the occurrence, distribution, and quality of coal continue to be wanting."[571]

The suggestion that coal formation had anything to do with the Flood has been discarded outright by most geologists since the age of Lyell. Stutzer and Noe expressed:

"The theory of formation of coal beds from transported material is very old. In the Middle Ages many scholars looked for evidence of the Great Flood mentioned in the Bible. When the viewpoint of an origin of coal from plant remains became established, it was natural that many

569. Grady et al. "Brown Coal Distributions." In *Coal-Forming Environments*. 1993, p. 64.

570. Cobb and Cecil. *Coal-Forming Environments*. 1993, p. 1.

571. Cecil et al. "Allogenic Coal-Bearing Strata." In *Coal-Forming Environments*. 1993, p. 3.

scientists should consider the coal beds to be accumulations of plants caused by the water currents of the Great Flood.

In later years the accumulation of vegetable matter was explained otherwise."[572]

The fact that modern geologists explain it "otherwise" does not necessarily mean that their explanation is more accurate.

Steve Austin, PhD, shared some astounding findings. A summary of some of his research, particularly interesting to this subject, is provided in a book he co-authored with John Morris titled *Footprints in the Ash*. In it, they wrote:

> Creationists have speculated that coal may have been formed as a result of Noah's flood, during which massive amounts of vegetation were scraped from the continents. Floating as a mat of vegetation on the world ocean, logs would have abraded against each other and decayed, accumulating a peat deposit beneath the floating mat. During the Flood year, abundant volcanic action produced clays which mixed in with peat. Subsequent deep burial by oceanic muds would have applied the pressure and heat needed to alter them rapidly into coal.... Unfortunately, no such floating mat existed for creationists to study— until Mount St. Helens erupted.[573]

Austin went on to describe the finding of huge amounts of bark and other vegetal matter on the lake-bottom beneath the log mat which was floating on Spirit Lake. Prior to that time he had successfully defended his PhD thesis on a theory he proposed of a larger-scale floating log mat having provided the materials for the Mississippi coal basin.[574] The research at Spirit Lake subsequently demonstrated the plausibility of his thesis.

---

572. Stutzer and Noe. *Geology of Coal.* 1940, p. 153.

573. Morris and Austin. *Footprints in the Ash.* 2003, pp. 82–86.

574. Austin. "Mount St. Helens." DVD. Institute for Creation Research.

horizontal floating tree

upright floating tree

upright trees on bottom in different "layers"

horizontal tree on bottom

Figure 8.6. Morris and Austin's depiction of logs floating and deposited in the rapidly accumulating sediments of Spirit Lake.[575]

In relating coal formation to the Flood, it is noteworthy that samples taken from the great peat bogs of equatorial Indonesia and Sumatra were "determined" to be from about one thousand to six thousand years in age.[576] What happened on Earth at that time—to start the process of peat accumulation? The Flood just may have caused a clean sweep, and afterwards, there was a restarting of the growth processes. Without correcting for the distortions in the carbon dating method (described in the Carbon Dating chapter), even the oldest age-estimates reported by Supardi et al. (6040 ± 180 years),[577] are relatively close to the 2,344 BC date often given for the Flood in Bible chronologies.

---

575. Morris and Austin. *Footprints in the Ash.* 2003, p. 99.

576. Supardi et al. "Peat Resources of Sumatra." In *Modern Coal-Forming Environments.* 1993, p. 50.

577. Ibid.

Oil Formation

Oil formation experiments were described by Elizabeth Pennisi. She noted that popular theory had supposed that oil also formed over millions of years. But, Andrew Kaldor "realized that ideas about oil and coal formation had evolved many years ago and had not really been updated to include new chemical and biological knowledge."[578] He and Michael Siskin decided to test the new ideas by experiment. They gathered oil shale samples and heated them under pressure. "These hotter-than-natural conditions sped up the transformation from a geologic time frame of millions of years to one measured in days and hours."[579]

Another researcher, Michael D. Lewan, had shown that oil formation was enhanced if water was added. "Without water, 'the products are seldom like that in natural crude oil.'"[580] Thus, water acts as a catalyst and oil can be formed much more quickly than had previously been thought. "Not only do the ideas buck tradition, but, if right, they will require the revision of time parameters in computer programs now used to predict locations of new reserves."[581]

Diamond Formation

An interesting commentary on man-made and natural diamond formation is found in the Nova program called "The Diamond Deception." It shows technology used to make diamonds in a very short time—measured in days, not millions of years as supposed in popular theory. A report by C. R. Hammond in 1991 indicated

---

578. Pennisi. "Water, Water Everywhere." *Science News,* Feb. 20, 1993, pp. 121-125.
579. Ibid.
580. Ibid.
581. Ibid.

that "about 30% of all industrial diamonds used in the U.S." were then "made synthetically."[582]

Abery noted another discovery about diamond formation: "Diamonds are not always formed deep inside the Earth. Millions of minute ones were formed from condensing plumes of vaporized carbonaceous material when a large meteorite impacted the Earth… to form the 24 km wide Reis crater."[583] Speaking of the world's largest diamond, she indicated it "is a peculiar black diamond known as a carbonado. Their source and formation has long been a puzzle although it seems agreed that they are very old. It has now been suggested that they result from fiery impacts, but one geologist has gone one better and suggested that they come from space, forming in the shock waves of exploding stars and falling to Earth as meteors."[584]

Conclusion

When geologists study a rock formation, it can be said that they are observing and recording facts. But where the materials came from to make up that formation, how they got to that place in that position, and how quickly, are all matters of conjecture based on facts—and assumptions.

Experiments have shown that coal, oil, diamonds and petrified wood can all be formed in a very short time by the application of varying degrees of heat and pressure. And, that catalysts, such as hot water (for oil) and clay (for coal) enhance the process. The Flood/continental shift hypothesis (mentioned in The Flood chapter) seems to fit better with the data—and is much more consistent with a literal reading of the scriptures—than is the conventional model. Not only were the raw materials available in

---

582. *CRC Handbook of Chemistry and Physics*, 72nd ed. 1991–1992, p. 4.7.

583. Abery. "Impact Diamonds." *C&C Review*. SIS, 1996:1, p. 42.

584. Abery. "More Diamond Anomalies. *C&C Review*. SIS, 1996:2, p. 33.

vast quantities, but the mechanism for quickly converting those raw materials into coal and oil was also present. Plentiful were the sources of heat (friction and volcanism), compression, (shifting of large land masses), and water. Wood and other vegetal material were moved about sometimes violently, sometimes gently floating and sloshing around in the great slurry of the Flood.

The Flood/continental shift model provides a feasible explanation of many of the problems left unanswered by the more popular approach. As more scientists dare to seriously consider the evidence for, and the implications of such models, major progress toward resolving the conflicts will be made.

Who can better expound on the truths of geology, a prophet who "beheld the earth, yea, even all of it; and there was not a particle of it which he did not behold, discerning it by the spirit of God" (Moses 1:27) or a geologist, trained in facts which have been woven into a tapestry along with threads of theory, surmise, speculation, and assumption? To literal believers, it is the one who has seen things as they really were. Although the prophets have written little about geological issues, they have recorded events with direct and profound relevance.

History or Myth?

We have no right to treat "history" as the true and accurate image of things.

Like science and religion, history must argue its case on evidence.

—Hugh Nibley, *The Temple and the Cosmos*

The developers of the carbon-14 dating technique were surprised that historical records did not go back as far as they had expected. Willard Libby remembered:

> Arnold and I had our first shock when our advisers informed us that history extended back only for 5000 years. We had thought initially that we would be able to get samples all along the curve, back to 30,000 years.... In fact, the earliest historical date that has been established

with any real certainty is about the time of the 1ˢᵗ Dynasty in Egypt.[585]

While a young man, it dawned on me that although the scriptures speak of Noah's Flood as a real event, there had been no mention of it in any of the history classes I'd taken. Why? I found a Bible chronology listing the time of the Flood at about 2340 BC. While the Roman and Greek civilizations were much later than that date, according to history books in the late 1960s, the First Dynasty of Egypt started in 3100 BC. I reasoned: if the description of the Flood in the Bible is true, as I'd been taught since childhood, either the Egyptian history should mention it, or one or both chronologies were in error. This led me to a multi-year spare-time study of ancient chronology. It turns out that Egyptian sources do mention the Flood—before the First Dynasty. I also learned that the popular Egyptian chronology at that time was being challenged. More on this later in this chapter.

History: Unbiased Facts or Selective Descriptions?

Often times, history is thought of as a recounting of facts and dates of past events. It does include them, but consider Nibley's exceptionally well-informed perspective:

> "What is our knowledge of the past and how do we obtain it?" asks the eminent archaeologist Stuart Piggott, and answers: "The past no longer exists for us, even the past of yesterday…. This means that we can never have direct knowledge of the past. We have only information or evidence from which we can construct a picture." The fossil or potsherd or photograph that I hold in my hand may be called a fact—it is direct evidence, an immediate

---

585. Libby. "Radiocarbon Dating." *Science*, March 3, 1961, p. 624.

experience; but my interpretation of it is not a fact, it is entirely a picture of my own construction. I cannot experience ten thousand or forty million years—I can only imagine, and the fact that my picture is based on facts does not make it a fact, even when I think the evidence is so clear and unequivocal as to allow no other interpretation.[586]

Another of Nibley's insights, although specifically written about church history, also applies to history in general:

Anyone who writes church history has the inescapable and dangerous obligation of deciding somehow just what evidence shall be made available to his readers and what shall not; obviously, he cannot include it all. Now anyone who takes it upon himself to withhold evidence is actually determining what the reader's idea of church history is going to be—he is controlling the past. And when the evidence held back is a thousand times more extensive than what is brought before the jury, it is plain that the historian is free to build up any kind of case he desires.

Is there no alternative to this commission of all but absolute power to a few notoriously partial authorities? There is none. The only completely fair presentation of church history would be a *full* display of all known evidence laid out. . . .[587]

By now some American college professors know that conventional Roman history is largely a pious party fiction, made-to-order history that bucks the evidence at every turn. Likewise the whole body of Greek literature that has come down to us has had to pass the scrutiny of generations of narrow and opinionated men: it is not the literature of the Greeks that we have inherited but a puree made from that fraction of their writings which the

---

586. Nibley. *Old Testament and Related Studies.* 1986, p. 26.
587. Nibley. "Controlling the Past." *Improvement Era.* Jan, 1955, p. 5.

doctors have felt proper to place in the hands of students after much abridgment and revisal.[588]

Thus, it seems, history is only a glimpse at the past—a glimpse obscured by a limited number of real facts and the bias of mortals! Is it possible for mortals to write unbiased history? No! People can attempt to record things as they really were, but to one degree or another, whether intentional or not, our words are a product of subjective thoughts. Nibley commented:

> The historians' problem was... [they] had an enormous heap of documents dumped in their laps. They were tremendously excited about the new treasure and saw immediately that the whole pile would have to be gone through piece by piece and word by word.... The only legitimate question is: "By what method can one properly examine the greatest possible amount of material in a single lifetime?"...
>
> ... History is all hindsight; it is a sizing up, a way of looking at things. It is not what happened or how things really were, but an evaluation, an inference from what one happens to have seen of a few scanty bits of evidence preserved...... What makes the study of history possible today I call the Gas Law of Learning, namely, that any amount of information, no matter how small, will fill any intellectual void no matter how large. It is as easy to write a history of the world after you have read ten books as after you have read a thousand—far easier, in fact.[589]

---

588. Nibley. "Controlling the Past, part 4." *Improvement Era*. Feb, 1955, p. 2.
589. Nibley. *Temple and Cosmos*. 1992, pp. 439–442.

Bible Chronology

"Chronology is the backbone of history."[590] This statement was made by Edwin Thiele, the author of a highly regarded study of chronology of the kingdoms of Israel and Judah. It seems very applicable, because—if the chronology is inaccurate—the history is distorted.

Everyone who has read the scriptures has encountered the "begat sections." For example: "And Adam lived an hundred and thirty years, and begat a son in his own likeness, after his image; and called his name Seth. And the days of Adam after he had begotten Seth were eight hundred years; and he begat sons and daughters" (Gen. 5:3-4). Although these sections are usually skimmed over, or completely ignored, some scholars have made extraordinary studies. Archbishop James Usher is famous (and among his critics, infamous) for his dating of Adam at precisely 4004 BC. He apparently had access to some great sources, and did some very fine work. Below is a compilation of some of the key dates estimated from the Bible and other ancient sources.

4000 BC	Adam
3378 BC	Enoch
3313 BC	Methuselah
2944 BC	Noah
2344 BC	The Flood
2277 BC	Eber
2243 BC	Peleg
2052 BC	Abraham
1952 BC	Isaac
1892 BC	Jacob/Israel
1803 BC	Joseph
1627 BC	Moses

590. Thiele. *Mysterious Numbers of the Hebrew Kings.* 1983, p. 33.

1547 BC	Exodus
1063 BC	David
1023 BC	Solomon
600 BC	Zedekiah
1	Jesus

In studying Bible chronology over the years, some challenging issues have arisen. One cause for uncertainty is discrepancies between the Hebrew Bible and the Greek version known as the Septuagint (abbreviated LXX). For instance, the King James Version (KJV), mostly derived from the Hebrew and subsequent translations, says Adam was 130 years old when Seth was born while the LXX lists 230 years for the same event. Several such 100-year discrepancies exist between the two versions.[591] Which is correct?

Another source of confusion in Bible chronology is the number of years attributed to Israel's time in Egypt. Exodus 12:40 (KJV) states: "Now the sojourning of the children of Israel, who dwelt in Egypt, was four hundred and thirty years." This verse seems to be quite clear in saying that the descendants of Jacob/Israel were in Egypt that long. However, other versions suggest the 430 years was from Abraham's entry into Canaan to the Exodus. A key phrase not in the Hebrew Bible and subsequent translations based on it appears in the LXX. It is translated: "and in the land of Canaan." Thus, according to the earlier LXX version, the 430-year period included both the time in Canaan and in Egypt and included more than just Jacob's descendants. The apparent error was popularized and further confused in Cecil B. DeMille's famous movie, *The Ten Commandments*. As the Exodus began, the movie's "Joshua" mentioned they had been "in bondage 400 years."

Here are some applicable references:

---

591. Barrois. "Chronology, Metrology, Etc." In *The Interpreter's Bible*, Vol. 1, 1952, p. 143.

430 years   "The sojourning of the children of Israel, who dwelt in Egypt, was four hundred and thirty years" (Exodus 12:40) (KJV).

430 years   "The sojourning of the children of Israel... in the land of Egypt *and in the land of Canaan*" (Exodus 12:40) (LXX). (emphasis added).

430 years   "To Abraham and his seed... the covenant, that was confirmed... four hundred and thirty years after" (Galatians 3:16-17).

430 years   "They left Egypt... four hundred and thirty years after our forefather Abraham came into Canaan, but two hundred and fifteen years only after Jacob removed into Egypt."[592] A footnote to this account of Josephus states: "Why our Masorete copy[593] so groundlessly abridges this account... to ascribe 430 years to the... Israelites in Egypt, when it is clear even by that Masorete chronology elsewhere, as well as from the express text itself, in the Samaritan, Septuagint, and Josephus, that they sojourned in Egypt but half that time."[594]

400 years   "And he said unto Abram... thy seed shall be a stranger in a land that is not theirs, and shall serve them; and they shall afflict them four hundred years." (Gen. 15:13)

---

592. *Josephus.* "Antiquities of the Jews," Book II, Chapter XV:2. 1960, p. 62.

593. Masorete. "Much of the work of preserving the Hebrew Scriptures through the centuries after Christ was accomplished by the Masoretes, traditional Jewish scholars who worked in Palestine and Babylon between the sixth and tenth centuries A.D." Read. *How We Got the Bible.* 1985, p. 21.

594. *Josephus.* "Antiquities of the Jews," Book II, Chapter XV:2. 1960, p. 62.

400 years "And God spake... that his seed [Abraham's] should sojourn in a strange land; and that they should bring them into bondage, and entreat them evil four hundred years" (Acts 7:6).

210 years "The sojourning of the children of Israel who dwelt in the land of Egypt in hard labor, was two hundred and ten years" (Jasher 81:3).

David Rohl wrote: "In most commentaries or popular books on the Old Testament you will read that the Israelite Sojourn in the land of Egypt lasted four hundred and thirty years. However, this figure is by no means certain. In fact, there is clear evidence that the true period of the Sojourn was no more than two hundred and fifteen years."[595]

By comparing the ages of key characters in the scriptures and related sources, I compiled a list showing 210 years for Israel in Egypt (see figure 9.1). The 430-year count extends from Abraham's covenant (at the time of his entry into Canaan) to the Exodus. The 400-year period is from Isaac's birth to the Exodus, and the 210 years from the time Jacob/Israel entered Egypt to the Exodus. Since Jacob's son Joseph lived 71 years after Jacob entered Egypt, and since the bondage didn't start until after he died (Exodus 1:6-11), it appears that the bondage was less than 139 years. And it is obvious that I am not the only one who has mixed up details of the lives of Abraham, Isaac, and Jacob or used the term "Israelites" or "children of Israel" to include not only Jacob's descendants but also some of his ancestors.

595. Rohl. *Pharaohs and Kings*. 1995, p. 329.

Abr	430y	400y	210y in Eg	Isaac	Israel	Levi	Joseph	Kohath	Amram	Aaron	Moses	Joshua	Caleb	
70	0													The Lord appeared to Abraham in his 70th y, he built an altar. Jasher 13:17-20
101	31	1												1 Isaac born when Abraham was 100. Gen 17:21; Jasher 23:80; Josephus 36
141	71	41												41 Isaac 40, marries Rebecca. Jsr 24:40, 45
161	91	61		61										1 Jacob & Esau born when Isaac was 60 y old. Jsr 26:15-16, Dem 2:2
175	105	75		75										15 Abraham died in 15th y of Jacob (lived 175 yrs Josephus 39) Jsr 26:29
	177	147		147	87									1 Levi b in 10th y 6th m of Jacob in Haran. Dem 2:3 (137 in 93rd yr of Israel in Egypt. Jsr 63:1)
	181	151		151	91	5								1 Joseph & Dinah b in 14th y 8th m of Jacob in Haran. Dem 2:5
	197	167		167	107	21								17 Joseph 17 sold into Egypt. Gen 35; Jsr 41:9, 44:1
	198	168		168	108	22								18 Joseph cast into prison for 12y after serving Potiphar for ~1 1/2y. TLT 45, 52, 58, 63
	210	180		180	120	34								30 Joseph 30 Prime Minister. Gen 41:46. 7 good years begin
	214	184			124	38								34 Ephraim & Manasseh born in 34th yr of Joseph. Jsr 50:15
	221	191	1e		131	45								41 Jacob enters Egypt at 130. Jsr 55:26
	236	206	16e		146	60	56							1 Kohath b, Levi 60 (36 TLT197), Jacob d. Dem 2:19
	237	207	17e		147	61	57							2 Jacob d 147, 17th yr in Eg. Gen 47:28 Levi 60y, Joseph, 56 Dem 2:19
	251	221	31e			75	71							16 Joseph's pharaoh d when Joseph was 71y old. TLT169
	273	243	53e			97	93	38						1 Amram b when Kohath was ~40. Dem 2:19
	291	261	71e			115	111	56						19 Joseph died at 110. Gen 50:22 71st yr of Isr in Eg. Jsr 59:25
	313	283	93e			137		78						41 Levi died at 137 in 93rd yr Isr in Eg. Jsr 63:1; TLT198, Dem 2:19
	350	320	130e					115	78					1 Moses b when Amram 78. Dem 2:19
	392	362	172e						120		43			1 Caleb b (~40 when spied land) Josh 14:6-10
	425	395	205e								76			34 Moses m Zipporah. Jsr 77:28-51
	427	397	207e								78			36 Moses to Eg, returns to Midian for 2y TLT 295
	429	399	209e								80		38	
exo	exo	exo	exo	exo	exo	exo	exo	exo	exo	exo	exo	exo	exo	Exodus
														40 Spies sent out in 2nd y of exodus. Num 10:11-12

Figure 9.1 Israel's time in Egypt. Key: Abr = Abraham; b = born; d = died; Dem = Demetrius the Chronographer;[596] Eg = Egypt; exo = Exodus; Jsr = Jasher; m = married; TLT, Ginzberg's *The Legends of the Jews*, Vol. 2.[597]

Another bit of confusion comes from the frequency of "forty-year" references in the Bible which seems more than coincidental. For instance:

"And the land had quietness 40 years in the days of Gideon" (Judges 8:28).

"David… reigned 40 years" (2 Samuel 5:4).

"And the time that Solomon reigned… was 40 years" (1 Kings 11:42).

In a revealing article about the frequent use of "forty years" in the Bible, P. J. Crowe pointed to evidence suggesting that

---

596. In *Old Testament Pseudepigrapha*, Vol. 2, 1983, pp. 843–854.
597. Patterned after similar charts by Dennis Clawson.

the term translated as "forty years" was an expression signifying "many years." He reasoned:

> If 40 was always used as a natural number, we would expect it to occur roughly as often as the numbers 35 to 39 and 41 to 45. This clearly is not the case...
>
> Compared with this total of 12 separate periods of 40 years there are no instances whatsoever of periods in the OT of 31-39 and 41-49 years that are not men's ages.
>
> After the number of occurrences of 40 years... is reduced... to adjust for duplicate references... the 40-year period still clearly has a grossly distorted frequency of occurrence. We can conclude from this statistical investigation, beyond reasonable doubt, that 40, as applied [to] a period of years, is not a naturally occurring number. Therefore the 40-year periods should not be taken literally.[598]

Indeed, in H. W. F. Gesenius's Lexicon, he indicated "forty... like seven and seventy, is used by the Orientals as a round number."[599]

During the divided kingdoms of Judah and Israel, the Bible describes the beginning of the reign of one king using the year of the other king's reign. For example: "In the twentieth year of Jeroboam king of Israel reigned Asa over Judah" (1 Kings 15:9). Such references thus provide a relatively precise chronology; however, there are minor problems. One is the uncertainty of exactly when the reign of a king began. In some cultures, rather than the reign starting when a king's predecessor died, he was not officially made king until the beginning of a new year.

---

598. Crowe. "The Biblical 40-Years Periods." *C&C Review*. SIS, 2001:2, pp. 32–34.

599. Gesenius, *Hebrew and Chaldee Lexicon*. 1857, reprint 1991, p. 75.

A complication was noted by Thiele: "Customs were not the same. In Assyria, Babylon, and Persia, when a king first came to the throne, the year was usually called the king's *accession* year, but not till the first day of the first month of the next new year did the king begin reckoning events in his own first year.... In other places a king began to reckon his first year from the day he first came to the throne."[600]

He pointed out another problem: evidence suggests that in the kingdoms of Judah and Israel, the official years of a king's reign began in different months. And, perhaps a more significant issue obscuring precise dating is "the existence of a number of co-regencies and overlapping reigns."[601] For example, when did David's reign begin? When he was anointed to be king by the prophet Samuel, when Saul died, or some other time?

Even considering the difficulties mentioned above, the question may be asked: which source is to be trusted more for the early periods of history, scriptural (based on an imperfect but inspired rendering), or secular chronology (based on surmise)? Each historian has a particular view of things. Truth is still truth, but it is often a challenge to wade through the scanty details, and the distortions, to find it.

John Pratt has meticulously studied Bible chronology. He has come up with some impressive data pointing to a chronology very close to that of Archbishop Usher.[602]

---

600. Thiele. *Mysterious Numbers of the Hebrew Kings.* 1983, p. 43.
601. Ibid., p. 61.
602. See Pratt. *Divine Calendars.* 2002. See also http://www.johnpratt. com, (last accessed 9/4/12).

The Importance of Egyptian Chronology

The ancient chronologies of many cultures are linked to—and dependent upon—the Egyptian, which was believed to be the longest and most securely established. According to Clube and Napier:

> In ideal circumstances, it should be possible to set up independent systems of dates for each of the nations of the ancient world using internal evidence alone.... Then... confirmed by a study of contemporary artefacts traded between the nations and events like battles in which two or more peoples participated. Unfortunately, the internal evidence is often not good enough to establish independent chronologies of sufficiently tolerable quality. As a result, there is still a tendency in practice for much of the approved dating of the prehistoric world, especially prior to the first millennium BC, to be correlated with and ultimately derived from just one single internal scale, namely that of the Egyptian civilization. It is natural that this should be so since it is of the Egyptian civilization that we have the longest, the most continuous and the best-preserved remains.... [However,] quite simply, the confidence with which conventional Egyptian chronology is upheld by modern experts seems out of all proportion to the certainty with which it has been established.[603]

Eminent Egyptologists have recognized major problems with the Egyptian dating. In the early days of Egyptology, dating was based mainly on the record of an Egyptian historian named Manetho, who lived in the third century BC. "Unfortunately" wrote Egyptologist Michael A. Hoffman, "no complete copies

---

603.   Clube and Napier. *Cosmic Serpent.* 1982, p. 226.

of Manetho's work have ever been found. The earliest reference is contained in the writings of Josephus and dates to the mid-first century A.D."[604]

Early Egyptologists took what they could find of Manetho's dynasties and added one to another to produce chronologies identifying 5224 BC as the supposed date of the "Hornet-dynasty of Lower Egypt."[605] In 1909, James H. Breasted described "the accession of Menes and the union of Egypt" at 3400 BC. Then he wrote about other date estimates:

> The extremely high dates for the beginning of the dynasties current in some histories are inherited from an older generation of Egyptologists; and are based upon the chronology of Manetho, a late, careless and uncritical compilation, which can be proven wrong from the contemporary monuments in the vast majority of cases.... Its dynastic totals are so absurdly high throughout, that they are not worthy of a moment's credence, being often nearly or quite double the maximum drawn from contemporary monuments, and they will not stand the slightest careful criticism.[606]

The accepted or "conventional" chronology has subsequently been adjusted even further, and by 1968 the First Dynasty was said to have begun 3100 BC.[607] Since then, scholars have convincingly argued that several of the dynasties were not in succession, but simultaneous, or at least overlapping, and in different parts of the land. Hoffman expressed his regret:

---

604. Hoffman. *Egypt Before the Pharaohs.* 1984, p. 12.

605. Weigall. *A History of the Pharaohs,* Vol. 1. 1925, p. 41

606. Breasted. *A History of Egypt,* 2nd ed. 1909, p. 23.

607. Sewell. *Egypt Under the Pharaohs.* 1968, p. 10, and David. *The Egyptian Kingdoms.* 1975, p. 8.

Although, roughly speaking, each of Manetho's dynasties represents a separate ruling family, it is unclear whether Manetho himself realized that, during periods of civil war, several dynasties ruled at the same time. This makes it impossible to reconstruct an accurate chronology for Egyptian history by simply stringing together all the reigns of all the kings of the thirty dynasties and then counting back from a known date.... Several earlier historians who tried this approach overestimated the beginning of the First Dynasty by as much as 2,500 years![608]

Donovan Courville noted: "Eusebius... states that the reign of Mena [Menes] was preceded by the reigns of 10 kings of This (Thinis). Strangely, historians would have these 10 kings reign in sequence. But if the kings before the dynastic period ruled in sequence, then from what was Egypt unified?"[609]

As seen above, even the history of Egypt is subject to much confusion and controversy. This is especially true for the predynastic period. Some Egyptologists list names of predynastic rulers, but according to John A. Wilson, "no one knows how long the succession of predynastic periods lasted in Egypt, from the crude little village of Merimdeh to the beginnings of the dynasties. Let us assume that this stretch of time occupies two thousand years."[610] Or would another assumption bring it closer to the truth?

"In the great days of 'scientific' scholarship... the only safe and respectable position for any man of stature to take was to give a flat 'no' to any suggestion that the Bible might contain real history." Nibley then noted that Eduard Meyer startled his colleagues by declaring "that the Old Testament was not only history but very good history—by far the most accurate, reliable,

---

608. Hoffman. *Egypt Before the Pharaohs*. 1984, p. 12.
609. Courville. *Exodus Problem*, Vol. 2, 1971, p. 148.
610. Wilson. *The Burden of Egypt*. 1951, p. 37.

and complete history ever produced by an ancient people, with the possible exception of the Greeks, who came much, much later. Time and research have strikingly vindicated this claim."[611]

The History of Israel

Because the history of Israel is so closely associated with the Bible, much of it has been discounted by antitheistic scholars. A popular rendition says that the early parts of the Bible were simply passed down by word of mouth, and Moses was the first to write them down. Nibley countered that argument:

> The favorite creed that the early history of Israel rested entirely on oral tradition was blasted by discoveries proving widespread literacy in the earliest days of Israel.... ... It was quite suddenly in the late 1800s that such documents began to appear, and then it was like the coming of our spring floods, with the great collections of stuff—no mere trickle—pouring out year after year in a breathtaking sequence that appears not yet to have reached its crest....
> ... The Ugaritic texts of Ras Shamra... showed Professor Peet to be wrong in attributing the growth of Hebrew literature to an evolutionary process, leading the great orientalist A. H. Sayce to confess that his own conception of the primitive beginnings of the record was a mistaken one: "There is no longer any difficulty," he wrote, "in believing that there were abundant literary documents for compiling the earlier books of the Old Testament.... Consequently there is no longer any need of our believing as I formerly did that cuneiform tablets lie behind the text of the earlier Biblical books."[612]

611. Nibley. *Old Testament and Related Studies.* 1986, p. 11.
612. Ibid., 1986, pp. 11–14.

Synchronizing Egyptian and Israelite Chronology

Ironically, some of the mistakes in synchronizing biblical and Egyptian chronologies appear to be due to over-zealous religious people trying to confirm the connections between Israel and Egypt. There is ongoing debate about who the pharaoh of the Exodus really was. The Bible does not mention a pharaoh named Rameses, but it does speak of the "land of Rameses" (Genesis 47:11) as well as the "treasure cities, Pithom and Rameses" (Exodus 1:1). Because of these references, it has been popular to suppose that one of several Pharaohs named Rameses was the pharaoh of the Exodus, but this connection does not conform to the evidence. Did the kings who used "Rameses" as one of their many official names do so because they were from "the land of Rameses"? They apparently lived long after the time the treasure city was built. David Rohl observed:

> The first page of the *Memorandum and Articles of Association* of the Egypt Exploration Fund, founded by Amelia Edwards in 1891.... expressly stated that the Fund's objectives should include the promotion of surveys, explorations and excavation work which would be "for the purpose of elucidating or illustrating the Old Testament narrative."
>
> ... This need to "find" the Bible in Egypt was the principal reason why the earliest digs initiated by the Egypt Exploration Fund were concentrated in the Nile delta. Edwards' committee purposefully selected sites which were strong candidates for Raamses and Pithom— the store-cities of Exodus 1:11 built by the Israelites during their Bondage in Egypt.[613]

---

613. Rohl. *Pharaohs and Kings.* 1995, p. 113.

Rohl then presented evidence refuting the premise that Rameses II was the Pharaoh of the Oppression and remarked:

> It is clear how scholars came to these conclusions. But there is other "historical" material contained in the Old Testament which undermines this apparently straightforward biblical link with Egypt—material which was... dismiss[ed] in favour of the superficially attractive chronological synchronism.... There is no compelling evidence to demonstrate that Ramesses II was either the biblical Pharaoh of the Oppression or Exodus. The mention of the store-city of Raamses, upon which these identifications are based, may simply be anachronistic.[614]

Nibley noted an aspect of Ramses II's life and character that has caused a great deal of confusion. He claimed that Ramses had deliberately manipulated the records:

> For many years scholars were convinced that Ramses II was just about the greatest builder and warrior king that ever lived. Ramses planned it that way. While his stone-cutters conscientiously effaced from buildings and monuments the names of their real builder (that is, where other enterprising monarchs had not already beaten him to it) and substituted in their place the name of the ruling Ramses, his historians were busy writing up the accounts of battles that had turned out badly for the king in such a way as to transform them into glorious victories. That was controlling the past in the grand manner, a practice as old as Egypt itself.[615]

---

614. Ibid., pp. 114, 117. Anachronism: the use of a familiar name for a location that was not in use during the time mentioned (e.g. using "America" before the land was thus named. That is, before Amerigo Vespucci, for whom America received its name).

615. Nibley. "Controlling the Past part 4." *Improvement Era.* 1955, p. 2.

Another erroneous link was apparently made in an attempt to synchronize biblical and Egyptian chronologies. It was the identification of "Shishak, king of Egypt," (1 Kings 11:40; 14:25–26) with one of the Shoshenks, from Egyptian sources. Although the names do have a striking resemblance, the details from Israelite sources of Shishak's time do not match those of Shoshenk from Egyptian records. For details, see Rohl's discussion on the subject, which he summarized with the following:

> Scholars are underpinning Egyptian chronology with a biblical synchronism. They readily accept the name-equation Shoshenk = Shishak and proclaim a correspondence between the Year 20 campaign of Shoshenk I and the Shishak assault upon Jerusalem. In doing so they dismiss the obvious discrepancies of fact between the two sources. If you are going to use biblical data to establish both the chronology of Egypt and the... Levantine[616] archaeology, you cannot then go on to arbitrarily disregard selected sections of the historical material contained in the biblical source simply because they do not fit your theory. Surely, if this were any sort of reliable historical synchronism, the facts from both sources, supposedly recording a single historical event, would agree in a substantial way. As it stands they do not agree at all... ... Scholars of the last century had taken the wrong path right at the beginning of their own journey of discovery. That false trail sign posted to "Raamses" and "Shishak", led modern scholarship into a quagmire of confusing anomalies in the chronology and archaeology of the ancient world.... We decided to take the alternative road sign.... It was not very long before we arrived at an entirely different ancient world—one with a much greater potential for biblical and archaeological synthesis. The irony was that although the conventional chronology had

---

616. Levant: The land region at the eastern end of the Mediterranean.

been based on two key biblical synchronisms it produced an unhappy marriage between excavation results and the Old Testament narratives.[617]

After criticizing what he called the four pillars on which conventional Egyptian chronology is built, Rohl concluded with: "Of the four chronological supports for Egyptian history, only Pillar One—the 664 BC sacking of Thebes by the Assyrians—is sound.... There are therefore no safe fixed points in the chronology of Egypt earlier than 664 BC."[618] He then very convincingly described his rationale for forty-two new synchronisms tying biblical characters and events with his revised Egyptian chronology. In the conclusion to his book, he wrote:

> Not everything in myth and tradition is true, but I believe this study has shown that it would be imprudent for scholars of ancient world history to underestimate the significance and tenacity of our legendary past. Without initially starting out to discover the historical Bible, I have come to the conclusion that much of the Old Testament contains real history. It has certainly been an interesting exercise for this Egyptologist who has found himself wandering into many unfamiliar areas of old world research in his quest for history. Only time will tell if the New Chronology, tentatively proposed here, is correct in most of its details.[619]

Joseph in Egypt

Many years ago, Sir Alan Gardiner mentioned a rock-inscription relating a tale of "a seven-year famine that had afflicted the land,

---

617. Rohl. *Pharaohs and Kings.* 1995, pp. 127, 327.
618. Ibid., p. 135.
619. Ibid., p. 367.

[the king] sought counsel from the wise Imhotep."[620] Could this "Imhotep" be an Egyptian version of Joseph, who the Bible says interpreted pharaoh's dream of the seven years of plenty and the seven years of famine? In conventional Egyptian chronologies, the pharaoh at that time, Djoser, reigned somewhere between 2630 and 3150 BC while according to Bible chronologies, Joseph became prime minister of Egypt about 1740 BC. There are remarkable parallels between the biblical and Egyptian accounts. Nibley also noted similarities between the accounts of Imhotep and Joseph:

> There was a school of Imhotep in operation at Memphis, and he was venerated right into the nineteenth century at nearby Saqqareh, where he had begun his career more than forty-five hundred years before![621] Significantly his shrine at that place is a ruin called "the Prison of *Joseph*." This puzzles Wildung, who writes: "We cannot describe the reason why the temple was referred to as the prison of the Biblical Joseph." For a clue... the worship of the two heroes began at their tombs, which as the objects of pilgrimage became shrines and temples. But Moslems and Christians would not repair to the tomb of an unknown pagan (Imhotep).... There was Joseph, a great favorite with humble Christians, Jews, and Moslems alike; was not he too like Imhotep... the grand vizier of Egypt, the highest officer in the land, riding forth with Pharaoh to the wild cheers of the populace whom he had saved from a seven-year famine just as Imhotep had done? Does not the great canal, a triumph of ancient engineering that watered the land for hundreds of miles parallel to the Nile, to this day bear the name of Joseph's Canal?[622]

---

620. Gardiner. *Egypt of the Pharaohs.* 1966, p. 76.
621. Here Nibley used conventional Egyptian dating.
622. Nibley. *Abraham in Egypt.* 1981, p. 105.

This Imhotep may very well be an Egyptian rendering of the biblical Joseph.

Rohl identified what he believes is a different Egyptian version of Joseph (the numbers in parentheses refer to pages in his book):[623]

- The seven-year famine was in year twenty of Amenemhat III of Egypt (p. 335).
- It was in Amenemhat's reign that massive hydraulic projects were initiated. "This important water channel still runs parallel to the great river for over two hundred kilometres... What is the traditional name of this 'second river Nile'? Why, the Bahr Yussef ('waterway of Joseph') of course!" (pp. 346–347).
- Yakkub, "is clearly the biblical name Jacob, father of Joseph" (p. 352).
- Ishpi was the name "'Yaseph' (Joseph/Yusef). However, they [scholars] were obviously prevented from identifying this name with *the* Joseph simply because of the chronological" discrepancies which then existed (p. 352).
- Joseph's Palace (pp. 356–358).
- The Tomb of Joseph—where his remains were placed after his embalming until the time of the Exodus (pp. 360–365).

So how could Joseph's story be as though it happened in different dynasties, under different pharaohs, and during different time periods? Velikovsky claimed that some of the Egyptian "periods" were just variations of the same stories: "Ancient history is distorted.... Because of the disruption of synchronism, many figures on the historical scene are 'ghosts' or 'halves' and 'doubles'. Events are often duplicates: battles are shadows; many speeches

---

623. Rohl. *Pharaohs and Kings.* 1995.

are echoes; many treaties are copies."[624] Stories of Joseph may vindicate this aspect of Velikovsky's many unusual assertions. Joseph just might be one of those who was revered in different parts of Egypt, with details handed down differently by diverse groups. Later, each rendition was mistakenly considered to be of a separate and distinct time.

Rohl's remarkable correlations between biblical and Egyptian records were generally unrecognized by his scholarly predecessors. He proposed other logical connections, and his work seems particularly well researched and documented and includes spectacular photos. He wrote: "Many people continue to hope that evidence will come to light confirming the existence of David, Solomon and even the earlier charismatic leaders of Israel such as Joseph and Moses. However, it is my belief that it is no longer necessary to wait for such evidence—all we need do is take a look at the archaeological material we already possess from the new perspective of a revised Egyptian chronology."[625]

Although he claims to be "without the sustaining support of any particular religious belief,"[626] Rohl declared that he was prepared to accept the Old Testament as a valid source for ancient history for reasons including:

- "All ancient documents are written by humans, and therefore.... susceptible to errors of fact, political bias, economy of truth and miscopying."
- "The objective... is to argue straightforwardly that the narratives contained in the Old Testament are consistent with the general cultural setting revealed through

624. Velikovsky. *Ages in Chaos*. Abacus edition. 1973, p. 22.
625. Rohl. *Pharaohs and Kings*. 1995, p. 34.
626. Ibid., p. 8

Egyptian and Levantine archaeology—once the correct chronology is applied."[627]

Another of the great connections between Israel and Egypt is of course the plagues and miracles associates with the Exodus. Velikovsky was a pioneer in bringing forth evidence suggesting that the life of a particular lesser-known pharaoh actually synchronizes well with the exodus events described in the scriptures. He mentioned a Papyrus Ipuwer that appears to be an Egyptian account of the plagues associated with the exodus.[628] He also proposed a rational explanation for the "miracles" having been a result of a close encounter with a comet. He took a literal approach to scriptural descriptions and found unusual but plausible explanations and proposed new synchronisms between Bible and Egyptian chronologies. Not all his connections have been vindicated over the years, but many do ring true to this day.[629]

Calendars

Most of us take for granted the Christian Calendar. People in general are not aware that most of the ancients did not use a fixed date as a point of reference over more than one generation. With each new king their date-reckoning often started over. Converting these relative dates to the modern calendar is a challenging process.

The Gregorian calendar (named for Pope Gregory the XIII) was introduced to replace the old Roman calendar (the Julian, named after Julius Caesar). It was adopted in four countries in

---

627. Ibid., p. 38.
628. Zecher. "The Papyrus Ipuwer, Egyptian Version of the Plagues." *The Velikovskian.* January 1997.
629. See Velikovsky. *Ages in Chaos.* 1973, *Peoples of the Sea.* 1980. *Ramses II and His Time.* 1980. *Worlds in. Collision.* 1977.

1582, and Pope Gregory decreed that the day after October 4 of that year became October 15 to correct for the ten days of accumulated error as a result of the lack of precision of the Julian calendar. The Gregorian also re-instituted the Roman practice of having the new-year start on January first. In many ancient cultures, the new year began in the springtime. In England and its colonies, this was the case until the Gregorian calendar was adopted in 1752, when the day after September 3 became September 14. Prior to 1752, New Year's Day in the British Empire was March 25. While researching family history, I was surprised to see dates like "1 Mar 1750/1" (meaning the date in the old English Parish Register showed it as March 1, 1750, but according to modern reconing, it would be March of 1751. Under the old style (prior to 1752), a child born say on March 25, 1750 (the first day of 1750), could have had a younger brother born one day less than a year later on March 24 1750 (the last day of 1750).

	New Year's Day	Last Day of Year	"Year" Length
1750	March 25	March 24	12 mo.
1751	March 25	Dec. 31	~9 mo.
1752	January 1	Dec. 31	12 mo.

Some countries phased in the change to the Gregorian calendar over time, and Russia didn't adopt it until 1918.[630] Thus, calendar confusion is not restricted to ancient times.

Carl Roebuck of Northwestern University described the challenge of converting ancient dates to the modern Christian system:

It is a difficult and highly technical task to fix the time of the events which they [the ancients] recorded in terms

---

630. http://en.wikipedia.org/wiki/Gregorian_calendar, (last accessed 9/4/12).

of our own Christian era. Not only are the gaps in our information numerous and large, but each people of antiquity had its own methods of reckoning time and dating events. The Christian era itself came into use only in the sixth century after Christ. About A.D. 540 a monk, Dionysius Exiguus, calculated by historical methods that the 248th year of the era of the Roman Emperor Diocletian, in which Dionysius lived, was the 532nd year from the birth of Christ. Even so, it was not until the eighteenth century that the practice of expressing events as occurring before the birth of Christ (B.C.) became regular in the western world.[631]

Referring to the reprinted chronicles of the Assyrians, Greeks, and Romans, Roebuck continued with: "From such records as these it is possible for historians to establish a relative chronology, to arrange events in the order of their occurrence in the history of a single people. But how do we transfer such relative schemes into the Christian era?"[632] He mentioned some of the means used in making correlations. How accurate are they? The farther back one goes, the less sure they are.

The Length of a Year

In the book of Enoch, the year was said to be "precisely three hundred and sixty-four days."[633] If true, was either the rotation of the earth or its orbit around the sun perturbed? Some scientists are claiming that events such as the Chilean 8.8 earthquake in 2010 or the 8.9 magnitude Japanese earthquake of 2011 have caused a slowdown in Earth's rotation—though only a few millionths of a second. Other accounts suggest that things such as the vast

631. Roebuck. *World of Ancient Times.* 1966, p. 23, footnote 1.
632. Ibid.
633. Laurence, trans. *The Book of Enoch.* 1883, p. 97.

quantities of water stored in man-made reservoirs have sped up Earth's spin—shortening "the day by about eight millionths of a second."[634] Could some catastrophic event have altered it much more significantly?

Other ancient texts also bring into question whether a year has always been approximately 365 days. According to a fragment found among the Dead Sea Scrolls: "On that day, Noah went out of the ark, at the end of a complete year of three-hundred and sixty-four days."[635] Such a minor difference as 364 versus 365 days doesn't seem very significant. But over one hundred years, using one length if the other was the actual, would make the calendar one hundred days out of season, adding to the confusion.

In the conclusion to an article about ancient calendars, Bob Johnson noted a potentially more significant issue: "There is a considerable amount of evidence that the year consisted of only 360 days during a period prior to 700 BC." In support of his assertion, he cited:

1. The Mayan cycles including "18 months of 20 days" and their Long Count system of tuns of 360 days.
2. "Chinese mathematicians are known to have based their geometry, as we do, on a 360 degree circle based on the annual movement of the sun."
3. The Chaldeans, "experts in astronomy in the first millennium BC, also had a year of only 360 days."
4. "The Assyrians used a year of 360 days."
5. "The Indian texts of the Veda use a year of 360 days divided into 12 months of 30 days."

634. McInnis. "Reservoirs Speed Up Earth's Spin." *Earth*. June, 1996, p. 14.

635. Martinez. *Dead Sea Scrolls Translated*, 2nd ed. 1994, p. 214. (Genesis Pesher.)

6. "From approximately 700 BC, the Hindus used a civil year of 365.25 days but retained a sacred year of 360 days."

7. "The Persians used a year of 360 days until the 7th century BC, when they added 5 extra days."

"In every case, the additional days were added to the year of 360 days and were thought to be unpropitious."[636] Why did so many peoples reckon the year as 360 days prior to about 700 BC?

Where Does Myth End and History Begin?

There are no clear distinctions between history, prehistory, legend, and myth. R. J. Braidwood expressed, "the establishment of a 'real' chronology for this borderline range between late prehistory and early history is seen to be far from precise."[637] Nibley discussed some of the difficulties: "The prevailing view of the past is controlled not by evidence but by opinion. The[y]... have believed what they wanted to believe.... They... decided that if we must take history we can at least make it into a thing expressive of our own experience; this led to the existentialism of today, in which the individual rejects as myth anything he does not feel inclined to accept."[638] Furthermore, the "myths became a plaything for all sorts of irresponsible poets, priests, and quacks to kick around, but behind them, Plutarch assures us, lies the core of historic events that really took place if we could only get back to them."[639]

Although archaeological evidence of specific prophets is hard to come by, Nibley noted, historical and literary evidence is abundant.

636. Johnson, B. "Origin of the 260 Day Calendar." *C&C Review*. SIS, 2001:1, p. 25.

637. Braidwood. "Prehistory into History." In *Proceedings of 12th Nobel Symposium*. 1970, p. 81.

638. Nibley. *Old Testament and Related Studies*. 1986, pp. 4–5.

639. Nibley. *Abraham in Egypt*. 1981, p. 161.

Along with a sudden resurgence of interest in the Old Testament in the 1970s comes an unparalleled concern for Abraham. In the new studies, the whole problem of discovering Abraham is one of fitting things together.... We never shall know what really happened or exactly what it was like back then, but consistency of sources keeps the game going... The Abraham legends turn up in Egyptian, Babylonian, and even Greek traditions of great antiquity with a richness of detail that can hardly be accidental.[640]

Though archaeology may conceivably confirm the existence of a prophet... it can never prove or disprove the visions that make the prophet a significant figure. Former attempts to explain the scriptures in terms of nature-myths,... and psychology had nothing to do with reality.[641]

Many have taken the stance that people and events associated with myth and legend are just fanciful imaginings. However, evidence has come to light, indicating that ancient myths and legends were based on actual events, though obscured to varying degrees. Anthony Larson wrote: "Though there may be many similarities between the myths of man and the accounts kept by the Prophets of God, the myths are only the remnants."[642] Similar thoughts were expressed by Nibley:

In the mid-nineteenth century the folklorists were beginning to notice that the same myths and legends turned up everywhere in the Old and New Worlds....
... Archaeology had made us progressively aware of the oneness of our world with successive discoveries... each one tying all the great Near Eastern civilizations closer... together .... And the Bible is right in the center of it: the patriarchs who had been reduced to solar myths by the

---

640. Ibid., p. 50.
641. Nibley. *Old Testament and Related Studies*. 1986, p. 33.
642. Larson. *And there Shall Be a New Heaven*. 1985, p. 70.

higher critics suddenly turned out to be flesh-and-blood people.... ... It already appears that the ancient myths, wherever they turn up, have a tendency to fit together into the same picture, supporting and confirming each other due to the solid ground on which they stand—the reality of ritual, by which history becomes a religious phenomenon—as is markedly the case in the annals of the Pharaohs. This leads us to conclude that there is a serious historical reality behind the myths as a whole, in spite of the adjusting and romancing that sometimes effaces them almost beyond recognition.

The myths thus provide us with a new and powerful tool for searching into hitherto inaccessible recesses of the past.[643]

"H. M. Chadwick pointed out what should have been obvious to everyone, namely, that epic literature, a large and important segment of the human record, is the product not of unrestrained poetic fancy but of real years of terror and gloom through which the entire race has been forced to pass from time to time."[644] "The unearthing of the oldest known villages gives us a new and unexpected picture of a civilization that 'seems to have come into being with relative (even revolutionary) suddenness.'"[645]

The Advent of the Written Record

At what point did writing take over and the telling of tales decline? Generally, it appears that the written records and the oral traditions were simultaneous even in the earliest times. It seems that in all periods of human existence, some people have known writing, though much of the population did not. Nibley wrote:

---

643. Nibley. *Old Testament and Related Studies.* 1986, pp. 30–32, 47.

644. Nibley. *The Ancient State.* 1991, p. 33.

645. Nibley. *Old Testament and Related Studies.* 1986, p. 10.

The written records should be as old as the human race itself, for... "a book of remembrance was kept... in... the language of Adam".... Now what do the ancients themselves have to say on the subject? Surprisingly, a great deal.... The oldest writing appears side by side with the oldest legends about writing. Wouldn't normal curiosity suggest a hearing of those legends?...

Why is it that the ancients are unanimous in attributing the origins of writing, including the alphabet, to a heavenly source.

Why are the earliest written documents always found in temples? Why do they always deal with religious matters?[646]

The translator of the Book of Jasher remarked: "the art of writing appears to have been known and practised from the earliest periods."[647]

Nibley described an event with an unusual twist on the subject of the invention of an alphabet:

A cover story appeared in the prestigious journal *Science* recounting the strange achievement of an Apache Indian by the name of Silas John, who not only claimed to have had a whole writing system revealed to him in a dream for holy purposes, but actually produced the system, which turns out to be a highly efficient one; an instant alphabet, not out of nothing, but out of a dream. If it could happen in 1904 to a semi-literate Apache, could it not have happened earlier?

Only such evidence could break the vicious circular argument which has long prevented serious investigation into the origins of writing. Many writers in scientific journals have recently deplored the way in which scientific

---

646. Nibley. *Temple and Cosmos.* 1992, pp. 453, 478–479.
647. Jasher. Translator's Preface, p. v.

conclusions reached long ago and held as unimpeachable truths turn students away from avenues of research which might well prove most fruitful.[648]

One thing many do not understand is that the most ancient of records have very strong religious ties. One prime example was given by the Egyptologist Rosalie David: "Towards the end of her civilization, despite a succession of foreign invaders, Egypt still retained her religious beliefs.... Religion was the cornerstone of Egyptian civilization."[649] Religion was truly a main feature of not only Egyptian and Israelite writings but ancient writings of other cultures as well:

What the outside texts prove is the antiquity and universality of the gospel and its central position in the whole history of civilization. It is not a local or tribal tradition on the one hand, nor is it the spontaneous expression of evolving human intelligence on the other, but is the common heritage of all ancient civilizations, battered, corrupted, and distorted in most cases, to be sure, but always recognizable in its main features and much too ingenious and elaborate to be the product of independent discovery.[650]

A primordial revealed religion... has passed through alternate phases of apostasy and restoration which have left the world littered with the scattered fragments of the original structure, some more and some less recognizable, but all badly damaged and out of proper context. The early fathers of the Church gave such an explanation for the disturbingly close resemblances between Christianity and

648. Nibley, *On the Timely and the Timeless.* 1978, p. 101.
649. David. *The Egyptian Kingdoms.* 1975, p. 78.
650. Nibley. *On the Timely and Timeless.* 1979, p. 41.

other, notably Egyptian, beliefs and practices—all are the remnants of another age.[651]

It would be helpful if analysis of the past could include eye-witness accounts, and audio/video recordings from several different vantage points. Such was the case with the 1989 San Francisco earthquake. It may have been the best-documented natural disaster up to that time. Available for study are videos of events as they happened, as the damage was assessed, and as aftershocks occurred. Seismic measurements from diverse locations are available, yet a precise cause for the earth moving in that manner and at that time and place is still a matter of conjecture. Since precise data is not available for the distant past, reliance on inference, estimate, assumption, and theory is an absolute necessity. The ancient records which have survived are vastly inferior in terms of factual details. Even so, their descriptions are worth considering."'Pale ink,' said Confucius, 'is better than the most retentive memory.'"[652]

According to Nibley:

> The documents first started coming out in great numbers with the Council of Constance (1414-1418) and finally with the fall of Constantinople in 1453. Vast numbers of ancient documents that had been reposing in the East and in various places for a long time suddenly poured into Europe. They were collected and organized in great... royal, and imperial libraries.... But unfortunately for the books, about this same time the Book of Nature[653] was discovered.

---

651. Nibley. *The Message of the Joseph Smith Papyri.* 1975, p. xii.

652. Mertz. *Pale Ink.* 1953, p. 21.

653. The Book of Nature is used here as a metaphor for those trying to "read" history by observing natural phenomena.

... [It] is much easier to read, in a way. The men who could read it would become the great geniuses of the world.... But the average man could read it just as well as anybody else. After all, the beginnings of geology were simply by a Scotch farmer, James Sutton, who went out and started guessing about the rocks on the beach near his home. And anyone could play that game. On the other hand, [to read] the written records.... you had to know or pretend to know the languages.... The result was that everybody wanted to play... because everyone's guess was as good as anybody else's; and you can guess like mad...

Joseph Justus Scaliger, who died in 1608, was the last man ever to make a serious attempt to read what the written human record said.... The human race has documented its doing for a long time, and no one pays any attention to the record.... Oh, it's a librarian's paradise: we classify, we photograph, we reproduce, we store and preserve, and we transfer. We can do all the tricks electronics can do today, but nobody reads the records. Nobody knows what is actually in these books. I mean this literally.... It's a most interesting thing the way these records have been shamefully pushed aside.[654]

Modern Myth

People of religion tend to get set in their ways. So do scientists. For example, a very popular theory has been that the ancestors of Native Americans had migrated across a land-bridge from Asia, at what is now called the Bering Strait.

I took an Archaeology of Mesoamerica class at Arizona State University. The dating of certain key events fit well with Bible chronology—that is, back to about 2000 BC. Older dates were separated by fantastic jumps of many thousands of years, throwing out any synchronization with scriptural chronology.

---

654. Nibley. *Old Testament and Related Studies*. 1986, pp. 115–117.

On the first day of class, the instructor mentioned the Bering Strait theory as though it was a demonstrated fact and the one and only way people got to the Western Hemisphere before Columbus. I asked if any other theories would be discussed, such as that found in Thor Heyerdahl's *Ra Expeditions*. The answer given was an astounding no. The reason: because Heyerdahl was outside mainstream archaeology. (He actually demonstrated the plausibility of his theories. In this instance, he built a ship out of bundles of papyrus reeds, patterned after those found on Egyptian wall paintings and sailed it from Africa to South America, where he had actually seen smaller boats also made of bundles of reeds.)[655] Dismissing the possibility of long distance boat travel in ancient times, as the professor did, is illogical—especially considering the numerous islands that have been inhabited since early times.

The infatuation with the Bering Strait theory was mentioned by Abery in her review of a book titled *Red Earth, White Lies*:

> Most archaeologists stoutly defend the theory that man only entered the Americas at the end of the last Ice Age, about 12,000 years ago, via a land bridge from Asia across what is now the Bering Strait... The author found that this theory has been around so long that students simply refer to it without question. He also notes that "the immense knowledge and factual proof of many scientific theories does not exist.
>
> Many theories and facts recited by scholars and scientists today are merely academic folk lore which professors heard in their undergraduate days and have not examined at all."[656]

---

655. Heyerdahl. *The Ra Expeditions*. 1971.

656. Abery. Reviews: "*Red Earth, White Lies* by Vine Deloria." In *C&C Review*. SIS, 1996:1, pp. 55–56.

Nibley also commented on the Bering Strait theory:

> The *real* origin is a migration via the Alaskan land-bridge
> or Bering Straits—a still unproven hypothesis. This is
> presented as the confrontation of crude 19th century
> superstition with the latest fruits of modern science. And
> that, too, is misleading. For in 1835 Josiah Priest wrote
> in his *American Antiquities*: "The manner by which the
> original inhabitants and animals reached here, is easily
> explained, by adopting the supposition, which, doubtless,
> is the *most* correct, that the northwestern and western
> limits of America were, at some former period, united to
> Asia on the *west*, and to Europe on the east."
>
> Therewith, for Priest, the question was settled… the
> theory of settlement by the Alaska land bridge was the
> final solution. And as such it has been accepted by North
> American anthropologists to this day, even though their
> colleagues in Europe and South America may shake their
> heads in wonder at such naïve and single-minded devotion
> to a one-shot explanation of everything. We may find it
> strange that back in 1835, with no evidence to go by but
> the configuration of the map, anyone could have settled
> for such finality—the *problem* was real and wonderful, the
> *conclusion* premature and untested."[657]

Conclusion

Polybius, who lived about 208–126 BC, expressed:

> There are plenty of mistakes made by writers out of ignorance,
> and which any man finds it difficult to avoid. But if we
> knowingly write what is false, whether for the sake of our
> country or our friends or just to be pleasant, what difference
> is there between us and the hack writers? Readers should be

---

657. Nibley. *Since Cumorah*. 1967, p. 245.

very attentive to and critical of historians, and they in turn should be constantly on their guard.[658]

Written histories, at best, are filtered by the compilers' knowledge and biases, and also by the sources to which they had access. At worst, they can be gross misstatements of facts, distortions, and deliberate falsifications. "But however vast the accumulation of facts may become, our picture of the past and the future will always be, not partly but wholly, the child of our own trained and conditioned imaginations."[659]

Many assume—because of the pervasiveness of the evolutionary view of the past—that early man was less intelligent. Portrayals of cave men bumbling around like apes have been overly abundant. If the scriptures are accurate, many of the ancients could be described as having been superintellects.

As we piece together our own perceptions about history, we should recognize that ancient literature provides important clues. Also, that the distinction between history and myth is far from clear.

658. Bartlett. *Bartlett's Familiar Quotations*, 15th ed. 1980, p. 95.
659. Nibley. *Old Testament and Related Studies*. 1986, p. 27.

10

Evolution and Creation

Evolution is a flexible word. It can be used by one person to mean something as simple as change over time, or by another person to mean the descent of all life forms from a common ancestor.... In its... biological sense, however, evolution means a process whereby life arose from non-living matter and subsequently developed entirely by natural means. That is the sense that Darwin gave to the word.

—Michael J. Behe, *Darwin's Black Box* (1996)

What Part of Evolution Is Fact?

In order to begin to reconcile evolution and Creation, it is particularly important to distinguish between fact and theory. John A. Widtsoe noted that one major obstacle is the wide range in usage of the word "evolution." He made an important distinction between "the law of change" (sometimes called "evolution") and the "theories of evolution":

> Among people generally, as well as by a group of scientists who should know better, the word [evolution] is used with unpardonable looseness. Especially should the difference between the law of evolution and the theory or theories of evolution be stressed whenever the word is used.
>
> In its widest meaning evolution refers to the unceasing changes within our universe. Nothing is static; all things change. Stars explode in space; mountains rise and are worn down... The law of change, an undeniable fact of human experience, is the essence of the law of evolution.[660]

Thus, when "evolution" is used to mean "change," it is not in dispute. Similarly, when "evolved" is used to mean "developed," no problem. However, not all of the processes that usually fall under the heading "evolution" have unanimous acceptance.

One method of subdividing the meaning of "evolution" is the use of "microevolution" when referring to the small-scale changes which are known to occur, and "macroevolution" for the major theoretical changes. Salkeld described: "The grand evolutional progressions, such as the transformation of a fish into a man, are examples of macroevolution. They remain out of reach, accessible only at the end of an inferential trail." He continued by discussing a problem with macroevolution: "Ardent Darwinian evolutionists say that macroevolution is just 'microevolution with unlimited time'; although some added: 'plus possibly, an 'X' (i.e. unexplained) factor.'"[661]

Phillip Johnson noted some of the difficulties in standardizing the definition of "evolution." He pointed out that minor changes within a species are often cited as "proof" of the whole theoretical realm associated with the word.[662]

---

660. Widtsoe. *Evidences and Reconciliations*, 1943, p. 149.
661. Salkeld. "Intelligent Design?" *C&C Review.* SIS, 2009, p. 2.
662. Johnson, P. *Darwin on Trial.* 1991, p. 151.

Biologist Caroline Crocker challenged the Darwinist view and taught her students of her belief that:

> The development of antibiotic resistance in bacteria is often cited as evidence for evolution. But this is, at best, microevolution. It would be invalid to extrapolate the results to claim they prove macroevolution.... a species of bacteria called *E. coli* has undergone 150 years of intensive culture and experimentation, including being genetically engineered. Since bacteria grow very quickly, multiplying from one to millions in a day, it could be expected that evolution into a different form would be evident. Dr. R. Lenski grew this bacterium for 20,000 generations and did not find even one new molecular machine... As biologist Michael Behe pointed out...*E. coli* is still *E. coli* and not another species of bacteria, much less something besides a bacterium.[663]

She was also said to have taught:

> The scientific establishment was... disguising an atheistic view of life in the garb of science...
> ... No one has ever seen a dog turn into a cat in a laboratory.[664]

According to Phillip Johnson, Darwin acknowledged that to some degree evidence was "not easy to reconcile with his theory" but he argued "that the common ancestry thesis was so logically appealing that rigorous empirical testing was not required."[665]

---

663. Crocker. *Free to Think*. 2010, p. 30.
664. Vedantam. "Eden and Evolution." http://www.washingtonpost.com/wp-dyn/content/article/2006/02/03/AR2006020300822_pf.html, (last accessed 9/4/12) 3 Feb. 2006, pp. 1–2.
665. Johnson, P. *Darwin on Trial*. 1991, p. 149.

Norman Macbeth spoke of a conference of biologists convened in 1980 to address the problem of the lack of evidence for macroevolutionary changes:

> The evolutionists had long neglected this problem preferring to concentrate on changes in coat-color and bristle-number rather than on how a tiny shrew could evolve into a whale or a reptile into a bird. They were convinced that such evolution must have occurred, but they knew of no mechanism by which to explain how it was done. After three days of earnest debate in Chicago, the 150 biologists still had no mechanism. Their Darwinian tools could not cope with the problem.[666]

Jonathan Wells shared his view of an attitude underlying much of evolution: "The whole Darwinian story... was driven by a... commitment to materialistic, antitheistic philosophy. The pattern of evolution was not something that had been inferred from overwhelming evidence in paleontology, molecular biology and embryology, but something that was assumed to be true from the start."[667]

Spontaneous Change—From Disorder to Order?

The theory of evolution does deal with facts, but those facts are organized on an intricate framework built with materials including assumptions, inferences, and all manner of variations. What aspects of evolution are really true, which are interpretations of facts, and which are just suppositions? It is surely true that things change; it seems that nothing in mortality remains constant for

---

666. Macbeth. "How to Defuse a Feud." *Kronos,* Vol. VII, no. 4, 1982, p. 3.
667. Wells. "Common Ancestry on Trial." In *Darwin's Nemesis.* 2006, p. 6 of Chapter 11.

very long. But do things spontaneously change from simple to complex, as suggested in some branches of evolutionary theory?

When I have shown a simple stone arrowhead to a group of students and asked them to identify it, they all seem to know it is an arrowhead. When told that it evolved into that shape, the response has been humorous disbelief. If it isn't reasonable that something as simple as an arrowhead can form without deliberate effort, how is it that so many people believe that all forms of life did just that?

In a chapter titled "The Law of Increasing Disorder," Juliana Boerio-Goates made an applicable observation: "A diver never dives *upward* from a swimming pool, just as scrambled eggs never spontaneously unscramble and a pet dog doesn't get younger. Our experience in everyday life shows us that nature tends to run in one direction."[668] And that direction is toward disorder.

The theory supposing that living things spontaneously changed from simple to complex seems contrary to the Second Law of Thermodynamics. Speaking of this conflict, Hugh Nibley shared this perspective:

> What many are pointing out today is that the mechanistic-evolutionary theory *reverses* both the direction of time and the order of nature. By the laws of thermodynamics, "left to itself, everything tends to become more and more disorderly, until the final and natural state of things is a completely random distribution of matter."
>
> "Selectivity... includes a tacit assumption... of positive action, of building up the improbable and more complex from the more probable, less complex and of actually increasing stability as complexity increases."...

---

668. Boerio-Goates. "Law of Increasing Disorder." In *Physical Science Foundations*, 2nd ed. 2006, p. 214.

… In the words of P. T. Matthews, "The sorting process— the creation of order out of chaos—*against* the natural flow of physical events is something which is essential to life."[669]

On another occasion, Nibley wrote:

When the biologist said that life was wildly improbable, a rare unreasonable event, who would have guessed how improbable it really was? "A human being," writes Matthews, "is at very best, an assembly of chemicals constructed and maintained in a state of fantastically complicated organization of quite unimaginable improbability." So improbable that you can't even imagine it. So "wildly improbable" that even to mention it is ridiculous. So we have no business being here. That is not the natural order of things.... So the physical scientists and the naturalists agree that if nature has anything to say about it, we wouldn't be here. This is the paradox of which Professor Wald of Harvard says, "The spontaneous generation of a living organism is impossible. . . ." The chances of our being here are not even to be thought of, yet here we are.... ... Nikolai Kozyrev, has been working for years on this question. He claims that the second law of thermodynamics is all right, but ... something works against it, something stronger. He says, "Some processes unobserved by mechanics and preventing the death of the world are at work everywhere, maintaining the variety of life."[670]

Science delves into the realm of the mortal or natural state of things. That state is one of disorder and decay. A new car can be purchased, and even if it is kept in a climate-controlled garage,

---

669. Nibley. *The Ancient State*. 1991, pp. 450, 453–454.
670. Nibley. *Temple and Cosmos*. 1992, pp. 4–6.

parts will decay. If left to natural processes, rust and corrosion ultimately claim it.

A realm often touted as evidence in support of speculative parts of evolution is genetic mutations. Wells suggested otherwise, indicating they

> are almost always harmful. Sure, a few are beneficial to the organisms that carry them in cases of resistance to antibiotics, pesticides or herbicides. Such cases, however involve only minor biochemical changes. I found absolutely no evidence that genetic mutations can produce beneficial changes in anatomy, of the sort needed by evolutionary theory. Nor did I find evidence that mutations (any more than selection) could produce new species.
>
> So by 1978 I had become convinced that the new-Darwinian mechanism of evolution was scientifically unsupported. Yet most biologists continued to promote and defend it, and liberal theologians continued to accommodate their views to it.[671]

Is there really any compelling evidence that one species evolved into another? Or is it just that fossilized remains of creatures with similar features are found, then strung together on the assumption that one is descended from another? Nibley wrote:

> The paleontologist... cannot observe processes but only results. He has no regular sequence of pictures before his eyes but only a few badly blurred snapshots of the earth over the last three million years. Studying these, the specialists try to tell us just what happened. Am I willing to stake my eternal salvation on their highly conflicting opinions? The little pictures are very few in number, very far apart, and very badly damaged. Every authority today emphasizes

---

671. Wells. "Common Ancestry on Trial." In *Darwin's Nemesis*. 2006, pp. 2–3 of Ch. 11.

that, more than ever before. In the place of connections between the specimens, we have only resemblances, and it is on them that we base our whole story—classification, taxonomy, biosystematics—it is all a question of endlessly debated definitions.[672]

Natural Selection

A problem with one of the main components of the theory of evolution, natural selection, was noted by James Strickling.

Most species seem to be capable of extreme variation in the structure and general appearance (morphology) of individual members. But in all of the years of observation in the field and experiment in the laboratory, not a single new species of animals has been seen to arise as a result of selection.... Countless mutations have been introduced into *Drosophilia* (fruit flies), but they never accumulate sufficiently to even lead in the direction of a new organism, let alone produce one.... Nowhere in the fossil record is there to be found an orderly grading of one species into another. It is generally claimed that the record is at fault, rather than the evolutionary concept.[673]

Berlinski similarly stated:

A detailed and continuous record of transition between *species* is missing, those neat sedimentary layers, as Gould noted time and again, never revealing precisely the phenomena that Darwin proposed to explain.... Robert Carroll observes quite correctly that "most of the fossil record does *not* support a strictly gradualistic account"

---

672. Nibley. "Before Adam." http://maxwellinstitute.byu.edu/publications/transcripts/?id=73, (last accessed 9/4/12). 2011, p. 5.
673. Strickling. "Natural Selection and Speciation." *Aeon*, Vol. 1, no. 3, 1988, pp. 28, 31.

of evolution.... ... Nothing can induce a chicken to lay a square egg or to persuade a pig to develop wheels mounted on ball bearings.[674]

Diversity

One fact of change seems to be diversity. Are any two individuals exactly alike? How many dogs were on Noah's ark? Maybe only two. How many breeds are there now? Hundreds. How did there get to be such diversity? Many varieties have been deliberately bred. To a degree, fast dogs can be bred with fast dogs to yield faster dogs. Big dogs bred with big dogs beget bigger—within certain limits—as the breeding of larger and larger dogs has not resulted in a horse (other than in the artistic renditions in some texts). Widtsoe described:

> It has been possible, within historic times, to domesticate many animals, often with real changes in bodily form, as various breeds of cattle, sheep, or dogs. Besides, isolated animals, as on the islands of the sea, have become unique forms, differing from those on connected continents.
> These facts, so claim the proponents of the theory of evolution, all point to the common origin, and an advancing existence, of all animal forms on earth. To many minds these observations, upon which in the main the theory of evolution rests, are sufficient proof of the correctness of the theory of evolution. It is indeed an easy way of explaining the endless variety of life.... Yet, at the best, the doctrine of the common origin of all life is only an inference of science. After these many years of searching, its truth has not been demonstrated.[675]

---

674. Berlinski. *The Devil's Delusion.* 2009, pp. 188–189.
675. Widtsoe. *Evidences and Reconciliations.* 1943, pp. 151–152.

In November 2004, the *National Geographic* published an issue with several articles positive toward evolution. The editor, Bill Allen, introduced the subject with a statement that may have relevance to the diversification of life forms after the Flood (although that was obviously not his intent): "Humans are not descended from apes. But then Charles Darwin never claimed we are.... What Darwin actually said was that the myriad species inhabiting Earth are a result of repeated branching from common ancestors—a process that came to be called 'evolution.'"[676] To a degree, Darwin's branching concept fits quite nicely with the scriptures.

If we all descended from Noah and his three sons, how did humans of one group get traits quite dissimilar from those of another? A clue seems to be found in Numbers 36:6–11: "Let them marry to whom they think best; only to the family of the tribe of their father shall they marry... for... the daughters of Zelophehad, were married unto their father's brothers' sons." There are a number of instances in the scriptures where people married close relatives, in this case, first cousins. Of course Adam's children didn't have much choice. Many of Noah's grandchildren would have married first cousins. Abraham, Isaac, and Jacob all married close relatives.

It is interesting that "royal" families throughout history tended to marry relatives to preserve the "royal blood." In Egypt, it was often siblings. An article by Zahi Hawass, describes how DNA studies have shown that King Tut's parents were brother and sister and that he had a congenital clubfoot. "Inbreeding may have caused the deformity."[677] Union with close relatives may

---

676. Allen. "Humans are not descended from apes." *National Geographic*, Nov. 2004, front matter.

677. Hawass. "King Tut's Family Secrets." *National Geographic*. Sep. 2010, p. 57.

have been a major contributor to the development of groups with peculiar characteristics.

In some states and countries, marrying relatives as close as first cousins is prohibited. Presumably, the laws were enacted for fear of dominant and recessive traits being accentuated by closely matched gene pools. Are such issues to be called evolution? Some suppose they are evidence of the overall theory. The answer seems to hinge on how broadly one defines the word "evolution."

The Zealous Atheistic Form of Evolution

It may be helpful to know some of the claims made by outspoken atheistic evolutionists:

> Lamarck, before he even came up with his explanation of the creation, was animated "by a severe... philosophical hostility, amounting to hatred, for the tradition of the Deluge and the Biblical creation story, indeed for everything which recalled the Christian theory of nature." And Darwin writes of himself in his twenties: "I had gradually come, by this time, to see that the Old Testament from its manifestly false history of the world... was no more to be trusted than the sacred books of the Hindoos [sic], or the beliefs of any barbarian.... This disbelief crept over me at a very slow rate, but was at last complete. The rate was so slow that I felt no distress, and have never since doubted for a single second that my conclusion was correct."[678]

Henry Morris called Julian Huxley's address at the Darwin Centennial Convocation in 1959 the "manifesto of the worldwide humanistic religion of evolution" and quoted some of Huxley's remarks:

---

678. Nibley. *Old Testament and Related Studies.* 1986, p. 23.

This is one of the first public occasions on which it has been frankly faced that all aspects of reality are subject to evolution, from atoms and stars to fish and flowers... to human societies and values—indeed, that all reality is a single process of evolution.

In 1859, Darwin opened the passage leading to a new psychosocial level, with a new pattern of ideological organization—an evolution-centered organization of thought and belief.... In the evolutionary pattern of thought there is no longer either need or room for the supernatural. The earth was not created, it evolved. So did all the animals and plants that inhabit it, including our human selves, mind and soul as well as brain and body. So did religion.... Finally, the evolutionary vision is enabling us to discern, however incompletely, the lineaments of the new religion that we can be sure will arise to serve the needs of the coming era.[679]

Another author who preached the atheistic view of evolution with evangelic fervor was mentioned by Salkeld:

Gavin de Beer, writing for the centenary exhibition at the British Natural History Museum, said "so soundly was the theory of evolution by natural selection grounded, that research does nothing but confirm the links in its chain of evidence, and the inferences to be drawn from them, with the same confidence as it accepts the affirmative demonstration of the movement of the earth round the sun and Newton's formulation of the laws of this movement. Science can now celebrate the centenary of the first general principle to be discovered applicable to the entire realm of living beings."

20 years later everything changed. Alvarez found a line of clay-like material containing a vast amount more

---

679. Morris, H. *A History of Modern Creationism*. 1984, pp. 71–72.

iridium than it should do. The iridium must have come from an extraterrestrial source. The interesting thing to me was: why were the paleontologists and evolutionary biologists so unwilling to accept this explanation that virtually the rest of science said made good sense. I came up with a few reasons…

a. Darwinism has never been well-defined: the original theory shifted around so often that it's become more of a religion than a scientific discipline and, as a result, as soon as any evidence came up that undermined it, it was like attacking a religion.…

b. Even the most ardent Darwinist realized you couldn't have any amount of adaptation to fit anyone to survive a global catastrophe; all you're left with is "survival of the survivors, if any," which says nothing of much value.

c. Extinction due to asteroid impact would by definition be a sudden geological event; in that case gradualism, a hallmark of Darwinism, would have to be modified.[680]

It seems those who write in favor of Darwin's theory are particularly poor in distinguishing fact from theory. And a great number of them are zealously trying to win converts to their position. Nibley remarked:

Students commonly assume that it was the gradual amassing of evidence that in time constrained such men to part company with the Bible. Exactly the opposite is the case: long before they had the evidence, they brought to their researches such an unshakable determination to discredit the book of Genesis that the discovery of the evidence was a foregone conclusion. It was Darwin's bosom friend and spokesman who blurted out the real

680. Salkeld. "Genesis and the Origin of Species." *C&C Review.* SIS, 2002:1, p. 11.

issue with characteristic bluntness: "Darwin himself avoided attacking the Bible, but for Huxley..."writes J. C. Greene, "the battle against the doctrine of inspiration... was the crucial engagement in the fight for evolution and for freedom of scientific inquiry." The battle was against revelation, and evolution was the weapon forged for the conflict. We must not be misled by that inevitable tag about "freedom of scientific enquiry." When a Tennessee high-school teacher was fired for teaching evolution in 1925, the whole civilized world was shocked and revolted at such barbaric restriction on freedom of thought; yet at the same time there was not an important college or even high school in the country that would hire a man who dared to preach against evolution. Freedom of thought indeed.[681]

A television program was shown in 2009 about the Scopes trial (the trial involving the same Tennessee high school teacher). It concluded with the phrase: "evolution became an undisputed scientific fact."[682] Why would competent TV journalists make such a dogmatic statement? Is it because the theory has become so popular? It certainly isn't because all aspects of evolutionary theory have been proven, or that no one disputes any parts of the theory, nor is it because the artistic lineage charts, so frequently put before our eyes, are fact.

A book titled *The Evolution-Creation Struggle* (Harvard University Press, 2005), was reviewed by Karen Armstrong:

> The clash between those who adhere to the scientific theory of evolution and those who believe that the biblical story of the six-day creation is literally true is a struggle between two religions. So concludes Michael Ruse...

---

681. Nibley. *Old Testament and Related Studies.* 1986, p. 24.
682. "Turning Points in History" aired Oct. 2, 2009 on KUEN DT Channel 9.1, Salt Lake City.

... He says, scientists have offered up an alternative vision of the nature of reality, and those among them who are most opposed to religion can proselytize with as much zeal as an evangelical Christian.

For Richard Dawkins, contemplation of the natural world through the eyes of science is a religious experience .... Yet Dawkins regards faith as one of the world's great evils, "comparable to the smallpox virus but harder to eradicate".[683]

One of the major points made in the DVD *Expelled: No Intelligence Allowed* is that there are only two choices for how life began on Earth: one is that life sprang into existence as a result of random chance (natural processes), and the other is: by some sort of planned intervention (intelligent design). The latter is neither allowed in the colleges nor in mainstream scientific literature. Therefore, students hear only one side of the argument.

The National Center for Science Education (NCSE) "provides information and advice as the premier institution dedicated to keeping evolution in the science classroom and creationism out."[684] Eugenie Scott, anthropologist and executive director of the NCSE was interviewed in *Expelled*. When asked if it was true that there were no peer-reviewed articles published that speak of intelligent design, she responded with a startling answer: "You are correct."[685] If her statement was accurate, the question arises: is it because no competent scientists have written articles referring to intelligent design? Or could it be because the peer review committees will not accept them since they express a view contrary to the dominantly popular position?

---

683. Armstrong. "Two Paths to the Same Old Truths." *NewScientist.* July 30, 2005, p. 42.
684. Scott. http://ncse.com/.
685. "Expelled: No Intelligence Allowed." Premise Media Corp. DVD. 2008, 49:04.

In another startling interview, biologist P. Z. Meyers, who runs a pro-Darwin, antireligion blog, said:

> Religion is an idea that gives some people comfort, and we don't want to take it away from them. It's like knitting, people like to knit.... We're not going to take away their churches. But what we have to do is get it to a place where religion is treated at the level it should be treated. That is, something fun that people get together and do on the weekend. And really doesn't affect their life as much as it has so far.
>
> Greater science literacy which is going to lead to the erosion of religion, and we'll get this positive feedback mechanism. Whereas religion slowly fades away, we get more and more science to replace it.[686]

When Dr. Peter Atkins, Professor of Chemistry at Oxford University, was interviewed by Stein he said: "Religion... is just fantasy basically. It's completely empty of any explanatory common sense, and it's evil as well."[687]

Richard Dawkins claimed: "Since the evidence for evolution is so absolutely, totally overwhelming, nobody who looks at it could possibly doubt it—if they were sane and not stupid." Later in the program, Dawkins said of his book *The God Delusion* (which has sold over a million copies), it "is my long-expected, long-worked-on full frontal attack on religion. To me, science... and religion... [are] about trying to explain existence. It's just that religion gets the wrong answer."[688] The climax to the Dawkins interview seemed to be when he declared: "when I discovered Darwinism, I realized there was this magnificently elegant... explanation. I didn't quite understand at the beginning; when I

---

686. Ibid., 1:02:06, 1:03:54.
687. Ibid., 1:03:21.
688. Ibid., 30:50, 54:38

did understand, then that finally killed off my remaining religious faith."[689]

Dr. Will Provine, Professor of the History of Biology at Cornell University, was another outspoken atheist interviewed by Stein. He spoke of his first evolution class and how after studying the text, he immediately gave up on deity. He said, "No God, no life after death,… no ultimate meaning in life, and no human free will, are all deeply connected to an evolutionary perspective. You're here today and gone tomorrow. And that's all there is to it."[690] What a discomforting thought!

In an article titled "How to Live with Evolution," Susan Bury suggested, "It's time we finally wring out the public debate over whether evolution occurred and gave rise to the living world. Evolution is real, and we are among its products. Let's get over it [the aversion to evolution], get with it, and get on with it."[691] Wait—does her advice make things clearer, or is she doing just what Widtsoe cautioned people against—failing to distinguish the facts from the hypothetical explanation of those facts? Why should she be so insistent on people accepting a theory? Will people live better lives for heeding her advice? Bury went on to say: "If we're taught anything in school, it should be evolution and its meaning in our lives."[692] What is its meaning in our lives? How does belief in that theory make the world a better place?

Nibley shared an extraordinary perspective of evolution as it relates to the meaning of life:

> The old Darwinian view is being puffed today for all it is worth in a half dozen prestigious TV documentaries in which we are treated to endless footage of creatures…

---

689. Ibid., 1:02:29.
690. Ibid., 58:03.
691. Bury. "How to Live with Evolution." *Skeptical Inquirer.* March/April 2001, p. 56.
692. Ibid.

soberly crunching, munching, swallowing, and ingesting other insects, fishes, birds, and mammals. This, we are told again and again, is the real process by which all things were created. Everything is lunching on everything else, all the time and that... is what makes us what we are; that is the key to progress. And note it well, all these creatures when they are not lunching are hunting for lunch—they all have to work for it: There is no free lunch in the world of nature, the real world. Lunch is the meaning of life, and everything lunches on something else.[693]

He went on to describe how evolutionary theory has spread so far as to affect economic thought:

Malthus had shown that there will never be enough lunch for everybody, and therefore people would have to fight for it; and Ricardo had shown by his Iron Law of Wages that those left behind and gobbled up in the struggle for lunch had no just cause for complaint. Darwin showed that this was an inexorable *law* of nature by which the race was actually *improved*.... In this... game of grabs, to share the lunch-prize would be futile, counter-productive, nay immoral. Since there is not enough to go around, whoever gets his fill must be taking it from others.[694]

Phillip Johnson expressed his view that scientists accepted evolution "before it was rigorously tested," and many have sought "to convince the public that naturalistic processes are sufficient to produce a human from a bacterium, and a bacterium from a mix of chemicals. Evolutionary science became the search for confirming evidence, and the explaining away of negative."[695] This, of course, is not quite the way the scientific method is intended.

---

693. Nibley. *Approaching Zion*. 1989, pp. 205–206.
694. Ibid., pp. 206–207.
695. Johnson, P. *Darwin on Trial*. 1991, p. 150.

"The two big questions today, Dobzhansky says, are (1) the mechanisms of evolution—the very question that Darwin was supposed to have answered for all time, and (2) 'the biological uniqueness of man,' which is the real Adam question. How do you define man?"[696] Is man really the offspring of an apelike creature who, in turn, was the offspring of a more ape-like creature, and so on? Or did man come from God—after his image? Do people really have spirits, or are all aspects of humans just evolved stuff?

Eugenie Scott wrote: "The United States stands out among developed countries in its low acceptance of one of the major organizing principles of science [evolution]." She continued: "because of its deep religious and historical roots, creationism will not go away any time soon."[697] Why is it that so many believers are reluctant to accept the whole evolutionary package? If there was no fall of Adam, would there be a need for the atonement? If man is just a product of chance, what are the ramifications? Is there really any meaning to life? What hope is there for a life after death and a judgment of real justice and mercy?

Evolution's Far-Reaching Influence

The theory of evolution has permeated society far beyond the scientific world. It pops up in unexpected places. Shockingly—but not surprisingly— a network news program aired an interview about the infidelity of a popular athlete. The author of a book titled *Decoding Love* expressed his opinion whether the athlete's marriage could be saved, then added: "Evolution has shaped men to be sexual opportunists."[698] Was he intimating that immoral behavior is just a product of evolution? If so, does evolutionary

---

696. Nibley. *Old Testament and Related Studies.* 1986, p. 59.

697. Scott. "Not (Just) in Kansas Anymore." *Science*, May 5, 2000, pp. 813–814.

698. Trees. "Is Tiger Woods' Marriage Over." *The Early Show*, CBS, December 16, 2009.

theory justify immorality? If so, what are the implications regarding sin, repentance, and forgiveness? Haven't physical desires been given to us for a reason? Aren't the teachings valid that we should "bridle our passions"? Is there any consequence for infidelity—besides the misery it causes the betrayed families? Berlinski noted that many now believe: "The idea that human behavior is 'the product of evolution'... is now more than a theory, it is a popular conviction."[699]

Examples given by Nibley demonstrate how the theory of evolution has influenced the study of ancient history: "As in so many other fields, the neat and easy rule of evolution, that greatest of time- and work-savers, explained everything."[700]

Also speaking of the broad acceptance of evolution, Salkeld shared a similar perspective:

> Popularisations had carried the case to millions in a persuasive manner. However, the fact that chemical evolution cannot be falsified means that its apparent plausibility can easily be exaggerated beyond its true status as speculation, and be regarded instead as knowledge....
> The substantial case questioning the plausibility of chemical evolution has been all but muted.[701]

In trying to reconcile certain aspects of evolution and religion, some suppose that evolution is the means God used in the creation process. However, Widtsoe cautioned:

> The doctrine of the common origin of life on earth is but a scientific theory, and should be viewed as such.... Honest thinkers will not attempt to confuse law and theory in the minds of laymen. The man, learned or unlearned, who

699. Berlinski. *The Devil's Delusion.* 2009, p. 166.
700. Nibley. *Since Cumorah.* 1967, p. 24.
701. Salkeld. "Intelligent Design?" *C&C Review.* SIS, 2009, p. 6.

declares the doctrine of the common origin of life on earth to be demonstrated beyond doubt, has yet to master the philosophy of science. The failure to differentiate between facts and inferences is the most grievous and the most common sin of scientists.[702]

If Widtsoe's statement is true that the failure to adequately distinguish facts and inferences is "the most grievous and the most common sin of scientists," vast improvement is needed.

According to C. D. Darlington, Charles Darwin's *Origin of Species* purported that "all living things were derived...from common origins many millions of years ago. Hence, to the dismay of serious Christians, the Biblical story of Creation seemed in danger of falling to the ground."[703] Nibley observed:

> Upstairs in the old Education Building...there stood for many years a tall, thin, glass showcase. On the top shelf was a human skull; below it was the cast of a Cro-Magnon skull; then Neanderthal; and so on until we got to a skull of a gorilla. Here before our very eyes was an unimpeachable sermon on how man came to be. But things have changed now. ". . . The numerous fossils now known offer alternative interpretations." Not so compellingly simple as before, but how many alternative interpretations? "The number of possible hypotheses are both theoretically and practically unlimited."[704]

Stephen Gould of Harvard wrote: "The family trees which adorn our text books are based on inference, however reasonable,

702. Widtsoe. *Evidences and Reconciliations.* 1943, p. 153.
703. Darlington. "The Origin of Darwinism." *Scientific American,* May, 1959, p. 60.
704. Nibley: *Old Testament and Related Studies.* 1986, p. 55.

not the evidence of fossils."[705] And, from Nibley: "In biology, thanks to Darwin, science 'gives the false impression that we know much more about the origin of life than we actually do.'"[706]

Natural Selection and Survival of the Fittest

The chief cornerstone of evolutionary theory is that of natural selection. "The hypothesis of natural selection has... gradually acquired a not altogether healthy degree of prestige, which is hard to break down. It has become, if only by reiteration, so firmly ensconced as part of our general outlook on nature that it needs real determination to cast doubt on it. Biologists are conditioned to it from their earliest education."[707]

Darlington published an article noting, "two shafts of criticism struck Darwin more directly than the outside world was allowed to know."[708] They involved natural selection. Richard de Mille was quoted: "Darwin himself was plenty worried about it [natural selection]. *How, he wondered, could something as complicated as the human eye evolve by tiny adaptive steps, when it couldn't serve any adaptive purpose until it was fully evolved?*"[709] (emphasis added)

The fossil record shows that there were many more life forms in the past than are now living on Earth—apparently due to massive extinction events. What does that say about natural selection? "Karl Popper would deny this so-called law of nature even the title to a scientific theory: '. . . It is far from clear what

705. Petersen. *Unlocking the Mysteries of Creation.* 1986, p. 91.
706. Nibley. *The Ancient State.* 1991, p. 423.
707. Ibid., p. 399.
708. Darlington. "The Origin of Darwinism." *Scientific American,* May, 1959, p. 60.
709. Ellenberger. "How to Defuse a Feud." *Kronos,* Vol. VII, no. 4, 1982, p. 37.

we should consider a possible refutation of the theory of natural selection."[710]

The tenet of survival of the fittest, in a real sense, is merely circular reasoning. Macbeth described ideas of the philosopher R. H. Brady:

> Despite varying twists of language, natural selection meant simply that the fittest species had survived, but the theory never specified how fitness was to be determined. The traditional answer to this embarrassing question was that fitness meant leaving the most offspring. But this was only a roundabout way of saying "by surviving". It produced a circle: the surviving species survived because they were the fittest, and they were adjudged to be the fittest because they had survived. There was no independent criterion of fitness, so the term meant only that those who survived had survived. This statement was correct, but uninformative; it explained nothing and was therefore useless.[711]

Tom Bethell also addressed the issue of survival of the fittest using similar logic:

> Darwin proposed no criterion of fitness other than that of survival itself. Nor did any of Darwin's followers in the years and decades since.... If this is true, as I have no doubt that it is, it follows that "the survival of the fittest" is not a testable theory, but a tautology. Which ones survive? The fittest. Who are they? Those that survive... ... Every week ecologists perform experiments testing hypotheses about the usefulness of various animal traits, and frequently such hypotheses are not confirmed. In no instance, however, do they then make the claim that Darwin's theory has been overthrown. And in fact no experimental observation will

710. Nibley. *The Ancient State.* 1991, p. 449.
711. Macbeth. "How to Defuse a Feud." *Kronos,* Vol. VII, no. 4, 1982, p. 2.

ever lead to such a claim, precisely because Darwin's theory is immune—logically immune—to falsification.

There is one final point. If it is true that the theory of natural selection is so vacuous that no experiment can in principle either verify or falsify it, then how has it managed to survive as satisfactorily as it has for over 120 years? I think the reason why biologists cling to it so tenaciously is that, if natural selection were swept away, then the general theory of evolution itself—the theory that evolution has occurred—would stand perilously exposed to doubt. (It is of course nonsense to say, as some ardent evolutionists do, that the general theory of evolution is now a "fact". . . .)[712]

Spontaneous Generation

What is spontaneous generation? Doesn't "spontaneous" still mean "from an unknown cause"? If so, did life form just by chance, or might there be a yet-to-be-identified cause behind a "spontaneous" phenomenon? How can such a theory be tested? A famous experiment was performed in 1952 by Stanley L. Miller and Harold C. Urey. They combined molecules of elements believed to simulate primordial conditions through which they ran an electric current. After a week, they "observed that as much as 10–15% of the carbon was now in the form of organic compounds.[713] "Two percent of the carbon had formed some of the amino acids which are used to make proteins."[714] Madeleine Nash described the experiment, then mentioned:

---

712. Bethell. "Darwin's Unfalsifiable Theory." *Kronos*, Vol. VII, no. 4, 1982, pp. 33–36.

713. Organic: sometimes the word is used to mean living, or components of living things. But in chemistry, and as used here, it simply signifies that it is to do with carbon compounds.

714. http://www.chem.duke.edu/~jds/cruise_chem/Exobiology/miller. html. (last accessed 9/29/12)

Now this textbook picture of how life originated,... is under serious attack.... Still unanswered is the riddle of how these molecules came to reproduce.... ... The molecule in Joyce's lab, after all, is not as sophisticated as a virus and is still many orders of magnitude less complex than a bacterium.[715]

Salkeld discussed "experiments which attempted to simulate" the hypothesized process by which life is thought to have originated on Earth from "natural processes alone." He reiterated information from a book by Thaxton, Bradley, and Olson whom he refers to as "TBO." He mentioned that they acknowledged that experiments had produced "19 of the 20 amino acids found in proteins" and "essential sugars, such as glucose."

On the basis of these experiments, many scientists had become convinced that the primitive ocean was full of organic compounds. However, TBO did not share such views. They wrote "In contrast to the conclusion usually drawn from these experiments, a credible alternative scenario can be presented which argues strongly against chemical evolution".... ... "It is becoming clear that however life began on earth, the usually conceived notion that life emerged from an oceanic soup of organic chemicals is a most implausible hypothesis. We may therefore with fairness call this scenario the 'myth of the prebiotic soup'"....

TBO contrasted the considerable success in synthesizing amino acids in simulation experiments and the consistent failure to synthesize protein and DNA.... Amino acids are quite simple compared to proteins and there would be a reasonable expectation of getting some yield of amino acids, even by chemical reactions that occur in rather random fashion. The same approach would

715. Nash. "How Did Life Begin?" *Time*, Oct. 11, 1993, pp. 68–74.

obviously be far less successful in producing complex protein and DNA molecules... ... A minimum of 20–40 proteins as well as DNA and RNA are required to make even a simple replicating system....

Finally, TBO considered ideas about proto-cells—the supposed link between the appearance of macromolecules and the appearance of the first living cells... In all cases the proto-cell systems... provided no genuine steps to bridge the gap between living and non-living... In summary, TBO considered that the assessment of David Green and Robert Goldberger... "was still appropriate: the macromolecule-to-cell transition is a jump of fantastic dimensions, which lies beyond the range of testable hypotheses. In this area, all is conjecture."[716]

M. G. Rutten asserted: "These large organic molecules cannot at present exist on their own... they cannot be formed regularly, or even rarely, in natural inorganic chemistry and even if this would be possible, they are liable to immediate destruction." He also commented: "I want to warn against... the basic assumption... that what is more simple... is more primitive and consequently older in the history of life. This assumption is entirely unjustified."[717]

Scientists in Darwin's day did not understand the incredible complexity of living cells. They likely presumed that cells were very simple, and had not heard of such things as DNA molecules. Francis Collins, a former atheist, was one of the team of scientists studying DNA and was privileged to announce a breakthrough:

The human genome consists of all the DNA of our species, the hereditary code of life. This newly revealed text was 3 billion letters long, and written in a strange

716. Salkeld. "Intelligent Design?" *C&C Review.* SIS, 2009, pp. 3–5.
717. Nibley. *The Ancient State.* 1991, pp. 449–450.

and cryptographic four-letter code. Such is the amazing complexity of the information carried within each cell of the human body.... ... It's a happy day for the world. It is humbling for me, and awe-inspiring, to realize that we have caught the first glimpse of our own instruction book, previously known only to God.... So perhaps the "battle" between science and religion is not as polarized as it seems? Unfortunately, the evidence of potential harmony is often overshadowed by the high-decibel pronouncements of those who occupy the poles of the debate.[718]

How could the incredibly intricate complexity of DNA form spontaneously? Michael J. Behe wrote: "Science has made enormous progress in understanding how the chemistry of life works, but the elegance and complexity of biological systems at the molecular level have paralyzed science's attempt to explain their origins. There has been virtually no attempt to account for the origin of specific, complex biomolecular systems, much less any progress."[719]

Intelligent Design

The expression "intelligent design" is used by many to suggest that life didn't just spring up by random chance.

Harlow Shapley's escape clause: Life occurs automatically wherever the conditions are right. Therefore there is no need for explaining the origin of life in terms of the miraculous or the supernatural. "Where conditions are right, there is chemical evidence that essential complex materials which appear spontaneously leave no reason whatever to invoke the miraculous." Here the unknown-x

718. Collins. *The Language of God.* 2006, pp. 1, 3, 4.
719. Behe. *Darwin's Black Box.* 1996, p. x.

"spontaneous" takes the place of unknown-x "miraculous." What is the difference?—purely… attitude.[720]

Reid Bankhead wrote: "The whole squabble about evolution centers upon two questions. Did life on earth come by chance or by divine will? If by divine will, is God limited to one process? These questions are as old as history."[721]

Creation

A harsh judgment against Creation was voiced by Darlington, who suggested that the theory of evolution has "released thinking men from the spell of a superstition, one of the most overpowering that has ever enslaved mankind."[722] Are believers to abandon the scriptures and label the account of Creation "superstition" because of an exceedingly popular theory? And are people to be excluded from the category of "thinking men" if they don't? Is belief in Creation really a form of enslavement?

Believers in Creation are at a distinct disadvantage in discussions with evolutionists because so little is known about the creation process. In the Bible, the Creation is described in 55 verses (Genesis, chapters 1 and 2), while variations of the evolutionary doctrine are discussed on literally millions of pages.[723] What can be said of the details of how Creation took place? Not much.

Contributing to the challenge of reconciling evolution and Creation is the difficulty of trying to understand the scriptural

---

720. Nibley. *The Ancient State*. 1991, p. 398.
721. Bankhead. *Fall of Adam, Atonement of Christ, and Organic Evolution.* (undated), p. 10.
722. Darlington. "The Origin of Darwinism." *Scientific American,* May, 1959, p. 60.
723. On September 18, 2011 an Internet Google search on "evolution" showed 420 million results.

verses relating to the subject. For instance, the first verse of the Bible: "In the beginning God created the heaven and the earth." Was it, as some believe, the beginning of everything? If not, the beginning of what? If there was no universe before this beginning, what was there? What role did God play? Was He the God of nothing?

The likely assumption for many is that Genesis 1:1 is referring to the beginning of this Earth as we know it. Or is it? When it was created, we are told, it was in a different state than it is now. What was the paradisiacal state like—from a scientific perspective? Wasn't it substantially different than the terrestrial state we are now living in? Nibley spoke of the Creation as "taking place as it did at a time and place and in a manner that we cannot even imagine. Then comes the garden of Eden—a paradise and another world beyond our ken [knowledge]."[724]

When the earth was formed, many believe, it was formed from "unorganized" matter. That matter consisted of various chemical elements. On the third day, an abundance of life was brought forth. Much of the carbon available at the surface of the earth was incorporated into those abundant life forms. At the Fall of Adam, according to the Bible, death was introduced. Was it also introduced into the plant and animal kingdoms? What were conditions like, and what are the implications? Could a distinct physical change have been initiated when Adam and Eve fell? Again, there are more questions than answers.

To many people of religion, "creation" literally means to make something out of nothing. Nibley found another view of the subject from the ancients: "Justin Martyr, the earliest Christian apologist... emphatically says, in the *Apology*, the early Christians did not believe in Creation out of nothing, but believed that when God created the world, He organized matter."[725]

---

724. Nibley. *Old Testament and Related Studies*. 1986, p. 33.
725. Ibid., p. 124.

At a new creation there is a reshuffling of elements, like the rearranging of notes in the musical scale to make a new composition; it is even suggested, as we have noted, that old worlds may be dismantled to supply stuff for making of newer and better ones.

Beginning with the very old Egyptian idea, recently examined by E. A. E. Reymond, that the creation of the world was really a re-creation by "transforming substances" that had already been used in the creation of other worlds, the Jewish and Christian apocryphal writers envisage a process by which the stuff of worlds is alternately organized into new stars and planets and when these have served their time, scrapped, decontaminated, and reused in yet more new worlds.... The Creation is compared to the smashing of inferior vessels to use their substance for better ones... or the melting down of scrap-metal for reuse.[726]

In whichever manner the elements were gathered, the process was a spectacle of grand proportions. Pictures can be imagined of rocks slamming together and asteroids crashing into what had formed so far, and as the globe grew, conglomerates of various materials came together. At some point, Roche's limit would have come into play, and smaller bodies would have been broken apart and incorporated into larger ones. There is no doubt that such slamming and crashing would cause immense heat due to frictional and compressional energies. This seems consistent with the theory that when first formed, the earth was in a molten state. Remember that according to Genesis 1:9, it wasn't until the third "day" of Creation that the "dry land" appeared. A curious reference is found in an ancient text called the Pseudo-Philo:

Zenez recalls to his hearers' minds the state of things at the creation of the earth; he sees "flames of fire that did

---

726. Nibley. *On the Timely and the Timeless.* 1978, pp. 57, 76 (note 79).

not consume and fountains bursting forth from their slumbers when there was as yet no foundations for men to live on." When a foundation at last appears between the upper and lower worlds, a voice tells Zenez, "These are the foundations prepared for men to inhabit for seven thousand years to come."[727]

In recent years, astronomers have proposed that the seeds of life on Earth may have come from comets, meteors, or asteroids:

> Now released for serious discussion by recent discoveries, is that human life may have been transplanted directly from some other planet. Speculating on the subject, we have... Carl Sagan; Leslie E. Orgel of the Salk Institute; Francis H. C. Crick, a Nobel laureate; and others. One eminent scientist, Albert Rosenfeld, confesses, "I'm somehow not surprised at the idea that someone out there put us here. And if such a magical, mysterious, and powerful intelligence exists that is utterly beyond human imagining, can you give me a good reason why I shouldn't call it God?"[728]

In William Lee Stokes' book *The Creation Scriptures* he presented some novel interpretations. One was particularly impressive:

> The time seems right to reassess the evidences for the truth of the creation scriptures. And I must take the position that they are true. By this I mean they are the authentic and authoritative message of God and when understood properly, they do not contradict any fact or facts that have been or ever will be discovered by man.... Certainly, the thing to do if one theory proves fruitless is to try another; this is the scientific method. The apostle Paul said it well:

---

727. Nibley. *Since Cumorah.* 1967, p. 325.
728. Nibley. *Old Testament and Related Studies.* 1986, p. 82.

"Prove all things; hold fast to that which is good." (1 Thessalonians 5:21)[729]

How Long Is a Day?

Of course a day on Earth is twenty-four hours, the time it takes for the earth to rotate on its axis. Was it always that long? Certainly not—at least not during the formation process. Can it be determined when Earth's rotation reached its current rate? Innumerable assumptions can be made, but precise knowledge is beyond our reach.

What is meant by the "days" of Creation? Many religious people contend that each day of Creation was also twenty-four-hours. Is this interpretation correct? One line of reasoning to the contrary lies in the fact that according to Genesis, although God said, "Let there be Light" on the first day of Creation, it wasn't until the fourth day that He said:

> Let there be lights in the firmament of the heaven to divide the day from the night: and let them be for signs, and for seasons, and for days, and for years...
>
> And God made two great lights; the greater light to rule the day, and the lesser light to rule the night: he made the stars also.
>
> And God set them in the firmament of the heaven to give light upon the earth,
>
> And to rule over the day and over the night, and to divide the light from the darkness: and God saw that it was good.
>
> And the evening and the morning were the fourth day. (Genesis 1:14–29)

So, if the sun and moon were not "in the firmament" for "days and for years" until the fourth "day," by what measure was a

---

729. Stokes. *The Creation Scriptures*. Salt Lake City. 1979, pp. 34–35.

"day" reckoned prior to that time? What was the source of light? Further, it wasn't until the sixth "day" that the Lord told Adam: "But of the tree of the knowledge of good and evil, thou shalt not eat of it: for in the day that thou eatest thereof thou shalt surely die" (Gen. 2:17). Since Adam lived 930 years (according to Genesis 5:5), the "day" reckoned in the verse above must have been a period of at least that long.

The Apostle Peter may have given an important clue: "But, beloved, be not ignorant of this one thing, that one day is with the Lord as a thousand years, and a thousand years as one day" (2 Peter 3:8). It isn't clear just what Peter meant, but it may suggest that the day of the Lord's reckoning has something to do with a thousand Earth years.

Jubilees may provide some additional insight:

> At the end of the nineteenth jubilee in the seventh week, in the sixth year, Adam died. And all of his children buried him in the land of his creation.... And he lacked seventy years from one thousand years, for a thousand years are like one day in the testimony of heaven and therefore it was written concerning the tree of knowledge, "In the day you eat from it you will die." Therefore he did not complete the years of this day because he died in it.
>
> Jubilees 4:29-30[730]

Since the ancients seem to have used what has been translated as "forty" to mean "many," might they also have used "one thousand" to mean something like "very many"? Gesenius indicated that a thousand is often used as "a round number."[731] In Nibley's words: "Until Adam underwent that fatal change of habitat, body chemistry, diet, and psyche that went with the Fall, nothing is to be measured in our years.... Until then, time

---

730. In *Old Testament Pseudepigrapha*, Vol. 2. 1985, pp. 63–64.
731. Gesenius. *Hebrew and Chaldee Lexicon*. 1857, reprint 1991, p. 54.

is measured from their point of view, not ours. As far as we are concerned, it can be any time."[732]

What is time to the Lord anyway? Whatever turns out to be the reality, for now, it appears that the "days" of Creation were not the same twenty-four hour periods so precisely measured with modern technology, but they might very well have been at least a thousand years long.

Conclusion

The task of reconciling evolution and Creation is very challenging—if only from a standpoint of word meanings. When believers in Creation hear or see references to evolutionary concepts, we must keep in mind that the word has a very broad usage. The theory encompasses facts as well as inferences, assumptions, and conjectures. Writers are notoriously poor at clearly distinguishing what is what. Even though there seems to be no practical way to get clear distinctions in word usage to be adopted generally, at least those serious about reconciling the conflicts can keep the differences in mind.

Widtsoe cautioned: "The noisy babble about evolution, often disgraceful to both sides, since Darwin wrote the *Origin of Species*, has been confined almost wholly to speculations or guesses concerning the cause, methods and consequences of the law of evolution [change]. The law itself has not been challenged."[733]

One aspect of evolution is definitely unacceptable according to Bankhead: "Any theory that leaves out God as a personal, purposeful Being, and accepts chance as a first cause, cannot be accepted."[734]

732. Nibley. "Before Adam." http://maxwellinstitute.byu.edu/publications/transcripts/?id=73, (last accessed 9/4/12). 2011, p. 17.

733. Widtsoe. *Evidences and Reconciliations*, 1943, p. 150.

734. Bankhead. *The Fall of Adam, The Atonement of Christ, and Organic Evolution.* (undated), p. 10.

If aspects of Darwinian evolution really aren't correct, why are they taught as part of the package of this presently dominant theory? Kenneth Bock may have identified at least part of the answer: "Evolution was found wanting, but there was nothing to take its place, so 'this theoretical bankruptcy has forced us back into the evolutionist fold in spite of ourselves.'"[735]

Wells claimed that the most convincing evidence he had been given in support of evolution turned out to be merely someone's faulty portrayal of embryos:

> I had been shown drawings of vertebrate embryos showing that they look almost identical in their early stages. The common ancestry of humans and fish was supposedly obvious in the striking resemblance between their embryos. As a graduate student in developmental biology, however, I learned that the actual embryos didn't look like the drawings in the textbooks. What Charles Darwin had considered "by far the strongest class of facts" in favor of his theory turned out not to be facts at all.[736]

A clear distinction should be made between the facts and theories associated with evolution. It is a fact that things tend to change over time, and that diversity occurs in new generations. However, the supposed spontaneous changes—without God's influence—from chemicals to living things and from simple to complex have not been demonstrated. On the contrary, it appears that in mortality, unless there is intelligent intervention, things go in the opposite direction—from order to disorder.

Macbeth described a problem in reconciling evolution and Creation:

---

735. Nibley. *The Ancient State*. 1991, p. 427.
736. Wells. "Common Ancestry on Trial." In *Darwin's Nemesis*. 2006, p. 5 of Chapter 11.

This country has long been plagued by an acrimonious controversy between two large segments of the population. Evolution, if it is taught at all in high schools and colleges, is apt to be taught on the basis of textbooks that portray evolution and natural selection as demonstrable scientific facts. The creationists... object to this situation, contending that equal time or balanced treatment should be given to their view that everything was created by divine powers. The evolutionists... reply that creationism is religious rather than scientific, hence should not be taught in public schools or in science courses. Unfortunately, at the same time they usually imply that creationism is nonsense and that its advocates are dim of wit.... The creationists freely admit that they are relying on revelation and that their view requires an act of faith. The evolutionists ought to admit that they are relying largely on speculations and that speculations should not be taught as hard science.[737]

I certainly don't want nonbelievers teaching my children about Creation, nor do I like them teaching theories as though fact—and particularly in such a way as to discredit the Bible. I would appreciate it if the purveyors of scientific information would clearly distinguish fact from theory, and observational data from the inferences drawn therefrom.

Nibley wrote:

Must modern man be an improvement on him [Adam]? Such is that absurd doctrine of cultural evolution with which the schools have been saddled for a century....
... "Gradually" and "step by step," repeated incessantly, are aimed at covering an ignorance that is both vast and surprising.... Are we superior to the ancients?... Which takes us back to the issue with which the Adam question

---

737. Macbeth. "How to Defuse a Feud." *Kronos,* Vol. VII, no. 4, 1982, pp. 1–2.

began and which has always been the central issue of human paleontology: a matter of definitions. They may seem trivial, secondary, naïve—but the experts have never been able to get away from it. Evolution and natural selection were never defined to Darwin's satisfaction. Today all the specialists are trying to agree on a clear definition for man: when is a *homo* a *homo*?

"Considerable academic debate surrounds the date for the appearance of modern man," Washburn tells us. "By 35,000 years ago, however, the hunting populations of western Europe were biologically indistinguishable from modern man." Yet he also tells us that "man began when populations of apes, about a million years ago, started the bipedal, tool-using way of life." In the same volume of essays, H. de Lumley reports on the 350,000-year-old village of Terra Amata... R. G. Klein... goes on to describe one of some 100 Pleistocene sites in the Ukraine between 80,000 and 75,000 years old.... Which is it to be, 2 million years, 1 million years, half a million years, 50,000 years, or 35,000 years?[738]

Many believers have tried to reconcile this controversy in their minds by supposing that God must have used evolution in the creation process. Surely He did use some of what falls under the broadly defined umbrella of "evolution." But certainly, He did not just leave it all to random chance. Didn't God direct the process, and somehow set it in motion? The details won't be known until He reveals them, but consider:

1. The theory of evolution is not beyond reproach. It is an exceedingly popular framework on which vast amounts of data are organized, but it does not answer all the questions.

738. Nibley. "Before Adam." http://maxwellinstitute.byu.edu/publications/transcripts/?id=73. 2011, (last accessed 9/4/12) pp. 22–23, 9–10.

2. It is not a theory conducive to proof or disproof.
3. Several scriptures and messages from inspired religious leaders suggest incompatibilities between certain aspects of evolution and the plan of salvation.
4. Many "believers" tend to discount the scriptures in favor of theory.
5. And perhaps the most serious problem: many attribute their loss of faith in God to evolution.

If the extinction of the dinosaurs (as well as numerous other creatures) really took place 65 million years ago as is commonly taught, why haven't some of the extinct life forms re-evolved or new species formed? Isn't sixty-five million years sufficient time?

The information summarized in this book suggests that there are abundant problems with some aspects of the theory of evolution—at least the way it is commonly taught. Once the details are revealed, evolution and Creation will cease to be a conflict. Until then, we are left with a great deal of uncertainty.

11

Astronomy and Cosmological Curiosities

Mathematics may be compared to a mill of exquisite workmanship, which grinds you stuff of any degree of fineness; but, nevertheless, what you get out depends on what you put in; and as the grandest mill in the world will not extract wheat-flour from peascods, so pages of formulae will not get a definite result out of loose data.

— T. H. Huxley (1869)

Astronomy: A Glimpse into the Past

On a clear night, away from city lights, it is amazing to gaze at the night sky and realize that the stars are not seen as they are now, but as they once were. Objects viewed outside our solar system are so far away that even at the speed of light (about 670 million miles per hour) it takes years for the light to travel to Earth. When we "look at" the North Star, we are seeing light that left that star about three hundred years ago. It probably still appears the same (since most stars don't change much in three hundred years), but maybe not. Suppose the North Star exploded today—observers on Earth wouldn't know about it for three hundred years.

Some objects of interest are:

Name	Est. Distance From Earth	Time its light takes to travel to Earth
Alpha Centauri (the star closest to our Solar System)	4.3 ly	4.3 years
Sirius (brightest star seen from Earth)	8 ly	8 years
Altair	16 ly	16 years
Vega	26 ly	26 years
Arcturus	40 ly	40 years
Antares	520 ly	520 years
Deneb	1,600 ly1,	600 years
Andromeda Galaxy	2.5 million ly	2.5 million years

The moon is close enough (at about two hundred fifty thousand miles) that it only takes a little over a second for light to travel between it and Earth. It takes about eight minutes for light to travel from the Sun to Earth, and about thirty-five to fifty minutes from Jupiter, depending on where it and Earth are in their respective orbits.

How are such vast distances as those between stars and galaxies measured? They aren't. They are estimated. The techniques invented by scientists are quite ingenious; nevertheless, the greater the actual distances, the less sure are their estimates.

How Much of Astronomy Is Fact and How Much Is Theory?

John Pratt wrote about one difficulty with astronomy: "The problem is not that scientists try to explain the past and the future. After all, the objective of the scientific method is to be able to predict the outcome of future experiments. The problem occurs when (a) science cannot perform the experiment to predict the future and (b) it then declares with absolute certainty just what the past and future are, even those it has no solid basis of experiments to do so."[739]

The Star of Bethlehem

Ancient people considered conjunctions of planets[740] to be events of major significance. Pratt noted a conjunction at about the time of Jesus's birth:

> When astronomers have searched the... skies, aided by computers which can calculate planetary positions for any date, they have found a conjunction of Jupiter and Saturn which looked like a promising possibility. Actually, the astronomer Johannes Kepler suggested that possibility, coupled with a "nova" or exploding star, centuries before computers were available. That suggestion has been the traditional story since Kepler, although it has also been noted that there was a comet in 5 B.C. which might better fulfill the description that "the star, which they saw in the east, went before them, till it came and stood over where the young child was. (Matthew 2:9)"[741]

Thus, the signs of Jesus's birth may have included a conjunction, a nova, and a comet. Pratt pointed out that it was not likely that the star hovered over Bethlehem as is sometimes portrayed in nativity artwork, but the combination of the three within a

---

739. Pratt. "Has Satan Hijacked Science?" *Meridian Magazine.* 16 Nov 2005, p. 6.

740. A conjunction occurs when two or more planets appear to be close to one another from Earth's perspective.

741. Pratt. *Divine Calendars.* 2002, pp. 100–101.

particular constellation could have been a sign to them fulfilling prophesy.[742]

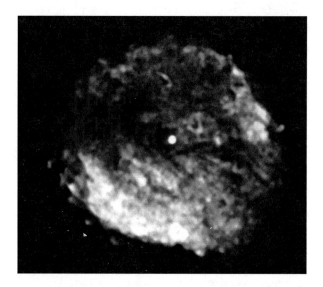

Figure 11.1. X-ray image of RCW 103,[743] the remnants of a supernova that scientists believe was visible from Earth about two thousand years ago.

Have scientists discovered remnants of "the star of Bethlehem"? Figure 11.1 was described: "A new X-ray image shows the 2,000 year-old-remnant of such a cosmic explosion, known as RCW 103, which occurred about 10,000 light years from Earth."[744] Or more accurately stated: It is estimated to have exploded about 12,000 years ago, and since it was about 10,000 light years away, it would have been visible from Earth about 2,000 years ago.

It is impressive to think that this object (now only detectable from Earth with very sophisticated equipment) could be what

742. John P. Pratt (personal communication).
743. Courtesy of NASA/CXC/Penn State/G. Garmire et al. http://chandra.harvard.edu/photo/2007/rcw103/, (last accessed 9/4/12).
744. ibid.

is left of the "new star" which was visible at the time of Jesus's birth. Had it been in the constellation Coma it might be a more likely candidate. (The ancient version of Coma was described by Joseph Seiss as representing "a young woman whose Persian name denotes a pure virgin, sitting on a throne, nourishing an infant boy... having a Hebrew name... Ihesu... which in Greek is called Christ.")[745]

Paul Gorenstein and Wallace Tucker described exploding stars and suggested:

> A sizable number of supernova remnants should always be present in our galaxy At least two dozen such remnants have now been identified.... The supernova of 1572...was immediately sighted by Tycho Brahe. He wrote, "the nova was brighter than any other fixed star. It was even brighter than Jupiter.... It maintained approximately its luminosity for almost the whole of November. On a clear day it could be seen... even at noon."[746]

Why don't the Gospels of Mark, Luke, or John mention the star? Matthew's account of the words of the wise men, or "men from the east," who came to see the king of the Jews includes: "Where is he that is born king of the Jews? for we have seen his star in the east, and are come to worship him" (Matthew 2:2). What about that star caused them to call it "his star," and why did they consider him important enough that they wanted to "worship him" as a king in a different nation?

Pratt proposed that the prophecies associated with the constellations were still had among them, but had been lost to the Jews. Many of the people in the land of Jerusalem may not have even noticed the "new star" much less recognized its significance.

---

745. Seiss. *The Gospel in the Stars.* (1882.) Republished, 1972, pp. 28–29.

746. Gorenstein and Tucker. "Supernova Remnants." *Scientific American*, July, 1971, p. 74.

In modern times, relatively few people would pay attention to a "new star," and fewer still would associate it with a particular constellation unless it was well-known like the Big Dipper. Only those familiar with the constellations and the motions of the planets would be aware unless it was exceedingly bright, or a news report of the phenomena caught their attention.

The Ancient Zodiac: A Mnemonic (Memory Assist)

Greek myths are closely connected to the constellations. The Greeks apparently received them from the much older Egyptian versions, and, in the Book of Abraham (as well as other sources), the tale is told that seems to reveal where the Egyptians got at least some of their astronomy:

> I, Abraham...
>
> ... saw the stars, that they were very great, and that one of them was nearest to the throne of God.... And he said unto me... behold I will show you all these. And... I saw those things which his hands had made, which were many; and they multiplied before mine eyes, and I could not see the end thereof.... And the Lord said unto me: Abraham, I show these things unto thee before ye go into Egypt that ye may declare all these words. (Abraham 3:1, 2, 12, 15)

Josephus also mentioned that Abraham "delivered to them [the Egyptians] the science of astronomy."[747] Thus, it appears that Abraham taught the Egyptians astronomy, and perhaps the constellations and even the early prophetic versions of their "myths."

John Pratt has given presentations about how the constellations and their associated stories were originally given as memory devices—to help the ancients remember the gospel, prophecies of Christ and his mission. Being one who was introduced to the

---

747. Josephus, p. 33

constellations at a very young age by my sister Miriam, I was fascinated—indeed awestruck—by what Pratt shared! He spoke of the writings of Joseph Seiss who lived 1823–1904. What Seiss published provides an exceptional perspective of the night sky.

Seiss observed that certain skeptics had found ancient traditions that had common elements with the Christian gospel. He reported that these skeptics used their research in a manner "to throw contempt on Christianity as a mere accommodation of certain old mythic ideas common to all primitive peoples." Seiss, however, noted that their research could also be used in support of a conclusion opposite to what they intended:

> These men adduced a large amount of traditional and astronomic lore, proving the great antiquity of the constellations and showing a striking correspondence between them and the subsequent scriptural story of Christ and salvation.... But though the[ir] argument ... is false and worthless, it does not follow that the materials collected to build it are the same... and the gathering of them was a valuable contribution to a better cause. The showings made of the close likeness between the old constellations and the Gospel are well founded.... But instead of proving Christianity a mere revival of old mythologies, they give powerful impulse toward the conclusion that the constellations and their associated myths and traditions are themselves, in their original, from the very same prophetic Spirit whence the Sacred Scriptures have come, and that they are of a piece with the biblical records in the system of God's universal enunciations of the Christ.[748]

Seiss discussed the concept taught in Genesis 1:14 that God gave "lights in the firmament of the heaven" not only "to divide the day from the night" but also "for signs, and for seasons." He

---

748. Seiss. *The Gospel in the Stars.* 1972, p. 6.

also pointed out that through the centuries stories associated with the constellations had been corrupted:

> For ages this whole field has been almost entirely left to a superstitious and idolatrous astrology, which has befouled a noble and divine science.... And when I look at the deep and almost universal hold which a spurious and wicked treatment of this field has so long had upon mankind, I have been the more led to suspect the existence of some original, true, and sacred thing back of it, out of which all this false science and base superstition has grown, and of which it is the perversion.... It is the spoliation of some better thing going before it. And so there is reason to think that there is, after all, some great, original, divine science connected with the stars.[749]

Seiss taught: "all the great doctrines of the Christian faith were known, believed, cherished, and recorded from the earliest generations of our race, proving that God has spoken to man, and verily given him a revelation of truths and hopes precisely as written in our Scriptures."[750] His message rings true for those familiar with the concept taught in the scriptures that every prophet prophesied of the Messiah.

In his book, Seiss discussed the twelve signs of the zodiac and each of their three decans (sub-constellations), for a total of forty-eight original constellations. Some of the connections he described are particularly impressive:

1. Virgo. Many have wondered if somehow the symbolism associated with this constellation was a handed-down distortion of the prophecy of Mary, the virgin mother of Jesus. Apparently it was. In its original, uncorrupted form, it did represent the prophecy of Mary, and the decans of

---

749. Ibid., p. 11.
750. Ibid., p. 15.

Virgo represented the Divine Child: Coma—the Infant, the Branch, the Desired one (later Coma was changed to Coma Bernices—Bernice's Hair—to appease a queen named Bernice who had lost her hair). Centaurus—the centaurs in mythology represented beings that were half immortal and half mortal. And Bootes—anciently, the great Shepherd or Harvester. Thus each decan appears to have originally been a symbol of the Messiah.

2. Scorpio. The scorpion obviously represents a dangerous or deadly enemy. The decans of Scorpio: The Serpent (struggling with the hero Ophiuchus); Ophiuchus (contending with the Serpent in his hands, stung in one heel by a Scorpion, and crushing the scorpion with the other); and Hercules, also wounded in his heel, the other foot over the Dragon's head. These bring to mind Genesis 3:15: "And I will put enmity between thee and the woman, and between thy seed and her seed: it shall bruise thy head, and thou shalt bruise his heel."

3. Capricornus. Half-dead goat, and half-live fish. It represented the dying redeemer, with the live fish signifying the resurrected Lord. Decans: Sagitta, the Arrow, or killing dart; Aquila, the Eagle, pierced and falling; Delphinus, the Dolphin, springing up, raised out of the sea. Thus representing the death and resurrection of the Messiah.

4. Cancer. Connected to the church. Its decans included: Ursa Major (the Big Dipper) which was anciently the Greater Sheepfold and Ursa Minor (the Little Dipper), anciently the Lesser Sheepfold.

It is ironic that the research done by those who used it to defame religious beliefs has brought to light some wondrous details about the ancient versions of the myths. In these and many other stories handed down regarding the constellations, it seems the symbolism was indeed intended to represent the Messiah and his divine birth and mission.

The Big Bang Theory

As mentioned in the Evolution and Creation chapter, a notion held by many religious people is that the universe was formed out of nothing ("ex nihilo"). Such a belief, other than the timing, fits nicely with the very popular big bang theory. It supposes everything in the universe flashed into existence billions of years ago in a stupendous explosion of who knows what. According to Corey S. Powell, "The big-bang theory rests on observations of redshifts that are interpreted as evidence that the universe is expanding."[751] Because redshifts are observed in the light of numerous stars and galaxies, and that fact can indicate that a light source is moving away from the observer,[752] Edwin Hubble proposed that stars and galaxies are moving away from one another. If the relative movement is actually the sole cause of the redshifts, it was reasoned, all the material in all of the galaxies must have been together at some time in the far-distant past.

Other evidence suggests that a portion of the observed redshifts found in starlight have other causes. One in particular is matter between the stars refracting the light. Some scientists

---

751. Powell. "The Redshift Blues." *Scientific American.* January, 1990, p. 18.
752. Light can be separated into a rainbow of colors by shining it through a prism. Depending on what elements produce the light, patterns of dark lines block out parts of the spectrum. For instance, a flame from burning hydrogen produces a rainbow spectrum with a different pattern of dark lines than a flame produced by natural gas (since natural gas contains hydrogen, some of the dark lines would be the same, but others, different). If a light source is moving away from an observer, the pattern of dark lines appears shifted toward the red end of the spectrum (thus a "redshift"). If the light source and the observer are moving toward one another, the pattern is shifted away from the red. This phenomenon is called the Doppler effect.

now believe that more matter exists unseen between the stars than that which is within them. If there was such a thing as the "big bang," what was the universe like before that singular event?

The second verse in the Bible says: "And the earth was without form and void; and darkness was upon the face of the deep" (Genesis 1:2). One definition of "void" is "containing no matter; empty."[753] Many use such a definition to support the notion of creation out of nothing. Alternate definitions of "void" suggest "barren, unoccupied, or abandoned."

The big bang is another scientific theory that is often taught as though certain. Silk et al. described: "A consistent account of that distribution [of matter in the universe] and its evolution must be developed within the context of the big-bang theory, since there is almost universal consensus among cosmologists and astrophysicists."[754] Note that here is another instance where the reason it "must be" based on that particular theory is simply because of its "consensus" status—in this instance—"among cosmologists and astrophysicists." Astrophysics, although making use of facts and higher math, is heavily reliant on theory, and cosmology may be the most speculative and untestable of all branches of science. Therefore, its suppositions may not even be close to accurate—and those portions that contradict the scriptures appear to be spurious.

The big bang theory is by no means universally accepted. Wal Thornhill wrote: "We are expected to believe that which can't be detected. Meaningless terms and phrases (the fabric of space time, the Big Bang) punctuate a new secular catechism." He also reported that Dr. Halton Arp "was regarded in his early career as

---

753. Void. *American Heritage Dictionary*, 1995.

754. Silk et al. "The Large-Scale Structure of the Universe." *Scientific American*, October, 1983, p. 72.

a leading young astronomer, but he made the poor career move of proving the Big Bang never happened."[755]

Marcus Chown reported on "the first ever Crisis in Cosmology conference in Moncao, Portugal," June 2005:

> What if the big bang never happened? Ask cosmologists this and they'll usually tell you it is a stupid question. The evidence, after all, is written in the heavens.... ... A small band of researchers is starting to ask questions no one is supposed to ask.... They argued that cosmologists' most cherished theory of the universe fails to explain certain crucial observations.... It is time for some serious investigation into the big bang's validity and its alternatives.
>
> "Look at the facts," says Riccardo Scarpa of the European Southern Observatory in Santiago, Chile.... For Scarpa and his fellow dissidents, the tinkering has reached an unacceptable level. All for the sake of saving the notion that the universe flickered into being as a hot, dense state. "This isn't science," says Eric Lerner.... "Big bang predictions are consistently wrong. . . ." So much so, that today's "standard model" of cosmology has become an ugly mishmash.[756]

On the other hand, if there really was a "big bang," what was before it? Nibley wrote: "We talk a lot about the second law [of thermodynamics], but what about the first law—the law about the conservation of energy, which is the conservation of mass and matter, in all their forms. It is important too."[757] Are we to give a theory (the big bang) precedence over a law (first law of thermodynamics)?

---

755. Thornhill. "Astronomy has little to celebrate in 2009." *C&C Workshop.* SIS, 2009:1, p. 27.

756. Chown. "End of the Beginning." *NewScientist.* July 2, 2005, p. 30.

757. Nibley. *Temple and Cosmos.* 1992, pp. 8–9.

Berlinski commented: "As far as most physicists are concerned, the Big Bang is now a part of the established structure of modern physics.... [It] has come to signify virtually a universal creed."[758] How is this creed to be tested? Who can go back in time billions of years ago to see what really happened? How can the supposed grand explosion be replicated? This seems an unlikely conflict: on one side the laws of thermodynamics and the scientific method and on the other, the big bang theory.

What Lies Beyond?

Another question related to the issue is this: "how could there be no end to space?" In my youth, I remember struggling, trying to comprehend how there could be no end. A thought came: suppose there was an end out there somewhere. I imagined a signpost that said "The End." Then came the next question: what lies beyond? If scientists hadn't actually seen to the edge of the universe when the first telescope was made, or with each one larger and more powerful, how can they now suppose that they have actually seen to the edge of the universe? With each improvement in space technology, more distant galaxies are discovered. Will there ever be a time when the end is actually seen, or is it just that nothing more can be detected using the equipment available at that time? Furthermore, if the distant galaxies are really billions of light years away, and what is seen now is only a view of light that has been traveling through space for billions of years, what are they like now?

Consider the Implications

Many remember the prophecies that "immediately after the tribulation of those days shall the sun be darkened, and the moon shall not give her light" (Matthew 24:29). Not as much attention

---

758. Berlinski. *The Devil's Delusion.* 2009, p. 70.

is paid to the rest of the passage: "and the stars shall fall from heaven, and the powers of the heavens shall be shaken." The sun and the moon being darkened may refer to their appearance when obscured by debris from volcanic and/or impact activity. The stars falling from heaven could certainly be a description of an intense meteor shower or, as some have suggested, the earth moving (at speeds otherwise seen only in the movies) while the stars remain in their relative positions.

Conclusion

Much is known about the cosmos, but almost infinitely, more is not known by mortals on Earth. The gap between the known and unknown is filled with speculation.

12

What Does It All Mean?

We don't know a millionth of 1% about anything.

—Thomas Edison

This book has not proved or disproved anything. It has, however, described weaknesses in some of the very popular scientific theories that tend to conflict with a literal reading of the scriptures. Some aspects of the "consensus theories," such as the rates at which Earth processes have taken place, the big bang, and certain segments of evolution, deserve criticism. They have eroded the faith of a staggering number of people. There are other conflicts not mentioned herein, but it is comforting to know that one day the kernels of truth will be sorted from the chaff of error.

Most people rarely hear certain theories expressed accurately: "the *theory* of evolution," "the *hypothesized* mantle convection currents," or "the big bang *theory*." These are regularly spoken of, and written of, as though they are the tested, proven, unbiased facts, and many scientists seem to believe they are. It is clear that even the way the word "fact" is often used in science is not consistent with most people's understanding of the word, and distinctions between facts and theories are far too often blurred.

Which processes played the most significant roles in Earth's history, those that were slow and uniform or those that were sudden and catastrophic? It is obvious now that the assumption of uniformity should be more generally supplemented by catastrophes.

When a passage in scripture is not consistent with popular theory, what should be done? Should the scripture be resigned to the status of fable, or should the scientific theory and its underlying assumptions be questioned? Which is more likely to stand the test of time?

With the present state of knowledge, it should now be clear to literal believers that estimating the age of the earth or a rock is highly speculative. Claims that geologic ages can be "calculated," and that the techniques are "self checking," are overly optimistic at best, and strongly misleading at worst. Until details are revealed as to where the matter used in forming the earth came from, how it got here, its history prior to, during, and since then, scientific dating techniques will continue to be speculative estimations. Furthermore, those estimates are based on theories which are based on assumptions that disregard what has been revealed on the subject. Until God reveals more details about physical conditions when the earth was created, and when it was in a paradisiacal state, one can assume whatever he pleases, and be just about as wrong as anyone else.

An anti-God version of science has gained undue prominence. Some people insist that science should be the study of natural processes without regard for God and his influence. They say that, by definition, science is so. Why should science ignore clues provided by God through his prophets?

Rather than basing science on a foundation without God's hand in things, what if the scriptures are used to provide clues to real events, and what if God is recognized as the creator?

Wouldn't the perspective of most scientists be significantly improved? Such a shift need not alter the scientific method—just give some inspired direction as to which theories to explore and which to discount. If the vast brain and technology resources in the scientific world were more often channeled by inspiration, what progress might be made?

Still, we should recognize that some answers won't be known until He comes and reveals all things. "Albert Einstein said, 'What I see in nature is a magnificent structure that we can comprehend only very imperfectly, and that must fill a thinking person with a feeling of humility. This is a genuinely religious feeling.'"[759]

We should remember that one of the challenges for those seeking to defend the truth involves the adversary: "It has always been a well-known principle among the Jews and Christians that Satan's tactic is not the frontal attack but the clever counterfeit. The devil inverts the truth."[760]

The Atheistic Approach to Science

An astounding aspect of the broad acceptance of popular theories is the misguided attempt to push atheistic views, not only on adults, but on little children. My son Alan showed me a DVD given to his four-year-old son titled *Here Comes Science.* Teaching young children to enjoy science and begin learning some fundamentals sounds great. But using a catchy tune called "Science is Real" sung by the group They Might Be Giants, with cartoon images attractive to little ones, came some alarming messages. Much of the song is a repetition of the words used in the title "Science is Real," with highly objectionable phrases being interwoven. In a very upbeat manner, it mentions the big bang and evolution (which are real—that is, real theory). One phrase

---

759. Brown, R. *Setting the Record Straight.* 2008, p. 16.
760. Nibley. *Temple and Cosmos.* 1992, p. 81.

deserves special criticism: it lumps angels into the same category as elves and unicorns, calling them "stories." This is contrasted to "facts," "truth," and "proof" as the domain of science. Isn't that teaching little children that angels, like unicorns and elves, are outside the realm of reality, and that science is the real source of truth? Should speculative theories be grouped together with precise and accurate science and then be referred to as "truth"?[761]

The tune includes another objectionable phrase which appears to be a rhymed version of one published by the National Academy of Science (NAS). The NAS's version is: "In scientific terms, 'theory' does not mean 'guess' or 'hunch' as it does in everyday usage. Scientific theories are explanations of natural phenomena built up logically from testable observations and hypotheses."[762] Yes, that's the ideal, but "built up logically" doesn't necessarily mean true. And testable observations don't necessarily yield correct surmises. Furthermore, many scientific theories are not conducive to either proof or disproof. Facts are an important part of science, but that doesn't mean everything given the label "scientific" is fact. Further, more confusion results when the word "fact" is used to mean "theory."

Revealed Versus Human Knowledge

Which sources of information are the most reliable for real truth? If God is real, and if He has revealed things to prophets throughout the ages, aren't the accounts they've shared on a much surer footing than the theories of men? This seems especially pertinent to those theories that deliberately exclude reference

761. Flansburgh, John C., John Linnell; "Science Is Real" They Might Be Giants.
http://www.metrolyrics.com/science-is-real-lyrics-they-might-be-giants.html#ixzz0vbHsGwHf. (last accessed 9/4/12)
762. National Academy of Sciences. *Science and Creationism,* 2nd Edition. 1999, p. 28.

to God. "Sir Isaac Newton taught that 'truth had been given by God in the beginning, but had been fragmented and corrupted in the course of time; its traces survived in enigmatic form in these different sorts of literature, but had to be recovered.'"[763]

It must be remembered that science is the study of "natural" or mortal things and rarely considers the immortal and cannot detect the spiritual. To mortals, some things are beyond reach, but to God, all things are within His grasp. According to Moses 6:35–36, Enoch was permitted to see "the spirits that God had created, and he beheld also things which were not visible to the natural eye." That statement is either true or it isn't. If this or similar statements are true, there is a whole realm of reality which science knows nothing about.

Use of the Scriptures

It is true that, as Kowallis put it, "the holy scriptures are not textbooks of science, nor were they ever intended to teach scientific principles."[764] And as James E. Talmage wrote, they "were never intended as a text-book of geology, archaeology, earth-science, or man-science."[765] However, the scriptures do contain many descriptions with major scientific implications! Those scientists who ignore the descriptions of real catastrophic events contained therein, or dismiss them as myth or fable, miss critically important clues! They choose to overlook certain answers that are actually given—like in a math book. If a student completes a math problem, but the solution doesn't agree with the answer given in the back of the textbook, someone made an error. Rarely the text is wrong, and much more often, it is the student who made the error. Similarly, if science contradicts the scriptures, an error has been made, and what is the most likely

763. Nibley. *Temple and Cosmos.* 1992, p. 415.
764. Kowallis. "Things of the Earth." In *Of Heaven and Earth.* 1998. p. 38.
765. Ibid.

source of that error?[766] Too many people bypass the test-checks from the Master and thus miss key details crucial to determining which scientific theories are the most promising.

Since revelations from God come through mortal men, they are subject to errors. However, God's revelations have the backing of truth. Pearson and Bankhead described it this way:

> Man is at an inestimable disadvantage when pitting his knowledge against God's knowledge. In the very best of circumstances man must reason from the part (his world) to the whole (God's world)... Man must constantly extrapolate, interpolate, and guess. God knows all things. He sees things in their entirety, in their true perspective. Hence the most reliable knowledge we have is that which God reveals or has revealed through his prophets.[767]

It is well to remember the following teachings of the prophet Isaiah:

> For my thoughts are not your thoughts, neither are your ways my ways, saith the Lord.
> For as the heavens are higher than the earth, so are my ways higher than your ways, and my thoughts than your thoughts. (Isaiah 55:8-9)

The role of the Holy Spirit should be considered in any search for understanding. Pratt expressed his view of the concept in this manner:

> The Lord has revealed many truths in the scriptures which can be used as an absolute standard against which

---

766. This concept is attributed to Dr. Melvin A. Cook, who utilized it in his scientific studies, and who shared it with me on several occasions. Private communication.

767. Pearson and Bankhead. *Building Faith.* 1994, p. 69.

scientific theories may be measured. If any theory denies a truth which the Lord has clearly told us, then that theory is not likely to endure.... The two obvious outcomes are that either a false theory will be abandoned or we will find out that we had misunderstood the revelation.[768]

The pioneer, colonizer, and church leader Brigham Young had a candid approach to God, nature, and the truth. He taught:

Our religion measures, weighs, and circumscribes all the wisdom in the world—all that God has ever revealed to man.... Our religion is simply the truth. It is all said in this one expression—it embraces all truth, wherever found, in all the works of God and man that are visible or invisible to mortal eye.... Our Father, the great God, is the author of the sciences, he is the great mechanic, he is the systematizer of all things, he plans and devises all things, and every particle of knowledge which man has in his possession is the gift of God, whether they consider it divine, or whether it is the wisdom of man; it belongs to God, and he has bestowed it upon us.[769]

Some individuals have had a hint of how a prophet can receive an incredible amount of information in a very short time. They've experienced a trauma with a remarkable side effect. In my case, immediately before an auto accident the events of my life up to that point almost instantly flashed into my consciousness. It was as though time was suspended while the review took place. Perhaps such an experience gives a glimpse of how the human mind can be quickened sufficiently to see the "vision of all" which was reported to have been seen by some of the chosen prophets, including:

---

768. Pratt. "Strengths and Weaknesses of Science." *Meridian Magazine.* 28 Dec 2000, p. 1
769. Discourses of Brigham Young. 1973, pp. 2–3.

Adam	Moses 5:10
Enoch	Moses 7:21, 1 Enoch 81:2[770]
Moses	Moses 1:27–28
Isaiah	Isaiah 29:11

Who knows more about the cosmos, one who has been given a vision of all things from God, or one who looks at vast collections of data and postulates fine theories as to what it all means? No matter how scientific, elegant, or rational the theories may seem, if they conflict with the revelations of God, something is wrong.

Revelation and inspiration are and have been considered an important source of knowledge of the truth for many. For example:

> None is more insistent on the need for revelation than Plato... Both Plato and Aristotle, according to Jaeger, "placed inspiration above reason... because it comes from God"—for while reason is far from infallible, "the sureness of inspiration, on the other hand, is like lightning".... ... "When I was young,"... Socrates say[s], "I was fanatically devoted to the intellectual quest which they call natural science. Filled with pride and youthful conceit... I was convinced that I could know the reason for everything.... I was always experimenting to discover the secrets of nature and life." He was convinced... "that no one need look any farther than science for the answers to everything. . . ." Then it was, he says, that he read the passage that completely changed his point of view: "There is a mind that orders things and causes all things to be."[771]

Does Satan Play a Role in Science?

Is there any realm of mortality which is immune to Satan's influence, or does he get involved wherever he can, including

---

770. In *The Old Testament Pseudepigrapha*, Vol. 1. 1983, p. 59.
771. Nibley. *The Ancient State*. 1991, pp. 326–329.

science? Is he real? Is he really intent on causing people to stumble and divert them from truth? Does he really seek to distort and pervert truth, whether in religion or science or any other earthly realm? Consider more of John Pratt's perspective:

> For many reasons, it not only appears that Satan is interested in science, he may well be attempting to hijack all of science and attempt to force it to become the foundation of his new official state atheistic religion.... How can Satan get away with avoiding the Scientific Method, while purporting to do science? He does it by *focusing on the past and on the future* which are both areas beyond direct observation of the present, the realm of science.
>
> Satan can fabricate all sorts of complete nonsense about the origins of the universe, the solar system, the earth and all of the creatures that live on it. None of these theories can be tested, but that does not stop him from proclaiming them as absolute truth.... Satan's theories of the origin of the earth and life are almost entirely based on unfounded speculation, that often contradict all of the actual evidence.
>
> Another "smoking gun" which strongly points to Satan's involvement becomes obvious when materialists use force to teach speculation as truth. That is, they pass laws which require teaching that science is based on atheism.[772]

In Summary

My sharing of things critical to established ideas and procedures has resulted in harsh criticism from experts in some fields. It has been amazing to see the defensive and hostile position some have taken. Their reaction seems to be due to the sharing of ideas that challenge concepts and procedures they have rigorously studied

---

772. Pratt. "Has Satan Hijacked Science?" *Meridian Magazine.* 16 Nov 2005, pp 2, 5.

for years and have grown accustomed to. This is understandable since their colleagues have railed against many of the authors quoted in this book—even though they attained solid academic credentials in their fields. Some have been alarmed that anyone would dare bring up subjects they consider to have already died and been buried.

It seems that the majority of scientists in this age subscribe to theories contradictory to the scriptures. Many of them are not specifically trying to undermine faith, but others are, and a majority seem to oppose a literal approach to the scriptures. They consider themselves to be open-minded and enlightened as to the workings of nature. In many ways, and in many subjects, they are far more knowledgeable than most laymen. That does not mean that the theories they have so diligently studied and mastered are 100 percent correct. What most laymen and many scientists tend to lose sight of is the vast network of assumptions on which much of modern science is built. Yes, experimental science and technology have reached wondrous heights; however, the deductions and inferences of theoretical science have not.

There is no doubt that many scientists accept some of the beliefs of "creationists" and it is understandable that they don't accept all of them. However, have they given a fair hearing to the evidence "creationists" have found pointing to weaknesses in popular scientific date estimations? In light of the information summarized in this book, it seems that more scientists should be outside the mainstream of scientific thought. If the popular scientific thought is opposed to a literal reading of Genesis, isn't there a need for substantial improvement? The question posed by some—"why so many people cling to Biblical literalism?"—may be answered: it is because no matter how many bits of factual data are collected, if they are pieced together without taking into account God's hand, it is incomplete. And because believers are convinced that the scriptures are a more reliable source of truth than the theories of men, literally!

If a literal approach to the scriptures isn't taken, what approach should prevail? Certainly the scriptures contain much more than mere parables, allegories, and myths. When Noah's Flood is described—with no hint of it being anything other than an account of a real event—who is so intellectually gifted that he can know what among the prophets' writings should be discounted? On what basis should people distinguish what is truth and what is myth? If a Bible description doesn't seem reasonable to someone who is learned in the ways of the world, does that mean it didn't happen as described?

Details found in the scriptures don't always fit with our personal perceptions of what ought to be. However, rather than discarding them, wouldn't it be better to just "put them on the shelf" until we obtain sufficient knowledge to adequately understand them?

Dr. Philip F. Low made some profound observations which, although not his intent, serve as a nice summary for many of the ideas presented in this book:

> Since truth and error can be intermixed in any scientific or religious philosophy, the challenge is to determine which aspects are true and which are false. This seldom can be done with certainty.
>
> Many people have the impression that scientific findings are indisputable because they can be repeated again and again and are obtained with the five senses or with instruments that extend those senses. But this impression is contrary to fact. Some degree of uncertainty always exists about the reliability of experimental results. This uncertainty may arise because the method of measurement disturbs the system being measured.... Uncertainty also may arise because the measuring device used in an experiment may not be sufficiently sensitive.[773]

---

773. Low. "Perspectives on Science and Religion." In *Of Heaven and Earth*. 1998, p. 8.

He added:

> Regardless of how many experiments support a given concept, there is always the possibility that the next experiment will disprove it or require that it be modified.... As evidence accumulates, the idea may achieve the status of a theory and, eventually, of a law. Even so, the idea can never be proved unequivocally.
>
> In addition to any uncertainty about the reliability of experimental results, there is uncertainty about their interpretation. Experimental results are seldom so definitive that only one interpretation is possible. Depending on their previous experience and prejudices, different scientists will have different interpretations. Thus opposing schools of thought develop, and reconciliation of these schools of thought occurs very slowly. I am inclined to agree with the famous German physicist Max Planck, who said, "A new scientific truth does not triumph by convincing its opponents and making them see the light, but rather because its opponents eventually die, and a new generation grows up that is familiar with it."[774]

Reconciling Some of the Issues

Here is a review of some of the issues discussed in this book:

1. Not all miracles need be thought of as supernatural. Just because the cause of an event isn't yet understood, it should not necessarily be relegated to a realm beyond reality. Nor should an event be declared nonmiraculous because its mechanism is later learned. It seems more accurate and consistent with scientific findings, to think of many miracles as miraculous because of their timing. How God parted the Red Sea (although many enjoy

---

774. Ibid., pp. 8–9.

speculating about it) is not nearly as important as the fact that He knew and, at just the right time, inspired Moses so he "stretched out his hand over the sea; and the Lord caused the sea to go back" (Exodus 14:21).

2. The fundamental assumption of uniformity is taught and accepted by popular science as though it were a law of nature. However, in reality, it is only applicable part of the time. It seems that more scientists should cease being "willingly ignorant" of catastrophic events, especially those described in the scriptures. Scientific evidence is mounting that a substantial portion of Earth's features were formed in catastrophic processes.

3. Carbon dating is a wonderful tool for estimating the ages of once-living specimens. However, the older the artifact, the less accurate is the age estimate. The term "absolute" is often used in conjunction with dates—but it does not assure accuracy. It is used for ages estimated in years in contrast to relative dates. The ± symbol, as used in published radiometric date estimations, suggests a specific degree of accuracy. However, it only takes into consideration one of the four components of the estimation formula—and the most precise one at that. Therefore, the use of the terms "absolute date" and the ± symbol are not reliable indicators of the accuracy of scientific date estimations. Furthermore, if chronologies derived from the Bible and the catastrophic events associated with the Flood are reasonably accurate, any "carbon date" beyond about 4,000 years ago is grossly distorted.

4. By assuming that growth rings in trees are strictly tied to annual cycles, dating by ring counting can produce significant errors. Experiments have shown that some trees, particularly those subject to wide fluctuations in water availability, can grow multiple rings within a year. Thus ring counts can be gross exaggerations of the

actual ages of particular trees. Although highly confident statistical claims are made of the accuracy of cross-dating, those claims rest on assumptions, judgment, and subjective interpretations.

5. Some scientific dating systems are harmonious with a literal reading of the scriptures, but the radiometric dating of rocks seems contradictory. The various forms of the technique fail to take into account very important scientific findings, and they completely exclude revealed truths. Study of the research of reputable scientists has led me to conclude that too much of science is built on a foundation of faulty assumptions. If a foundation is weak, no matter how high-tech the process or how enchanting the theory sounds, sooner or later, it will fail.

6. The effects comets, meteors, and asteroids have had on the earth and its features have long been ignored. In recent years, however, ever-growing banks of evidence are coming forth showing that they have played significant roles—especially in explaining how major physical changes can happen very quickly.

7. Theories and data abound that are harmonious with the scriptural accounts of Noah's Flood although the evidence to support them is interpreted differently by mainstream science and attributed to drastically older time periods. One challenge is to find theories that are in harmony with revealed truths and, when possible, test them.

Maybe a comfortable sense of security is felt when scientists suppose that they understand slow, steady processes. Granted, it is quite disconcerting to recognize that certain events, like a massive volcanic eruption or interaction with a comet, could throw the earth into a calamitous condition for months or years. However, the evidence clearly indicates that catastrophes have happened, and there is no compelling reason to suppose that they won't in the future.

Questions without Good Answers

1. What was the earth like prior to the Fall of Adam—the physical state of things?

2. What is time? Highly sophisticated instruments measure time with great precision, but what is it? It seems to move forward at a continuous rate, indeed, time is as natural to mortals as breathing. It is taken for granted and assumed to be a uniform process. Yet, certain descriptions suggest there is more to it. From Revelation 10:5-6 comes a curious statement: "And the angel...sware by him that liveth for ever and ever...that there should be time no longer." Another, this one from Moses 1:6: "And all things are present with me, for I know them all." How can this be? It seems these references are far beyond mortals' ability to comprehend. In this case, it will likely not be understood until it is experienced. Yet, even in scientific circles, unusual ideas about time are being contemplated. The title to a recent article is revealing: "Could Time End? Yes, and No: For time to end seems both impossible and inevitable."[775]

3. What is gravity? Its effects are known, and scientists can calculate its strength, but what causes it? Is it reversible?

4. Why is the magnetic north pole different than Earth's axis of spin? Or as Delair posed the question:

   Why doesn't the inclination of its axis coincide with that of Earth as a whole (cf. the different locations of the geographical and magnetic poles)? It strains credulity to suppose that any Earth-like planet, undisturbed by external

---

775. Musser. "Could Time End?" *Scientific American.* Sept. 2010, p. 84.

influences for millions of years, could have naturally acquired, unaided, a tilted axis, an offset magnetic field, variable rotation, or a Chandler Wobble.[776]

The Future

If atheists are right, what will believers have lost? Maybe a little "fun"! What really are the rewards of belief or disbelief? Collingridge shared an old rendition: "according to Pascal's wager, if there is no God, then the rewards of believing and not believing are the same. If, on the other hand, God lives, then the rewards of believing and accepting Him are much greater than the rewards of choosing not to believe."[777]

Isaiah prophesied concerning the last days: "Moreover the light of the moon shall be as the light of the sun, and the light of the sun shall be sevenfold, as the light of seven days in the day that the Lord bindeth up the breach of his people, and healeth the stroke of their wound" (Isaiah 30:26). That points to a catastrophic change of unprecedented proportions.

> But the day of the Lord will come as a thief in the night; in the which the heavens shall pass away with a great noise, and the elements shall melt with fervent heat, the earth also and the works that are therein shall be burned up.
>
> Seeing then that all these things shall be dissolved, what manner of persons ought ye to be in all holy conversation and godliness...
>
> Nevertheless we, according to his promise, look for new heavens and a new earth, wherein dwelleth righteousness.
>
> 2 Peter 3:10-13

Maybe such a melting process is not observable to mortal eyes. It is probably beyond "laws of nature" as they are now understood.

---

776. Delair. "Planet in Crisis." *C&C Review.* SIS, 1997:2, p. 9.
777. Collingridge. *Truth and Science.* 2008, p. 91.

The National Geographic Society has produced some excellent, substantially factual DVDs. Two particularly impressive programs, as to their candid descriptions of facts and events—without frequently presenting theory as though fact—are: *Volcano: Nature's Fury* (2003) and *Asteroids: Deadly Impact* (2003). A more recent one, *Journey to the Edge of the Universe* (2008), has some great information, but much of it is highly speculative. To its credit, it does hint of the reliance on theory a number of times, with expressions like "may be," and "could have been."

Other things mentioned in the program are in need of qualifying remarks, or substantial editing. One particularly offensive statement was made by the narrator: "Everything we do is controlled by the Sun, depends on it... For millions of years this was as close as it got to staring into the face of God... But one day, all this will stop. The sun's fuel will be spent. And when it dies, the earth will follow. This god that creates life destroys it and demands that we keep our distance."[778] Part of that statement is clearly false doctrine—in direct conflict with the testimonies of prophets. Another statement is a curious inconsistency: "We must go back through time to the very first chapter to learn how the universe began." And, since we can't, we speculate. The program did share a profound truth: "Sometimes it feels like the more we see, the less we know."[779]

How Should the Reconciling Proceed?

It seems there is a need for more scientists who are willing to try to explore a literal approach to the scriptures. Even for those who believe the scriptures are literally true, many are reluctant due in part to the danger to them personally—

---

778. "Journey to the Edge of the Universe." *National Geographic* DVD. 2008.
779. Ibid.

since doing so often involves noting weaknesses in popular scientific theories which can make enemies of colleagues. Others consider science (facts, theories, and inferences) to be so secure that they must discount events described in the scriptures. In doing so, they miss out on very important clues provided by God through his prophets and inspired leaders. It appears that many within the creationist and catastrophist communities are doing an admirable job in exploring channels beyond the main stream, and defending a literal approach to the Bible. They don't have all the answers, but at least, they are willing to ask many of the right questions, to do the research, and seek the answers. Of course, some dismiss their work outright because they have been branded with a modern secular version of the word "heretic."

In the words of Francis Collins:

> It is time to call a truce in the escalating war between science and spirit. The war was never really necessary. Like so many earthly wars, this one has been initiated and intensified by extremists on both sides.... Science is not threatened by God; it is enhanced. God is most certainly not threatened by science; He made it all possible. So let us together seek to reclaim the solid ground of an intellectually and spiritually satisfying synthesis of *all* great truths.[780]

It is my hope that readers of this book are now more aware of the need to distinguish fact from inference and to be better able to do so. Also, that their horizons have been expanded. Whether or not the alternate theories described herein turn out to be reasonably accurate, they are at least possibilities that are more consistent with a literal reading of the scriptures.

---

780. Collins. *The Language of God.* 2006, pp. 233–234.

Appendix 1

Other Problems with
C14 Date Estimates

Estimating the fourth of the facts essential to accurate carbon dates (whether anything besides radioactive decay has affected the C14 content of a specimen) needs more attention. Some of the problems are described below.

Contamination

Various sources of contamination in samples have been identified. For instance, radon contamination was mentioned by Stuiver and Pearson: "Tree-ring ^{14}C determinations back to 2500 BC made at the... Laboratory of the University of Washington need corrections because previously undetected minor amounts of radon released by ovens during sample preparation have to be taken into account."[781]

---

781. Stuiver. "Calibration of the Radiocarbon." In *Radiocarbon after Four Decades*. 1992, p, 19.

One method used to "discern" whether contamination has occurred is highly suspect: "Either modern or ancient carbon can often be clearly discerned if the result of a measurement deviates considerably from the expected value.... About one-fifth of the samples whose age could be historically checked differed by more than 200 years from the expected age."[782] If a C14 date is rejected because it differs from what was expected, how valid is the system? It could be that the error is in the expectation, or both.

Constancy of the Atmosphere

Because of unexplained discrepancies, scientists proposed that C14's production rate in the atmosphere must have varied.[783] Cook wrote: "While Libby contended that the cosmic ray flux has been constant for millions of years, today dendrochronologists are claiming wide fluctuations in cosmic ray intensities, resulting in great variations of ^{14}C in the earth's atmosphere."[784] Since experiments have not shown such variations, only a constant cosmic ray flux, the problem was attributed to alterations in the earth's magnetic field which might have allowed different amounts of cosmic rays to reach the atmosphere. Lingenfelter and Ramaty expressed the problem along with what has become the popular "solution":

> Since the... factors which determine the C14 production are known at best only at the present and possibly over a relatively short time period in the past, arbitrary assumptions would have to be made about the radiocarbon production in the more distant past. However, we can

---

782. Neustupny. "Accuracy of Radiocarbon Dating." In *Proceedings of 12th Nobel Symposium.* 1970, p. 25.

783. Bard et al. "Calibration of the ^{14}C Timescale." *Nature.* May 31, 1990, p. 409.

784. Cook. *Scientific Prehistory.* 1993, p. 13.

eliminate the need for such arbitrary assumptions by introducing a parameter... equal to the present ratio between production and decay in the total reservoir."[785]

It is intriguing to suppose that it might be possible to "eliminate" the need for the "arbitrary assumptions" by introducing another assumption. This is especially peculiar since both the new one and the old seem contrary to the experimental evidence.

Minute Amounts of C14

There is such a small amount of C14 present in living things at any given time that small errors can mean big differences in the age estimations. According to Bard et al., there is less than a ton of C14 in the atmosphere while the ocean contains more than forty tons. "Subtle changes in the reservoir sizes and/or rates of exchange between reservoirs could have significantly affected the ^{14}C content of the atmosphere."[786]

Hedges and Gowlett also pointed out that the amount of C14 in a specimen after 40,000 years is so minute that "small quantities of modern carbon can severely skew the measurements."[787]

785. Lingenfelter and Ramaty. "Astrophysical Variations in C14 Production." In *Proceedings of 12th Nobel Symposium.* 1970, p. 520.

786. Bard et al. "Calibration of the ^{14}C Timescale." *Nature.* May 31, 1990, p. 408.

787. Hedges and Gowlett. "Radiocarbon Dating by AMS." *Scientific American,* Jan. 1986, p. 107.

Appendix 2

Carbon 14's Effect
on Longevity

Dr. Melvin A. Cook proposed that higher levels of C14 in the biosphere since the Flood contributed to a significant decrease in human lifespans. To understand the ramifications, recall that carbon is a primary building block of life on Earth. Although radioactive carbon (C14) is only estimated to be .00000000010% of the total of naturally occurring carbon,[788] like other radioactive elements, the decay process can damage living cells. Life forms apparently do not distinguish C14 from C12 or C13. As they assimilate carbon in the growth process, they do so in the same proportion it is found among other isotopes of available carbon.

At some time in Earth's history, a vast portion of the total carbon in the biosphere was "locked out." That is, it was removed from the reach of living things by burial. The vast coal, oil, natural

---

788. Higham. "Radiocarbon Web-info." http://www.c14dating.com/int. html, (last accessed 9/4/12).

gas, limestone, and similar deposits that lie beneath the surface of the earth attest to that fact. Although there is no dispute that vast quantities of carbon were removed from the biosphere, there is ongoing debate about whether that burial was slow or sudden. It has been proposed that the carbon was locked out suddenly in conjunction with the Flood/continental shift event.

Before the carbon was buried, there was a substantially larger amount of total carbon available for living things to assimilate at or near Earth's surface. Thus, C14 was much more dilute, having been mixed with a much larger carbon pool at that time. So prior to the great Flood, as living things ingested carbon, they did so at a significantly lower dose of radioactivity.

To understand, an analogy may be helpful: Picture a large aquarium filled with non-radioactive carbon atoms (C12 and C13). Imagine that carbon has the appearance and properties of clear water. Now suppose that C14 atoms also have the properties of water, but are a very dark-purple color, and toxic. Then, an apparatus starts to drip the dark purple C14 atoms into the aquarium at a rate of one drop each hour. Because the dark purple fluid would dissipate throughout, it would take quite some time before the clear water-like substance would start to discolor.

Now suppose that half of the mixture in the aquarium is suddenly removed and buried. Immediately after removal, the remaining half would have the same concentration as before, but as the drops of the radioactive C14 continue to be added each hour, the mix continues to discolor. Since no more C12 or C13 atoms are added, and since the C14 is dispersing amidst a smaller volume of carbon, its concentration increases at a faster rate.

Compare this analogy with the C14 forming and mixing amongst the other carbon atoms remaining in the biosphere after the Flood. Apparently, since Creation, C14 has been building as a result of the cosmic rays' interaction with Earth's atmosphere, but C12 and C13 have not. As C14 atoms were formed, they mixed with the other available carbon isotopes in the reservoir. Since that reservoir was much larger before the Flood/continental shift event, the concentration of radioactive carbon within the carbon mix was much less. After the Flood, a much smaller reservoir was available in which newly forming C14 could disperse. Over time, the reservoir became more and more concentrated until it reached its current level. Therefore, before the Flood any living thing absorbing carbon did so from a mixture much less concentrated in C14. After the Flood, anything obtaining carbon from the reservoir (which was increasing in C14 concentration more rapidly), would have receive a higher dose of radioactive carbon.

If the continents did slide suddenly, there is no doubt that some things would have subducted (or been buried) beneath other parts of the crust. Although the common tectonic theory is generally associated with the assumption of slow continental movement, if its timing is modified, it seems to fit with the flood hypothesis proposed earlier in this book.

Ham et al. summed up the idea quite nicely: "The Genesis flood would have greatly upset the carbon balance. The Flood buried a huge amount of carbon, which became coal, oil, etc., lowering the total [carbon]… in the biosphere…. Whereas no terrestrial process generates any more ^{12}C, ^{14}C is continually being produced…. Therefore the $^{14}C/^{12}C$ ratio in plants/animals/ the atmosphere before the flood had to be lower."[789]

Since radioactivity damages living cells and can cause cancer and other diseases, if radioactive C14 really has been increasing in concentration since the Flood, the higher levels of C14 in humans would naturally decrease longevity.

---

789. Ham et al. "How Accurate are Carbon-14 and Other Radioactive Dating Methods?" http://christiananswers.net/q-aig/aig-c007. html?zoom_highlight=how+the+carbon+clock+works. (last accessed 9/4/12)

Appendix 3

A Personal Experience

In pursuit of obtaining permissions to use copyrighted material in this book, I had an interesting experience. I wanted to use a couple of photos and e-mailed the copyright holder seeking permission. I mentioned the subject of my book: "trying to reconcile some of the conflicts between science and religion." The copyright holder responded with:

> The topic of your book is certainly intriguing and one upon which I've thought quite often. Of course, dendrochronology has been heavily critiqued by individuals because the continuous tree-ring chronologies date prior to the Great Flood. No doubt you are familiar with this debate. Before I grant permission to use my photo(s), could you tell me a little about how dendrochronology is treated in your book? As you may have guessed, I've been heavily criticized for supplying graphics and images to authors who then turn around and completely bash my field of inquiry, thus damaging my reputation. I have to look out for myself and I hope you understand.

I responded:

> In one of my sections I specifically discuss some scientists who have been ostracized and ridiculed for their out-of-the-ordinary positions on some subjects (especially as they pertain to popular theory vs. the Bible). Thus I do understand your concern. I don't want your reputation tarnished by allowing me to use your photos.... My view is truth is truth. Once we can get past the erroneous scientific theories and the scriptural misunderstandings, we really do have some great clues—though not all of the answers.
>
> I have a chapter devoted to C14 dating, in which I discuss its strengths and weaknesses. In the next chapter, titled "Other Scientific Age Estimations" I have a section on dendrochronology, which I've divided into three main categories: (1) Dating of tree-stumps, (2) Estimating the age of living trees (this is where I'd like to use the photos... noting the difficulty of estimating the ages of very old living, or partially-living trees), and (3) Cross dating. I mention that there is hardly any conflict between Bible chronology and tree-stump, or living tree estimates (with some specific exceptions—particularly some of the early estimates), but most of the conflicts are due to cross-dating results. And to be honest, I am critical of some of what I've learned about cross-dating.

The holder of the copyright responded:

> I hope you understand, but I'll have to pass on supplying the images, but I'm sure you can easily procure others. Again, I have to be careful with my reputation amid criticisms lofted against me for seemingly innocent permissions I gave in the past. I wish you the best of luck with your book!

Thinking this might happen, I got the idea of using his refusal, rather than his photos, and responded to his e-mail:

Thanks, and I do understand. It is tragic that some are so quick to criticize. As I mentioned, I have a section in my book on just that subject. If you don't object, I'd like to use this dialogue as an example of reputable scientists fearing the repercussions from their colleagues (leaving you unnamed, but using the words you've written me).

The response came back: "No problem, but please do leave my name out of it, as that in itself would perhaps be far more damaging!"

Glossary

The definitions herein are a composite of various sources, usually simplified, including, but not limited to the following:

American Heritage Dictionary, on CD. Softkey International Inc., based on the American Heritage Dictionary of the English Language, 3rd ed., 1992, 1995.

Dictionary of Geological Terms. American Geological Institute. Garden City, New York: Dolphin Books, 1962.

McGraw-Hill Dictionary of Scientific and Technical Terms. Daniel N. Lapedes, editor. New York: McGraw-Hill Book Co. 1974.

McGraw-Hill Concise Encyclopedia of Science & Technology, Parker, Sybil P. Editor in Chief. 4th Edition. 1997.

Random House Dictionary of the English Language. 2nd ed., Unabridged. New York: Random House. 1987.

Webster's New World College Dictionary, 4th Edition. Cleveland: Wiley Publishing, 2005.

A

a priori: deductive, based on theory or logic, rather than experience or experiment.

absolute time: denotes time estimates expressed in years. In contrast, relative time which indicates if an event was before or after another. It should be realized that the terms "absolute time" and "absolute date" do not assure certainty or correctness, merely an estimate expressed in years.

acrimonious: bitter and caustic.

AMS. Accelerator Mass Spectrometry: a highly sophisticated scientific technique designed to measure different elements and even to distinguish rare isotopes of particular elements. Of interest is its ability to identify quantities of the rare C14 relative to the abundant C12.

accretion: growth, by addition from without.

anachronism: mention of a particular place using a name that was not given until a later time. For example, using "America" to describe a location on the western hemisphere prior to Amerigo Vespucci, after whom America received its name.

anathema: greatly detested, viewed as accursed or damned.

anthricite: a hard coal formed from nearly completely dehydrated vegetal matter. It is the highest of the four common ranks of coal.

asteroid: one of numerous "minor planets" usually found in the asteroid belt between Mars and Jupiter. However, many are now known to have orbits which cross that of the earth.

B

basalt: a fine-grained igneous rock dominated by dark-colored minerals. Much of the floor of the oceans is basalt and represents a mixture of mantle and granite.

big bang theory: a popular theory of the origin of the universe in which it is thought to have begun with a primeval super-explosion.

biosphere: that part of the earth where life is found (at its surface, atmosphere, and oceans).

bituminous coal: the second of the four main ranks of coal. It is soft and, relative to anthracite, a low-grade coal mostly formed from partially dehydrated wood.

breccia: rock consisting of angular or sharp granular fragments held in fine-grained material.

C

Cambrian: a grouping of geological strata characterized by widespread fossils of hard-shelled animals associated with salt water and sea plants. Trilobites are found in the lower Cambrian levels in Europe, but these formations do not necessarily coincide with the Cambrian beds in North America. Cambrian rocks include sandstones, limestones, shales, and conglomerates; slates, marbles, and quartzites; and ignious rocks.

carbon-14: a radioactive isotope of carbon with a half-life of about 5,730 years. It is used to estimate the dates of once-living things by comparing the current concentrations of ^{14}C found in their remains to the levels assumed to have been at their time of death. (Note: for simplicity, in this book carbon-14 is usually written "C14," however, when variants such as "C14," "^{14}C" or "C-14" appear within a quote, they are shown as they were published.)

chain reaction: a series of reactions in which secondary reactions are initiated by the energy produced in one or more preceding reactions.

coalification: the process by which coal is formed from plants subject to intense pressure and/or heat.

comet: a body, believed to be composed of ice and dust, which orbits around the sun in an elliptical path. When a comet comes near the sun, some of its material vaporizes, forming a large coma of gas and often a tail.

conglomerate: a rock made up of more or less rounded fragments of such size that an appreciable percentage of the volume of the rock consists of particles of granule size or larger. It often has a concrete-like appearance.

continental shift: a sudden shifting of the continents likely caused by a temporary tilting of Earth's axis.

convection current: a current formed by the rising of a warmed fluid or gas and the movement of denser, cooler fluid or gas sinking to take its place.

cosmic rays: highly energetic subatomic particles coming to Earth from all directions.

Cretaceous: a series of geological strata characterized by an abundance of chalk. It is commonly thought to represent a period from 65 to 140 million years ago, the end of which corresponded with the extinction of the dinosaurs.

cross-section: a view of an object which had been sliced through or depicted as though it had.

D

dark matter: particles of matter in interstellar space. Some scientists believe it comprises over 90 percent of the mass of the universe. The particles tend to obstruct light and may cause a red shift indistinguishable from the doppler effect.

daughter nuclide: an atom resulting from the radioactive decay of a heavier element. Some are radioactive and others are stable.

decay constant: a constant relating the rate of radioactive decay of a substance compared to the number of atoms present.

dendrochronology: the comparative study of growth rings in trees and wood samples. It is used to estimate ages.

discontinuity: distinct changes in one or more of the physical properties of the materials in the earth's crust.

doppler effect: a change in the frequency of sound or light waves caused by the relative motion of a source and an observer. For example, the pitch of a jet engine appears to change as it passes an observer. Light can be separated into a rainbow of colors by shining it through a prism. Depending on what elements produce the light, patterns of dark lines are seen blocking out parts of the spectrum. For instance, a flame from burning hydrogen produces a rainbow spectrum with a different pattern of dark lines than a flame produced by natural gas (since natural gas contains hydrogen, some of the dark lines would be the same, but others, different). If a light source is moving away from an observer, the pattern of dark lines appears shifted toward the red end of the spectrum (thus a "redshift").

E

ecliptic: the plane of the earth's orbit around the sun.

element: a unique combination of protons, neutrons, and electrons that cannot be broken down by ordinary chemical methods. The fundamental properties of an element are determined by its number of protons.

empirical: based on observation and experiment rather than theory.

enigmatic: baffling, perplexing, cryptic, ambiguous.

epigraph: a motto or quotation, as at the beginning of a chapter, setting forth a theme.

equilibrium: a state of balance where the rate of buildup is matched by the rate of removal.

exosphere: the outermost part of the atmosphere, from which certain elements were once thought to be lost into space (such as helium).

explicable: explainable, understandable.

extrusive rock: a rock that has moved from within the earth out to, or near, the surface (e.g. magma).

F

falsify: generally involves trying to prove or disprove a theory.

flood basalt: basalt which poured out from fissures in a molten state and then hardened.

fusion (nuclear):	the nuclear process in which two atoms unite to form an atom of a different substance, with the release of energy. This is the process commonly thought to be the source of the sun's energy.

G

geologic time-scale:	a theoretical chronological sequence based on the geologic strata and the assumption of uniformity.
granite:	a coarse-grained igneous rock consisting of quartz, feldspars, and mica.
graphite:	a soft, dark, lustrous form of carbon used for lead in pencils, lubricants, etc. It consists of almost completely dehydrated ligno-cellulose material.

H

half-life:	the estimated time it takes for one half of the radioactive nuclei in a sample to decay.
helio:	a prefix referring to the sun. For example: Heliocentric means the system recognizing the sun as the center of the solar system.
Hilt's law:	the rank of coal generally increases with its depth of burial due to pressure and heat.
hydrocarbon:	an organic compound consisting of the elements hydrogen and carbon. It reacts in air to form water and oxides of carbon. Petroleum is a complex mixture of hydrocarbons.

hypothesis:
a tentative theory or supposition, devised to provide a basis for further investigation. It is advanced to explain certain facts or phenomena and should be subjected to tests. Some hypotheses cannot be directly verified or refuted.

I

ice sheet:
a broad moundlike mass of glacier or polar ice of considerable extent that has a tendency to spread radially under its own weight, sometimes that spreading occurs in great surges.

igneous rock:
rock which was formed in intense heat, such as magma, that solidifies into granite or basalt.

incontrovertible:
undeniable, indisputable.

infer:
to conclude or deduce from something known or assumed; derived by reasoning.

intrusion:
in geology, the invasion of a liquid such as molten rock into or between solid rocks. A body of rock resulting from such an invasion.

intrusive rock:
a rock that solidified from a mass of magma that invaded the earth's crust but did not reach the surface.

ion:
an atom (or group of atoms) that has lost or gained one or more electrons, so that it has an electric charge.

Iridium:
a metal that is very rare in Earth's crust but common in meteorites.

isochron:
a graphical representation of data points which form a straight line. It

is used to derive an estimate of the initial composition of the radioactive and radiogenic elements within rock formations. Although some claim it provides a "self checking" system, it is based on the assumption that the original composition of the matter from which the rocks formed is known. For radioactive dating methods, that belief seems to be wishful thinking.

isostasy: the tendency of the earth's crust to move toward a vertical balance. A great load from a lake or an ice sheet causes the land under it to depress. If the load is removed the crust gradually moves toward its preload position.

isotope: any of two or more forms of an element having the same or very similar chemical properties.

K

KT: the boundary between the levels of strata called Cretatious and Tertiary. It contains unusual amounts of iridium.

L

lahar: layered deposits often associated with mudflows.

lattice: a three-dimensional pattern, particularly the atoms or molecules in a crystal.

law of conservation of energy: the total amount of energy remains the same during all energy changes.

layered solidification:	the process of solidification of elemental layers as the earth's crust cooled. It is a result of the respective melting temperatures of the elements and their tendency to coalesce while liquid.
leaching:	the removal of certain elements from a substance by the passage of fluid.
Levant:	The land region at the eastern end of the Mediterranean, between Egypt and Mesopotamia.
lignin:	an organic substance which acts as a binder for the cellulose fibers in wood and other plants and adds strength and stiffness to the cell walls.
lignite:	a low-grade brown coal in which the texture of the original wood can often still be seen. It consists of about 70 percent carbon and 20 percent oxygen
limestone:	a sedimentary rock consisting mainly of calcium carbonate, often containing organic remains of sea animals such as mollusks, and corals. Limestones often contain fragments of other rocks, and a particularly crystalline texture is common. When exposed to sufficient heat and pressure it becomes marble.

M

magma:	a liquid or molten rock which becomes igneous rock when cooled.
mantle:	the intermediate zone of the earth's interior between the crust and the core.
meteor:	the luminous phenomenon observed when matter enters the earth's

atmosphere and usually burns up due to the heat of friction; popularly called a "shooting star" or a "falling star."

meteorite: a stony or metallic fragment of interplanetary matter that falls to Earth's surface.

micro: a prefix meaning very small, or often more specifically: one millionth or 10^{-6}.

Milky Way: the galaxy which contains this Earth and the solar system. All of the stars seen from Earth (unaided) are within the Milky Way. On a clear night—away from city lights—a faint band of light can be seen in the sky. It is due to the many stars and diffuse nebulae lying near the plane of the Milky Way galaxy but which are so distant that they cannot be individually resolved by the naked eye.

Moho (Mohorovicic Discontinuity): the name given to the base of the crust marked by abrupt increases in velocities of shock waves. It is estimated to be about eight kilometers (five miles) below the ocean floor and thirty-two kilometers (twenty-miles miles) below the continents on average. It is named after the Yugoslavian geophysicist Andrija Mohorovicic who found evidence of it in 1909.

molecule the smallest unit quantity of matter which can exist by itself and retain all the properties of the original substance.

N

nebula: a gigantic cloud of interstellar gas or dust.

neutrino: a subatomic particle of which neither its mass nor its charge has been measured, but that carries energy in certain nuclear transformations.

neutron: a particle composed of a proton and an electron combined. It is electrically neutral. If isolated, it beta-decays to form a proton and an electron, with a half-life of about twelve minutes.

nova: an explosion of a star, increasing its luminosity by hundreds to thousands of times.

nuclear: referring to the nucleus or core of atoms.

nuclear fission: the splitting of an atomic nucleus into smaller nuclei.

nucleus (of an atom): the dense central core of an atom in which most of the mass and all the positive charge is concentrated. Electrons seem to orbit the nucleus of an atom.

nuclide: an isotope of an element that is identified by its number of protons and neutrons, and its energy state (e.g. carbon-14).

O

order of magnitude: a range of magnitudes of a quantity extending from a relatively small value to a multiple of the quantity (usually a multiple of 10).

organic: although organic is a term often used to signify living, once-living, or derived-from-living matter, in chemistry it is also used to designate chemical compounds containing carbon (which is one of the building blocks of living things on Earth).

P

palynology: The study of spores, pollen, microorganisms, and microscopic fragments in sediments.

peat: partially reduced plant or wood material containing approximately 60 percent carbon and 30 percent oxygen.

permeability: the degree to which water or other fluids can filter through a substance, by way of spaces within it or between its components.

plastic: in a flexible or changing state.

plate tectonics: in conventional geology, believed to be the slow and ongoing motion of plates or segments of the outer layer of the earth's crust over the underlying mantle.

primordial: first, earliest, from the beginning.

proton: a subatomic particle of matter with a positive electrical charge of 1 unit (equal in amount but opposite in effect to the charge of an electron).

R

radioactive: spontaneous breakup of atomic nuclei.

radiogenic: produced by radioactive decay, e.g. radiogenic leads (Pb206, Pb207, and Pb208) are the stable end-products of the radioactive decay of uranium and thorium.

replicate: to repeat, duplicate, or reproduce.

Roche limit: a method for estimating how close two massive objects (in space) can be without one being broken apart by the gravitational forces of the other. Its formula is complex, considering mass, density, and rigidity of the objects. A simplified version is: If two massive bodies of similar composition come within about 3 radii of the larger, the smaller will likely break apart.

S

sandstone: a medium-grained sedimentary rock consisting primarily of sand which has been compressed and hardened.

second law of thermodynamics: general application—all natural processes flow from order to disorder.

sedimentary rock: rock formed from accumulations of sediment, which may consist of rock fragments of various sizes, the remains or products of animals or plants, the product of chemical action, evaporation, heat, and pressure. Sedimentary rocks cover about 75 percent of the land area of the world.

seismic waves: vibrations traveling through parts of the earth. They are a result of earthquakes and other strong disturbances.

shale: A very fine-grained sedimentary rock consisting of fragments of other rock, formed by the hardening of muck or clay. It splits easily into thin layers.

sic: signifies a problem, such as a typographical error, misspelled, or wrongly used word within quoted text.

spall: the breaking off a layer or layers roughly parallel to a surface caused by a shockwave traveling through the substance.

supernova: a stellar explosion in which a star suddenly increases its brightness by from hundreds of thousands to hundreds of millions of times.

T

tacit: implied, understood.

tautology: a needless repetition of an idea. The restated version seems intended to establish the validity of the first. For instance: creatures survived a calamity because they were the fittest, and they are judged the fittest because they survived.

tektite: a small glassy body found at locations around the world, believed to have originated in meteorite impacts.

terrestrial: relating to the earth.

Tertiary: The geological strata commonly thought to represent a period of time from two to sixty-five million years ago. The time aspect of the layer is not supported in this book.

theory: a convenient model, designed to categorize and explain a set of related observations or phenomena.

thermodynamics: the branch of physics that deals with heat and heat transfer among bodies.

thermodynamics, laws of: First, when mechanical work is transformed into heat or heat into work, the amount of work is always equivalent to the quantity of heat (conservation of energy). Second: It is impossible by any continuous self-sustaining process for heat to be transferred from a colder to a hotter body. As it applies to natural processes on the earth, the general tendency from order to disorder.

U

uniformitarianism: the assumption that the present is the key to the past. It supposes that the processes now operating are the same as those that have also caused changes in the past. The changes are usually assumed to have been at the same rate. It seems to dominate modern conventional scientific thought.

universe: all matter and radiation and the space occupied thereby. Each time a more powerful telescope is built, the estimated size of the universe has increased.

V

varve: a pair of thin sedimentary beds, one coarse and one fine. This couplet of beds has been interpreted as representing a cycle of one year or an interval of thaw followed by an interval of freezing in lakes and fiords near glaciers. In certain conditions, varves can be formed more frequently.

viscosity: the resistance of a substance to flow. All fluids possess a definite resistance to change of form and some solids show a gradual yielding to forces tending to change their form.

Index

clean	172, 217, 270
climate	19, 116, 126, 129, 133, 138, 140, 141, 177, 190, 229, 232, 248, 254, 267, 316
clobbered	230
cloud	61, 68, 111, 178, 212, 213, 405
clubfoot	320
clue	28, 41, 66, 69, 111, 138, 169, 175, 185, 189, 205, 212-214, 219, 220, 240, 248, 254, 256, 294, 310, 320, 343, 364, 367, 380, 390
cling	30, 179, 334, 372
clusters	157
coal	177, 225, 263-273, 285, 287, 394-396, 400, 403
code	336, 337
coelacanth	259
coesite	163
coincidental	283
cold	77-79, 88, 141, 210, 211, 220, 227, 409
collaborators	93
collapse	68, 142, 209, 212
colleague	16, 32, 45, 48, 53, 83, 199, 288, 309, 372, 380, 391
collide	91, 155, 158, 165, 179, 193, 198, 222, 246
collision	48, 49, 91, 155, 164, 165, 177, 186, 198, 199, 216
colonies	298
Columbus	40, 308

distort	183, 194, 248, 270, 279, 284, 285, 295, 305, 310, 356, 371, 375
diverse	16, 17, 184, 205, 296, 306, 345
diversification	219, 320
diversity	319, 345
divine	39, 217, 338, 346, 356-358, 369
division	218, 236
Djoser	294
DNA	320, 335-337
doctrine	41, 66, 67, 69, 75, 178, 251, 268, 319, 324, 330, 331, 338, 346, 356, 379
document	46, 53, 55, 117, 162, 278, 289, 296, 304, 306, 307
documentary	19, 25, 52, 71, 327
dog	219, 313, 315, 319
dogma	39, 49, 53, 70, 200, 215, 253
dogmatic	15, 41, 46, 49, 58, 324
dominant	63, 69-71, 76, 257, 260, 321, 325, 345
dominate	69, 395, 410
dominion	207
doubt	29, 34, 37-39, 53, 56, 57, 71, 85, 128, 149, 163, 160, 170, 184, 188, 192, 207, 208, 217, 224, 251, 284, 309, 321, 326, 331-334, 340, 372, 387, 389
dove	226
dowser	37
drain	138, 199, 226, 229, 231, 240
drawbacks	133

fixity	178
flagrant	50
flash	175, 358, 369
flat	40, 288
flexible	311, 406
float	171, 187, 209, 227, 238, 258, 261, 262, 273
floating log mat	261, 269, 270
flood basalt	159, 189, 399
flood layer	205
fluid	187, 190, 244-246, 252, 253, 386, 397, 403, 406, 410
folk lore	308
food	78, 220
force	36, 66, 73, 159, 168, 177, 182, 184, 186, 187, 189, 190, 195, 198, 200, 243, 244, 248, 371, 407, 410
forced	39, 71, 303, 345
forgiveness	330
foregone	323
Fortuna strip-mine	267
forty	73, 74, 205, 209, 214, 235, 277, 283, 284, 293, 294, 343, 356, 383
fossil	57, 177, 193, 204, 225, 254-256, 258, 259, 260, 276, 317, 318, 331, 332, 395
fossil catfish	254
fossil forest	262
fountains	210, 211, 213, 225, 341
fourth day	342

genealogical	218
General Sherman	122, 123
generally accepted	31, 46, 86
genetic	313, 317
genius	307
genome	336
geochronology	146, 152
Geological Column	256, 257
geological dating	143-152, 257
geological society	41, 73, 229
geometry	300
German	128-130, 219, 244, 264, 374
geyser	210, 211
Gibeon	169, 173, 174
gift	369
gifted	373
glacial	189, 231, 238
glacier	136, 220, 229, 237, 238, 401, 410
glimpse	217, 278, 337, 349, 369
global	76, 78, 183, 184, 192, 203, 204, 211, 222, 223, 237, 323
globe	92, 160, 175, 188, 214, 243, 340
glucose	335
gold	78, 193
Gondwana	186
gorge	142
gorilla	331
Gospel	20, 22, 42, 133, 305, 353-355
GPS	183, 184
grading	253, 318

palynology	137, 406
papyrus	169, 297, 308
parable	23, 373
paradise	43, 153, 307, 339, 364
paralyzed	188, 337
parameter	271, 383
partial	75, 111, 115, 147, 182, 197, 263, 277, 390, 395, 406
Pascal's wager	378
passion	56, 330
passively	53
pasteurization	235
pattern	111, 112, 115, 124, 126, 127, 129, 131, 132, 192, 193, 214, 216, 230, 308, 314, 322, 358, 398, 402
peace	139, 209, 226
pearls	78
peascods	349
peat	267-270, 406
peer	17, 56, 325
Peleg	232, 236, 279
pendulum	70
Pennsylvania	98, 265
perception	35, 57, 61, 71, 83, 310, 373
perilously	334
permafrost	192, 193
permanent	50, 178
permeable	116, 246, 406
permeated	329
permissions	389, 390

radiometric	88, 109, 149, 153, 256, 375, 376
rainbow	211, 212, 358, 398
Rameses	290, 291
ramifications	64, 107, 329, 385
random	130, 163, 315, 325, 335, 337, 347
rapid	72, 137, 143, 184, 199, 221, 226, 246, 250-252, 254-256. 258, 259, 269, 270, 387
rare	16, 55, 62, 76, 90, 116, 127, 138, 158, 164, 201, 258, 259, 315, 336, 363, 367, 394, 401
rational	19, 51, 56, 297, 370
rationale	66, 293
raw material	267-273
razor-sharp	256
RCW 103	352
realistic	33, 106, 189
reality	21, 25, 37, 43, 56, 58, 72, 74, 141, 168, 175, 187, 207, 211, 218, 221, 226, 250, 302, 303, 322, 325, 344, 366, 367, 374, 375
realize	22, 23, 59, 105, 106, 134, 158, 165, 167, 183, 200, 216, 217, 235, 271, 288, 323, 326, 337, 349, 394
realm	25, 30, 34, 35, 37, 43, 46, 52, 61, 63, 101, 131, 135, 312, 316, 317, 322, 366, 367, 370, 371, 374
reasonable	35, 36, 133, 186, 219, 220, 233, 239, 284, 315, 331, 335, 373
reasoning	35, 130, 151, 265, 333, 342, 401
rebound	109, 136, 137, 206, 243

recede	142, 143, 228, 250
recessive	321
reckoning	298
recognition	268, 303
recognize	16, 22, 30, 32, 38, 58, 67, 69, 83, 94, 104, 106, 107, 110, 124, 138, 139, 145, 156, 157, 159, 163, 177, 182, 208, 233, 240, 251, 266, 286, 305, 310, 353, 364, 365, 376, 400
reconcile	15-17, 34, 41, 46, 61, 107, 178, 311, 313, 330, 338, 344, 345 347, 374, 379, 389
re-creation	340
Red Rock Canyon	228
Red Sea	374
redshift	358, 398
reel to and fro	172, 175, 176
reflection	205, 242, 245
refracting	358
refute	35, 291, 333, 401
region	110, 113, 114, 116, 117, 135, 136, 140, 165, 192, 195, 196, 203, 205, 206, 215, 229, 230, 232, 237, 243, 244, 266, 403
reinterpret	163
reiterate	237, 332, 335

Shishak	292
shock	55, 76, 160, 163, 196, 275, 324, 329
shockwave	193, 196-198, 206, 215, 242, 243, 252, 253, 272, 404, 408
Shoshenk	292
showcase	331
shuffle	172
Siberia	193, 236
sign	78, 145, 211, 233, 234, 245, 256, 262, 292, 342, 351, 352, 355, 356, 361
signal	117, 126
signature	76, 127, 128
signed	45
significant	17, 27, 55, 62, 72, 76, 82, 90, 94, 97, 106, 107, 129-131, 133, 135, 146, 151, 152, 156, 170, 205, 209, 212, 231, 233, 235, 238, 265, 266, 285, 293, 294, 300, 302, 351, 353, 364, 365, 375, 376, 383, 385, 386
signify	18, 126, 284, 334, 357, 361, 406, 408
silt	249, 254
Silurian	73
similar feature	317
simple	35, 83, 84, 93, 124, 168, 171, 187, 188, 190, 217, 243, 311, 315, 331, 335, 336, 345, 396
simplify	62, 81, 96, 134, 149, 168, 188, 263, 407

Bibliography

1 Enoch (Ethiopic Apocalypse of Enoch). In *The Old Testament Pseudepigrapha*, Vol. 1. Translated by E. Isaac. Edited by James H. Charlesworth. Garden City, NY: Doubleday & Co., Inc., 1983.

2 Enoch (Slavonic Apocalypse of Enoch). In *The Old Testament Pseudepigrapha*, Vol. 1. Translated by F. I. Andersen. Edited by James H. Charlesworth. Garden City, NY: Doubleday & Co., Inc., 1983, pp. 91–221.

The Book of Abraham. In the *Pearl of Great Price*. Salt Lake City, Utah: The Church of Jesus Christ of Latter-day Saints. 1981 edition.

Acheson, Mel. "Suddenly." *Chronology & Catastrophism Workshop*, Society for Interdisciplinary Studies (SIS), 2010:1, pp. 33–34.

Ababneh, Linah N. "Analysis of Radial Growth Patterns of Strip-Bark and Whole-Bark Bristlecone Pine Trees in the White Mountains of California: Implications in Paleoclimatology and Archaeology of the Great Basin." PhD dissertation, University of Arizona, 2006. http://www.geo.arizona.edu/

Antevs/Theses/AbabnehDissertation.pdf. (last accessed 9/6/12)

Abery, Jill. "Impact Diamonds." *Chronology & Catastrophism Review.* SIS, 1996:1, p. 42.

Abery, Jill. "Inside Science: Fakes." *Chronology & Catastrophism Review.* SIS, 2001:1, p. 38.

Abery, Jill. "Japanese Fraud." *Chronology & Catastrophism Review.* SIS, 2001:2, p. 46.

Abery, Jill. "Tottering Tectonics." *Chronology & Catastrophism Review.* SIS, 2001:1, p. 38.

Abery, Jill. "Suspicious Sedimentation." *Chronology & Catastrophism Review.* SIS, 1997:2, p. 44.

Abery. Jill. Reviews: "*Red Earth, White Lies,* Native Americans and the myth of scientific fact." Vine Deloria, 1995. In *Chronology & Catastrophism Review.* SIS, 1996:1, pp. 55–56.

Abery, Jill. Reviews: "*Silencing Scientists and Scholars in Other Fields: Power, Paradigm Controls, Peer Review and Scholarly Communications,* by G. Moran." Ablex Publishing Corp. 1998. In *Chronology & Catastrophism Review.* SIS, 2001:1, p. 50.

Abery. Jill. "Return to Catastrophism—the Flood did happen." *Chronology & Catastrophism Workshop.* SIS, 1993:2, p. 29. From Dr. Horst Friedfriech's review of *Und die Sintflut gab es doch,* by Alexander and Edith Tollmann, Munich: Droemer-Knaur. 1993.

Aitchison, T. C., and E. M. Scott. "A Review of the Methodology for Calibrating Radiocarbon Dates into Historical Ages." In *Applications of Tree-Ring Studies: Current Research in Dendrochronology and Related Subjects.* Edited by R. G. W. Ward. Oxford, England: BAR International Series 333. 1987, pp. 187–201.

Alder, Robert. "Under the Ice." *NewScientist.* May 6, 2000. http://www.newscientist.com/article/mg16622370.700-under-the-ice.html.

Allan, Derek S. "An Unexplained Arctic Catastrophe." *Chronology & Catastrophism Review.* SIS, 2001:2, pp. 3–7.

Allen, Bill. "From the Editor: Humans are not descended from apes." National Geographic, Nov. 2004.

Amante, C., and B. W. Eakins, ETOP01 1 Arc-Minute Global Relief Model: Procedures, Data Sources and Analysis. NOAA Technical Memorandum NESDIS NGDC-24, March 2009. 19 pp. http://www.ngdc.noaa.gov/mgg/image/etopo1_large. jpg. (last accessed 9/6/12)

American Heritage Dictionary, on CD. Softkey International Inc., based on the American Heritage Dictionary of the English Language, 3rd ed., 1992, 1995.

Armstrong, Karen. "Two Paths to the Same Old Truths." *NewScientist.* July 30, 2005, pp. 42–43. http://www. newscientist.com/article/mg18725101.900-reviewed-the-evolutioncreation-struggle-by-michael-ruse.html.

Arnold, James R. "The Early Years with Libby at Chicago: A Retrospective." In *Radiocarbon After Four Decades: An Interdisciplinary Perspective.* Edited by R. E. Taylor, A. Long, and R. S. Kra. New York: Springer-Verlag. © 1992, pp. 3–4. All Rights Reserved. With kind permission of Springer Science & Business Media.

Associated Press. "Asteroid Zips by Unseen." Deseret News. March 21–22, 2002.

Associated Press. "Huge Alaska Glacier Halts Seaward Surge." *Deseret News.* December 7, 1994.

Associated Press. "'Living Fossil' Tree Found in Australia." *Deseret News.* December 16, 2000.

Associated Press. "Topping Mother Nature: Lab Makes Petrified Wood in Days." *USA Today,* January 1, 2005. http://www. usatoday.com/tech/science/discoveries/2005-01-25-petrified_x.htm?csp=15. (last accessed 9/6/12)

Atlas of the Bible Lands, New Edition. Hammond World Atlas Corporation, part of the Langenscheidt Publishing Group. 1990.

Austin, Steven A. "Mount St. Helens: Explosive Evidence for Catastrophe." DVD, 2012. Copyright © Institute for Creation Research, www.icr.org. Used by permission.

Austin, Steven A. "The Declining Power of Post-Flood Volcanoes." *Acts & Facts*. 27 (8) August 1998, pp. i–iv. Copyright © 1998 Institute for Creation Research, www.icr.org. Used by permission.

Bailey, D. K. "Pinus Longaeva." http://www.conifers.org/pi/Pinus_longaeva.php. (last accessed 9/6/12)

Baillie, M. G. L. *Tree-Ring Dating and Archaeology*. University of Chicago Press. 1982.

Baillie, M. G. L., and J. R. Pilcher. "The Belfast 'Long Chronology' Project". In *Applications of Tree-Ring Studies: Current Research in Dendrochronology and Related Subjects*, Edited by R. G. W. Ward. Oxford, England: BAR International Series 333. p. 203–211, 1987.

Baillie, Michael G. L. "A Recently Developed Irish Tree-ring Chronology." *Tree-ring Bulletin*, Vol. 33, 1973, pp. 15–28.

Baker, James M. Photo: "The Teton Fireball of Aug 10, 1972." Used with permission.

Baker, Vic. "Joseph Thomas Pardee and the Spokane Flood Controversy." *GSA Today*, V. 5, no. 9, Sept. 1995. http://gsahist.org/gsat2/pardee.htm. (last accessed 9/6/12)

Bankhead, Reid E. *The Fall of Adam, The Atonement of Christ, and Organic Evolution*. Pleasant Grove Utah: National Research Group. (undated)

Bard, Edouard; Bruno Hamelin; Richard G. Fairbanks; and Alan Zindler. "Calibration of the ^{14}C timescale over the past 30,000 years using mass spectrometric U-Th ages from Barbados corals." *Nature*. Vol. 345, May 31, 1990, pp. 405–410.

Barrois, Georges A. "Chronology, Metrology, Etc." In *The Interpreter's Bible*, Vol. 1. New York: Abingdon Press, 1952, pp. 142–164.

Bartlett, John. *Bartlett's Familiar Quotations*, 15th edition. Boston: Little, Brown and Company. 1980.

Baumgardner, John. "Exploring the Limitations of the Scientific Method." *Acts & Facts*. 37 (3): March 2008, pp. 4–5. Copyright © 1998 Institute for Creation Research, www.icr.org. Used by permission.

Beal, Alasdair N. "A Bit Creaky? – Tree Rings, Radiocarbon and Ancient History." *Chronology & Catastrophism Review* Vol. XIII. SIS, 1991, pp. 38–42.

Beal, Alasdair. "Editor's Notes." *Chronology & Catastrophism Review*. SIS, 1997:2, p. 2.

Beal, Alasdair. "How Old Is Greenland's Ice Cap?" *Chronology & Catastrophism Workshop*. SIS, 1992:1, pp. 10–11.

Beal, Alasdair. "Lies, Damned Lies and. . . ." *Chronology & Catastrophism Workshop*. SIS, 1990:2, pp. 20–23.

Beal, Alasdair. "The Great 250,000 Year Ice Core." *Chronology & Catastrophism Workshop*. SIS, 1993:2, pp. 7–8.

Becker, Berndt. "The History of Dendrochronology and Radiocarbon Calibration." In *Radiocarbon After Four Decades: An Interdisciplinary Perspective*. Edited by R. E. Taylor, A. Long, and R. S. Kra. New York: Springer-Verlag. © 1992, pp. 34–48. All Rights Reserved. With kind permission of Springer Science & Business Media.

Begley, Sharon. "The Science of Doom: Space is Filled with Objects that Threaten Earth." *Newsweek*, November 23, 1992, pp. 56–60.

Behe, Michael J. *Darwin's Black Box: The Biochemical Challenge to Evolution*. New York: Touchstone. 1996.

Berlinski, David. *The Devil's Delusion: Atheism and Its Scientific Pretensions*. New York: Basic Books. 2009.

Bethell, Tom. "Darwin's Unfalsifiable Theory." *Kronos: A Journal of Interdisciplinary Synthesis.* Vol. VII, no. 4, 1982, pp. 33–37.

Birch, Francis. "Heat from Radioactivity." In *Nuclear Geology: A Symposium on Nuclear Phenomena in the Earth Sciences.* New York: John Wiley & Sons. 1954, pp. 148–174.

Boerio-Goates, Juliana. "The Law of Increasing Disorder." In *Physical Science Foundations,* 2nd Edition. Managing Editor Jennifer Berry. Provo, Utah: BYU Academic Publishing. 2006. Used with permission.

Braidwood, R. J. "Prehistory into History in the Near East." In *Radiocarbon Variations and Absolute Chronology: Proceedings of the Twelfth Nobel Symposium held at the Institute of Physics at Uppsala University,* Edited by Ingrid U. Olsson. New York: John Wiley & Sons, Inc. 1970, pp. 81–91.

Breasted, James Henry. *A History of Egypt: From the Earliest Times to the Persian Conquest,* 2nd ed. New York: Charles Scribner's Sons. 1909.

Brier, Bob. *Ancient Egyptian Magic.* New York: Quill. 1981.

Broad, William and Nicholas Wade. *Betrayers of the Truth.* New York: Simon and Schuster. 1982. The quotes from *Betrayers of the Truth* are reprinted by permission of SLL/Sterling Lord Literistic, Inc. Copyright by William Broad and Nicholas Wade.

Brown, Walt. *In the Beginning: Compelling Evidence for Creation and the Flood,* 7th edition, 2001. An online edition may be seen at http://www.creationscience.com (last accessed 9/6/12). A video with Dr. Brown summarizing his theory may be seen on www.youtube.com (Google search "hydroplate"), and on the DVD "The Incredible Discovery of Noah's Ark" by Grizzly Adams Family Entertainment, 2005.

Brown, Rodney J. *Setting the Record Straight: Mormons & Science.* Orem, Utah: Millennial Press. 2008.

Bury, Susan. "How to Live with Evolution." *Skeptical Inquirer.* March/April 2001, pp. 56–57.

Campbell, Bernard G. "Conceptual Progress in Physical Anthropology: Fossil Man." In *Annual Review of Anthropology*, Vol. 1, 1972, pp. 27-54.

Carey, S. Warren. *The Expanding Earth*. Amsterdam: Elsevier Scientific Publishing Co. 1976.

Carney, Scott. "Did a Comet Cause the Great Flood?" *Discover Magazine*, November 2007, pp. 66–67.

Cecil, C. Blain; Frank T. Dulong; James C. Cobb; and Supardi. "Allogenic and Autogenic Controls on Sedimentation in the Central Sumatra Basin as an Analogue for Pennsylvanian Coal-Bearing Strata in the Appalachian Basin." In *Modern and Ancient Coal-Forming Environments*. Edited by James. C. Cobb and C. Blain Cecil. Boulder, Colorado: Geological Society of America Special Paper 286. 1993, pp. 3–22.

Chandra X-Ray Observatory. Courtesy of NASA/CXC/Penn State/G. Garmire et al. http://chandra.harvard.edu/photo/2007/rcw103/. (last accessed 9/6/12)

Chicago Manual of Style, 15th Edition. University of Chicago Press. 2003.

Chang, Alicia (Associated Press). "NASA craft braved comet ice storm during flyby." *Deseret News*. November 19, 2010.

Chappell, Robert H. Jr. "The Day the Sun Stood Still: A Comparative Analysis." *Catastrophism and Ancient History*, Vol. XIII, July 1991, pp. 102–112.

Choi, D. R.; B. I. Vasil'yev; and M. I. Bhat. "Paleoland, crustal structure, and composition under the northwestern Pacific Ocean." In *New Concepts in Global Tectonics*. Edited by Sankar Chatterjee and Nicholas Hotton III. Lubbock: Texas Tech University Press. 1992, pp. 179–191.

Chown, Marcus. "End of the Beginning." *NewScientist*. July 2, 2005, pp. 30–35. http://www.newscientist.com/article/mg18625061.800-did-the-big-bang-really-happen.html.

Clapham, Phillip. "Sea Level Changes." *Chronology & Catastrophism Review*, SIS, 1997:2, p. 12.

Clark, David L. *Of Heaven and Earth: Reconciling Scientific Thought with LDS Theology.* Salt Lake City: Deseret Book. 1998.

Clube, Victor and Bill Napier. *The Cosmic Serpent: A Catastrophist View of Earth History.* New York: Universe Books, 1982. Text reprinted courtesy of Rizzoli International Publications, Inc, New York.

Cobb, James C. and C. Blaine Cecil. *Modern and Ancient Coal-Forming Environments.* Boulder, Colorado: Geological Society of America Special Paper 286. 1993.

Cohen, Michael P. *A Garden of Bristlecones: Tales of Change in the Great Basin.* Reno, Nevada: University of Nevada Press. 1998.

Collilieux, X.; Z. Altamimi; J. Ray; T. van Dam; and X. Wu. "Effect of the Satellite Laser Ranging Network Distribution on Geocenter Motion Estimation." *Journal of Geophysical Research,* Vol. 114. 2009, pp. 1–17. Reproduced by permission of American Geophysical Union. http://www.ngs.noaa.gov/CORS/Articles/itrf2005_geoc_JGR09.pdf. (last accessed 9/6/12)

Collingridge, Dave S. *Truth and Science: An LDS Perspective.* Springville, Utah: Cedar Fort, Inc. 2008.

Collins, Francis S. *The Language of God: A Scientist Presents Evidence for Belief.* New York: Free Press. 2006.

Cook, Edward R. and Neil Pederson. "Uncertainty, Emergence, and Statistics in Dendrochronology." In *Dendroclimatology: Progress and Prospects,* Malcolm K. Hughes, Thomas W. Swetnam and Henry F. Diaz, eds. Dordrecht: Springer. 2011, Vol. 11, Part 2 pp. 77–112. With kind permission of Springer Science & Business Media.

Cook, M. Garfield. *Science and Modern Revelation.* Phoenix Publishing, Inc. 1981.

Cook, Melvin A. "Continental Drift: Is Old Mother Earth Just a Youngster?" *The Utah Alumnus,* Vol 40, no. 1. 1963, pp. 10–12.

Cook, Melvin A. *Noah's Flood, Earth Divided and Earthquakes at the Crucifixion.* Salt Lake City: Privately printed. 1995.

Cook, Melvin A. *Prehistory and Earth Models.* London: Max Parrish. 1966.

Cook, Melvin A. *Scientific Prehistory.* Bountiful, Utah: Family History Publishers. 1993.

Cook, Melvin A. *The Autobiography of Melvin A. Cook,* Vol. 2. Salt Lake City: published privately by the author. 1977.

Cook, Melvin A. "Where is the Earth's Radiogenic Helium?" *Nature,* no. 4552, January 26, 1957, p. 213.

Courville, Donovan A. *The Exodus Problem and its Ramifications: A Critical Examination of the Chronological Relationships Between Israel and the Contemporary Peoples of Antiquity,* Vols 1 & 2. Loma Linda, California: Challenge Books, 1971.

CRC Handbook of Chemistry and Physics, 72nd edition. David R. Lide, Editor-in-Chief. Boca Raton: CRC Press. 1991.

Crittenden, Max D. Jr. "Effective Viscosity of the Earth Derived from Isostatic Loading of Pleistocene Lake Bonneville." *Journal of Geophysical Research,* Vol. 68, no. 19, October 1, 1963, pp. 5517–5530. Reproduced by permission of American Geophysical Union.

Crocker, Caroline. *Free to Think: Why Scientific Integrity Matters.* Southworth, Washington: Leafcutter Press, Publisher. 2010.

Crowe, P. J. "The Biblical 40-Years Periods." *Chronology & Catastrophism Review.* SIS, 2001:2, pp. 31–35.

Curie, Marie. *Radioactive Substances.* Westport, Connecticut: Greenwood Press. 1961, reprint edition 1971.

Dalrymple, G. Brent. *The Age of the Earth.* Stanford University Press. 1991.

Damon, Paul E., Austin Long, and Donald C. Grey. "Fluctuation of Atmospheric C14 During the Last Six Millennia." In *Proceedings of the Sixth International Conference Radiocarbon and Tritium Dating.* Compiled by Roy M. Chatters and

Edwin A. Olson. Pullman, Washington. June 7–11, 1965, pp. 415–428.

Darlington, C. D. "The Origin of Darwinism." *Scientific American*, Vol. 200, no. 5, May 1959, pp. 60–66.

David, A. Rosalie. *The Egyptian Kingdoms*. Oxford: Elsevier Publishing. 1975.

Dayton, John E. "Ice Cores and Chronology." *Chronology & Catastrophism Review*. SIS, 1995, pp. 12–18.

de Santillana, Giorgio, and Hertha von Dechend. *Hamlet's Mill: An Essay on Myth and the Frame of Time*. Boston: David R. Godine, Publisher, paperback edition. 1977.

Delair, J. B. "Planet in Crisis: The Earth's Last 12,000 Years." *Chronology & Catastrophism Review*. SIS, 1997:2, pp. 4–11.

Demetrius the Chronographer. In *The Old Testament Pseudepigrapha*, Vol. 2. Translated by O. S. Wintermute. Edited by James H. Charlesworth. Garden City, NY: Doubleday & Co., Inc., 1983. pp. 843–854.

Discourses of Brigham Young: Second President of The Church of Jesus Christ of Latter-day Saints. Selected and Arr. by John A. Widtsoe. Salt Lake City: Deseret Book. 1954, 1973 edition.

Dorf, Erling. "Tertiary Fossil Forests of Yellowstone National Park, Wyoming." *Billings Geological Society 11th Annual Field Conference*. September 7–10, 1960.

Dunning-Davies, Jeremy. "Science in Turmoil—Are we Funding Fraud?" http://www.thunderbolts.info/thunderblogs/guest_jdd.htm. (last accessed 9/6/12)

Editorial. "Breaking the Laws: Much of What We Think Is Immutable May Be Nothing of the Kind." *NewScientist*. April 29, 2006, p. 5. http://www.newscientist.com/article/dn9085-editorial-breaking-the-laws-of-nature.html.

Elias, C. N.; P. R. Rios; and A. W. Romero. "Spall of Differently Treated High-Strength Low-Alloy Steel." In *Shock-Wave and High-Strain-Rate Phenomena in Materials*. Edited by Marc A.

Meyers, Lawrence E. Murr, and Karl P. Staudhammer. New York: Marcel Dekker, Inc. 1992, pp. 733–739.

Ellenberger, C. Leroy. "How to Defuse a Feud: Editorial Postscript." *Kronos: A Journal of Interdisciplinary Synthesis.* Vol. VII, no. 4, 1982, pp. 5–7, 37.

Encarta Encyclopedia Deluxe. 2004.

Engels, Joan C. "Effects of Sample Purity on Discordant Mineral Ages Found in K-Ar Dating." *Journal of Geology,* Vol. 79, 1971, pp. 609–616.

"Expelled: No Intelligence Allowed." Premise Media Corp. DVD. 2008.

Eyring, Henry. *Reflections of a Scientist.* Salt Lake City: Deseret Book. 1983.

Eyring, Henry. *The Faith of a Scientist.* Salt Lake City: Bookcraft. 1967.

Farmer, Molly. "Science Should Include God, Scholar Says." *Deseret News.* May 14, 2009.

Farrer, Austin. "The Christian Apologist." In *Light on C. S. Lewis.* Edited by Jocelyn Gibb. New York: Harcourt Brace Jovanovich. 1965, pp. 23–43.

Faul, Henry, editor. *Nuclear Geology.* New York: John Wiley & Sons. 1954.

Faure, Gunter. *Principles of Isotope Geology.* New York: John Wiley & Sons. 1977.

Ferguson, C. W. "A 7104-Year Annual Tree-Ring Chronology for Bristlecone Pine, *Pinus Aristata,* from the White Mountains, California." *Tree-Ring Bulletin.* 1969, Vol. 29, no 3–4, Tucson, Arizona: Tree-Ring Society. pp. 3–29. http://www.treeringsociety.org/TRBTRR/TRBvol29_3-4_3-29.pdf. (last accessed 9/6/12)

Field, T. William. "Evidence of an Inversion Event?" *Aeon,* Vol. II, no. 1, 1989, pp. 5–22.

Flansburgh, John C. and John Linnell. They Might Be Giants. Science Is Real. http://www.metrolyrics.com/science-is-real-lyrics-they-might-be-giants.html#ixzz0vbHsGwHf. (last accessed 9/4/12)

Fleury, Maureen K. "The Year Without a Summer 1816." http://www.suite101.com/content/the-year-without-a-summer-1816-a54675. May 21, 2008, pp. 1–3.

Foster, Lee. "1816 – The Year Without Summer." http://www.erh.noaa.gov/car/Newsletter/htm_format_articles/climate_corner/yearwithoutsummer_lf.htm. (last accessed 2/4/13)

Francis, Wilfrid. *Coal.* London: Edward Arnold Ltd. 1954.

Gardiner, Sir Alan. *Egypt of the Pharaohs.* New York: Oxford University Press. Paperback edition 1966.

Gesenius, H. W. F. *Gesenius' Hebrew and Chaldee Lexicon to the Old Testament Scriptures.* Translated by Samuel Prideaux Tregelles. Grand Rapids, Michigan: Baker Book House. 1857, reprint, 1991.

Gibbs, W. Wayt. "Great Expectations." *Scientific American,* December 1995, p. 18.

Ginenthal, Charles. "The Extinction of the Mammoth." *The Velikovskian.* Special edition. 1997, p. 160.

Ginzberg, Louis. *The Legends of the Jews,* Vol. 1. Translated by Henrietta Szold. Philadelphia: The Jewish Publication Society of America, 1909.

Glock, Waldo S., R. A. Studhalter, and Sharlene R. Agerter. "Classification and Multiplicity of Growth Layers in the Branches of Trees at the Extreme Lower Forest Border." *Smithsonian Miscellaneous Collections,* Vol. 140, no. 1. Washington D.C.: The Smithsonian Institution. June 17, 1960.

Goodfriend, Glenn A., and Darden G. Hood. "Carbon Isotope Analysis of Land Snail Shells: Implications for Carbon Sources and Radiocarbon Dating." *Radiocarbon,* Vol. 25, no. 3, 1983, pp. 810–830.

Gorenstein, Paul and Wallace Tucker. "Supernova Remnants: Radiation Emitted by the Debris Left Over from Catastrophic

Stellar Explosions May Yield Clues to Many Astronomical Puzzles." *Scientific American*, Vol. 225, no. 1, July, 1971, pp. 74–85.

Gould, Jay. "What Is a Species?" *Discover Magazine*, December, 1992.

Grady, William C., Cortland F. Eble, and Sandra G. Neuzil. "Brown Coal Maceral Distributions in a Modern Domed Tropical Indonesian Peat and a Comparison with Maceral Distributions in Middle Pennsylvanian-age Appalachian Bituminous Coal Beds." In *Modern and Ancient Coal-Forming Environments*. Ed. J. C. Cobb and C. B. Cecil. Boulder, Colorado: Geological Society of America Special Paper 286. 1993, pp. 63–82.

Grant, A. C. "Intracratonic tectonism: key to the mechanism of diastrophism." In *New Concepts in Global Tectonics*. Edited by Sankar Chatterjee and Nicholas Hotton III. Lubbock: Texas Tech University Press. 1992, pp. 65–73.

Gray, Bennison. "Alternatives in Science: The Secular Creationism of Heribert Nilsson." *Kronos: A Journal of Interdisciplinary Synthesis*. Vol. VII, no. 4, 1982, pp. 8–25.

Grieve, Richard A. F. "Impact Craters: When will enough be enough?" *Nature*, Vol. 363, June 24, 1993, pp. 670–671.

Grissino-Mayer, Henri D. "Evaluating Crossdating Accuracy: A Manual and Tutorial for the Computer Program COFECHA." *Tree-Ring Research*. Vol. 57(2), 2001, pp. 205–221.

Hall, Carl T. "Staying Alive: High in California's White Mountains grows the oldest living creature ever found." http://www.sfgate.com/default/article/Staying-Alive-High-in-California-s-White-2995266.php. (last accessed 9/4/12)

Halupnik, Teresa. "An Analysis of Tracheid Length Versus Age in a 4842-year-old Bristlecone Pine Called Prometheus." PhD Dissertation University of Texas at Arlington, 2008. http://webcache.googleusercontent.com/search?q=cache:hA

ki8rBhiHkJ:dspace.uta.edu/bitstream/handle/10106/1844/
Halupnik_uta_2502D_10103.pdf%3Fsequence%3D1+prom
etheus+bristlecone+pine+slab+dimensions&cd=4&hl=en&
ct=clnk&gl=us&client=firefox-a&source=www.google.com.
(last accessed 9/4/12)

Hamburg, Morris. *Statistical Analysis for Decision Making.* New
York: Harcourt, Brace & World. 1970.

Hamilton, E. I. and R. M. Farquhar. *Radiometric Dating for
Geologists.* London: Interscience Publishers. 1968.

Hapgood, Charles. *Earth's Shifting Crust: A Scientific Key to Many
of Earth's Mysteries.* With a foreword by Albert Einstein. New
York: Pantheon Books. 1958.

Hawass, Zahi. "King Tut's Family Secrets: DNA evidence reveals
the truth about the boy king's parents and new clues to his
untimely death." *National Geographic.* September 2010, pp.
34–61.

Hayatsu, Ryoichi, Robert L. McBeth, Robert G. Scott, Robert
E. Botto, Randall E. Winans. "Artificial Coalification Study:
Preparation and Characterization of synthetic Macerals."
Organic Geochemistry. Vol. 6, 1984, pp. 463–471.

Hedges, R. E. M. "Sample Treatment Strategies in Radiocarbon
Dating."In *Radiocarbon After Four Decades: An Interdisciplinary
Perspective.* Edited by R. E. Taylor, A. Long, R. S. Kra. New
York: Springer-Verlag. © 1992, pp. 165–181. All Rights
Reserved. With kind permission of Springer Science &
Business Media.

Hedges, Robert E. M. and John A. J. Gowlett. "Radiocarbon
Dating by Accelerator Mass Spectrometry." *Scientific
American,* January 1986, pp. 100–107.

Hendrickson, Nancy L. "Space in the Desert: Arizona's Meteor
Crater and the Lowell Observatory bring visitors visions of
earthly impacts and distant planets." *Astronomy.* November
1998, pp. 92–97.

Hennigan, W. J. "'Capabilities We Haven't Seen Yet': GPS Upgrade Aims for Accuracy, Reliability." *Los Angeles Times.* In *Deseret News,* May 30, 2010.

Heyerdahl, Thor. *The Ra Expeditions.* Trans. Patricia Crampton. New York: Signet. 1971.

Higham, Thomas. "Radiocarbon Web-info." http://www.c14dating.com/agecalc.html.

Hoesch, William A. "Galloping Glaciers." *Acts & Facts.* 36 (12) December, 2007, p. 14. Copyright © 2007 Institute for Creation Research www.icr.org. Used by Permission.

Hoffman, Michael A. *Egypt Before the Pharaohs: The Prehistoric Foundations of Egyptian Civilization.* New York: Alfred A. Knopf. 1984.

Homrighausen, Elmer G. "The Second Epistle of Peter." In *The Interpreter's Bible.* Vol. 12. New York: Abingdon Press. 1957, pp. 166–208.

http://en.wikipedia.org/wiki/Charles_Lyell. (last accessed 9/6/12)

http://en.wikipedia.org/wiki/Comet_Hale-Bopp. (last accessed 9/6/12)

http://en.wikipedia.org/wiki/File:General_Sherman_Tree_wide.jpg. (last accessed 9/6/12). Famartin at en.wikipedia (http://en.wikipedia.org)

http://en.wikipedia.org/wiki/File:Benldmeteorite.jpg. (last accessed 9/6/12). Shsilver at en.wikipedia. (http://en.wikipedia.org)

http://en.wikipedia.org/wiki/File:India_topo_big.jpg. (last accessed 9/6/12) This image file is licensed under the Creative commons Attribution-Share Alike 3.0 Unreported (http://creativecommons.org/licenses/by-sa/3.0/deed.en) licence.

http://en.wikipedia.org/wiki/Polystrate_fossil. (last accessed 9/6/12)

http://en.wikipedia.org/wiki/Pierre-Simon_Laplace. (last accessed 9/6/12)

http://en.wikipedia.org/wiki/Pistis_Sophia. (last accessed 9/6/12)

http://science.nasa.gov/science-news/science-at-nasa/2000/ast06oct_1/. (last accessed 9/6/12)

http://www.chem.duke.edu/~jds/cruise_chem/Exobiology/miller.html. (last accessed 9/29/12)

http://www.daviddarling.info/encyclopedia/R/Rochelimit.html. (last accessed 9/4/12)

http://www.dinosaurc14ages.com/hughpet.htm. (last accessed 9/10/12)

http://www.huffingtonpost.com/2011/06/27/asteroid-today-2011_n_885052.html. (last accessed 9/4/12)

http://www.newworldencyclopedia.org/entry/Dead_Sea_scrolls. (last accessed 9/4/12)

http://www.niagaraparks.com/media/geology-facts-figures.html. (last accessed 9/4/12)

http://www.pbs.org/wgbh/nova/transcripts/2511longitude.html. (last accessed 9/4/12)

http://www.sacred-texts.com/chr/apo/jasher/index.htm. (last accessed 9/4/12)

http://www.nps.gov/cebr/images/20070823131458.jpg. (Photo by Paula Hamilton) (last accessed 9/7/12)

Hubbert, M. King and William W. Rubey. "Role of Fluid Pressure in Mechanics of Overthrust Faulting." *Bulletin of the Geological Society of America*, Vol. 70, February 1959, pp. 115–166.

Internet Encyclopedia of Science: http://www.daviddarling.info/encyclopedia/R/Rochelimit.html.

Jasher, The Book of. Salt Lake City: J. H. Parry & Company, 1887, Photo Lithographic Reprint, 1973.

Johnson, Bob. "The Origin of the Sacred 260 Day Calendar of the Early Mesoamerican Civilisations: A Hypothesis." *Chronology & Catastrophism Review.* SIS, 2001:1, pp. 22–26.

Johnson, Paul. *The Civilization of Ancient Egypt.* New York: Atheneum. 1978.

Johnson, Phillip. *Darwin on Trial.* Downers Grove, Illinois: InterVarsity Press. 1991.

Josephus: Complete Works. Trans. William Whiston. Grand Rapids, Michigan: Kregel Publications. 1960.

"Journey to the Edge of the Universe." *National Geographic* DVD. 2008.

Jubilees. In *The Old Testament Pseudepigrapha*, Vol. 2. Translated by O. S. Wintermute. Edited by James H. Charlesworth. Garden City, NY: Doubleday & Co., Inc., 1983.

Judson, Sheldon, and Marvin E. Kauffman. *Physical Geology,* 8th edition. Englewood Cliffs, New Jersey: Prentice Hall, 1990.

Jueneman, Frederic. "Will the Real Monster Please Stand Up." *Industrial Research and Development*, September, 1972, p. 15.

Keith, M. L. and G. M. Anderson. "Radiocarbon Dating: Fictitious Results with Mollusk Shells." *Science,* Vol. 141, no. 3581, 1963, pp. 634–637.

Kerr, Richard A. "Looking Deeply into the Earth's Crust in Europe." *Science,* Vol. 261, July 16, 1993, pp. 295–297. Copyright 1993 by the American Association for the Advancement of Science. Reprinted with permission from AAAS. http://www.sciencemag.org/content/261/5119/295.extract?sid=9532ee98-bced-4851-8cc2-037df07a1a5f

Keys, David. *Catastrophe: An Investigation into the Origins of the Modern World.* New York: Ballantine Books. 1999.

Kious, W. Jacquelyne and Robert I. Tilling. *This Dynamic Earth: The Story of Plate Tectonics.* Denver: U. S. Geological Survey. (undated).

Kistler, S. S. "Dear Editor." *The Utah Alumnus.* December/January Vol. 40, no. 2, 1964, p. 4.

Knight, Hal. "Behind the Legend, There's a Man." *Deseret News.* September 1, 1976.

Kowallis, Bart J. "Earth's Interior." In *Physical Science Foundations*, 2nd Edition. Managing Editor Jennifer Berry. Provo, Utah: BYU Academic Publishing. 2006. Used With Permission.

Kowallis, Bart J. "Geologic Time." In *Physical Science Foundations*, 2nd Edition. Managing Editor Jennifer Berry. Provo, Utah: BYU Academic Publishing. 2006. Used With Permission.

Kowallis, Bart J. "Things of the Earth." In *Of Heaven and Earth:Reconciling Scientific Thought with LDS Theology*. Edited by David L. Clark. Salt Lake City: Deseret Book. 1998. pp. 29–46.

Kulp, J. Laurence. "Geological Chronometry by Radioactive Methods." In *Advances in Geophysics*, Edited by H. E. Landsberg. New York: Academic Press. 1955, pp. 179–214. With permission from Elsevier.

Kulp, J. Laurence and Walter R. Eckelmann. "Discordant U-Pb Ages and Mineral Type." *American Mineralogist*, 42, 1957, pp. 154–164.

Lamb, Michael P. and Mark A. Fonstad. "Rapid Formation of a Modern Bedrock Canyon by a Single Flood Event." *Nature Geoscience*, 3, 2010, pp. 477–481, http://www.nature.com/ngeo/journal/v3/n7/abs/ngeo894.html. (last accessed 9/6/12)

Lammerts, Walter E. "Are the Bristle-cone Pine Trees Really so Old?" *Creation Research Quarterly* 20(2). Chino Valley, Arizona: Creation Research Society. 1983, pp. 108–115.

Lanner, Ronald M. *The Bristlecone Book: Natural History of the World's Oldest Trees*. Missoula, Montana: Mountain Press Publishing Co. 2007.

Larson, Anthony E. *And the Earth Shall Reel To and Fro: The Prophecy trilogy*, Vol. 2. Orem, Utah: Zedek Books. 1983.

Larson, Anthony E. *And there Shall Be a New Heaven and a New Earth: The Prophecy trilogy*, Vol. 3. Orem, Utah: Zedek Books. 1985.

Larson, Kristine M., Jeffrey T. Freymueller, and Steven Philipsen. "Global Plate Velocities from the Global Positioning

System." *Journal of Geophysical Research,* Vol. 102, no. B5, May 10, 1997, pp. 9961–9981. Reproduced by permission of American Geophysical Union.

Lasken, Jesse E. "Misusing Radiocarbon: A Case Study." *Chronology & Catastrophism Review* Vol. XIV. SIS, 1992, pp. 17–19.

Lasken, Jesse E. "Should the European Oak Dendrochronologies be Re-examined?" *Chronology & Catastrophism Review* Vol. XIII. SIS, 1991, pp. 30–35.

Laurence, Richard, translator. *The Book of Enoch The Prophet.* London: Kegan Paul, Trench & Co. 1883. Photographic copy, San Diego: Wizards Bookshelf. 1983. Also available online at http://www.johnpratt.com/items/docs/enoch.html.

Lemon, Roy R. *Principles of Stratigraphy.* Columbus: Merrill Publishing Co. 1990.

Lemonick, Michael D. "Supernova! Scientists are agog over the brightest exploding star in 383 years." *Time,* March 23, 1987, pp. 60–68.

Lewis, John S. *Rain of Iron and Ice: The Very Real Threat of Comet and Asteroid Bombardment.* Reading, Massachusetts: Addison-Wesley Publishing. 1996.

Libby, Willard F. "Accuracy of Radiocarbon Dates: Apparent discrepancies are examined for geophysical significance and for a general principle of correction." *Science,* Vol. 140, no. 3564, April 19, 1963, pp. 278–280.

Libby, Willard F. "Natural Radiocarbon and Tritium in Retrospect and Prospect." In *Proceedings of the Sixth International Conference: Radiocarbon and Tritium Dating.* Compiled by Roy M. Chatters and Edwin A. Olson. Pullman, Washington. 1965, pp. 745–751.

Libby, Willard F. *Radiocarbon Dating,* 2nd Edition. University of Chicago Press. 1955.

Libby, Willard F. "Radiocarbon Dating: The method is of increasing use to the archaeologist, the geologist, the meteorologist, and the oceanographer." *Science,* Vol. 133, March 3, 1961, pp. 621–629.

Lingenfelter, R. E. "Production of Carbon 14 by Cosmic-Ray Neutrons." *Reviews of Geophysics.* February 1, 1963, pp.35–55.

Lingenfelter, R. E. and R. Ramaty. "Astrophysical and Geophysical Variations in C14 Production." In *Radiocarbon Variations and Absolute Chronology: Proceedings of the Twelfth Nobel Symposium held at the Institute of Physics at Uppsala University.* 1970, pp. 513–533.

Lombardi, Michael A. "Why is a minute divided into 60 seconds, an hour into 60 minutes, yet there are only 24 hours in a day?" *Scientific American.* March 5, 2007.

Low, Phillip F. "Perspectives on Science and Religion." In *Of Heaven and Earth: Reconciling Scientific Thought with LDS Theology.* Edited by David L. Clark. Salt Lake City: Deseret Book. 1998.

Lowman, Paul D. Jr. "Plate tectonics and continental drift in geologic education." In *New Concepts in Global Tectonics.* Edited by Sankar Chatterjee and Nicholas Hotton III. Lubbock: Texas Tech University Press. 1992, pp. 3–9.

Macbeth, Norman. "How to Defuse a Feud." *Kronos: A Journal of Interdisciplinary Synthesis.* Vol. VII, no. 4, 1982, pp. 1–4.

Martinez, Florentino Garcia. *The Dead Sea Scrolls Translated: The Qumran Texts in English,* 2nd edition. Wilfred G. E. Watson, translator. Grand Rapids: William B. Eerdmans Publishing Co., 1994.

Matthews, Mark. "Evidence for Multiple Ring Growth per Year in Bristlecone Pines." *Journal of Creation* 20(3). Creation Ministries International: Eight Mile Plains, Australia. 2006, pp. 95–103. http://creation.com/images/pdfs/tj/j20_3/j20_3_95-103.pdf. (last accessed 9/6/12)

Maxwell, Cory H., editor. *The Neal A. Maxwell Quote Book.* Salt Lake City, Bookcraft. 1997, p. 294.

McGraw-Hill Concise Encyclopedia of Science & Technology, Parker, Sybil P. Editor in Chief. 4th Edition. 1997.

McGraw-Hill Dictionary of Scientific and Technical Terms. Edited by Daniel N. Lapedes. New York: McGraw-Hill Book Co. 1974.

McInnis, Doug. "Reservoirs Speed Up Earth's Spin." *Earth.* June, 1996, p. 14.

McKenzie, Dan. "Spinning Continents." *Nature,* Vol. 344, 8 March 1990, pp. 109–110.

McKinney, Michael L. and Robert L. Tolliver editors. *Current Issues in Geology: Selected Readings.* St. Paul Minnesota: West Publishing Co. 1994.

McKnight, Tom L. *Physical Geography: A Landscape Appreciation.* Englewood Cliffs, N. J.: Prentice Hall. 1990.

Melosh, H. J. "Acoustic Fluidization: Can Sound Waves Explain Why Dry Rock Debris Appears to Flow Like a Fluid in Some Energetic Geologic Events?" *American Scientist,* Vol. 71, no. 2, March-April, 1983, pp. 158–161.

Melosh, H. J. and P. Schenk. "Split Comets and the Origin of Crater Chains on Ganymede and Callisto." *Nature,* Vol. 365, October 21, 1993, pp. 731–733.

Mertz, Henriette. *Pale Ink: Two Ancient Records of Chinese Exploration in America.* Paperback edition, Bibliobazaar, 2008.

Meyerhoff, Arthur A. et al. "Origin of midocean ridges." In *New Concepts in Global Tectonics.* Edited by Sankar Chatterjee and Nicholas Hotton III. Lubbock: Texas Tech University Press. 1992, pp. 151–178.

Milton, Earl R. "Physics, Astronomy and Chronology." *Chronology & Catastrophism Review.* SIS, 1987, pp. 24–33.

Mirov. N. T. *The Genus Pinus.* New York: The Ronald Press Co. 1967.

Monastersky, Richard. "Mysteries of the Orient: A half-billion years ago the remarkable complex forms of animals we see today suddenly appeared. A new bonanza of Chinese fossils may finally tell us why." *Discover Magazine,* April 1993.

Monastersky, Richard. "Oxygen Upheaval: The crashing of continents may have shaped the atmosphere." *ScienceNews,* December 12, 1992, p. 342.

Monitor. "Conductive and Energetic Earth." *Chronology & Catastrophism Workshop,* SIS, 2009:1, p. 22. Information from *NewYork Times,* July 25, 2008.

Monitor. "Death of a Comet: Shoemaker-Levy 9 Hits Jupiter." *Chronology & Catastrophism Workshop.* SIS, 1994:2, p. 19.

Monitor. "Enceladus—Mystery Moon." *Chronology & Catastrophism Workshop,* SIS, 2009:1, p. 21. Information from *Scientific American,* December, 2008, pp. 26–35.

Monitor. "Lignin + Clay = Coal." *New Scientist.* September 1, 1983, p. 623.

Monitor. "Wind or Water and Impact." *Chronology & Catastrophism Workshop,* SIS, 1994:2, p. 28.

Montigny, Raymond. "The Conventional Potassium—Argon Method." In *Nuclear Methods of Dating.* Edited by Etienne Roth and Bernard Poty. Dordrecht: Kluwer Academic Publishers. © 1989, pp. 295–324. All Rights Reserved. With kind permission of Springer Science & Business Media.

Moody, J. Ward. "Forces in Fluids." In *Physical Science Foundations,* 2nd Edition. Managing Editor Jennifer Berry. Provo, Utah: BYU Academic Publishing. 2006. Used With Permission.

Moody, J. Ward. "Knowledge, Science, and the Universe." In *Physical Science Foundations,* 2nd Edition. Managing Editor Jennifer Berry. Provo, Utah: BYU Academic Publishing. 2006. Used With Permission.

Moore, E. S. *Coal: Its Properties, Analysis, Classification, Geology, Extraction, Uses and Distribution,* 2nd Ed. New York: John Wiley & Sons, Inc. 1940.

Morris, Henry M. *A History of Modern Creationism.* San Diego California: Master Book Publishers, 1984. Copyright ©

1984 Institute for Creation Research, www.icr.org. Used by permission.

Morris, John, and Steven A. Austin. *Footprints in the Ash: The Explosive Story of Mount St. Helens.* Green Forest, AR: Master Books. Second printing 2005. Used with permission from the publisher. 2003.

Morrison, Philip. "Wonders: On Neutrino Astronomy." *Scientific American,* November 1995, pp. 108–109.

Murakami, Motohiko, Kei Hirose, Hisayoshi Yurimoto, Satoru Nakashima, Naoto Takafuji. "Water in Earth's Lower Mantle." *Science,* Vol. 295, March 8, 2002, pp. 1885–1887.

Murphie, Dale F. "Critique of David Rohl's A Test of Time." *Chronology & Catastrophism Review.* SIS, 1997:1, pp. 31–33.

Musser, George. "The Paradox of Time: Why It Can't Stop, But Must: For time to end seems both impossible and inevitable. Recent work in Physics suggest a resolution to the paradox." *Scientific American.* September 2010, pp. 84–91. http://www.scientificamerican.com/article.cfm?id=could-time-end.

NASA, ESA, and H. Weaver and E. Smith (StSci). http://hubblesite.org/gallery/album/solar_system/pr1994026c. (last accessed 9/6/12)

Nash, J. Madeleine. "How Did Life Begin? In bubbles? On comets? Along ocean vents?" *Time,* October 11, 1993, pp. 68–74.

National Academy of Sciences. *Science and Creationism: A View from the National Academy of Sciences* 2nd Edition. Washington DC: National Academy Press. 1999.

Nemes, J. A., and J. Eftis. "Rate-Dependent Modeling of Multidimensional Impact and Post-Spall Behavior." In *Shock-Wave and High-Strain-Rate Phenomena in Materials.* Edited by Marc A. Meyers, Lawrence E. Murr, and Karl P. Staudhammer. New York: Marcel Dekker, Inc. 1992, pp. 723–739.

Nemiroff, Robert and Jerry Bonnell. "Astronomy Picture of the Day." http://apod.nasa.gov/apod/ap090302.html. (last accessed 9/6/12). Used with permission.

Neuzil, Sandra G., Supardi, C. Blain Cecil, Jean S. Kane, and Kadar Soedjono. "Inorganic Geochemistry of Domed Peat in Indonesia and its Implication for the Origin of Mineral Matter in Coal." In *Modern and Ancient Coal Forming Environments*. Edited by James C. Cobb and C. Blain Cecil. Boulder, Colorado: Geological Society of America Special Paper 286. 1993, pp. 23–44.

Newgrosh, Bernard. "Calibrated Radiocarbon and the 'Methodological Fault-Line.'" *Chronology and Catastrophism Review* Vol. XIII. SIS, 1991, pp. 35–37.

Newgrosh, Bernard. "Scientific Dating Methods and Absolute Chronology." *Journal of the Ancient Chronology Forum*, Vol. 2, 1988, pp. 60–68.

Newhall, Christopher G. "Mount St. Helens, Master Teacher." *Science.* May 19, 2000, pp. 1181–1183.

Nibley, Hugh. "A New Look at the Pearl of Great Price" part 8. *Improvement Era.* October, 1969, p. 89.

Nibley, Hugh. *Abraham in Egypt.* Salt Lake City: Deseret Book. 1981.

Nibley, Hugh. *An Approach to the Book of Abraham.* Salt Lake City: Deseret Book. 2009.

Nibley, Hugh. *Approaching Zion.* Salt Lake City: Deseret Book. 1989.

Nibley, Hugh. "Before Adam." Provo, Utah: Maxwell Institute. 2011, 26 pp. http://maxwellinstitute.byu.edu/publications/transcripts/?id=73. (last accessed 9/6/12)

Nibley, Hugh. "Controlling the Past (a Consideration of Methods)" *Improvement Era.* Jan. 1955.

Nibley, Hugh. "Controlling the Past" part 4. *Improvement Era.* Feb. 1955.

Nibley, Hugh. *Enoch the Prophet.* Salt Lake City: Deseret Book. 1986.

Nibley, Hugh. *Nibley on the Timely and the Timeless: Classic Essays of Hugh W. Nibley.* Provo Utah: Religious Studies Center Brigham Young University / Salt Lake City: Bookcraft, Inc., 1979.

Nibley, Hugh. *Old Testament and Related Studies.* Salt Lake City: Deseret Book. 1986.

Nibley, Hugh. *Since Cumorah.* Salt Lake City: Deseret Book. 1967.

Nibley, Hugh. *Temple and Cosmos: Beyond This Ignorant Present.* Salt Lake City: Deseret Book. 1992.

Nibley, Hugh. *The Ancient State.* Salt Lake City: Deseret Book. 1991.

Nibley, Hugh. *The Message of the Joseph Smith Papyri.* Salt Lake City: Deseret Book. 1975.

Notes and Queries. "Tutankhamun radiocarbon dates." *Chronology and Catastrophism Review.* SIS, 1996:1, p. 34.

Nova: *Bone Diggers.* Air Date June 19, 2007. www.pbs.org/wgbn/nova/nature/bone-diggers.html. (last accessed 9/19/12)

Oberbeck, Vern R. "Impacts and Global Change." *Geotimes,* September 1993, pp. 16–18. (© 1993 American Geological Institute and used with their permission. www.agiweb.org.)

Orowan, Egon. "The Origin of the Oceanic Ridges." *Scientific American.* November 1965, pp. 103–119.

Otlet. "Environmental Impact of Atmospheric Carbon-14 Emissions Resulting From the Nuclear Energy Cycle." In *Radiocarbon After Four Decades: An Interdisciplinary Perspective.* Edited by R. E. Taylor, A. Long, and R. S. Kra. New York: Springer-Verlag. © 1992, pp. 519–534. All Rights Reserved. With kind permission of Springer Science & Business Media.

Owen, James. "Oldest Living Tree Found in Sweden." *National Geographic News,* April 14, 2008, p. 1. http://news.

nationalgeographic.com/news/2008/04/080414-oldest-tree. html. (last accessed 9/6/12)

Palmer, Trevor. "Uniformitarianism, Catastrophism and Evolution." *Chronology & Catastrophism Review.* SIS, 1996:1, pp. 4–13.

Parfit, Michael. "The Floods That Carved the West." *Smithsonian.* April 1995, pp. 45–41.

Patten, Donald Wesley. *The Biblical Flood and the Ice Epoch: A Study in Scientific History.* Seattle: Pacific Meridian Publishing Co. 1966.

Patten, Donald W. and Samuel R. Windsor. "Catastrophic Theory of Mountain Uplifts: A Crustal Deformation Theory." *Catastrophism and Ancient History.* Vol. XIII, January 1991, pp. 17–41.

Pearson, G. W., J. R. Pilcher, and M. G. L. Baillie. "High-Precision [14]C Measurement of Irish Oaks to Show the Natural [14]C Variations from 200 BC to 4000 BC." *Radiocarbon,* Vol. 25, 1983, pp. 179–186.

Pearson, Glenn L., and Reid E. Bankhead. *Building Faith with the Book of Mormon.* Provo, Utah: Joseph Educational Foundation, 1994.

Pease, Roland. "Supernova Brightens the Horizon." *Nature,* Vol. 362, April 15, 1993, p. 585.

Pendleton, Yvonne J. and Dale P. Cruikshank. "Life from the Stars?" *Sky & Telescope,* March 1994, pp. 36–42.

Pennisi, Elizabeth. "Water, Water Everywhere: Surreptitiously converting dead matter into oil and coal." *ScienceNews,* February 20, 1993, Vol. 143, pp. 121–125.

Peteet, Dorothy M. "Major Contributions of Radiocarbon Dating to Palynology: Past and Future." In *Radiocarbon After Four Decades: An Interdisciplinary Perspective.* Edited by R. E. Taylor, A. Long, and R. S. Kra. New York: Springer-Verlag. © 1992, pp. 454–472. All Rights Reserved. With kind permission of Springer Science & Business Media.

Petersen, Dennis R. *Unlocking the Mysteries of* Creation, Vol. 1. South Lake Tahoe, California: Creation Resource Foundation.

Pipkin, Bernard W. *Geology and the Environment.* Minneapolis: West Publishing Co. 1994.

Pitman, Sean D. "J. Harlen Bretz—and the Great Scabland Debate." http://www.detectingdesign.com/harlenbretz.html. (last accessed 9/6/12)

Porter, R. M. "Ai, Jericho and 'Deviant' C14 Dates." *Chronology & Catastrophism Review.* SIS, 1992, p. 26.

Porter, R. M. "Recent Developments in Near Eastern Archaeology." *Chronology & Catastrophism Review,* SIS, 2002:1, pp. 14–17.

Powell, Corey S. "The Redshift Blues: New redshift theory challenges both physicists and cosmologists." *Scientific American.* January, 1990, pp. 17–18.

Poty, Bernard. "Geological Conditions Governing the Use of Dating Methods." In *Nuclear Methods of Dating.* Edited by Etienne Roth and Bernard Poty. Dordrecht: Kluwer Academic Publishers. © 1989, pp. 35–44. All Rights Reserved. With kind permission of Springer Science & Business Media.

Pratt, John P. "Did the Fish Die in the Flood?" *Meridian Magazine,* March 26, 1999. http://www.johnpratt.com/items/docs/lds/meridian/1999/flooded_fish.html. (last accessed 9/6/12)

Pratt, John P. *Divine Calendars: Astronomical Witnesses of Sacred Events.* Orem, Utah: AstroCal. 2002.

Pratt, John P. "Fact or Theory?" 1998, http://www.johnpratt.com/items/astronomy/science.html. (last accessed 9/6/12)

Pratt, John P. "Has Satan Hijacked Science?" *Meridian Magazine,* 16 Nov 2005. http://www.johnpratt.com/items/docs/lds/meridian/2005/satan.html. (last accessed 9/6/12)

Pratt, John P. "How Did the Book of Jasher Know?" *Meridian Magazine,* June 22, 2002. http://www.johnpratt.com/items/docs/lds/meridian/2002/jasher.html. (last accessed 9/6/12)

Pratt, John P. "Strengths and Weaknesses of Science." *Meridian Magazine*, 28 Dec 2000. www.johnpratt.com/items/docs/lds/meridian/2000/science.html. (last accessed 9/6/12)

Rafter Radiocarbon Laboratory GNS Science. http://www.gns.cri.nz/Home/Services/Laboratories-Facilities/Rafter-Radiocarbon-Laboratory/Measuring-Radiocarbon/Radiometric-Counting. (last accessed 9/6/12)

Rankama, Kalervo. *Isotope Geology.* New York: Pergamon Press. 1954.

Read, Lenet Hadley. *How We Got the Bible.* Salt Lake City: Deseret Book. 1985.

Renton, John J. "Continental Drift." Lecture 3 in *The Nature of Earth: An introduction to Geology.* Chantilly Virginia: The Great Courses. 2006.

Rinehart, John S., and John Pearson. *Behavior of Metals under Impulsive Loads.* Cleveland: The American Society for Metals. 1954.

Roebuck, Carl. *The World of Ancient Times.* New York: Charles Scribner's Sons. 1966.

Rohl, David M. *Pharaohs and Kings: A Biblical Quest* (Originally published in the United Kingdom and the rest of the world as: *A Test of Time: The Bible From Myth to History).* New York: Used by permission of Crown Publishers, a division of Random House, Inc. Any third party use of this material, outside of this publication, is prohibited. Interested parties must apply directly to Random House Inc. for permission. copyright © 1995.

Rose, Lynn E. "The Domination of Astronomy over Other Disciplines." *Kronos: A Journal of Interdisciplinary Synthesis.* Vol. II, no. 4, 1977, pp. 56–63.

Rose, Lynn E. "The Greenland Ice Cores." *Kronos: A Journal of Interdisciplinary Synthesis.* Vol. XII, no. 1, 1987, pp. 55–68.

Ross, Charles A., and June R. P. Ross, *Geology of Coal.* Stroudsburg, Pennsylvania: Hutchinson Ross Publishing Co. 1984.

Roth, Etienne. "Dating Methods Using Natural Radioactive Phenomena." In *Nuclear Methods of Dating*. Edited by Etienne Roth and Bernard Poty Dordrecht: Kluwer Academic Publishers. © 1989, pp. 1–34. All Rights Reserved. With kind permission of Springer Science & Business Media.

Salkeld, David. "Genesis and The Origin of Species." *Chronology & Catastrophism Review*. SIS, 2002:1, pp. 10–13.

Salkeld, David. "Intelligent Design?" *Chronology & Catastrophism Review*. SIS, 2009, pp. 2–17.

Salkeld, David. "Mythological/Historical Evidence for Earth Tilting?" *Chronology & Catastrophism Review*. SIS, 1996:2, p. 15.

Salkeld, David. "Shamir." *Chronology & Catastrophism Review*. SIS, 1997:1, pp. 18–22.

Säve-Söderbergh, T, and I. U. Olsson. "C14 Dating and Egyptian Chronology." In *Radiocarbon Variations and Absolute Chronology: Proceedings of the Twelfth Nobel Symposium held at the Institute of Physics at Uppsala University*. Edited by Ingrid U. Olsson. Stockholm: Almqvist & Wiksell. 1970, pp. 35–53.

Savino, John, and Marie D. Jones. *Supervolcano: The Catastrophic Event that Changed the Course of Human History (Could Yellowstone be Next?)*. Franklin Lakes, New Jersey: New Page Books. 2007.

Scott, Eugenie C. http://ncse.com/.

Scott, Eugenie C. "Not (Just) in Kansas Anymore." *Science*, Vol. 288, May 5, 2000, pp. 813–815.

Seiss, Joseph A. *The Gospel in the Stars*. 1882. Reprint edition: Grand Rapids, Michigan: Kregel Publications. 1972.

Sewell, Barbara. *Egypt Under the Pharaohs*. New York: G. P. Putnam's Sons. 1968.

Shackleton, N. J. et al. "Radiocarbon Age of Last Glacial Pacific Deep Water." *Nature*, Vol. 335, October 20, 1988, pp. 708–711.

Sharp, Robert P. "The Latest Major Advance of Malaspina Glacier, Alaska." *The Geographical Review.* Vol. XLVIII, no. 1, 1958, pp. 16–26.

Shermer, Michael. "When Scientists Sin: Fraud, Deception and Lies in Research Reveal How Science is (Mostly) Self-correcting." *Scientific American.* July 2010, p. 34.

Shill, Aaron. "New Look at Prophet's Cosmos." *Deseret News.* August 27, 2009.

SIS Study Group. *Chronology and Catastrophism Review.* SIS, 1997:1, pp. 53–54.

Slade, David A. "The Dust-up over Ice-cores." *Chronology and Catastrophism Workshop.* SIS, 1994:2, pp. 6–9.

Speer, James H. *Fundamentals of Tree-ring Research.* Tucson: The University of Arizona Press. 2010.

Standring, Paul. "Pot Pourri." *Chronology & Catastrophism Review.* SIS, 2001:2, pp. 49–52.

Stephenson, Nathan L. "Estimated Ages of Some Large Giant Sequoias: General Sherman Keeps Getting Younger." *Madrono,* Vol. 47. Berkeley: California Botanical Society, no. 1, 2000, pp. 61–67.

Stokes, William Lee. *The Creation Scriptures: A Witness for God in the Scientific Age.* Salt Lake City: Starstone Publishing Co. 1979.

Stokes, W. Lee, F. W. Christiansen, W. P. Hewitt, Harry D. Goode, and Richard A. Robison. "...And Dissenting Voices." *The Utah Alumnus,* Vol. 40, no. 2. December/January 1964, p. 4.

Stokes, M. A., and T. L. Smiley. *An Introduction to Tree-Ring Dating.* University of Chicago Press. 1968.

Storetvedt, K. M. "Rotating plates: New concept of global tectonics." In *New Concepts in Global Tectonics.* Edited by Sankar Chatterjee and Nicholas Hotton III. Lubbock: Texas Tech University Press. 1992, pp. 203–220.

Strickling, James E. "On the Nature of Natural Selection and Speciation." *Aeon: A Symposium on Myth and Science*, Vol. 1, no. 3, 1988, pp. 23–37.

Strickling, James E. "The Signature of Catastrophe (Reinterpreting the Geological Record)." *Aeon: A Symposium on Myth and Science*, Vol. 1, no. 2, February 1988, pp. 53–67.

Stutz, Bruce. "Rogue Waves: The Physics of Pure Hell at Sea." *Discover*. July 2004, pp. 48–55.

Stutzer, Otto, and Noe, Adolph C. *Geology of Coal*. University of Chicago Press. 1940.

Stuiver, Minze, and Gordon W. Pearson. "Calibration of the Radiocarbon Time Scale, 2500–5000 BC." In *Radiocarbon After Four Decades: An Interdisciplinary Perspective*. Edited by R. E. Taylor, A. Long, and R. S. Kra. New York: Springer-Verlag. ©1992, pp. 19–33. All Rights Reserved. With kind permission of Springer Science & Business Media.

Sukys, Paul. "Velikovskian Catastrophism: Science or Pseudoscience? Part III—Thomas Kuhn and the Myth of 'Mob Psychhology.'" *Chronology & Catastrophism Review*. SIS, 2009, pp. 18–28.

Supardi, A. D. Subekty, and Sandra G. Neuzil. "General Geology and Peat Resources of the Siak Kanan and Bengkalis Island Peat Deposits, Sumatra, Indonesia." In *Modern and Ancient Coal-Forming Environments*. Edited by James C. Cobb and C. Blain Cecil. Boulder, Colorado: Geological Society of America Special Paper 286. 1993, pp. 45–62.

Suzuki, David. In *If Ignorance is Bliss, Why Aren't There More Happy People? Smart Quotes for Dumb Times*. John Lloyd and John Mitchinson. New York: Harmony Books. 2008, p. 274.

Svitil, Kathy A. "It's Alive, and It's a Graptolite: From the seafloor off New Caledonia comes a strange colonial creature that was supposed to have been extinct for 300 million years." In *Current Issues in Geology: Selected Readings*. Edited by Michael L. McKinney and Robert L. Tolliver. St. Paul: West

Publishing Co. 1994, pp. 190–191. Reprint from *Discover Magazine*, July 1993.

Talcott, Richard. "Great Comets." *Astronomy*. May 2004, pp. 36–41.

Taylor, R. E. "Radiocarbon Dating of Bone: To Collagen and Beyond." In *Radiocarbon After Four Decades: An Interdisciplinary Perspective*. Edited by R. E. Taylor, A. Long, and R. S. Kra. New York: Springer-Verlag. © 1992, pp. 375–402. All Rights Reserved. With kind permission of Springer Science & Business Media.

Than, Ker. "Comet Smashes Triggering Ancient Famine." January 7, 2009. http://www.newscientist.com/article/mg20126882.900-comet-smashes-triggered-ancient-famine.html?full=tru&print=true. (last accessed 9/6/12)

"The Books of Enoch." In Martinez, Florentino Garcia. *The Dead Sea Scrolls Translated: The Qumran Texts in English*, 2nd edition. Wilfred G. E. Watson, translator. Grand Rapids: William B. Eerdmans Publishing Co., 1996.

The Planet Earth: The World Book Encyclopedia of Science. Chicago: World Book, Inc. 1984.

Thiele, Edwin R. *The Mysterious Numbers of the Hebrew Kings*. © Copyright1983 by Edwin Thiele Published by Kregel Publications, Grand Rapids, Michigan. Used by permission of the publisher. All rights reserved.

Thomas, Brian. "The Stones Cry Out: What Rocks and Fossils Say about the Age of the Earth." *Acts & Facts*. 40 (1) Jan. 2011, p. 17. Copyright © 2011 Institute for Creation Research, www.icr.org. Used by Permission.

Thornhill, Wal. "Astronomy has little to celebrate in 2009." *Chronology & Catastrophism Workshop*. SIS, 2009:1, pp. 27-28.

Totten, C. A. L. *Joshua's Long Day and The Dial of Ahaz*. Merrimac, Massachusetts: Destiny Publishers. 1968. Reprinted from the treatise Totten published in 1890.

Trees, Andrew. "Is Tiger Woods' Marriage Over." Interviewed by Harry Smith. *The Early Show*, CBS, December 16, 2009.

Trefil, James. "Stop to Consider the Stones That Fall From the Sky: More often than we once thought, huge comets and asteroids strike Earth with catastrophic effect—a few months ago, one barely missed us." *Smithsonian*. September 1989, p. 81–93.

Turner, Rodney. *This Eternal Earth: A Scriptural and Prophetic Biography*. Revised and edited version of *The Footstool of God*. 1983. Orem, Utah: Granite Publishing and Distribution, L.L.C, 2000.

Twain, Mark. *Life on the Mississippi*. New York: Harper & Brothers. Reprint ed. 1951. 1874. http://www.online-literature.com/twain/life_mississippi/. (last accessed 9/4/12)

Van der Merwe, J. *Carbon-14 Dating of Iron*. University of Chicago Press. 1969.

Van der Sluijs, Rens. "An Aristotelian Hangover." *Chronology & Catastrophism Review*. SIS, 2009, p. 39.

Van der Sluijs, Rens. "The Unwavering Truth about the Zodiacal Light." *Chronology & Catastrophism Workshop*. SIS, 2010:1, p. 40.

Vedantam, Shankar. "Eden and Evolution." Feb 3, 2006. http://www.washingtonpost.com/wp-dyn/content/article/2006/02/03/AR2006020300822_pf.html. (last accessed 9/6/12)

Velikovsky, Immanuel. *Ages in Chaos*. First published in 1953. London: Abacus edition. 1973.

Velikovsky, Immanuel. *Peoples of the Sea*. First published in 1977. London: Abacus edition. 1980.

Velikovsky, Immanuel. *Ramses II and His Time*. First published in 1978. London: Abacus edition. 1980.

Velikovsky, Immanuel. *Stargazers and Gravediggers: Memoirs to Worlds in Collision*. New York: Quill, 1984. The quotes from *Stargazers and Gravediggers: Memoirs to Worlds in*

Collision by Immanuel Velikovsky. Copyright © 1983 by Elisheva Velikovsky. Reprinted by permission of HarperCollins Publishers.

Velikovsky, Immanuel. *Worlds in Collision*. New York: Pocket Books. 1950. Page references are to the 1977 edition.

Vergano, Dan. "Saturn Holds a Tiny New Secret." *USA Today*. July 23, 2007.

Vitaliano, Dorothy B. *Legends of the Earth: Their Geologic Origins*. Bloomington: Indiana University Press. 1973.

Walden, John. "Dear Editor." *The Daily Utah Chronicle*. Feb. 3, 1964. In *Autobiography of Melvin A. Cook*. Vol. 2, 1977, p. 188.

Weaver, Kenneth F. "Meteorites: Invaders From Space." *National Geographic*. September, 1986, pp. 390–418.

Webster's New World College Dictionary, 4th edition. Cleveland, Wiley Publishing, 2005.

Weigall, Arthur. *A History of the Pharaohs*, Vol. 1. New York: E. P. Dutton. 1925.

Weissman, Paul. A review of: *Cosmic Catastrophes*, by Chapman and Morrison. *Sky & Telescope*. January, 1990, pp. 45–46.

Wells, Jonathan. "Common Ancestry on Trial." Taken from *Darwin's Nemesis* edited by William A. Dembski. Copyright © 2006 by William A. Dembski. Used by permission of InterVarsity Press, PO Box 1400 Downers Grove, IL 60515. www.ivpress.com. 2006, ch 11.

Wetherill, G. W. "Present Status of Geochronological Methods." In *Geochronology of North America*. Courtesy: National Science Foundation. 1965, pp. 1–15.

Whipple, Andrew P. "Science and Creationism." *Nature*, Vol. 333, June 9, 1988, p. 492.

Widtsoe, John A. *Evidences and Reconciliations: Aids to Faith in a Modern Day*. Salt Lake City, Bookcraft. 1943.

Wiencke-Lotz, Hildegard. "On the Length of Reigns of the Sumerian Kings." *Chronology and Catastrophism Review*. SIS, 1992, pp. 20–26.

Wiley, John P. Jr. "Phenomena, Comment and Notes: This Time the Comet Alarm was False, but Earth Moves in Heavy Traffic: Sooner or Later Our Luck Will Run Out." *Smithsonian.* March, 1993, pp. 21–25.

Wiley, John P. Jr. "Phenomena, Comment and Notes: While Comet Shoemaker-Levy 9 is History, Space Scientists are Just Beginning to Piece Together the Details of its Pyrotechnic Encounter With Jupiter Last July." *Smithsonian*, Vol. 25, no. 10, January, 1995, pp. 14–16.

Williams, Gordon. "Our Tilted Earth: A Geomorphic Analysis of Crustal Movement About the Poles, North America and Australiasia." *Chronology & Catastrophism Workshop.* SIS, 1994:1, pp. 9–15.

Wilson, J. Tuzo. "Mobility in the Earth." In *Continents Adrift: Readings from Scientific American.* San Francisco: W. H. Freeman and Co. 1970, pp. 1–3.

Wilson, John A. *The Burden of Egypt.* University of Chicago Press. 1951.

Wise, Donald U. "Creationism's Geologic Time Scale: Should the scientific community continue to fight rear-guard skirmishes with creationists, or insist that 'young-earthers' defend their model in toto?" *American Scientist,* Vol. 86, March-April 1998. pp. 160–173.

Wolfs, Frank. 1996. http://teacher.pas.rochester.edu/phy_labs/ AppendixE/AppendixE.html. (last accessed 9/6/12)

Woolley, C. Leonard. *The Sumerians.* New York: W. W. Norton & Co. 1965.

Zecher, Henry. "The Papyrus Ipuwer, Egyptian Version of the Plagues ~ A New Perspective." *The Velikovskian.* January 1997. http://www.henryzecher.com/papyrus_ipuwer.htm. (last accessed 9/6/12)

Zimmer, Carl. "What Is a Species?" *Scientific American.* June 2008, pp. 72–79. 1986.